Context

Nordrhein-Westfalen

Vokabeltrainer-App

Verfügbar für: iOS, Android und Windows Phone

Dieses Buch gibt es auch auf **www.scook.de/eb**

Es kann dort nach Bestätigung der Allgemeinen Geschäftsbedingungen genutzt werden.

Buchcode: ho957-3ne5t

Context · Ausgabe Nordrhein-Westfalen

Im Auftrag des Verlages herausgegeben von
Dr. Annette Leithner-Brauns, Dresden; Ingrid Becker-Ross, Krefeld; Prof. Hellmut Schwarz, Mannheim

Erarbeitet von
Irene Bartscherer, Bonn; Ingrid Becker-Ross, Krefeld; Friederike von Bremen, Hannover; Ulrike Elsäßer, Stuttgart; Gerit Fredrich, Meiningen; Prof. Dr. Britta Freitag-Hild, Potsdam; Veronika Gastpar, Mainburg; Dr. Peter Hohwiller, Landau; Markus Hözel, Köln; Ulrich Imig, Wildeshausen; Elke Jentsch, Reichenbach im Vogtland; Sylvia Loh, Esslingen; Dr. Paul Maloney, Hildesheim; Markus Marzinzik, Landau; Claudia Meixner, Erlangen; Neil Porter, Tel Aviv; Birgit Rietgraf, Backnang; Angela Ringel-Eichinger, Bietigheim-Bissingen; Victoria Schoeneberg, Köln; Dr. Andreas Sedlatschek, Esslingen; Claudia Spieler, Gießen; Marcel Sprunkel, Köln; Michael Thürwächter, Heidelberg; Inga Wittbrodt, Sankt Augustin

unter beratender Mitwirkung von
Martina Baasner, Berlin; Dr. Sabine Buchholz, Hürth; Bernd Koch, Marburg; Jochen Lüders, München; Gunthild Porteous-Schwier, Moers; Sieglinde Spranger, Chemnitz

in Zusammenarbeit mit der Englischredaktion
Elke Lehmann *(Projektleitung)*; Dr. Marion Kiffe, Laura Morgenthal, Dr. Georg-Christian v. Raumer, Ingrid-Maria Sauer, Anna Schwarz, Hartmut Tschepe, Ralph Williams sowie Katrin Gütermann, Berlin, und Neil Porter, Tel Aviv

Layoutkonzept
zweiband.media, Berlin

Layout und technische Umsetzung
designcollective, Berlin

Umschlaggestaltung
axeptDESIGN, Berlin; Michaela Müller für agentur corngreen, Leipzig

Weitere Bestandteile des Lehrwerks

- E-Book zum Schülerbuch
- Workbook (978-3-06-031667-0)
- VOCABI (978-3-06-033490-2)
- Vokabeltrainer-App
- Audio-CDs (+ MP3) (978-3-06-033487-2)
- Video-DVD (978-3-06-033488-9)
- Lehrerfassung des Schülerbuchs (978-3-06-031443-0)
- Handreichungen für den Unterricht (978-3-06-033483-4)
- Digitaler Unterrichtsmanager
- Vorschläge zur Leistungsmessung (978-3-06-034151-1)
- More Speaking Practice (Rollen- und Bildkarten) (978-3-06-031504-8)

Website zum Lehrwerk: **www.cornelsen.de/context**

Die Links zu externen Webseiten Dritter, die in diesem Lehrwerk angegeben sind, wurden vor Drucklegung sorgfältig auf ihre Aktualität geprüft. Der Verlag übernimmt keine Gewähr für die Aktualität und den Inhalt dieser Seiten oder solcher, die mit ihnen verlinkt sind.

Alle Drucke dieser Auflage sind inhaltlich unverändert und können im Unterricht nebeneinander verwendet werden.

Druck: Mohn Media Mohndruck, Gütersloh

1. Auflage, 1. Druck 2015
broschiert
ISBN 978-3-06-033482-7

1. Auflage, 2. Druck 2015
gebunden
ISBN 978-3-06-033489-6

PEFC zertifiziert
Dieses Produkt stammt aus nachhaltig bewirtschafteten Wäldern und kontrollierten Quellen.
www.pefc.de

PEFC
PEFC/04-31-1033

Contents

Contents

Contents

Contents

Contents

Contents

Abbreviations and labels used in *Context*

adj	adjective
adv	adverb
AE/BE	American English / British English
ca. *(Latin)*	circa = about, approximately
cf.	confer (compare), see
derog	derogatory *(abfällig, geringschätzig)*
e.g. *(Latin)*	exempli gratia = for example
esp.	especially
et al. *(Latin)*	et alii = and other people/things
etc. *(Latin)*	et cetera = and so on
f./ff.	and the following page(s)/line(s)
fml/infml	formal/informal English
i.e. *(Latin)*	id est = that is, in other words
jdm./jdn.	jemandem/jemanden
l./ll.	line/lines
n	noun
pt(s)	point(s)
p./pp.	page/pages
pl	plural
sb./sth.	somebody/something
sing	singular
sl	slang
usu.	usually
v	verb
vs. *(Latin)*	versus *(gegen, im Gegensatz zu)*

CC	Communicating across Cultures
EE	Everyday English
EP	Exam Practice
LP	Language Practice
SF	Skills File
PREVIEW	refers to the advance organizer (chapter preview) in the Lead-in of each chapter.
LANGUAGE HELP	gives you ideas, words and phrases to get started on tasks.
TROUBLE SPOT	points out language difficulties and common mistakes.
CHALLENGE	marks a more difficult task.
SUPPORT	refers you to the Support Pages (pp. 200–217) where you can find more help to do the assignment.
YOU CHOOSE	lets you decide which of the two given assignments you would like to do.
BASIC	marks a task that tests language skills you should already be familiar with.
*metaphor	indicates that a word or expression (here: *metaphor*) is explained in the Glossary (pp. 323–339).
▶ SF 21	directs you to the Skills File (here: Skill 21).
▶ LP 7	directs you to the Language Practice section (here: Language task 7).
🎧 **CD2** 04	indicates that the sound file can be found on the accompanying audio CD (here: CD2, track 4).
🎬 **DVD**	indicates that the film or video clip can be found on the accompanying video DVD.
🔊 **Webcode**	can be entered at www.cornelsen.de/webcodes to connect you to a website with additional material or support.

About the photograph on the cover of this book

The cover photo, taken in April 2013 near the junction of St Mary Axe and Leadenhall Street in London, shows a number of well-known buildings in the City of London's 'Tower Cluster' zone:

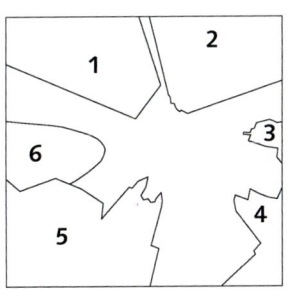

1 *St Helen's*, 1 Undershaft, Gollins Melvin Ward Partnership 1969, 28 storeys

2 *The Leadenhall Building (the Cheesegrater)*, 122 Leadenhall Street, Rogers Steark Harbour + Partners 2013, 48 storeys

3 *Lloyd's building*, 1 Lime Street, Richard Rogers 1986, 14 storeys

4 *Willis Building*, 51 Lime Street, Foster + Partners 2007, 26 storeys

5 *St Andrew Undershaft*, 1532

6 *30 St Mary Axe (the Gherkin)*, Foster + Partners 2003, 41 storeys

1 Modern Media – Tools or Tyrants?

Download a list of chapter vocab here:

 Webcode context-01

retard ['riːtɑːd] (*taboo, sl*) stupid person

▶ SF 13: Analysing cartoons

BEING FIVE *A kid who blogs using voice recognition software* by GEORGE SFARNAS ©2014 beingfive.blogspot.com

Panel 1: I'M A DIGITAL NATIVE, WHICH MEANS I WAS BORN IN THE AGE OF TECHNOLOGY...SO IT COMES NATURAL TO ME!

Panel 2: MY PARENTS ARE DIGITAL IMMIGRANTS, WHICH MEANS THEY CAN LEARN TECHNOLOGY, BUT THEY HAVE TO WORK AT IT!

Panel 3: AND MY GRANDPARENTS ARE DIGITAL RETARDS, WHICH MEANS THEY BARELY KNOW HOW TO USE A TOASTER!

1 Talking about a cartoon

a **THINK** Make a few notes on the message of the cartoon above.

b **PAIR** With a partner, collect examples to illustrate the degree of media literacy that is to be expected of each of the three groups referred to in the cartoon.

c **SHARE** Present your findings in class. Focusing on your peer group, agree on the three types of media you use most.

> I hate television. I hate it as much as peanuts. But I can't stop eating peanuts.
> **Orson Welles** (1915–1985)

> I fear the day technology will surpass our human interaction. The world will have a generation of idiots.
> **Albert Einstein** (1879–1955)

> The concept of surveillance is ingrained in our beings. God was the original surveillance camera.
> **Hasan M. Elahi** (born 1972)

> We're still in the first minutes of the first day of the internet revolution.
> **Scott Cook** (born 1952)

surpass sb./sth. [səˈpɑːs] (fml) be better or greater than sb./sth. else
surveillance [səˈveɪləns] careful watching of a person or place
ingrained firmly established and therefore difficult to change

2 MARKETPLACE (MILLING-AROUND ACTIVITY) **The digital age**

a Walk around your classroom. As soon as your teacher tells you to stop, turn to the student nearest to you and discuss one of the four quotes above. Say how much you agree or disagree with the statements by Welles, Einstein, Elahi or Cook. Justify your opinion (and take notes).
When your teacher gives a signal, swap partners. Repeat this activity until everyone has discussed all the four quotes.

b Present and evaluate the results of your discussions in class.

CD1 02

Listen to an audio version of the text on the CD or download it here:
Webcode context-02

Living interactive lives

Connected

In recent years a great many social networks have been developed to cater for people of different age groups and interests. Not only do they offer an easy way of staying in touch with friends and acquaintances, they also provide a platform to 'meet' like-minded people, exchange ideas and material, seek advice and   5
collaborate on a private and professional level. However, people's 'likes' and 'dislikes' are carefully stored, along with a great number of other details gathered about the users, to be exploited by businesses or political organizations. This pool of information allows for personalized ads as well as effective campaigning, but with it comes the danger of subtle manipula-   10
tion. Despite warnings as to the potential abuse of data inadvertently revealed, social networks continue to grow in popularity, especially among younger people, who have embraced a virtual lifestyle from an early age on and are therefore used   15
to sharing their everyday lives with an online community.

Digital media has also had a major impact on the educational system. Though banned or at least restricted at first, its   20
potential for supporting self-initiated learning has by now been recognized, turning it into a valuable teaching tool for research, cooperative learning and self-study, to name but a few of its   25
numerous uses. With the demand for media literacy increasing in every type of job and schools responding to the requirements of the 21st century, there has been a shift to a more media-based way of   30
teaching, which is more able to integrate students with special needs.

Surveillance

Digital media gives users access to a huge amount of un-filtered information. However, it also reveals details about individual   35
users, be it intentionally or by chance. Hence secret services have benefitted greatly from sophisticated surveillance technology. Moreover, CCTV is starting to be used in schools, both as a security measure and a means of quality control.

Reality TV   40

Even though most people show some degree of uneasiness when it comes to video or data surveillance, there seem to be fewer qualms about watching common people's lives exposed on TV for entertainment. The growing popularity of reality TV, which can turn anybody into a celebrity or failure depending on the audience's response, reflects the general trend of people's   45
more interactive approach to the media.

■ **TROUBLE SPOT**

the media (l. 34) + *singular verb or plural verb*
Digital media gives/give …
The media has/have …

▶ SF 2: Learning new words

1 Words in use

Find the <mark>highlighted</mark> words or phrases in the text that match these definitions:

1 engage in a way of life that is centred on the internet
2 encourage independent studying
3 make something available
4 feeling uncomfortable with something
5 work and study together
6 friends or contacts you don't know very well
7 show something that is usually hidden
8 unintentionally

2 Improving your style

a Gather phrases from the text that express the idea of 'a lot of'. Go beyond the highlighted words.

b Collect linking words from the text. Classify them in three categories according to their meaning:

▶ LP 15: Connecting your thoughts (sentence structure)

Adding a similar aspect	Introducing a contrast	Drawing a conclusion

c Fill in additional linking words that you know. Compare your results with those of your partner and present them in class.

3 Grammar and style: Participle constructions

▶ SF 4: Using a grammar book
▶ LP 15: Connecting your thoughts (sentence structure)

a Rewrite the underlined clauses using participle constructions.

1 People who use smartphones sometimes seem to become addicted to them.
2 As they are afraid that they might miss out on something, they constantly check their digital device.
3 They often annoy their parents or even friends by the fact that they are glued to their screen while they are having a conversation.
4 Although they realize that they may get into trouble if they use their phone in class, some of them just can't stop playing with their mobile anyway.

b How is the following participle construction different from the others in the text? How would you translate *with* here?
With the demand for media literacy increasing in every type of job and schools responding to the requirements of the 21st century, there has been a shift to a more media-based way of teaching, which is more able to integrate students with special needs. (ll. 26–32)

▶ LP 16: Avoiding Germanisms

c Rewrite this sentence, using *with* followed by a participle construction.
As the rules at school strictly forbid the use of mobile phones in class, teachers are required to take action against mobile phone use in their classrooms.

4 Discussion

Has Facebook changed the concept of 'friendship'? Discuss this question with a partner, using as many of the <mark>highlighted</mark> words from the text as possible.

Ms Moem

📽 **DVD**

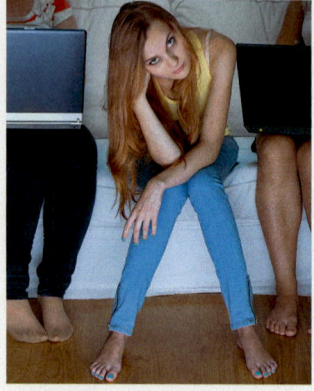

▶ SF 41: Mediation of written and oral texts

▶ SF 21: Analysing poetry

LANGUAGE HELP
• win a friend ⟷ lose a friend
• make friends with sb. = forge/form/develop/build a friendship with sb.
• cultivate a friendship
• a close/special/intimate ['ɪntɪmət] /trusted/loyal/true/lifelong/long-time/long-lost/new-found friend
• a fair-weather friend (= sb. who will let you down when you are in need)
• a casual acquaintance [ə'kweɪntəns] (= a person you don't know very well)

Dis-connected

A1 Lonely friends *Ms Moem*

Ms Moem is a contemporary English poet, who writes poems, rhymes and verses on all topics. She has her own poetry blog website.

- Watch and listen to Ms Moem's poem 'Connected' – a poem about Facebook, Twitter, YouTube and social media in general.

COMPREHENSION ◀

1 First impressions
  a Make notes on the effect of listening to the poem and watching its words unfold in the video clip. Then compare your experiences in class and discuss your first understanding of the content of the poem.
  b Sum up the essence of this poem as a Twitter message of no more than 140 characters.

2 Understanding the speaker's attitude towards social media
  a List the aspects that are important for the speaker with regard to social networks.
  b State how important the speaker considers her own role as a social media user. Give evidence from the text.

3 Mediation (English → German)
Your friend is fascinated with social networks and has shared Ms Moem's video clip with you and other friends on a social networking site. He recommended it because he feels it reflects his positive attitude towards social media. Outline to him in German what the poem actually says about social media.

ANALYSIS ◀

4 Poetic devices
Examine which means the poet uses to draw our attention to the influence of social media on our lives. **SUPPORT** ▶ p. 200

5 The message
Interpret what impact the internet has had on human relationships according to Ms Moem's poem.

BEYOND THE TEXT ◀

6 Creating images
In small groups, discuss how you could underline the message of the poem with video sequences or stills instead of showing the words in the video clip. You may also include ideas for background music. Present your ideas to each other.

7 Writing a comment
'Oh why can't we turn the time back.
It was simpler when we could just be friends, and that didn't depend on whether someone had accepted your friend request.'
Write a short comment in which you state why you do or do not agree with this statement from Ms Moem's poem. ▶ LANGUAGE HELP

CULTURE SPOT

New media art:
Viewpoint of Billions with Google Glass *(2013)*

- *American artist David Datuna was the first to incorporate internet-connected smartglasses ('wearable computing') into a piece of modern art.*
- *Four interactive cameras have been built into a 12-foot (3.67 m) flag of the United States of America. These will automatically connect with viewers wearing Google Glass.*
- *Photos, newspaper clippings and videos of famous moments in US history have been placed behind thousands of optical lenses. They will be projected to the wearer's 'third eye' when they look at the artwork.*
- *For up to three minutes viewers will have a unique experience, e.g. they can answer questions posed by Glass and have their responses and experiences recorded and uploaded onto the artist's website, YouTube and Tumblr.*

DVD Watch a video on David Datuna's interactive installation 'Viewpoint of Billions with Google Glass'.

1 Describe David Datuna's art installation. How is art created with new media?

2 Explain the title of the installation. Work in pairs and exchange your opinions on this work of art.

3 Discuss in class whether or not you would like to contribute to Datuna's interactive installation.

For another work of art based on the Stars and Stripes, see p. 140.

A2 Online learning in 2044 *Ernest Cline*

The following text is an extract from a science-fiction *novel. It's the year 2044, and Wade Watts, the teenaged *protagonist, escapes his depressing reality by spending his waking hours immersed in the OASIS, a virtual utopia where you can be anything you want to be on any of ten thousand planets, if you can pay for it.

4 **oasis** [əʊˈeɪsɪs] (here) retreat, pleasant place in the middle of sth. unpleasant
13 **thrift store** *(AE)* = *(BE)* **charity shop** shop selling second-hand clothing at low prices
16 **T-1000** fictional robot consisting of liquid metal and therefore capable of changing its shape; evil terminator in the film *Terminator 2*
19 **invariably** [ɪnˈveərɪəbli] always
21 **(run a) gauntlet** [ˈgɔːntlət] deal with a lot of people criticizing or attacking you
23 **sanity** [ˈsænəti] mental health
24 **a passing grade-point average** average of the grades achieved in all of the classes throughout a school year that is sufficient to proceed to the next year

I'd attended school in the real world up until the sixth grade. It hadn't been a very pleasant experience. I was a painfully shy, awkward kid, with low self-esteem and almost no social skills – a side effect of spending most of my childhood inside the OASIS. Online, I didn't have a problem talking to people or making friends. But in the real world, interacting with other people – especially kids my own age – made me 5
a nervous wreck. I never knew how to act or what to say, and when I did work up the courage to speak, I always seemed to say the wrong thing.

My appearance was part of the problem. I was overweight, and had been for as long as I could remember. My bankrupt diet of government-subsidized sugar and starch-laden food was a contributing factor, but I was also an OASIS addict, so the only exercise I usually got back then was running away from the bullies before and after 10
school. To make matters worse, my limited wardrobe consisted entirely of ill-fitting clothes from thrift stores and donation bins – the social equivalent of having a bull's-eye painted on my forehead.

Even so, I tried my best to fit in. Year after year, my eyes would scan the lunchroom 15
like a T-1000, searching for a clique that might accept me. But even the other outcasts wanted nothing to do with me. I was too weird, even for the weirdos. And girls? Talking to girls was out of the question. To me, they were like some exotic alien species, both beautiful and terrifying. Whenever I got near one of them I invariably broke out in a cold sweat and lost the ability to speak in complete sentences. 20

For me, school had been a Darwinian exercise. A daily gauntlet of ridicule, abuse, and isolation. By the time I entered sixth grade, I was beginning to wonder if I'd be able to maintain my sanity until graduation, still six long years away.

Then, one glorious day, our principal announced that any student with a passing grade-point average could apply for a transfer to the new OASIS public school system. 25

OPS #1873

The real public school system, the one run by the government, had been an underfunded, overcrowded train wreck for decades. And 30
now the conditions at many schools had gotten so terrible that every kid with half a brain was being encouraged to stay at home and attend 35
school online. I nearly broke my neck sprinting to the school office to submit my application. It was accepted, and I transferred to OASIS 40
Public School #1873 the following semester.

Prior to my transfer, my OASIS avatar had never left Incipio, the planet at the center of Sector One where avatars were spawned at the time of their creation. There wasn't
45 much to do on Incipio except chat with other noobs or shop in one of the giant virtual malls that covered the planet. If you wanted to go somewhere more interesting, you had to pay a teleportation fare to get there, and that cost money, something I didn't have. So my avatar was stranded on Incipio. That is, until my new school e-mailed me a teleportation voucher to cover the cost of my avatar's transport to Ludus, the planet
50 where all of the OASIS public schools were located.

There were hundreds of school campuses here on Ludus, spread out evenly across the planet's surface. The schools were all identical, because the same construction code was copied and pasted into a different location whenever a new school was needed. And since the buildings were just pieces of software, their design wasn't
55 limited by monetary constraints, or even by the laws of physics. So every school was a grand palace of learning with polished marble hallways, cathedral-like classrooms, zero-g gymnasiums, and virtual libraries containing every (school board-approved) book ever written.

On my first day at OPS #1873, I thought I'd died and gone to heaven. Now, instead
60 of running a gauntlet of bullies and drug addicts on my walk to school each morning, I went straight to my hideout and stayed there all day. Best of all, in the OASIS, no one could tell that I was fat, that I had acne, or that I wore the same shabby clothes every week. Bullies couldn't pelt me with spitballs, give me atomic wedgies, or pummel me by the bike rack after school. No one could even touch me. In here, I was
65 safe.

From: *Ready Player One*, 2012

43 incipio (*Latin*) I am beginning, I begin
44 spawn sth. produce sth.
45 noob (*sl*) a person that has just started doing sth. and is very inexperienced in it
49 ludus (*Latin*) game, school
55 monetary constraint financial restriction
57 school board-approved accepted by the institution in charge of local schools
63 pelt sb. with sth. attack sb. by throwing things at them
give sb. atomic wedgies (*infml*) pull sb.'s underwear up forcefully as a kind of bullying, usually performed on male victims
64 pummel sb. [ˈpʌml] keep hitting sb.

COMPREHENSION ◄

1 Understanding the situation
a Name Wade's reasons for wanting to attend the new OASIS public school.
b Describe the schools on Ludus.
c Point out what makes OPS #1873 so much better in Wade's opinion.

ANALYSIS ◄

2 Telling names
Refer to the annotations and analyse what the names reveal about the
*character and the *setting. **SUPPORT** ▶ p. 200

LANGUAGE AWARENESS ◄

3 Telling images
a Study the following (parts of) sentences in their contexts and paraphrase their meaning.

1 My bankrupt diet of government-subsidized sugar and starch-laden food was a contributing factor … (ll. 9–10)
2 … the social equivalent of having a bull's-eye painted on my forehead. (ll. 13–14)
3 For me, school had been a Darwinian exercise. A daily gauntlet of ridicule, abuse, and isolation. (ll. 21–22)
4 The real public school system, the one run by the government, had been an underfunded, overcrowded train wreck for decades. (ll. 26–30)

b The sentences in **a** all contain *images. Interpret what they tell you about the protagonist.
c **CHALLENGE** ▶ Write an analysis of the telling *images in the text, taking further examples into account.

▶ SF 9: Paraphrasing

WRITING FOCUS ON SKILLS

Writing an argumentative text

In argumentative writing, we present arguments for and against a topic in order to convince others of our point of view. Writing an argumentative text is often a requirement in both school-leaving and international language proficiency examinations. You usually have a time limit and must keep within a certain number of words.

A typical assignment could be:
'Discuss whether attending OASIS public school will solve Wade's problems.'

1 Examining the task

Before gathering any arguments, make sure you are familiar with the meaning of the keywords of the task, i.e. *OASIS public school* and *Wade's problems*. (Refer to your work on text **A2**, p. 17.)

2 Collecting arguments

Divide the class into two groups. One half of the class has to find at least three reasons why OASIS might be considered the perfect school for Wade, the other half has to collect at least three arguments supporting the idea that his problems will remain. Work on your own and make notes.

3 Developing a thesis and an antithesis

Arrange a central meeting point in the classroom, the so-called database. As soon as you have finished collecting your arguments, go to the database and pair up with a student from the other group. Exchange your arguments. Discuss and reach an agreement on how to answer the topic question. The position you support is called the thesis ['θiːsɪz], the one you reject is called the antithesis [æn'tɪθəsɪs].

4 Composing the argumentative text

1 Introduction

Start your text with an interesting example, quote, definition or statistic related to your topic in order to grab your reader's attention. Then introduce the topic itself with a clear statement or *rhetorical question. Compare and evaluate the following three introductions:

A   *Online schooling is a type of distance learning. You take courses without attending an actual school. Students and teachers interact via the internet, rather than meeting face-to-face. Wade sees this aspect as a big improvement on his old school. But will changing schools really solve his problems?*

B   *'On my first day at OPS #1873, I thought I'd died and gone to heaven.' This is Wade's first impression of his new online school, after leaving the bullies of his old school behind. But will his opinion change as he gets to know his new school better?*

C   *Statistically, one in four students is regularly bullied at school in the USA. So there are lots of real-life Wades looking for a way out of their difficult situation. Wade chooses to attend an online school to escape his problems at school. But will online-education really turn out to be a positive alternative for Wade?*

Either choose one of these introductions for your argumentative text or create your own.

2 Main part

On the basis of your notes from **3** on the opposite page, compose the main part of your argumentative text. Remember to start a new paragraph for every part of your text and avoid using contracted forms like *there's, she's, he'll,* etc.

Use some of the linking words from **Words in Context** to connect your ideas. Here are some additional phrases to help you structure your text:

► LP 11: Using the right register

► LP 14: Linking words and phrases

► LP 15: Connecting your thoughts (sentence structure)

Presenting various options	*on the one hand – on the other hand* *not only – but also* *either – or*
Giving reasons	*because* *as* *since ('da', 'weil')*
Giving examples	*for example (e.g.)* *for instance* *such as*

Complete the following sentences and add your own reasons and examples illustrating your arguments:

On the one hand, Wade's difficult situation may improve for a while because …
On the other hand, online education is unlikely to completely solve his problems as …

3 Conclusion

The purpose of the conclusion is to round off your argumentative text. For this reason you should not present any new arguments but rather draw a logical conclusion from your line of arguments in order to support your thesis, for example predict what will happen to Wade.

Summing up	*In brief ('kurz gesagt'), …* *To sum up, …* *In conclusion, I would like to say that …* *In the final analysis ('letztendlich', 'alles in allem'), …*

Complete the following conclusion by briefly stating your view and adding your own idea of how Wade might overcome his problem.

To sum up, in my opinion Wade's escape into the virtual world will only create more problems. Instead of trying to avoid all human interaction, he should rather …

Who wrote this essay, Perkins?
You or Google?

A3 Digital media at school *Gerhard Witossek*

The following text is from the home page of a German educational institution.
It includes information on the kinds of devices and services that are suitable for
school, their benefits and potential drawbacks.

Digitale Medien im Lehr- und Lernprozess

Im Wandel

Ist von digitalen Medien im Unterricht die Rede, heißt das in vielen Schulen die
Nutzung von Internet, Lernplattformen und Beamern. Diese sind in die Klassenräume
eingezogen und sind weitgehend Bestandteil modernen Unterrichts.

In den letzten Jahren hat sich die Veränderungsdynamik deutlich beschleunigt: In 5
der gegenwärtigen Diskussion geht es um die Nutzung von „interaktiven White-
boards", „Clouds", „Tablet-PCs" und „Smartphones". Insbesondere die Tablet-PCs,
großformatige Smartphones und die Arbeitsmöglichkeiten in der Cloud entwickeln
sich rasant weiter.

Dabei stellt sich die Frage, wie diese Medien zielgerichtet im Unterricht eingesetzt 10
werden können. Digitale Medien sollen nicht zum Selbstzweck werden, sondern den
Lehr-Lern-Prozess fördern. Darüber hinaus soll den Schülerinnen und Schülern ein
sinnvoller und reflektierter Umgang mit den neuen Technologien vermittelt werden.
Es gilt also, mediendidaktische, medienerzieherische und mediengestalterische Kompetenzen zu entwickeln und miteinander in Einklang zu bringen. 15

Im Unterricht

Digitale Medien sicher zu beherrschen, die neuen Entwicklungen zu verfolgen und
sinnvoll in den Lehr-Lern-Prozess zu implementieren, stellt für die einzelne Lehrkraft
eine große Aufgabe dar. Neben anderen und bewährten Medien und Methoden sollen
digitale Medien den Unterricht bereichern: Veranschaulichung, Handlungs- 20
orientierung oder die Förderung sozialer Kompetenzen sind nur einige Anfor-
derungen an den Unterricht, die leichter mit digitalen Medien erfüllt werden können.

Die Arbeit mit digitalen Medien ermöglicht auch neue Unterrichtsstrukturen. Die
üblichen 45-Minuten-Einheiten können besser verbunden werden. An Kreidetafeln
lebte das erarbeitete Ergebnis bislang meist nur in den Heften der
Schüler fort. Bedient man sich digitaler Tafeln oder Lernplattformen
zur Sicherung der Ergebnisse,
können diese wieder gezeigt,
verändert und weiterentwickelt
werden. Der „rote Faden" einer 30
Unterrichtssequenz wird da-
durch deutlicher und die
Entwicklungsschritte im Unterricht greifbarer.

Digitale Medien können 35
Schülerinnen und Schülern
auch ein anderes Lernen außer-
halb der Schule ermöglichen.
Beispielsweise können Unter-
richtsmaterialien in die Cloud gestellt, interaktive Übungen im Internet genutzt
oder Apps sinnvoll eingesetzt werden. [...]

False friends

Beamer
= video projector
Handy = mobile phone/
cellphone
(Lautsprecher-)Box
= (loud)speaker

Die Chancen

Der Einsatz digitaler Medien im Unterricht ist integraler Bestandteil zeitgemäßen
45 pädagogischen Handelns. Schülerinnen und Schüler wachsen mit den neuen
Technologien auf, sie gehören zu den Kulturtechniken unserer Gesellschaft. Deshalb
liegt es auch in der Verantwortung der Schule, dazu beizutragen, dass Kinder und
Jugendliche Medienkompetenz entwickeln können. Es darf auch nicht vergessen
werden, dass Jugendliche bereits von sich aus digitale Medien für die Schule nutzen.
50 Beispielsweise recherchieren sie mit Hilfe des mobilen Internets, tauschen sich per
Facebook über Unterrichtsinhalte aus oder stellen sich in der Cloud gegenseitig
Arbeitsmaterialien bereit. Diese generelle Bereitschaft zum Umgang mit digitalen
Medien kann für den Unterricht produktiv genutzt werden.

Digitale Medien können auch die Lehrkraft entlasten. Im Internet finden sich Un-
55 terrichtsmaterialien, Freeware, Apps oder Lernplattformen, die schnell verfügbar und
benutzerfreundlich sind. Zum Beispiel können der Tafelanschrieb am interaktiven
Whiteboard abgespeichert, interaktive Übungen nach Hause mitgegeben oder Ar-
beitsblätter online zur Verfügung gestellt werden.

Die Nutzung neuer Medien im Unterricht bereitet Jugendliche auf ihr Arbeits-
60 leben vor: In fast allen Berufen ist der Computer das Arbeitsmittel schlechthin. Die
hohe Veränderungsdynamik sorgt auch hier für schnelle Entwicklungen, auf die
Schülerinnen und Schüler vorbereitet werden müssen.

Die Risiken

Jugendliche werden häufig als „digital natives" bezeichnet, also als eine Generation,
65 die mit neuen Medien aufwächst und in deren Alltag die Nutzung digitaler Medien
ganz normal ist. Dies führt allerdings nicht automatisch zu einem reflektierten und
bedachten Umgang mit den Möglichkeiten der digitalen Welt. Beschäftigt man sich
im Unterricht näher mit dem Schutz persönlicher Daten in sozialen Netzwerken, so
zeigt sich sehr schnell, dass längst nicht alle Schülerinnen und Schüler die Risiken
70 überblicken.

From: *Münchner kommunaler Bildungsserver*, October 2014

Mediation (German → English)

Imagine you are spending a school year as an exchange student at a high school
in Oregon, USA. Your exchange school is about to introduce a new media
concept. In order to incorporate a wide range of ideas, all of its exchange
students are asked to outline the role of digital media at school in their home
countries. Use the German article as the basis for your English presentation to
the school board. Make some notes.

▶ SF 41: Mediation of written and oral texts
▶ SF 24: Giving a presentation

1

Part B

Being on display

B1 Should classrooms have video cameras?

- Work in pairs. Partner A deals with text **1** (T1), partner B with text **2** (T2). Read your text and take notes of the arguments you find.

T1 👍 YES

Cameras will protect students and teachers

Video cameras need to be in the classroom in order to protect the safety of both students and teachers. In today's society we have video cameras in lots of public spaces such as libraries, school buses, parks, beaches, public streets, etc. A public school is a public place just like any other public place so people are not entitled to privacy rights. 5

1. A video recording could be the one thing that saves a teacher's job when there are false accusations.

2. Video recording could protect a student who wants protection from a teacher who is abusing them. 10

3. A video recording could ensure students are being protected from wrongdoing by other students.

For people who are worried about the security of it, the camera data and controls could be kept in the Principal's office. For people complaining about privacy rights and 'Big Brother': in public property the right to privacy does 15 not exist. If you don't like it, you can either homeschool or pay to go to a private school. Oh by the way, the only eyewitness of the Boston Marathon Bombers? A video camera.

T1

6 **be entitled to (do) sth.** have the right to (do) sth.
8 **false accusations** being charged with sth. one has not done

T2

3 **police sth.** monitor sth. closely, keep control over sth.
interfere with sth. disturb sth., prevent sth. from succeeding
4 **benefit sb.** ['benɪfɪt] be to sb.'s advantage
11 **dehumanize sb.** [ˌdiːˈhjuːmənaɪz] make sb. lose their human dignity
train sth. on sb. aim a camera, gun, etc. at sb.
16 **deter sth.** [dɪˈtɜː] prevent sth. from happening
19 **resemble sth.** be similar to sth.
20 **trapped** unable to move or escape

▶ LP 11: Using the right register

COMPREHENSION ◀

1 Collecting arguments

Share your arguments with your partner and discuss which ones you consider most convincing.

LANGUAGE AWARENESS ◀

2 Using more formal language

Texts T1 and T2 contain some elements of informal language. In an argumentative text, you should aim at using more formal language. Rewrite the underlined parts of these sentences using a more formal *register:
1 A public school is a public place just like any other public place. (T1, l. 5)
2 A video recording could be the one thing that saves a teacher's job. (T1, ll. 7–8)
3 You're treating them like they are already criminals. (T2, l. 12)
4 Think about how you would feel if you had a camera on you. (T2, ll. 20–21)

CCTV (closed-circuit television) is a system in which television signals are not publicly broadcast but are monitored only by those people who have access to the system's content (**'closed circuit'** ['sɜːkɪt]). The primary purpose of CCTV is to reduce crime and anti-social behaviour, especially in public places and shops. With around 4.2 million CCTV cameras (one for every 14 people), Britain has become the most watched country in the world, a **'surveillance society'**.

What would be your immediate reaction to CCTV cameras in your classroom? Make notes and discuss them with a partner.

NO 👎 **T2**

The possibility of abuse of power is too great.
I do not believe that cameras in the classroom would be/will be used to prevent bullying and abuse, rather to police and interfere with teaching. It would be too easy to manipulate and use the tapes in a way that benefits
5 the administration and not the teacher. Furthermore, students and teachers should never be observed without their knowing, and I can see that becoming a problem.
You may wonder why teachers have such a problem with the invasion of privacy. It's not about having something to hide, after all, they are
10 frequently observed and, after all, the classroom is full of students. It's dehumanizing to have cameras trained on teachers and students at all times. You're treating them like they are already criminals, and I think students especially have enough to deal with.
Claiming that this will prevent/end teacher or student abuse ignores the
15 real problem. If there is abuse going on, there needs to be actual action taken. It's not enough to think that cameras will deter certain actions, as most people will not think of their actions as bullying, and if they do, they might be talented in hiding it.
I think schools resemble prisons enough as it is. I do not think students
20 need further reason to feel trapped and exposed. Think about how you would feel if you had a camera on you while trying to learn.

From: *Debate.org*

■ TROUBLE SPOT

the possibility of (doing) sth.
(l. 1)
the possibility that sth. may happen
Not: ~~the possibility to do sth.~~

■ TROUBLE SPOT

actual ['æktʃuəl] (l. 15) =
tatsächlich, wirklich, konkret
But: *aktuell* = **topical, current**

► LP 16: Avoiding Germanisms

◄ BEYOND THE TEXT

3 Discussing the pros and cons of surveillance at school
Get together in groups of four and do the following task:
As there have been some cases of bullying and vandalism at your school, the school board wants to introduce CCTV cameras inside and outside the school building (except for the private toilet cubicles) to monitor and protect the students.
As student representatives you are on a committee that will be heard before the school board's final decision.
a Discuss the pros and cons of the proposed idea.
b Develop a concept that you consider acceptable for your school.
c Present your concept to the school board (i.e. the class).
SUPPORT ► p. 200

► SF 27: Having a discussion
► SF 24: Giving a presentation

CD1 03

game changer sth. that changes a situation completely

B2 9/11 – a game changer   *Barack Obama*

The following extract is taken from remarks on US intelligence programmes by US President Barack Obama, on 17 January 2014.

- Study the word cloud below, which contains the most frequently used words in Obama's remarks. The size of the letters indicates the frequency of the words. Work with a partner and speculate on the general content of Obama's remarks, using as many words from the cloud as possible.

---

1 **intelligence** [ɪnˈtelɪdʒəns] secret information about an enemy

2 **President Truman (Harry S. Truman)** 33rd US President (1945–1953)

4 **avert sth.** [əˈvɜːt] prevent sth.

6 **anchor sth.** [ˈæŋkə] fix sth. firmly

7 **checks and balances** mutual control

> **TROUBLE SPOT**
>
> *ordinary*
> [*BE:* ˈɔːdnri, *AE:* ˈɔːrdneri] (ll. 7–8)
> = *gewöhnlich, durchschnittlich*
> But: *ordinär = **vulgar** [ˈvʌlgə]*

---

9 **informer** sb. who gives away secrets, usually for money

13 **revelation** [ˌrevəˈleɪʃn] act of disclosing secrets

15 **twilight** (here) final stage of sth. when it becomes weaker or less important than it used to be

18 **emerge** [iˈmɜːdʒ] appear, to become known

19 **proliferation** [prəˌlɪfəˈreɪʃn] rapid increase

Throughout American history, intelligence has helped secure our country and our freedoms. [...] (I)n the early days of the Cold War, President Truman created the National Security Agency, or NSA, to give us insights into the Soviet bloc, and provide our leaders with information they needed to confront aggression and avert catastrophe.

Throughout this evolution, we benefited from both our Constitution and our tradi- 5
tions of limited government. U.S. intelligence agencies were anchored in a system of checks and balances – with oversight from elected leaders, and protections for ordinary citizens. Meanwhile, totalitarian states like East Germany offered a cautionary tale of what could happen when vast, unchecked surveillance turned citizens into informers, and persecuted people for what they said in the privacy of their own homes. 10

In fact, even the United States proved not to be immune to the abuse of surveillance. And in the 1960s, government spied on civil rights leaders and critics of the Vietnam War. And partly in response to these revelations, additional laws were established in the 1970s to ensure that our intelligence capabilities could not be misused against our citizens. In the long, twilight struggle against Communism, we had been 15
reminded that the very liberties that we sought to preserve could not be sacrificed at the altar of national security.

If the fall of the Soviet Union left America without a competing superpower, emerging threats from terrorist groups, and the proliferation of weapons of mass destruction placed new and in some ways more complicated demands on our intelligence 20
agencies. Globalization and the Internet made these threats more acute, as technology erased borders and empowered individuals to project great violence, as well as great good. Moreover, these new threats raised new legal and new policy questions.

For while few doubted the legitimacy of spying on hostile states, our framework of
25 laws was not fully adapted to prevent terrorist attacks by individuals acting on their
own, or acting in small, ideologically driven groups on behalf of a foreign power.

The horror of September 11th brought all these issues to the fore. Across the political spectrum, Americans recognized that we had to adapt to a world in which a bomb
could be built in a basement, and our electric grid could be shut down by operators
30 an ocean away. We were shaken by the signs we had missed leading up to the attacks
– how the hijackers had made phone calls to known extremists and traveled to suspi-
cious places. So we demanded that our intelligence community improve its capabilities, and that law enforcement change practices to focus more on preventing attacks
before they happen than prosecuting terrorists after an attack.

35 It is hard to overstate the transformation America's intelligence community had to
go through after 9/11. Our agencies suddenly needed to do far more than the traditional mission of monitoring hostile powers and gathering information for policy-
makers. Instead, they were now asked to identify and target plotters in some of the
most remote parts of the world, and to anticipate the actions of networks that, by their
40 very nature, cannot be easily penetrated with spies or informants. [...]

From: the official website of the White House, 17 January 2014

24 **hostile** [*BE:* ˈhɒstaɪl, *AE:* ˈhɑːstl]
belonging to the enemy
26 **on behalf of** as a representative
of
27 **bring sth. to the fore** gain
public attention for sth.
38 **plotter** sb. making secret plans
to harm others

■ FACT FILE

9/11 refers to September 11th,
2001. On this date four planes
were hijacked by terrorists in
the USA. One plane crashed in
Pennsylvania, one destroyed
part of the Pentagon in
Virginia, and two flew into the
World Trade Center, New York
City. About 3,000 people were
killed in these attacks which
were conducted by the ex-
treme Islamic group Al Qaeda
[ælˈkaɪdə].

──────────── COMPREHENSION ◄

1 The structure of the text
   a Divide this extract into parts and give headings to each part.
   b Outline Obama's argumentation in your own words.

▶ SF 38: Writing a well-
structured text

──────────── ANALYSIS ◄

2 Understanding the title
Explain why 9/11 can be considered a 'game changer' with regard to US
security policy.

3 Analysing stylistic devices
   a The phrases in the box on the right are quotes from the
   text. Explain their meaning.
   b Point out what *stylistic device is used in all of these
   phrases and analyse the effect achieved by employing it.
   c Go over the text again and find at least one example of
   an *antithesis. Describe its effect on the reader.

▶ SF 17: Analysing stylistic devices
▶ Glossary, p. 323

- 'U.S. intelligence agencies were anchored in a system of
checks and balances' (ll. 6–7)
- 'states like East Germany offered a cautionary tale'
(ll. 8–9)
- 'the very liberties that we sought to preserve could not
be sacrificed at the altar of national security' (ll. 16–17)

──────────── BEYOND THE TEXT ◄

4 Evaluating a cartoon
   a Analyse the cartoon on the right, keeping in mind
   some of the information presented in Obama's
   speech.
   b CHALLENGE ▶ 'It is hard to overstate the transformation America's intelligence community had
   to go through after 9/11.' (ll. 35–36)
   Look for a cartoon on the internet that expresses the
   idea of the quote, print it and bring it along to class.
   Tape it to the wall of your classroom and analyse it
   orally with your classmates as they walk from cartoon
   to cartoon.
   After examining all the cartoons, stand next to the
   one you prefer in order to select the most popular
   cartoon. Be prepared to justify your choice.

▶ SF 13: Analysing cartoons

Reality TV

C1 Big Brother out of this world *Ellie Zolfagharifard*

Creators of a reality TV show plan to broadcast the selection and training of a group of candidates who will be sent on a one-way mission to Mars in 2025. Is Big Brother going to take on the red planet?

It takes a certain type of person to apply for a one-way ticket to Mars. Not only will they require mental and physical strength, but now, they will also need to have the makings of the next reality-TV star. Endemol, the production company behind Big Brother, has announced that it will document the progress of a group of hopefuls as they compete for a 2025 ticket to the red planet. 5

The reality series will follow the selection process of the privately-funded Mars One mission, which aims to launch 20 humans on Mars within the next decade. During the first selection round, more than 200,000 people signed up to be part of the first human colony on the red planet. The applicants have now been shortlisted to 705 candidates – 418 men and 287 women – who will undergo what is described as 'the world's toughest job interview'. 10

Darlow Smithson Productions (DSP), an Endemol company, will film the hopefuls as they are 'tested to the extreme as part of an elite training programme'. Candidates do not need to have any scientific qualifications and a Big Brother-style audience vote will be used to make the final choice. Any chosen Mars settlers will then be required 15 to dedicate eight years of their lives preparing for the 300 million-mile pioneering mission. The ticket is one-way and Mars One plans to send additional crews every two years to expand the colony.

DSP said its production will be seen around the world, with the first series likely to be appearing in early 2015. The plan is for the cameras to also follow the first human 20 settlers on the planet as they attempt to build a new society from scratch.

'Our team felt all along that we needed a partner whose strength lies in factual storytelling to an international audience,' Mars One co-founder Bas Lansdorp said in a statement. 'DSP will provide that to Mars One, while allowing our selection committee to maintain control of the applicant selection process.' [...] 25

The majority of applicants for the one-way trip to Mars came from the US, with India and China coming in second and third place. The second round will include an interview with Mars One committee members, and candidates advancing to the third round will compete against one another. The third round will include 30 a series of challenges to prepare candidates for the potential mission and will be broadcast on television and online.

The group said it aims to have a 35 human settlement on Mars within a decade. Journey time to Mars, which is approximately 40 million miles away depending on its position in orbit, would be around 200 days. 40

From: *Daily Mail*, 3 June 2014

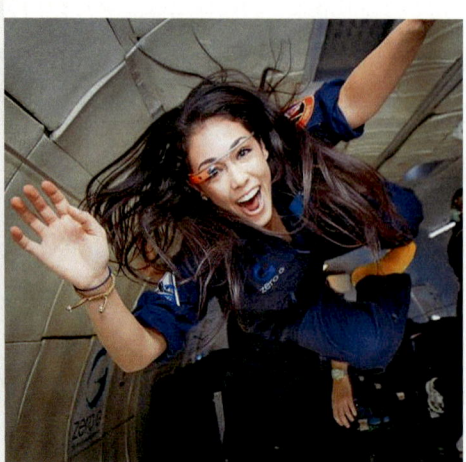

Bride-to-be Kellie Gerardi (25) says she will leave her fiancé on Earth if she is selected to live on the red planet forever as part of a reality TV show.

■ **FACT FILE**

Reality TV shows feature ordinary people instead of professional *actors or *actresses. There are basically two types. In one, participants are exposed to TV audiences 24/7 and are required to share an artificial environment with complete strangers for a limited period of time. The second type of show depicts a mixture of carefully selected 'scenes' from participants' real lives and acted-out events in order to create an entertaining and attention-grabbing story for viewers.

2 **require sth.** [rɪ'kwaɪə] need sth.
have the makings of sth. have the necessary qualities for becoming a particular type of person

4 **hopeful** (n) sb. who wants to succeed or is likely to win

7 **launch sb. on Mars** [lɔːnʃ] send sb. to Mars
decade ['dekeɪd, dɪ'keɪd] period of ten years

9 **be shortlisted** (BE) be selected from a longer list of applicants

10 **undergo sth.** experience sth. challenging or unpleasant

16 **dedicate sth.** ['dedɪkeɪt] give all of one's attention and effort to sth.
pioneering [ˌpaɪə'nɪərɪŋ] (adj) first of its kind

18 **expand sth.** make sth. grow larger

21 **from scratch** from the very beginning, with very little preparation

22 **factual** ['fæktʃuəl] based on facts

25 **maintain sth.** [–'–] make sth. continue

38 **approximately** [ə'prɒksɪmətli] nearly; more or less

▶ COMPREHENSION ◀

1 How the project works

  a Outline the basic idea of the project and the stages of the selection process.

  b Summarize the role reality TV plays in the project described in the text.

        ▶ SF 31: Writing a summary

▶ ANALYSIS ◀

2 What makes the text appealing?

Analyse the methods used to make the text appealing (e.g. heading, *register, *stylistic devices, quotes, bias/neutral position?). `SUPPORT ▶` p. 201

▶ LANGUAGE AWARENESS ◀

3 Word order and emphasis

  a Look at the beginning of the second sentence of the text again (ll. 1–2). Explain why the auxiliary *will* comes <u>before</u> *they* in the first half of the sentence (*will they require*) but <u>after</u> *they* in the second half (*they will … need*).

  b `CHALLENGE ▶` Write two more sentences about the Mars mission that start with *Not only … (but …)*.

        ▶ LP 13: Placing emphasis on key points

▶ BEYOND THE TEXT ◀

4 Applying for the Mars One astronaut selection programme

  a Work out a list of criteria that you consider important when selecting a potential settler on Mars. Try to decide on the three most relevant criteria.

  b Write a formal letter of application to the selection committee of Mars One trying to convince them to send you to Mars.

        ▶ SF 29: Writing a formal letter or email
        ▶ LP 11: Using the right register
        ▶ SF 26: Taking part in an interview

5 ROLE-PLAY The world's toughest job interview

Act out an interview between the members of the selection committee and four applicants for the Mars One project. The rest of the class then vote on the two applicants to be accepted and give reasons for their choice.

C2 The ultimate reality TV show *DBC Pierre*

Vernon Little is a teenager who has been wrongly convicted of murdering classmates and is now on death row. In his cell he is watching an interview on TV in which Lally (the nickname of Eulalio Ledesma), a journalist, explains his idea of 'the ultimate reality TV show' to the reporter Bob.

'So you're effectively proposing to fund the State's penal system by selling broadcast rights to the prisoners' executions? I mean – isn't a prisoner's last hour a little *personal?*'

    'Not at all – don't forget that all executions are witnessed, even today. We're
5 simply expanding the audience to include anyone with an interest in the proper function of law.' Lally puts a hand on his hip. 'Not so long ago, Bob, all executions were public – even held in the town square. Crime went down, public satisfaction went up. Throughout history it's been society's right to punish delinquents by its own hands. It makes plain sense to give that right back to society.'
10   'Hence the web-vote?'
    'Exactly. And we're not just talking executions here – we're talking the ultimate reality TV, where the public can monitor, via cable or internet, prisoners' whole lives on death row. They can live amongst them, so to speak, and make up their own minds about a convict's worthiness for punishment. Then each week, viewers across the
15 globe can cast a vote to decide which prisoner is executed next. It's humanity in action – the next logical step toward true democracy. ''But surely, due process dictates the fate of prisoners?'

be on death row [rəʊ] be a prisoner sentenced to death, waiting for the death penalty to be carried out

  1 **fund sth.** provide money for sth.
    penal ['piːnl] connected with lawful punishment
  8 **delinquent** [dɪ'lɪŋkwənt] criminal
  10 **hence** *(fml)* consequently
  12 **monitor sth.** watch and check sth.
  16 **due** *(adj)* right and proper

18 **tamper with sth.** interfere
with sth.
appeals process possibility of
taking a court case one has lost
to a higher court *(Berufungsrecht)*
19 **recourse** [BE: –'–, AE: '––] *(fml)*
sth. that may provide help in a
difficult situation
20 **roster** list
hooshy laugh (here) laughter
with loud breathing sounds
21 **momentous** [mə'mentəs]
important
25 **breach sth.** violate sth.
26 **forfeit** ['fɔːfɪt] loss of sth. as a
punishment
con *(infml)* convict, prisoner
27 **languish** ['læŋgwɪʃ] *(fml)*
suffer sth. unpleasant for a long
time
29 **expediency** [ɪk'spiːdiənsi]
sth. that is useful to achieve a
purpose
33 **nod at sb.** move one's head in
sb.'s direction
gear up for sth. prepare for sth.
34 **shot at sth.** *(infml)* attempt at
sth., effort for sth.

REALITY
TV

▶ SF 17: Analysing stylistic devices

▶ SF 13: Analysing cartoons

▶ SF 29: Writing a formal
letter or email

▶ SF 34: Argumentative writing

'Absolutely, and we can't tamper with that. But the new fast-track appeals process
means prisoners' last recourses at law are spent much sooner, after which I say the
public should have a hand in the roster of final events.' Lally lets fly a hooshy laugh at 20
the reporter, and spreads his hands wide. 'In the tradition of momentous progress,
it's blindingly simple, Bob: criminals cost money. Popular TV makes money. Criminals are popular on TV. Put them together and, presto – problem solved.'

The reporter pauses as a helicopter settles in the background. Then he asks, 'What
do you say to those who claim prisoners' rights will be breached?' 25

'Oh *please* – prisoners, by definition, live in *forfeit* of their rights. Anyway, cons today
can languish in institutions for years without knowing their fate – wouldn't you say
that was cruel? We're finally giving them what the law has always promised but never
delivered – expediency. Not only that, they'll have greater access to spiritual counsel,
and musical choices to accompany their final event. We'll even craft a special segment 30
around their final statement, with the background imagery of their choice. Believe me
– prisoners will welcome these changes.'

The reporter smiles and nods at Lally. 'And what of reports that you're gearing up
for a shot at the senate?'

I switch off the set. I ain't looking forward to cameras in here. We just have an open 35
toilet, see? I guess that's where the money gets made. Internet viewers will be able to
choose which cells to watch, and change camera angles and all. On regular TV there'll
be edited highlights of the day's action. Then the general public will vote by phone or
internet. They'll vote for who should die next. The cuter we act, the more we entertain, the longer we might live. I heard an old con say it'd be just like the life of a real 40
actor.

From: *Vernon God Little*, 2003

COMPREHENSION ◀

1 Lally's ultimate reality TV show
In pairs, briefly sum up the concept of Lally's ultimate reality TV show. With
a partner, exchange your opinions of it. Discuss whether you would have
asked similar questions if you had been the reporter.

ANALYSIS ◀

2 Lally's mode of argumentation
a Explain Lally's line of argumentation to convince the reporter and the
audience of his idea. SUPPORT ▶ p. 201
b Identify *stylistic devices that he uses to underline his point of view.

3 Vernon's reaction
Examine Vernon's reaction to the interview.

BEYOND THE TEXT ◀

4 Interpreting a cartoon
Compare the criticism of reality shows voiced in the cartoon on the left and
the novel extract above.

5 Responding to the interview
Imagine Lally/Eulalio Ledesma invited the viewers to send him some
comments on his project. Write him an email.

6 Commenting
'Your remote control is the most powerful weapon you have to show the
country what you want.' (Quotation from *Hazard County* by Allison Moore)
a Discuss this statement with a partner and make notes.
b CHALLENGE Write a comment on the statement.

Discussing the pros and cons of modern media

Write a text on the following topic:

> *Will the media change our lives for better or worse over the next ten years? Discuss.*

Instructions

1 Create four posters to place along the walls of your classroom. Each poster will have one of the following headings: **the internet – TV – school/work – surveillance**. Divide the posters vertically into two parts for the positive and negative aspects of the headings.

Find a tool to make your poster here: **Webcode** context-50

The internet
positive
negative

TV
positive
negative

School/Work
positive
negative

Surveillance
positive
negative

2 Choose one expert per poster.

3 The rest of the class walk from poster to poster, suggesting their ideas for each of the topics to the experts, who are to write down the entries on the posters.

4 Stand next to the poster which you would like to use as the basis for your text.

5 Discuss with your classmates who have chosen the same poster as you which aspects on the poster you consider most important.

6 Check Focus on Skills (pp. 18–19) and write an argumentative text, narrowing down the topic ('Will the media change our lives for better or worse over the next ten years?') to the heading of your chosen poster.

▶ SF 34: Argumentative writing

7 Having finished this task, exchange your text with a classmate who has chosen the same topic. Your teacher will give you an assessment sheet to fill work. Evaluate each other's work, keeping in mind what you have learnt in this chapter.

▶ SF 40: Proofreading

2 Science – Enhancing Life?

A

B

Biofuel

Transhumanism
human advancement through technology

Genetic engineering
manipulation or modification of organisms using biotechnology

Energy transition
the path to a sustainable economy, e.g. by using biofuels

Gene pharming
the use of genetically modified organisms to produce pharmaceutical products

C

D

Download a list of chapter vocab here: **Webcode** context-03

1 Identifying current trends in science

a Study the pictures, then match them to one of the topics in the box.

b THINK Pick the photo you find most interesting and speculate about which development in modern science it depicts.

c PAIR Find a partner who chose the same photo. Exchange your ideas, and on the basis of your findings make a chart outlining chances and risks these developments might have for the future.

d SHARE With your chart, move around the classroom. Find a couple who made a chart based on a different picture. Discuss your charts and decide together whether the developments you have discussed will have a positive or negative impact on the future.

E

F

G

H

2 A look into the future

Predicting the future is difficult, if not impossible. Use your imagination and look into the future.

YOU CHOOSE **Examining new technology**

a Choose a modern form of technology (such as Google Glass, 3D printers, driverless cars, etc.) and say why you think it has the capability to transform our society in the future. In small groups present and discuss your ideas.

 OR

b Make a ranking of new technologies according to their importance to you. In small groups compare your lists and together choose the three technological inventions that have the biggest potential in the future.

▶ SF 24: Giving a presentation

PREVIEW

In this chapter you will learn about attempts to improve human life through genetic engineering and technological advancements. You will also examine the challenges of acquiring energy.

Main topics
- Genetic engineering .... p. 34
- Mind- and body-enhancing drugs .... p. 42
- Transhumanism .... p. 45
- Future energy policy .... p. 47

Focus on Skills: READING and MEDIATION
- Using reading strategies (scientific text) ...... p. 41
- Mediating written texts .... p. 49

Chapter Task: Doing a WebQuest on genetically modified food .... p. 51

CD1 04

*Listen to an audio version of the text
on the CD or download it here:*

Webcode context-04

Science – motor of progress?

Feeding the world, healing deadly diseases and finding renewable sources of energy are some of the challenges we have to meet in the 21st century if we want to continue to live well. It is probably in the fields of science and technology that we will find answers to these problems.

Genetic Engineering   5
Scientists are now able to map the DNA sequence of the genes of many plants, animals and humans. They hope to use this information to improve the robustness or yield of crops and livestock and to cure human diseases.
Genetic engineering (GE) is the process by which the sequence of an organism's DNA is altered by technological means, e.g. by inserting   10
a foreign gene to produce a more desirable result.

'They used to be called sheep, and they produced wool. Now they're some sort of bioengineered creatures, and they produce antibiotics.'

In order to provide food for an increasingly faster growing world population the commercial use of GE in farming may help increase food production. The first genetically modified (GM) crop was introduced in 1995   15
– the slow-softening tomato. Others have been made more insect-resistant or disease-resistant. In 2013, GM crops, including maize, cotton and rice, were being grown on more than 175 million hectares in 29 countries. In medicine, genetic engineering may one day be used to   20
repair defect genes.
A new widely-debated approach is gene pharming. Pharma crops are genetically modified plants like maize that produce much-needed medicines. The genes for human proteins like insulin could be transferred to   25
animals, which then produce the protein in their milk. However, there are ethical concerns about genetic engineering:

- **Risk and safety:** Transgenic plants or animals (i.e. containing one or more foreign genes) may in the end prove to be unhealthy or even dangerous.   30
- **Meddling with reproduction:** In vitro fertilization (IVF) offers the opportunity to preselect an embryo that is free from genetic disorders. Many fear this will lead to custom-made designer babies – children designed to have a particular eye colour or IQ.

These are reasons why GE requires public approval and careful regulation.   35

Quenching the thirst for energy
With the rise of emerging countries like Brazil and India the global thirst for energy is growing rapidly. Since the Fukushima nuclear disaster of 2011 many nations have agreed on a nuclear power phase-out. Even though renewable sources of energy like solar, wind and hydropower do not seem to be cost-   40
efficient at the moment, experts are researching ways to switch from finite energy sources such as coal, gas and petroleum to sources that are sustainable and more environmentally friendly. This is seen as an important step to reduce humanity's carbon footprint and to stop global warming.
Using plants like rapeseed or palm oil to produce biofuels is another way to   45
avoid using fossil fuels. However, environmental and ethical concerns about such technologies are growing.

▶ SF 2: Learning new words

1 Information Stock Exchange

a Choose two of the issues in the text that you feel well-informed about. Write them on green cards.

b Write two terms on red cards that you would like to find out more about.

c Walk around the classroom and find two people with green cards that match your red cards. Ask them to give you the information you want.

d Explain the terms on your green cards to two students.

e On the blackboard arrange your cards in three columns:
  - Still lost: red cards with terms that still need clarifying
  - Lost and found: green and red matches
  - Information pool: green cards that were not talked about

2 Formal vs. informal language

▶ LP 11: Using the right register

Scientific reports strive for accuracy and precision, which is why they rarely use phrasal verbs. Try to substitute the phrasal verbs or informal expressions below with a formal verb from the text.

1 put sth. into sth.
2 move sth. from one place to another
3 make sth. different
4 make sth. less or smaller

3 Compound adjectives

▶ LP 10: Using adjectives and adverbs

Compound adjectives make texts more formal by condensing information.

a Find examples of compound adjectives such as *custom-made* (l. 33) in the text and categorize them according to their structure:
noun + adjective • noun + participle • adjective + adjective • adjective/ adverb + participle

b Make these sentences shorter by forming compound adjectives.
  1 Genetic engineering is a business that is growing fast.
  2 GE companies hope to make progress at a speed that will break all records.
  3 They hope to help farmers keep their fields free from pollution.
  4 The development took ten years before GE crops could hit the market.

> ■ TROUBLE SPOT
>
> Hyphenated compound adjectives are only used **before** nouns:
> *It was a well-written report.*
> ↔ *The report was well written.*

4 Writing

Describe the picture and discuss it with reference to genetic engineering.

The genetic engineering debate

A1 A saviour sibling   *Laura Roberts*

Genetic screening is a new technology that has been helping families with genetically transmitted diseases.

Megan Matthews, nine, received tissue donated by her 18-month old brother Max who was created specifically so that he could aid her medical treatment. [...]

Megan, from King's Lynn, Norfolk, was born with a rare blood disorder which can cause bone marrow failure and a worldwide search for a suitable bone marrow donor failed. The condition, Fanconi Anaemia, meant she needed transfusions every few weeks and was unable to fight infections.   5

Her parents Katie and Andy Matthews wanted another child but natural conception would have provided only a one in four chance that the sibling would be a perfect tissue match. The new child could also have been born with the same life-threatening genetic disorder. To avoid this, Cambridge, Bristol and Nottingham medical teams   10 were involved in a treatment which used donated cells from the specifically created baby and taken to treat Megan's disorder.

Two embryos were implanted into Mrs Matthews by CARE Fertility in Nottingham after they were checked for transplant suita-   15 bility. Initially umbilical cord blood was saved and after Max was born an operation was carried out to take bone marrow. The tissue transplant took place in July this year at Bristol Royal Hospital for Sick Children.   20 Compared to her frequent and invasive hospital visits, Megan now only requires a weekly check-up at Addenbrookes hospital in Cambridge.

Simon Fishel, managing director of Care   25 Fertility, said that ethical concerns over creating children with specific genetic material were outweighed by the benefits. He said: 'The ethical issues are in favour of doing this work. We are trying to save the life of a child   30 and achieve a family without the enormous burden of a child with this disorder who would die.' Mrs Matthews also said she had no ethical problems with the treatment her family had received. She said: 'Max is loved for being him and not for what he has done. He has completed our family and now I have a bubbly and healthy girl.'   35

The use of genetically engineered children for medical treatment has been widely criticised. Josephine Quintavalle, Director of Comment on Reproductive Ethics told the BBC: '[Max] owes his life to his capacity to be of therapeutic use to his sick sister, otherwise he would not have been chosen in the first place. This is the big ethical problem.' Sufferers of Fanconi Anaemia may suffer long-term health problems and   40 Megan may require further treatment.

From: 'First complete "saviour sibling" transplant carried out in the UK', *Daily Telegraph*, 22 December 2010

sibling brother or sister
1 **tissue** ['tɪʃuː] *Gewebe*
2 **specifically** intended for a particular purpose
3 **disorder** *Störung*
4 **bone marrow** *Knochenmark*
 donor *Spender/in*
7 **conception** *Empfängnis*
15 **suitability** [ˌsuːtəˈbɪləti] *Eignung*
16 **umbilical** [ʌmˈbɪlɪkl] **cord** *Nabelschnur*
32 **burden** sth. that gives a person a heavy responsibility
35 **bubbly** full of life and energy

SAVIOUR SIBLINGS HOW IT WORKS

Woman is given fertility drugs.

Eggs are fertilized to produce embryos.

Multiple eggs are produced.

Embryos are analysed for genetic defects and tissue compatibility.

Only healthy embryos are injected into uterus.

Mother gives birth to genetically healthy baby.

Transfusion of umbilical cord blood to sick child

▶ SF 10: Working with closed test formats

─────────────────────────────────── COMPREHENSION ◀

1 Understanding the concept of saviour siblings

Choose the statement which fits best and give the line that provides evidence for your choice.

   a A saviour sibling is a brother or sister …

      1 who has been specifically created for the purpose of curing a sick brother or sister.

      2 whose life was saved by receiving a transplant from a brother or sister.

   b Without a transplant Megan would …

      1 have died within a short period of time.

      2 have had to go in and out of hospitals to receive transfusions.

   c The use of IVF was necessary to …

      1 produce a healthy embryo.

      2 make sure that the baby would not suffer from Fanconi Anaemia.

   d The procedure has been widely criticized as …

      1 human beings seem to have been reduced to commodities.

      2 embryos are killed in the process.

2 Summarizing information

Use the drawing and the information from the text to explain how a saviour sibling is produced.

▶ SF 31: Writing a summary

─────────────────────────────────────── ANALYSIS ◀

3 Argumentative structure

   a Look at the last sentence of the article and decide whether the writer is in favour of the use of saviour siblings, whether she is against their use or whether he takes a neutral position.

   b Analyse the argumentative structure of the article, paying particular attention to the effect of the writer's use of direct and indirect speech.

     SUPPORT ▶ p. 202

▶ SF 18: Analysing non-fiction

──────────────────────────── LANGUAGE AWARENESS ◀

4 Using the passive

   a Scientific texts usually contain many passive constructions. Look at the use of the passive voice in ll. 2, 11, 13, 15, 16, 17–18, 28, 34, 36, 39, and analyse its effect. (Hint: it may help to transform one or two into the active voice to see the difference.)

   b In German, active sentences with *man* are often used instead of a passive sentence. In which cases do you think *man* might be better than the passive voice if you were to translate the sentences?

▶ LP 7: The passive

───────────────────────────────── BEYOND THE TEXT ◀

5 PLACEMAT ACTIVITY Case studies

Choose one of the cases below and use a placemat to note down the pros and cons for that case. Use the guidelines from the Fact File on p. 36 to consider the ethical dimensions of the topic. Discuss the issue with your group members and prepare a group statement in which you justify your position.

1 Megan's case (cf. text).

2 A pair of deaf parents wants to use genetic screening to ensure that their child is also deaf.

3 Parents who want to use genetic screening to test their foetus for genes that indicate a high risk of their child developing particular conditions, so that they can abort the foetus if they so wish.

▶ SF 24: Giving a presentation

■ FACT FILE

Ethics in science

Science is advancing at an ever-accelerating speed. New discoveries and new technologies are affecting all areas of our life. Many new
5 inventions or discoveries have sparked public discussions on whether their use is desirable or should be avoided.

In order to find out which course of action is the moral one, people turn to ethics. Ethics is
10 the branch of philosophy that studies the principles of what is morally right or wrong. When it comes to ethical decision making, the following questions can help you. You can use them to test whether your decision is morally 15
acceptable:

- Are the rights of everyone involved respected?
- Which solution would be the most just, fair or responsible?
- Which solution will probably have the best overall consequences, even if it means that 20 some will not benefit from it?
- Which solution will be most sustainable and help everyone?
- Think of the wisest person you know. What would he or she do in this situation? 25

Read the Fact File and write down: 3 words or expressions that are new to you and worth adding to your word bank on genetic engineering; 2 ethical principles that are particularly important when it comes to ethical decision making; 1 reason why ethical decision making is important.

The National Theatre's production of Nick Dear's Frankenstein

A2 You are mine to kill *Nick Dear*

The excerpt below is from Nick Dear's 2011 stage adaptation of Mary Shelley's novel Frankenstein *(1818). Considered by many to be one of the first horror stories, Shelley's gothic novel poses many moral and ethical questions about the role of science in a society that was beginning to change due to scientific advances. Victor Frankenstein, a young scientist, has succeeded in creating life. From dead bodies and with the help of newly-discovered electricity he has brought a creature to life. Appalled by its ugliness, he sends it away. After he learns that the creature has killed his brother William, he searches for it in the Arctic ice, where the creature has fled.*

- With a partner, come up with a list of guidelines that a responsible scientist should follow, e.g. whether they should make their findings publicly available.

There is a sound like a great exhalation of breath, as the glacier shudders and shifts. Through the snowstorm the Creature is suddenly visible, standing very still on the ice. He makes a great leap towards Victor.

VICTOR	My God! Muscular coordination – hand and eye – excellent tissue – perfect balance! And the sutures have held! I failed to make it 5 handsome, but I gave it strength and grace.

Victor circles the Creature. The Creature swivels to keep an eye on him.

	What an achievement! Unsurpassed in scientific endeavour! God, the madness of that night – the heat, the sweat, the infusions, the moment when I saw it crawl towards me, and I – and I – 10
CREATURE	You ran away.
VICTOR	What?
CREATURE	You abandoned me.
VICTOR *(stunned)*	It speaks!
CREATURE	Yes, Frankenstein. It speaks. 15
VICTOR	You know my name?

5 **suture** ['suːtʃə] *Naht*
7 **swivel** ['swɪvl] turn round quickly
8 **unsurpassed** better or greater than any other
endeavour *(n)* [ɪn'devə] attempt to do sth. new and difficult
10 **crawl** walk on your hands and knees
13 **abandon sb.** leave sb. with no intention of seeing them again

The Creature hands Victor the tattered journal.

	My journal!
CREATURE	Why did you abandon me?
20 VICTOR	I was terrified – what had I done?
CREATURE	Built a man, and given him life –
VICTOR	Well, now I have come to take it away –
CREATURE *(laughs)*	Oh, have you?
VICTOR	I have come to kill you!
25 CREATURE	To kill me? Why then did you create me?
VICTOR	To prove that I could!
CREATURE	So you make sport with my life?
VICTOR	In the cause of science! You were my greatest experiment – but an
	experiment that has gone wrong. An experiment that must be
30	curtailed!

Victor runs at him and attacks him with his stick, but the Creature swiftly disarms him and throws him to the ground.

CREATURE	Be still, genius! I have a request.
VICTOR	Damn you, you can't have requests!
35 CREATURE	Oh, I can! Listen to me. It's your duty.
VICTOR	I have no duty to a murderer.

From: *Frankenstein*, 2001

30 **curtail sth.** [–'–] (here) bring sth. to an end
31 **disarm sb.** take a weapon away from sb.

COMPREHENSION ◀

1 Creature and creator
Describe the situation as presented in this scene.

ANALYSIS ◀

2 Responsible or irresponsible scientist?
Examine the attitude of Victor Frankenstein to his creation. Use your list from above to judge whether his attitude shows him to be a responsible or an irresponsible scientist.

BEYOND THE TEXT ◀

3 CHALLENGE ▶ The experiment
Creature or human? Comment on this question taking into consideration ethical and legal aspects and the character of the Creature. Discuss the consequences this decision will have for the Creature and for possible punishments regarding Williams's death.

4 FOUR-CORNERS ACTIVITY Discussing statements
Assign each of the four positions below to a corner in your classroom. Then stand next to the statement that comes closest to your own opinion. With the others in your corner discuss the reasons why you each chose that position.

'We've created a teenager.'

▶ SF 27: Having a discussion

| Scientists should have complete freedom in their research and not be controlled by the government. | 'Science, in the very act of solving problems, creates more of them.' *Abraham Flexner* | 'Whenever science makes a discovery, the devil grabs it while the angels are debating the best way to use it.' *Alan Valentine* | It is not for humans to create life forms and use them for their own purposes. |

A3 At the lab

astigmatism optical defect
(*Hornhautverkrümmung*)

AT THE GENETIC ENGINEERING LAB

PERHAPS YOU COULD GIVE HIM A TOUCH OF ASTIGMATISM. KIDS WITH GLASSES ARE SOOO CUTE!

© Guy & Rodd/Distributed by Universal Uclick for UFS via CartoonStock.com

COMPREHENSION ◀

1 Describing a cartoon

Describe the cartoon and identify the topic the cartoon addresses.

ANALYSIS ◀

▶ SF 13: Analysing cartoons

2 Examining a cartoon

Analyse the means the cartoonist employs to make his point.

BEYOND THE CARTOON ◀

3 Comparing texts

Comment on how the topic of the cartoon is similar or different to the dilemma dealt with in *Frankenstein* (cf. **A2**).

4 YOU CHOOSE ▶ **Practising speaking**

When doing the following task, use the guidelines from the Fact File (cf. p. 36) to include the ethical dimension of the topic.

▶ SF 24: Giving a presentation
▶ SF 27: Having a discussion

a Prepare a monologue on whether designer babies are desirable or not.
   SUPPORT ▶ p. 202

OR

b Find a partner and discuss in front of the class whether designer babies are desirable or not, with one of you being in favour and one against.

▶ LANGUAGE HELP

Find a tool for improving your speaking skills here:

 Webcode context-51

The hyperrealistic sculptures by Australian contemporary artist Patricia Piccinini address ethical issues of genetic engineering in an often disturbing or provocative way.

The Long Awaited (2008)

Silicone, fibreglass, human hair, plywood, leather, clothing. 152 x 80 x 92 cm high. Courtesy of the artist and Tolarno and Roslyn Oxley9 Galleries

Patricia Piccinini on *The Long Awaited*:

'Empathy is at the heart of my practice. I don't think that you really can – or indeed should – try to understand the ethics of something without emotions […]. It is one thing to argue for or against cloning when it is just an intellectual issue. However, things change if you have a mother or son who might need it. I like to think that my work understands that the point at which "good" becomes "bad" does not stand still, which is why it is so difficult to find.'

1 Study the sculpture. Then discuss your reactions to it with a partner. Choose the adjectives from the list below to describe the sculpture and its effect on you.

aesthetic • calming • delightful • disturbing • embarrassing • harmonious • interesting • loving • obnoxious • quaint • shocking • supportive • tasteless • touching • tranquil • understanding • unsettling • warm

2 Analyse the relationship between the boy and the creature on the bench. Explain to what extent the sculpture illustrates Piccinini's comment.

3 Write a formal email to Patricia Piccinini in which you comment on *The Long Awaited* as a statement on genetic engineering.

A4 **Animals with bonus features** *Bob Holmes*

- FOUR-CORNERS ACTIVITY **Animal rights**
  Read the four statements displayed in four corners of your classroom, then stand next to the one you can identify with most. Explain why.
  1 Through breeding and selection humans have always changed domestic animals. Genetic engineering is basically no different.
  2 The genetic engineering of animals should be forbidden as it violates animal rights and is potentially harmful to the animal.
  3 Using genetically engineered animals to produce drugs is acceptable if it reduces severe human suffering.
  4 Animals with human DNA should be entitled to special rights.

The text below examines the genetic engineering of animals so that they may benefit humans in more ways than they do today.

6 **tedious** ['tiːdiəs] taking a long time and requiring a lot of work
18 **jumping gene** gene that can insert copies of itself into other DNA sites in the same cell
25 **omega-3** ['əʊmɪgə] type of fatty acid
32 **tack sth. on** add sth.
34 **antibody** *Antikörper*

Unless you live in Europe, your last meal probably contained genetically modified ingredients – 80 per cent of soya grown worldwide is now genetically engineered, for instance. Yet while modified plants are rapidly taking over the planet's farms, the same cannot be said for GM animals. [...]

The main reason is that the genetic engineering of animals – with the exception of mice – has been a slow, tedious process needing a lot of money and not a little luck. Behind the scenes, though, a quiet revolution has been taking place. Thanks to a set of new tricks and tools, modifying animals is becoming a lot easier and more precise. That is not only going to transform research, it could also transform the meat and eggs you eat and the milk you drink. The first transgenic animals were produced by injecting DNA into eggs, implanting the eggs in animals and then waiting weeks or months to see if any offspring had incorporated the extra DNA. Often fewer than 1 in 100 had, making this a long, expensive process. [...]

In mice, geneticists found a way round this problem: producing cells with the desired modification first, before growing entire animals. [...] At the same time, biologists have developed more efficient ways of adding DNA to cells, by hijacking natural genetic engineers such as viruses, and jumping genes capable of 'copying and pasting' themselves. All these advances mean the effort and cost needed to produce GM animals has decreased a hundredfold. [...] The ability to easily and precisely modify animals will undoubtedly lead to huge pay-offs in research and medicine. [...]

Genetically modified farm animals could provide us with more nutritious meat, milk and eggs, while causing fewer pollution problems, and perhaps suffering less too. Pigs whose muscles are enriched with omega-3s have already been created, and researchers are exploring similar options with milk. [...]

Genetic engineering is now a standard technique in the production of many protein-based drugs. Human insulin, for example, has long been produced by cultures of bacteria carrying the human insulin gene. Pharmaceutical companies are eager to turn animals into drug factories, too. That's because animal cells alter many of their proteins by tacking on sugars and other 'decorations', an extra step that bacteria cannot perform. As a result, many proteins – most importantly, antibodies – work much better if they are made in animal cells.

5

10

15

20

25

30

35 One such animal-produced protein has already been approved for clinical use by the US Food and Drug Administration. An anticoagulant called antithrombin III is purified from the milk of genetically engineered goats created by GTC Biotherapeutics, a biotech company in Framingham, Massachusetts. Many others are under development. [...] Open Monoclonal Technology of Palo Alto, California, has engineered 40 rats to produce human antibodies. Its first product, an anti-cancer antibody for treating lymphoma, should be in clinical trials within two to three years.

From: 'Altered animals: creatures with bonus features', *The New Scientist*,
14 July 2010

36 **anticoagulant** [ˌæntɪkəʊˈægjələnt]
Gerinnungshemmer
41 **lymphoma** [lɪmˈfəʊmə] *Lymph-drüsenkrebs*

READING FOCUS ON SKILLS
Using reading strategies (scientific text)

Scientific texts are challenging both in terms of content and language. The tips below can help you to get a detailed and thorough understanding of such texts.

1 Understanding the gist
Skim text **A4** on the previous page quickly to get a basic understanding of what the text is about. The first sentence of a paragraph is usually the topic sentence that states the main idea of the paragraph. Summarize to a partner what you think the text is about.

▶ SF 14: Reading strategies

2 Reducing the complexity of the text
Focus on the most relevant pieces of information only. Often it is not necessary to understand a sentence or paragraph word for word.
a Add headlines to the paragraphs to mark what they are about in general.
b The second and the third paragraphs deal with the advancements made in changing the genetic makeup of animals. In order to understand what these are, identify words that describe the development so that you will be able to explain it. (Hint: you can ignore technical details.)

3 Dealing with hard words
a Scientific texts are full of technical terms. Often they are of Latin or Greek origin and are similar to German words, e.g. 'precise' *(präzise)* in l.8. Find more examples in the text and explain their meaning.
b Scientific texts aim for accuracy. They use *formal instead of *informal style. Use the context to find the equivalent of these words in the text:

▶ SF 1: Dealing with unknown words

▶ LP 11: Using the right register

change sth. · put sth. into sth.· include sth. · being able · go down · offer sth./make sth. available · do sth. · accept · make sth. cleaner · create/design sth.

c Often the meaning becomes clear when you look at the word family, e.g. *purify* (v) – *pure* (adj). Now use this strategy to find the meaning of 'engineer' (l.2), 'nutritious' (l.22) and 'enrich' (l.24).

▶ LP 20: Word formation

4 Relating information
It is helpful to draw diagrams or flowcharts in order to understand processes. Try to draw a simple diagram or flowchart to illustrate the process of creating a transgenic animal as described in the second paragraph.

▶ SF 7: Making visual aids

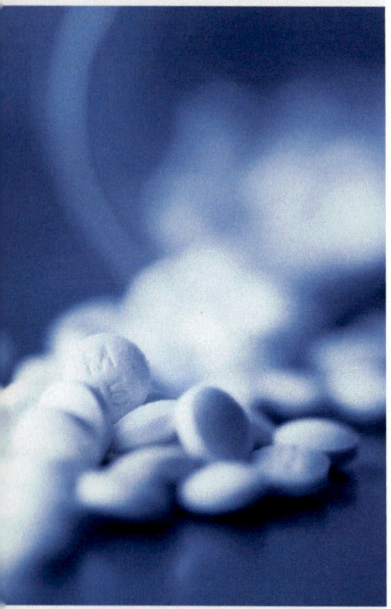

DVD

▶ SF 41: Mediation of written and oral texts

▶ SF 23: Analysing a film

Modifying mankind

B1 A brain-enhancing pill

Watch the short *news report on the use of Modafinil.

─────────────────────────────── COMPREHENSION ◀

1 Understanding the effects of a neuro-enhancing drug
Describe the positive and negative effects of the neuro-enhancing pill as mentioned in the video. Outline why the drug is popular despite the risks that come with it.

2 Mediation (English ➔ German)
A fellow student of yours believes that it's impossible to get such a drug without a prescription. Tell him or her (in German) what you have found out.

─────────────────────────────── ANALYSIS ◀

3 Examining the tone
Choose adjectives from the list below to describe the *tone of the report. Provide evidence for your opinion from the news report.

objective · neutral · biased · sensational · critical · exaggerated

─────────────────────────────── BEYOND THE TEXT ◀

4 SILENT-WRITING DISCUSSION What if there were 'smart pills'?
a Get together in groups of four (students A–D). Look at the questions below. Write your question at the top of a piece of paper, then answer it. Then pass the paper on to the student to your right. Add your answer to the next question on the paper you receive. Continue until every student has the paper again that he or she started with.

Student A: Imagine there were pills that could really make people smarter. Should those pills be given to everyone for free?	**Student B:** Imagine there were pills that could really make people smarter. If people took such pills before an exam, would you consider it to be cheating?
Student C: Imagine there were pills that could really make people smarter. Should parents be allowed to give such pills to school-age children?	**Student D:** Imagine there were pills that could really make people smarter. Would taking such pills to enhance your brain power be any different from drinking coffee or energy drinks, taking vitamins or going for a run?

b Now read the responses and sum up the comments for your group members.
c Discuss the impact of neuroenhancers on society and recommend how society should deal with them.

B2 Gene doping   *Tim Franks*

It seems the fight against doping in sport is an ever-losing battle. The text below points out how genetic engineering may make the fight for a clean sport even harder.

- Before reading the text, speculate about the connection between genetic engineering and doping, then skim the article and check whether your guess was correct.

This could be a battle like no other in sport. The authorities are so concerned, they have been preparing for it for more than 10 years. But it is still unclear whether they have the tools to test for it – or whether anyone has done it successfully. It is gene doping. The idea is simple: to alter our genetic makeup, the very building blocks of
5 who we are, in order to make us stronger or faster. The practicalities are highly complex.

Gene therapists – for example those treating very sick children at London's Great Ormond Street hospital – add a synthetic gene to the patient's genome, and reintroduce it into the bone marrow via a disabled virus. The new gene is expressed by the
10 patient's cells and acts like a medicine, permanently incorporated in the bone marrow. […]

Dr Philippe Moullier […] had shown it was possible to produce artificially one particular gene – the erythropoietin gene – and introduce it into the body. And as anyone who had
15 a vague brush with professional cycling in the 90s knows, the hormone erythropoietin, or EPO – which controls the production of red blood cells – was the illicit dope of choice for competitors. It was the wonder drug Lance Armstrong kept in his fridge, to boost his oxygen-carrying red-blood-cell
20 count.

But while injected EPO has been detectable for years, introducing the EPO gene would result in the body producing its own EPO. Could this be an undetectable way of improving oxygen delivery? […]
25 And while making a permanent change to the genome may be complex – using a disabled virus to carry the genetic medicine to the cells – Philippe Moullier says there is now a shortcut, which delivers temporary results: injecting the purified gene directly into your muscle. […]

Even better for the would-be doper, says Moullier, this type of temporary boost may,
30 after a few days, be hard for the authorities to detect. So what is the World Anti-Doping Agency (Wada) doing about it?

Back in 2003, Wada banned gene doping. The agency argues that the practice would not just be unfair, it could be lethal – introducing an extra copy of the EPO gene into your body could lead to too many red blood cells being produced and your blood thick-
35 ening into sludge. […]

But there is a deeper question. Even if there were to be or already is a legally and biologically fireproof test for gene doping, what should happen if gene therapy were to become much more widespread, even routine? What if we were all able to buy, over the counter, genetic medicine to slow muscle deterioration? Should we – could we –
40 stop athletes from using the medicine, to prolong their careers or speed a return from injury?

From: 'Gene doping: sport's biggest battle', BBC, 12 January 2014

9 **express** cause (a gene) to manifest its effects in other cells
10 **bone marrow** *Knochenmark*
12 **Philippe Moullier** French doctor who first showed the possibilities of gene therapy
15 **brush** occasion when you have contact with or experience sth.
19 **boost sth.** make sth. more powerful
35 **sludge** thick, soft, wet substance
39 **deterioration** [dɪˌtɪəriəˈreɪʃn] *Verschlechterung*
40 **prolong sth.** make sth. last longer

The hormone erythropoietin became the illicit dope of choice for competitors in the Tour de France, bringing the competition into disrepute.

▶ SF 31: Writing a summary

COMPREHENSION ◀

1 Getting the facts straight

Use the words below to summarize what the article is about. Include a definition of the term *gene doping*.

authorities · synthetic gene · erythropoietin or EPO · red blood cells · cycling · undetectable · injection · purified gene · lethal · ethical issue · genetic medicine

ANALYSIS ◀

▶ SF 18: Analysing non-fiction

2 Examining the tone

Illustrate how the writer's use of language reveals his attitude to the topic.

SUPPORT ▶ p. 203

LANGUAGE AWARENESS ◀

3 Speculating about effects and consequences

Gene doping is a new technology that is not yet in use but that could become important quite soon. That is why the article contains many speculations about its possible consequences.

Collect examples of modal auxiliaries used in the text to express probability or possibility. Compare their use with the use of the conditional sentences.

BEYOND THE TEXT ◀

4 Discussing doping in sports

a Collect arguments in favour of or against allowing doping in professional sports.

▶ SF 28: Having a debate

b **CHALLENGE ▶** Debate the motion 'This house believes the ban on doping should be lifted'. Before debating, search the internet for arguments for your position in the debate. Then meet with your partners and work out a strategy for how to convince the house to adopt your position. Make sure you anticipate your opponent's arguments and be prepared to counter them.

B3 Transhumanism *Zoltan Istvan*

The following text deals with the possibilities of transhumanist technology.

- Before reading, speculate what transhumanist technology means.

As long as they're earthbound, most people shrug off the idea of being anything other than a biological human. Some people are even repulsed or angered by the concept of scientifically tampering with the human body and brain too much. However, the time is coming when radical technology will allow us to expand and significantly
5 improve the abilities of our minds and the forms of our bodies. A transhumanist age is nearly upon the human race – an age where cyborgs, sentient robots, virtual lives based in computers and dramatically altered human beings may become commonplace.

Already, there are hundreds of universities, laboratories and companies around the
10 world where transhumanist projects are underway. A transhumanist is a person who aims to move beyond the human being via science and technology. Some of the most eye-opening projects are military-oriented, such as the 'Iron Man' armor suit being created for American soldiers. Trial runs of the suit are tentatively scheduled for this summer. Another well-known project
15 is at Chalmers University of Technology in Sweden where scientists are connecting robotic limbs to the human nervous system of amputees, essentially creating cyborg-like people. The first arm surgeries are scheduled to occur in less than 12 months. Of course, private companies like Google are also
20 very much involved in the broad field of transhumanism. They are spending many millions of dollars on creating artificial intelligence, which one day may have its own sentience and be thousands of times smarter than humans. [...]

Even though some of these technologies seem frightening
25 to the layperson, they should be here in a matter of years, not decades. One of the most exciting and controversial ideas of transhumanism is the complete integration of the human mind with a machine. Similar to the extraordinary technology featured in the movie *The Matrix*, humans may be able to download themselves into computers and live virtual existences.

An army veteran gives a thumbs up with a prosthetic arm.

From: 'Despite skepticism, many people may embrace radical transhumanist technology in the future', *The Huffington Post*, 18 February 2014

1 **shrug sth. off** treat sth. as if it is not important
2 **repulse sb.** [– ' –] *(fml)* make sb. feel strong disgust
3 **tamper with sth.** make changes to sth. when one should not
6 **sentient** ['senti̯ənt; 'senʃt] *(fml)* able to feel or see things through the senses
13 **trial run** test of sth. to see how well it performs
tentative ['tentətɪv] not certain or definite
25 **layperson** person who is not an expert in a particular field

▶ SF 10: Working with closed test formats

Find an online dictionary here:
🔲 **Webcode** context-52

1 Transhumanism defined

   a Define the term *transhumanism*.

   b List examples from the text of transhumanist technology.

   c Match them to the categories given in the chart below. (Tip: there are more categories than examples.)

A	augmenting	(adding removable attachments that boost capabilities)
B	boosting	(enhancing capabilities and improving intelligence)
C	embellishing	(changing an external part of a human for decorative purpose)
D	replacing	(permanently replacing an organ or limb)
E	adding	(integrating something additional into the human form)
F	altering	(changing the actual biological structure of a human)
G	redefining	(changing a human so much that the person is no longer recognizable as a human)

   d **CHALLENGE** Match the examples below with the categories from **1c**.

> *modified DNA • bionic legs • a piercing or tattoo • plastic surgery • consciousness upload • a brain chip • caffeine or steroids • Google Glass*

2 YOU CHOOSE New methods or new terms

   a Explain how the examples given in the text differ from popular enhancement techniques such as exercising or surgery.

   OR

   b Innovative new technologies require new words or new combinations of words to label them, e.g. the term *internet* first appeared in 1974. Such newly coined words are called neologisms (from Greek *neo* = new, *logos* = word, speech). Collect examples of neologisms from the text, check their origin and explain their meaning.

3 Using transhuman technologies

   a List the transhuman technologies you would embrace, and the ones you would reject. Discuss your views with a partner, explaining your reasons.

   b **CHALLENGE** Use the guidelines from the Fact File (cf. p. 36) to formulate some ethical guidelines for using transhumanist technologies.

Quenching the thirst for energy

C1 The global demand for energy

With an ever-increasing world population and the economic progress of emerging nations, the global demand for energy poses a challenge that includes environmental, political and technological aspects.

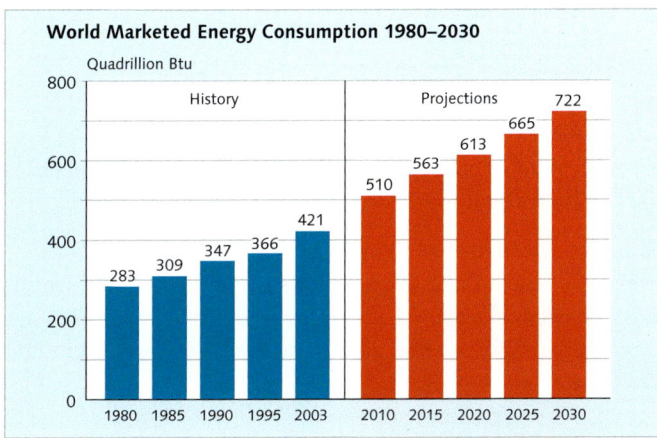

Btu = British thermal unit unit of energy, ca. 1055 joules

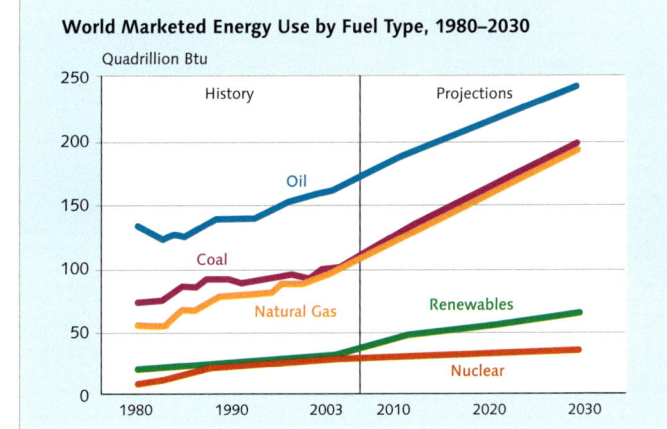

From: US Energy Information Administration, 2006

COMPREHENSION ◄

1 Understanding graphs

Study the graphs and state what information they give about future trends of energy consumption. ► LANGUAGE HELP

BEYOND THE TEXT ◄

2 Thinking about future trends

a In small groups discuss the positive or negative consequences these trends might have.

b Suggest ways how to tackle the problematic aspects that these trends could cause.

► SF 12: Analysing charts and graphs

LANGUAGE HELP
- The bar chart / line graph is about … / deals with …
- The chart gives/compares/ explains …
- The size / the number of …
- The number of … has increased sharply/ significantly
- Whereas in 2005 …
- In comparison with … / Compared to …

C2 The future of energy in Germany

You are taking part in an international youth conference about how different countries are reacting to environmental awareness. The conference intends to set up a website for young people dedicated to showing recent changes in global energy policies. You are to present the German Energiewende in a text of about 200 words, explaining the German position and the aims of the Energiewende. While searching for information you have come across the following text. Skim the text in order to get the gist of what it is about.

Die Energiewende ist der Kurzbegriff für eine fundamentale Wende in der Energie-versorgung: Das bisherige Energiesystem, das auf Kernenergie, Kohle, Öl und Gas beruht, wird abgelöst von einer neuen Energieversorgung auf Basis Erneuerbarer Energie (EE) – Windkraft, Sonnenenergie, Wasserkraft, Biomasse und Erdwärme. Die wesentlichen Gründe für diese Wende in der Energieversorgung sind: 5

• Risikovorsorge: Die Risiken der Kernenergie sind prinzipiell nicht beherrschbar. Dies haben die Reaktorkatastrophen in Tschernobyl und Fukushima gezeigt. Zudem ist der hochradioaktive Abfall aus Kernkraftwerken für Hunderttausende von Jahren äußerst giftig, ohne dass bisher eine Lösung für die Endlagerung gefunden wäre. 10
• Klimaschutz: Bei der Verbrennung von Kohle, Öl und Gas entstehen klimaschäd-liche Treibhausgasemissionen, die die Hauptverursacher für den Klimawandel sind.
• Knappe Ressourcen: Kohle, Öl und Gas sind endlich. Je knapper sie werden, desto teurer wird ein auf fossile Energieträger basierendes Energiesystem. 15
• Wertschöpfung vor Ort: Während ein großer Teil der bisherigen Energieträger (insbesondere Öl, Gas, Uran und Steinkohle) importiert wird, sind die Erneuer-baren Energien heimische Energien, die somit die Wertschöpfung vor Ort erhöhen und die Importabhängigkeit reduzieren.

Die Frage der Energieversorgung war lange ein zentraler politischer Streitpunkt – 20
insbesondere die Nutzung der Kernenergie war über Jahrzehnte Gegenstand hefti-ger Auseinandersetzungen. Seit den Beschlüssen des Bundestages vom Juni 2011 existiert in Deutschland jedoch ein parteiübergreifender Konsens, dass der Weg der Energiewende beschritten werden soll. So sind sowohl der Ausstieg aus der Kern-energie bis zum Jahr 2022 als auch konkrete Ziele für den Ausbau der Erneuerbaren 25
Energien im Strombereich gesetzlich festgeschrieben. [...]

Was sind die zentralen Themen und Herausforderungen?

Stromerzeugung und -verbrauch haben eine besondere Bedeutung für die Energie-wende, da die Erneuerbaren Energien hier die riskanten beziehungsweise CO_2-inten-siven Energieträger Kernenergie, Braun- und Steinkohle ersetzen müssen. Zudem 30
werden mittelfristig immer größere Anteile des Wärme- und Verkehrsbedarfs durch Strom bereitgestellt werden. Die Energiewende-Ziele im Stromsektor lauten:
• Erneuerbare Energien: mindestens 80 Prozent Anteil Erneuerbarer Energien an der Stromversorgung bis spätestens 2050 mit den Zwischenzielen von 40 Prozent bis 2025 und 55 bis 60 Prozent bis 2035. 35
• Energieeffizienz: Reduktion des Stromverbrauchs um 10 Prozent bis 2020 und 25 Prozent bis 2050 gegenüber dem Niveau von 2008.

From: agora-energiewende, 2014

MEDIATION FOCUS ON SKILLS

Mediating written texts

When mediating a text from one language into another, you always have to take into consideration the following aspects.

1 Content: What information do you want to get across?

Remember that when you are mediating, the final text is always shorter than the original text, as you are only mediating the important or necessary information.

Read the task in the introduction to text **C2** (cf. p. 48) again. What do you have to focus on?

Look at the statements below. Which are correct and which are incorrect?

> 1 I have to summarize all the information in the text.
> 2 I need to include the dates by which time goals must be met.
> 3 I have to explain why the *Energiewende* took place.
> 4 I can show what the aims are by also explaining what Germany intends to stop doing.
> 5 I need to discuss why it will be a challenge to meet the aims.
> 6 I need to discuss the political background.
> 7 I need to point out the future goals of the German energy policy.

▶ SF 41: Mediation of written and oral texts

2 Recipient: Who are you mediating for?

Decide who you are mediating for, and in which medium. Are you writing for people who speak English well? Are they experts on the matter?

3 Language: What style of language should you use?

a After deciding who your audience is, consider how this may affect the style and structure of your text. Is the style of the original text formal or informal? Should it be retained in your text? What about the vocabulary?

b In the text there are many words which you don't know in English. Try to translate or explain the following terms in English: *Erdwärme, Biomasse, Treibhausgas, Wasserkraft.* Check your results with a dictionary afterwards. For your audience, how might it be best to mediate theses terms?

c Are there any structural features (e.g. bullet points, boxes, headlines) that you need in your text?

▶ LP 11: Using the right register

▶ SF 9: Paraphrasing

Find an online dictionary here:
Webcode context-52

4 Intercultural aspects: Which aspects of the text might be hard to understand for people from a different culture?

Sometimes you have to explain things that are easy for you to understand but hard for other people, because they are specific to your culture.

a Think of the term *Energiewende*. Describe it in a way that would make its meaning clear to somebody with no idea what it is.

b Find other aspects in the text that would have to be adapted, stressed or explained, e.g. when mediating for a Japanese, African or Scottish person.

▶ CC 1: Cultural awareness

5 Write your text.

6 Peer Assessment

In groups of four evaluate your texts using the assessment sheet your teacher will give you.

🎧 **CD1** 05
▶ SF22: Listening
▶ SF10: Working with closed test formats

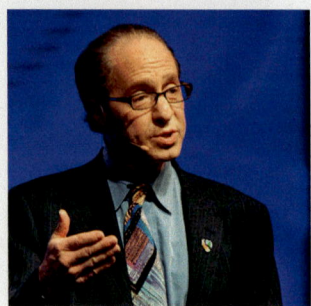

Raymond Kurzweil

FACT FILE

Biofuels are a type of energy derived from renewable plant and animal materials. Approximately 100 billion litres of biofuel are produced each year. Biofuels provide about 3% of the world's fuels for road transport.

🎬 **DVD**
▶ SF23: Analysing a film

▶ SF5: Doing research
▶ SF27: Having a discussion

C3 A possible future

COMPREHENSION ◀

1 Understanding an expert's perspective
Listen to the following interview with Raymond Kurzweil, an expert on technology, and say which of the following statements he made and which he did not.
1 Fossil fuels should be taxed to reflect the true cost they have on the environment.
2 Wind energy will be the most used renewable energy.
3 Within 14 years 100% of our energy needs will come from renewable sources.
4 Governments are unable to aid the change to renewable energies.

BEYOND THE TEXT ◀

2 Examining predictions
a The interview was made in 2008. Discuss to what extent Kurzweil's predictions have come true.
b Discuss how relevant his perspective is today.

C4 Biofuels – the green alternative?

The European Union has committed itself to producing 10% of its energy from renewable sources of energy by 2020. One way of achieving this goal is through the use of biofuels. This concept has been met with both approval and rejection.

COMPREHENSION ◀

1 Arguments for and against
Watch the two video clips about biofuels and note down arguments for and against biofuels.

ANALYSIS ◀

2 Comparing films
a Explain which of the two clips you found more convincing.
b Examine how the use of music, light, cinematic devices and the voiceover contributed to the ideas in the one you found most convincing.

BEYOND THE TEXT ◀

3 Having a discussion
In two groups find arguments in favour of and against biofuels. The motion could be as follows: 'Governments should subsidize biofuels.'
SUPPORT ▶ p.203

'No you can't turn your vegetables into bio-fuel.'

Doing a WebQuest

A supermarket in your hometown has announced their decision to stock genetically modified (GM) foods. The public is concerned.

- Do a quick opinion poll to find out what your class thinks about this issue.

In order to decide whether or not to take action, a Committee of Concerned Citizens agrees to consult experts: a scientist, a farmer, an environmentalist, and a nutritionist.

1 Get together in groups of four. Each of you researches the topic from the point of view of one of the experts (cf. the cards below). Make sure to also use German sources.

Find useful links here:
 Webcode context-05

As the **scientist**, you investigate the process of creating GM foods. You need to consider the following questions:
- How are GM foods produced?
- Is there a danger that this process might lead to unsafe products?
- What safeguards should be installed to prevent unsafe products?

As the **environmentalist**, you investigate the environmental aspects of GM foods. You need to consider the following questions:
- What environmental problems might be caused by GM foods?
- What safeguards should be installed to minimize these problems?

- As the **farmer**, you think of the consequences for farmers like yourself. You need to consider the following questions:
- What consequences will GM foods have for farmers (their health, cost of seeds, etc.)?
- What experiences have farmers had with GM foods so far?

As the **nutritionist** you investigate the nutritional aspects of GM foods. You need to consider the following questions:
- Do GM foods have the same nutritional value as natural foods?
- Could there be any nutritional problems or long-term health effects involved in eating GM foods?

---

2 In your group, exchange the results of your research. Decide whether or not to recommend stocking GM foods.

3 Prepare a presentation for the Committee in which you give a recommendation and justify your opinion (no longer than ten minutes). Make sure your listeners can follow your arguments – they are no experts on the matter!

▶ SF 24: Giving a presentation

4 Give your presentation.

5 After each group has given their presentation, the Committee (i.e. the class) discusses the recommendations and decides whether to take action.

▶ SF 27: Having a discussion

6 Repeat the opinion poll you conducted before the WebQuest.

7 Evaluate the presentations with the assessment sheet your teacher will give you.

3 Visions of the Future – Utopias and Dystopias

A

B

Download a list of chapter vocab here: 👆 **Webcode** context-08

1 Finding captions for pictures

a Look at the following captions and match them to the images above (there is one more caption than you need).
1 Paradise island
2 Life in a bubble
3 Taking care of you
4 Watch out for the enemy
5 Thought control
6 How I see the world

b Compare your ideas with a partner.

2 Researching topics

Get into groups of five. Within your group, assign a different picture to each member. Make notes on your image, think about what the image could represent and do some research. Present your findings to the others in your group.

▶ SF 11: Analysing pictures
▶ SF 5: Doing research

D

E

C

COLOR BY KATRIN IORIS 2003

3 An imaginary journey

  a Take another look at the pictures on these pages, then sit back, close your
     eyes and listen …

  b When you have opened your eyes again, picture one or two of the photos
     that you took when you stepped out of the phone box in the year 2121.
     Describe your photos to a partner and listen to your partner's descriptions.

  c Based on your imaginary journey, write a text about your impressions –
     were they positive or negative? You can add one or two images of the
     'photos' that you took.

🎧 **CD1** 07

PREVIEW

In this chapter you will you will examine works of *fiction in which writers have considered present-day
issues and transformed them into imaginary positive and negative depictions of the future.

Main topics

Focus on Skills: VIEWING and READING

Chapter Task: Creating your own piece

CD1 08

Listen to an audio version of the text on the CD or download it here:

 Webcode context-09

From utopia to dystopia

Exciting worlds

The term 'utopia' comes from Greek and means both 'no-place' and 'good-place'. In 1516 the English lawyer, philosopher and adviser to the king, Thomas More, wrote a work of *fiction describing a society on an island he named *Utopia*. From then on, the term was used to refer to imaginary, paradise-like 5 places, but also to a particular kind of narrative, known as utopian literature.

Today, the word 'utopia' is applied to a wide range of real places: from calm yoga retreats and beautiful holiday destinations to theme parks, shopping malls and other 10 centres of entertainment. Modern day utopias reflect key parts of our society, its lust for self-indulgence and constant excitement.

Peace and safety

In More's day, the imaginary and ideal utopias were 15 often distant, yet to be discovered islands – thus creating the illusion of actually existing. Such utopian societies were governed by strict sets of laws, forcing the individual to repress his unreliable nature and act for the good of society. 20
Early utopian literature was based on the desire for a better life and a society in which peace was guaranteed. During the Victorian era, political convictions such as socialism and the belief in scientific progress caused utopian literature to flourish. However, as the world had more or less been mapped out, the settings switched from 25 undiscovered territories to familiar places and how the author envisaged them in the future.

Oppressive governments

After two world wars and the horrors of the first half of the 20th century, former utopian ideals seemed absurd. Moreover, totalitarianism often led 30 to the establishment of dictatorships instead of benefitting mankind. As a consequence, the belief of heaven on earth turned into a nightmarish vision: the term 'utopia' was replaced by 'dystopia', meaning 'bad', or 'hard' or – to put it simply – a utopia gone wrong. The main aim of a dystopia is to portray images of the future as realistic and threatening possibilities. 35
In the 20th century, dystopia became the main form of visionary literature, mirroring society's failures and projecting today's divisive issues (such as capitalism, consumerism, self-indulgence, the power of science and technology and globalization) into the future. If dystopias cause despair, it is because writers want readers to think about the present and see their visions of the 40 future as a serious menace.
However, dystopias that leave no room for hope fail in their intention. Their true purpose is to make us realize that we should be committed to making a better society. For this reason, the distinction between utopian and dystopian literature has become increasingly unclear: dystopian literature often includes 45 utopian elements, and vice versa.

1 Definitions and derivatives

a Copy and complete the chart below. You may not be able to fill all gaps.

Nouns	Verbs	Adjective
narrative	*narrate sth.*	*narratable*
	portray sb./sth.	
		nightmarish
vision		
		divisive
	repress	
		imaginary

b The phrases below are definitions of words used in the text on p. 54. Identify these words, write them in added lines in the table above and complete the table where possible:

- a strong belief
- a type of literature that describes imaginary events and people
- a false idea or belief
- a threatening person or thing
- a system of government in which there is only one political party with complete power

2 Synonyms

a Match the formal phrases on the left with the corresponding informal phrases on the right. One informal definition is missing, so write your own definition in informal English. Check your solutions with a partner.

▶ SF 1: Dealing with unknown words

Formal style	Everyday English
1 undiscovered territories	a a certain type of story
2 mirror sth.	b be willing to work really hard for sth.
3 a particular kind of narrative	c making people think that
4 repress one's emotions	d show sth.
5 creating the illusion of	e places that haven't been found yet
6 be committed to sth.	f topics which often cause arguments
7 divisive issues	g …

b Fill in the gaps with phrases from the 'formal style' column:
1 Certain social media … privacy, but you never know who is reading your messages!
2 Dystopian literature often … negative aspects of today's society.
3 If we want to keep the earth habitable, we should … sustainability.
4 Science fiction stories are …
5 At present, data privacy and the legalization of cannabis are …

3 Speaking

Explain the development from utopian to dystopian literature in everyday English. Use as many words and expressions from the boxes above as possible.

Entertain me!

A1 Inside our heads   *M.T. Anderson*

Feed is a young adult science fiction novel written by M.T. Anderson. From the viewpoint of an American teenager, it shows the descent of the USA into a culture based mainly on advertising and consumerism.

When I wrote *Feed*, (in 2001) my intention wasn't really to predict future tech – but instead, to think about cultural conditions as they already were then.

All around us ads, TV shows, and movies nudge us with images of the high life, playing on our desire to belong. When I was a teen, this drove me crazy (as it bugs and worries many teens). There's always that subliminal message seducing us and bullying us: *if you just get this, and buy this, and order that, you'll be cool, and you'll be loved. See how much fun these kids are having? If you want to be wanted, then you need to want what other people want. And other people – what they want is this. Buy it. Buy it now.*

This marketing has become even more intense (and not just for teens!) now that most of us are connected all the time through devices of one kind or another. [...]

So I began to conceive a story in which these media connections and social networking connections weren't external, but within us all. What if we no longer needed the devices? What if we had an internet feed within us, so we were never disconnected?

From: *Feed*, 2002

5

10

15

Glossary

1 **predict sth.** say that sth. will happen
3 **nudge sb.** push sb. gently
4 **play on sth.** take advantage of sth. (e.g. fear or emotions) to get what you want
bug sb. annoy sb.
5 **subliminal** affecting your mind even though you are not aware of it
seduce sb. (here) persuade sb.
12 **conceive sth.** (here) imagine sth., think of sth.

COMPREHENSION ◀

1 The beginnings of a novel
    Outline how M.T. Anderson became a writer of dystopian fiction.

BEYOND THE TEXT ◀

2 YOU CHOOSE ▸ Giving your own opinion

a Justify why you would like to read the story (or why not).

b Comment on whether you agree with Anderson that 'There's always that subliminal message seducing us and bullying us' (ll. 5–6). Give examples.

A2 Don't let me get bored   *M.T. Anderson*

▶ SF 14: Reading strategies

Feed begins with a journey to the moon. Before reading the extract, make a few notes on what you would expect to find if you went there. Now compare your notes with what Anderson's protagonist finds.

We went to the moon to have fun, but the moon turned out to completely suck.

We went on a Friday, because there was shit-all to do at home. It was the beginning of spring break. Everything at home was boring. Link Arwaker was like, 'I'm so null,' and Marty was all, 'I'm null too, unit', but I mean we were all pretty null, because for the last like hour we'd been playing with three uninsulated wires that were coming out of the wall. We were trying to ride shocks off them. So Marty told us that there was this fun place for lo-grav on the moon. Lo-grav can be kind of stupid, but this was supposed to be good. It was called the Ricochet Lounge. We thought we'd go for a few days with some of the girls and stay at a hotel there and go dancing.

5

Glossary

2 **shit-all** (sl) nichts
3 **be null** (here) feel nothing
6 **ride shocks off sth.** get electric shocks from sth.
8 **ricochet** ['rɪkəʃeɪ] *abprallen*

10 We flew up and our feeds were burbling all sorts of things about where to stay and what to eat. It sounded pretty fun, and at first there were lots of pictures of dancing and people with romper-gills and metal wings, and I was like, *This will be big, really big,* but then I guess it wasn't so skip when we were flying over the
15 surface of the moon itself, because the moon was just like it always is, after your first few times there, when you get over being like, *Whoa, unit! The moon! The goddamn moon!* and instead there's just the rockiness and the suckiness, and the craters all being full of old broken shit, like domes nobody's using any more
20 and wrappers and claws.

The thing I hate about space is that you can feel how old and empty it is. Don't know if the others felt like I felt, about space? But I think they did, because they all got louder. They all pointed more and squeezed close to Link's window.
25 You need the noise of your friends, in space.

I feel really sorry for people who have to travel by themselves. In space, that must suck. When you're going places with other people, with this big group, everyone is leaning toward each other and people are laughing and they're chatting and things are great, and it's just like a commercial for jeans, or something with nougat.

From: *Feed*, 2002

10 **burble** (here) *babbeln*
12 **romper-gills** in the novel, device that allows you to breathe in space (gills = *Kiemen*)
14 **skip** (here) *toll*
19 **dome** *Kuppel*
20 **wrapper** piece of plastic that is wrapped around sth., e.g. food
claw (here) *Greifer*

COMPREHENSION ◀

1 Finding headings for the text
Match the following terms with the appropriate lines in the text (there are more headings than you need):

---

amusement · belonging · boredom · disappointment · excitement ·
fascination · loneliness · vandalism

▶ SF 10: Working with closed test formats

LANGUAGE AWARENESS ◀

2 Using formal English
Look at the narrator's language and put the following phrases from the text into more *formal English:
1 'the moon turned out to completely suck' (l. 1)
2 'there was shit-all to do at home' (l. 2)
3 'lo-grav' (l. 7)
4 'our feeds were burbling all sorts of things' (l. 10)
5 'it wasn't so skip' (l. 14)

ANALYSIS ◀

3 Analysing genre and technique
  a Examine what you consider to be utopian and dystopian elements in the text. Compare your findings with a partner.
  b Analyse Anderson's narrative technique. SUPPORT ▶ p. 204

▶ SF 36: Writing a text analysis
▶ SF 19: Analysing narrative prose

BEYOND THE TEXT ◀

4 YOU CHOOSE ▶ Creative writing

  a Re-write the text from the point of view of a third-person *narrator.

 OR

  b Choose a different futuristic context and write an *interior monologue for a teenager with a feed.

▶ SF 37: Doing a creative writing task

Film trailers are designed to capture our attention and to draw us to the cinema. Just like commercials, they are a means of advertising. The idea of the trailer is to summarize the film and to indicate what makes the film different from all the other films on the film circuit.

In contrast to a film clip, which shows a short but complete sequence from a film, in a trailer various scenes from the film are cut and arranged so that the audience is given a good idea of what the film will be about. It can establish the mood, introduce characters and the setting, and reveal the *plot and the main themes. [5]

Typical trailer features
- reveal something of the plot, but not too much,
- are fast-paced – short shots and quick cuts between key scenes, [10]
- do not show events in the correct order,
- use music and sound effects to manipulate emotions,
- build up to a climax, and then finish (cliffhanger), so the final shot leaves a lasting effect on the audience, [15]
- show the title of the film at the end, so that the audience will remember it.

1 *Choose what you consider to be the three most important features of a trailer.*

2 *Together with a partner, compare your ideas and agree on the three most important features.*

A3 The Hunger Games

The trailer you are about to watch is for the 2012 blockbuster film The Hunger Games, *based on the novel by Suzanne Collins and starring Jennifer Lawrence.*

1 Identifying key features of a trailer
Watch the trailer. Together with a partner, tick off the features that you noted down after working on the Fact File above. Share your findings with another pair. Were all of the features you listed in the trailer?

2 Viewing for detail
Work in groups of three. Copy the viewing log below and decide who is going to be responsible for which topic. Take notes on your topic as you watch.

Characters	Setting(s)	Plot and main themes
Information, behaviour, relationships	When and where is the film set? How is the setting established?	What is the film going to be about?

3 Discussing the trailer
a In groups of three, discuss whether or not the trailer is effective.
  ▶ LANGUAGE HELP
b CHALLENGE ▶ Make notes on the most effective, memorable or impressive parts of the trailer and present them to the class, giving reasons for your choices.

▶ SF 23: Analysing a film

▶ SF 27: Having a discussion

FOCUS ON SKILLS

Viewing films

▶ SF 23: Analysing a film

You will watch three extracts from the film The Hunger Games. *For each extract, you will focus on a different aspect important for film analysis.*

1 Analysing presentation of characters

a In groups of three, watch the first film extract and take notes on the key details regarding how the different characters are shown. Each person in your group should concentrate on one set of characters. Copy the viewing log below, which will help you keep track of what you see:

	Setting	Costumes and makeup	Facial expressions and body language	Camera angles
1 Tributes				
2 Audience				
3 Game makers Sponsors President Snow				

DVD

glimpse *(n)* quick look
overstate sth. exaggerate sth.
goosebumps *Gänsehaut*
have the odds in your favour
be lucky

b In your group, discuss how the viewer's impressions of the different groups are influenced.

DVD

2 Analysing suspense

a In groups of four, watch the next film extract, concentrating on how the film uses different techniques to create *suspense. Each one of you is responsible for one specific aspect:

 TROUBLE SPOT

technique = Methode
technology = Technik

1 Feelings: Katniss's emotions and how they are shown	2 Time: How the sense of time is conveyed	3 Sounds: e.g. music, voices, silence	4 Colours: darkness and light

b Discuss how different techniques create suspense in this extract.

DVD

starve die because you do not have enough food

3 The portrayal of themes

a In groups of three, watch the third extract and take notes on the following aspects:

The role of the game-makers	The role of the sponsors	How the tributes cope in the arena

b Examine which contemporary divisive issues are dealt with in *The Hunger Games*.

c Watch all the extracts again and note down utopian and dystopian elements. Compare *The Hunger Games* with reality TV shows you know and note down the similarities and differences.

A4 Flipping the bird at authority

This article from German media website Spiegel Online *reviews the second film in* The Hunger Games *series:* Catching Fire *(2013).*

„Die Tribute von Panem – Catching Fire": Sie zeigt den Mächtigen den Vogel

Die Dystopie von Panem gewinnt sicher keinen Preis für Originalität, zu offensichtlich orientiert sich Collins' Entwurf dafür an vertrauten Vorbildern aus der zivilisations- und autoritätskritischen Science-Fiction. Das ist aber kein Makel, denn die grimmige Welt mit ihrem grausamen Klassensystem erfüllt durchaus ihren Zweck. Simpler, materieller und greifbarer als andere Zukunftsvisionen, ist es der Schauplatz, an dem 5
Katniss, das widerständige „Girl on Fire", eine neue Art von Teen-Heldin sein kann.

    Als unfreiwillige Lichtgestalt des Lumpenproletariats ist sie weit entfernt von den elitären Zauberer- und Vampir-Aristokratien, die Fiktionen wie „Harry Potter" und „Twilight" bevölkern und deren Sorgen im Vergleich wie Luxusprobleme wirken. Katniss ist Geschöpf der sozialen, ökonomischen und moralischen Dauerkrise ihrer 10
Welt, und je mehr sie sich von den vermeintlich naturgegebenen Verhältnissen emanzipiert, desto bedrohlicher wird sie für die Herrschenden. Und mag sie auch sehr geschickt (und gefährlich) im Umgang mit Pfeil und Bogen sein, ihre wahren Waffen bleiben Intellekt, Intuition und das Wissen um die Macht von Gesten und Bildern. [...] 15

    Als Impresario der Hunger Games traktiert Heavensbee vom Regiepult aus die Tribute in der megalomanen Arena mit Flutwellen, Giftnebel, Blutregen und

sonstigem telegenen Terror. Die handfeste Survival-Action ist eindrucksvoll bebildert,
doch längst nicht so spektakulär wie der Kampf der Symbole, den Katniss mit dem
20 System austrägt. In seinen besten Momenten verbindet „Catching Fire" so großes
Melodrama mit offensiver Mediensatire und zeigt das staatstragende Gladiatoren-
spiel als sadistische Zuspitzung des Casting-Show-Phänomens.

Gegen das Drehbuch der Mächtigen die Deutungshoheit über das eigene Image
wiederzuerlangen, ist daher der wirksamste Akt der Rebellion.

25 So ist Katniss zuallererst die Marianne eines ästhetischen Aufstands, wenn sie in
ihren Auftritten das verbotene Bild des „Mockingjay" popularisiert, eines Vogels mit
besonderer Bedeutung für die Vergangenheit Panems. Selbiger ist konsequenter-
weise auch Leitmotiv der millionenschweren Werbekampagne von „Catching Fire",
eines Films, der wie sein Vorläufer weitaus besser ist, als er eigentlich sein müsste.
30 Eben weil er sein junges Zielpublikum nicht für dumm hält und unabhängig
vom Unterhaltungsdiktat eine Haltung einnimmt, die auch jenseits der Pubertät
begeistern kann.

Darum sollte man nach dem abschließenden Cliffhanger auch für die nächste Fort-
setzung dranbleiben: The revolution *will* be televised.

From: *Spiegel Online*, 2013

1 Paraphrasing difficult vocabulary

You want to help a friend who only speaks a bit of German to understand
the article. Explain the following words and phrases in English as simply as
possible.

1 'Deutungshoheit über das eigene Image' (l. 23)
2 'Drehbuch' (l. 23)
3 'Geschöpf der moralischen Krise' (l. 10)
4 'Klassensystem' (l. 4)
5 'Werbekampagne' (l. 28)
6 'sehr geschickt im Umgang mit Pfeil und Bogen sein' (l. 13)
7 'Zielpublikum' (l. 30)
8 'zivilisationskritisch' (ll. 2–3)
9 'Zuspitzung des Casting-Show-Phänomens' (l. 22)

▶ SF 9: Paraphrasing

2 Mediation (German → English)

You are spending a year at a US high school. In Media Studies class, each
student must present a film. You would like to present *The Hunger Games
– Catching Fire*. Although your teacher has never seen the film, she will not
allow you to present it as it 'glorifies violence'. Use arguments you found in
the article to write her an email to convince her that the film has qualities
making it suitable for the class. ▶ LANGUAGE HELP

▶ SF 41: Mediation of written
and oral texts

> **LANGUAGE HELP**
> - Taking into account … how about …?
> - I would greatly appreciate your permission to …
> - I would really appreciate it if …
> - I really understand your concern but …
> - Although you might not agree, I really feel that …
> - Have you considered that …?

3 YOU CHOOSE Writing

a Put yourself in the position of the teacher in **2** and write a response to an email written by someone else in your class.

 OR

b Choose a different film with dystopian themes and write a four-minute presentation for the media studies class. Describe the plot, themes and protagonist(s), and explain how the film portrays a dystopia.

Part B

Give me stability in the community

B1 Inside the Circle   *Dave Eggers*

In his 2013 novel, Dave Eggers depicts the Circle, a fast-growing digital corporation that offers a wide range of community attractions to its employees in the hope of binding them to the company. Mae Holland has just been hired thanks to her best friend Annie, who also works there, and on her first day is given a tour of the campus.

- Quickly list the internet companies you know and say what you have heard about their reputations.
- Discuss with a partner whether you would like to work for such a company, and what you roughly imagine your workday would be like.

Extract 1: A utopian workplace

The rest of the day was a blur of glass rooms and brief, impossibly warm introductions. Everyone she [= Mae] met was busy, just short of overworked, but nevertheless thrilled to meet her, so happy she was there, any friend of Annie's … There was a tour of the health center, and an introduction to the dreadlocked Dr. Hampton who ran it. There was a tour of the emergency clinic and the Scottish nurse who did the admitting. A tour of the organic gardens, a hundred yards square, where there were two full-time farmers giving a talk to a large group of Circlers while they sampled the latest harvest of carrots and tomatoes and kale. There was a tour of the mini-golf area, the movie theater, the bowling alleys, the grocery store. Finally, deep in what Mae assumed was the corner of the campus – she could see the fence beyond, the rooftops of San Vincenzo hotels where visitors to the Circle stayed – they toured the company dorms. Mae had heard something about them, Annie mentioning that sometimes she crashed on campus and now preferred those rooms to her own home. Walking through the hallways, seeing the tidy rooms, each with a shiny kitchenette, a desk, an overstuffed couch and bed, Mae had to agree that the appeal was visceral.

'There are 180 rooms now, but we're growing quickly,' Josiah said. 'With ten thousand or so people on campus, there's always a percentage of people who work late, or just need a nap during the day. These rooms are always free, always clean – you just have to check online to see which ones are available. Right now they book up fast, but the plan is to have at least a few thousand rooms within the next few years.'

'And after a party like tonight's, these are always full,' Denise said, with what she meant to be a conspiratorial wink.

The tour continued through the afternoon, with stops to sample food at the culinary class, taught that day by a celebrated young chef known for using the whole of any animal. She presented Mae with a dish called toasted pigface, which Mae ate and discovered tasted like a more fatty bacon; she liked it very much. They passed other visitors as they toured the campus, groups of college students, and packs of vendors, and what appeared to be a senator and his handlers. They passed an arcade stocked with vintage pinball machines and an indoor badminton court, where, Annie said, a former world champion was kept on retainer. By the time Josiah and Denise had brought her back around to the center of the campus, the light was dimming, and staffers were installing tiki torches in the grass and lighting them. A few thousand Circlers began to gather in the twilight, and standing among them, Mae knew that she never wanted to work – never wanted to be – anywhere else. Her hometown, and

5

10

15

20

25

30

> ### ■ TROUBLE SPOT
>
> ***give a talk to sb. on sth.*** (l. 7)
> = *speak in front of an audience about sth., give a speech on sth.*
> ***have a talk with sb.*** = *speak to sb., have a conversation with sb.*

1 **blur** *(n)* series of events that you cannot see or remember clearly
  brief quick
2 **thrilled** very happy
8 **kale** *Grünkohl*
11 **San Vincenzo** (here) Italian style of architecture
12 **dorm** building with rooms for people to sleep in
13 **crash** *(v) (sl)* sleep
14 **kitchenette** small kitchen
15 **overstuffed** *prall gepolstert*
  visceral ['vɪsərəl] relating to strong emotions
18 **nap** *(n)* short sleep
22 **conspiratorial** suggesting that a secret is being shared
23 **sample sth.** try sth.
24 **culinary** related to cooking and food
28 **vendor** seller
30 **keep sb. on retainer** pay sb. to make sure they will be available to do work when needed
31 **dim** *(v)* fade, get weaker
32 **tiki torch** *Gartenfackel*

35 the rest of California, the rest of America, seemed like some chaotic mess in the developing world. Outside the walls of the Circle, all was noise and struggle, failure and filth. But here, all had been perfected. The best people had made the best systems and the best systems had reaped funds, unlimited funds, that made possible this, the best place to work. And it was natural that it was so, Mae thought. Who else but utopians

40 could make utopia?

Extract 2: The company's core beliefs

The next day, Mae's team leader Dan explains the philosophy of the company.

'Mae, now that you're aboard, I wanted to get across some of the core beliefs here at the company. And chief among them is that just as important as the work we do here – and that work is very important – we want to make sure that you can be a human being here, too. We want this to be a workplace, sure, but it should also be a *human*

45 place. And that means the fostering of community. In fact, it must be a community. That's one of our slogans, as you probably know: *Community First*. And you've seen the signs that say *Humans Work Here* – I insist on those. That's my pet issue. We're not automatons. This isn't a sweatshop. We're a group of the best minds of our generation. Genera*tions*. And making sure this is a place where our humanity is respected,

50 where our opinions are dignified, where our voices are heard – this is as important as any revenue, any stock price, any endeavor undertaken here. Does that sound corny?'

'No, no,' Mae rushed to say. 'Definitely not. That's why I'm here. I love the "community first" idea. Annie's been telling me about it since she started. At my last job, no one really communicated very well. It was basically the opposite of here in every way.'

55 Dan turned to look into the hills to the east, covered in mohair and patches of green. 'I hate hearing that kind of thing. With the technology available, communication should never be in doubt. Understanding should never be out of reach or anything but clear. It's what we do here. You might say it's the mission of the company – it's an obsession of mine, anyway. Communication. Understanding. Clarity.'

From: *The Circle*, 2013

37 filth dirt
38 reap funds make money
41 be aboard (here) be a part of a new organization
45 fostering (n) strengthening
47 pet issue topic you feel strongly about
48 automaton [–'–––] robot
sweatshop ['swet-] place where people work for low wages and in poor conditions
51 revenue ['revənjuː] money made from business
corny (sl) silly and unoriginal
55 mohair type of soft wool

COMPREHENSION ◀

1 Mediation (English ➔ German)
You are working on an article for your school blog about young people's first days at new workplaces. In German, outline Mae's experience.

▶ SF41: Mediation of written and oral texts

LANGUAGE AWARENESS ◀

2 Compound nouns

a To emphasize a sense of community, Dan creates a new noun to describe the Circle as a '*human*place' – a *workplace* for *humans*. Compound nouns can be one word (e.g. *sunrise*), multiple words (e.g. *washing machine*) or multiple words joined by hyphens (e.g. *daughter-in-law*). Search for further compound nouns in the first extract.

b YOU CHOOSE ▶ Creative writing with compounds

1 Write an advertisement or slogan (not more than two sentences) for a utopian company, school or political party using two of the compound nouns you found in **a** plus at least three new ones.

OR

2 Write a short description of a utopian workplace, using two of the compound nouns you found in **a** plus at least three new ones.

▶ SF37: Doing a creative writing task

READING FOCUS ON SKILLS
Reading for analysis (novel extract)

The extracts from The Circle *in* **B1** *are from close to the beginning of the novel and form part of the introduction of the reader to the company and to a few key characters.*

1 Looking at the setting and what it means

Location can create mood, develop *characters or function as a *symbol. You can analyse literary *setting by considering how the location influences the characters, the *plot, and your own impression of the novel.

a Make a list of the facilities Mae is introduced to on her tour of the Circle campus (ll. 1–30), adding any additional information we are given about each one. Explain the effect the description of the tour has on you (as a reader).

b The company dorms are given the most space in the text. Discuss the effect of this, and explain what is meant by the sentence 'Mae had to agree that the appeal was visceral' (l. 15).

▶ SF 17: Analysing stylistic devices

c The tour ends at the beginning of a party (ll. 30–34). Examine the atmosphere at this point by looking at how it is created and the effect it has on Mae.

d Study the last lines of Extract 1, and evaluate their effect on your expectations about the novel.

2 Identifying key themes

The theme of a text is the message the author is trying to get across to the reader.

▶ SF 39: Quoting a text

a Look at the example in the table below, then find two more important quotations in Extract 1 which represent different themes and complete the table in a similar way:

Quotation	*'Mae knew that she never wanted to work – never wanted to be – anywhere else.' (ll. 33–34)*
Context	*Mae is standing in the twilight, surrounded by happy colleagues after a tour of the Circle campus.*
Themes	*utopia; a perfect workplace; realizing your dreams*

b Discuss your choices with a partner. Do you agree? Why / why not? Together, choose the two most important quotations.

▶ SF 19: Analysing narrative prose

3 Analysing key themes

a For each of the two quotations you chose in task **2b**, write a sentence explaining how it illustrates a key theme in the text.

b Explain the slogans 'Community First' and 'Humans Work Here' in the context of Mae's tour of the company and Dan's explanations about the company values. ▶ LANGUAGE HELP

4 Evaluation

Read Dan's final speech again (ll. 56–59). Evaluate the effect this speech has on Mae and is supposed to have on you as the reader.

■ **LANGUAGE HELP**

- The effect of … on the reader is to emphasize …
- The reader is given the impression that …
- Ultimately, Dan's words serve to …
- … creates an atmosphere of …
- Dan's use of … makes Mae / the reader …

🔵 CULTURE SPOT

A tower with its top in the sky (Genesis 11:1–9)

1. Match the titles and the captions with the right buildings. **Titles:** *Salisbury Cathedral; the tallest building in the EU; the Tower of Babel; 30 St Mary Axe*
   Captions: *the Gherkin; the tallest spire; an artist's impression; the Shard*

2. Bruegel intended his painting of the Tower of Babel to illustrate the story of human pride punished by God and the futility of human endeavour.
   a. Together with a partner, list examples of other human attempts 'to reach the sky'.
   b. Research the tallest buildings in the world over the centuries and make a list of the most impressive ones.
   c. Collect further examples of human endeavours to transgress human limitations.

3. Discuss whether all this inventiveness and activity is more suitable as a subject for dystopias or as a subject for utopias.

B2 Living in the compound *Margaret Atwood*

Margaret Atwood's novel Oryx and Crake *(2003) is set on the North American continent. In this extract, Jimmy looks back on his childhood when his father worked for a company called OrganInc.*

- Imagine that you are the planner or architect of a gated community, i.e. one that is fenced in and guarded. Note down a few ideas or make a sketch of the layout.

When Jimmy was really little they'd lived in a Cape Cod-style frame house in one of the Modules – there were pictures of him, in a carry-cot on the porch, with dates and everything, stuck into a photo album at some time when his mother was still bothering – but now they lived in a large Georgian centre-plan with an indoor swimming pool and a small gym. The furniture in it was called reproduction. Jimmy was 5 quite old before he realized what this word meant – that for each reproduction item, there was supposed to be an original somewhere. Or there had been once. Or something.

The house, the pool, the furniture – all belonged to the OrganInc 10 Compound, where the top people lived. Increasingly, the middle-range execs and the junior scientists lived there too.

Jimmy's father said it was 15 better that way, because nobody had to commute to work from the Modules. Despite the sterile transport corridors and the high-speed bullet trains, there was 20 always a risk when you went through the city.

Jimmy had never been to the city. He'd only seen it on TV – endless billboards and neon 25 signs and stretches of buildings, tall and short; endless dingy-looking streets, countless vehicles of all kinds, some of them with clouds of smoke coming out the back; thousands of people, hurrying, cheering, rioting. There were other cities too, near and far; some had better neighborhoods in them, said his father, almost like 30 the Compounds, with high walls around the houses, but those didn't get on TV much.

Compound people didn't go to the cities unless they had to, and then never alone. They called the cities the pleeblands. Despite the fingerprint identity cards now carried by everyone, public security in the pleeblands was leaky: there were people cruising around in those places who could forge anything and who might be anybody, 35 not to mention the loose change – the addicts, the muggers, the paupers, the crazies. So it was best for everyone at OrganInc Farms to live all in one place, with foolproof procedures.

Outside the OrganInc walls and gates and searchlights, things were unpredictable. Inside, they were the way it used to be when Jimmy's father was a kid, before things 40 got so serious, or that's what Jimmy's father said. Jimmy's mother said it was all artificial, it was just a theme park and you could never bring the old ways back, but

1 **frame house** *Holzhaus*
2 **carry-cot** small bed for a baby
4 **bother** (v) care
13 **exec** (infml) boss, manager
17 **commute** travel regularly from your home to your workplace
20 **bullet train** very fast train
25 **billboard** large advertisement
27 **dingy** ['dɪndʒi] dark and dirty
34 **leaky** (here) deficient, not very good
35 **cruise around** (here) be somewhere in order to do bad things
36 **loose change** (here) people who don't fit into the social hierarchy
  mugger violent thief
  pauper ['pɔːpə] (old use) very poor person
37 **foolproof** very well designed and unable to fail

Jimmy's father said why knock it? You could walk around without fear, couldn't you? Go for a bike ride, sit at a sidewalk café, buy an ice-cream cone? Jimmy knew his father was right, because he himself had done all of these things. [...]

Long ago, in the days of knights and dragons, the kings and dukes had lived in castles, with high walls and drawbridges and slots on the ramparts so you could pour hot pitch on your enemies, said Jimmy's father, and the Compounds were the same idea. Castles were for keeping you and your buddies nice and safe inside, and for keeping everybody else outside.

'So are we the kings and dukes?' asked Jimmy.

'Oh, absolutely,' said his father, laughing.

From: *Oryx and Crake,* 2003

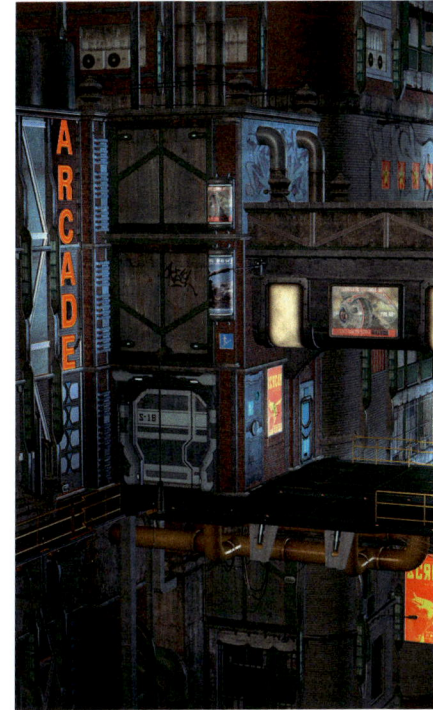

50 **knight** *Ritter*
51 **duke** *Herzog*
53 **drawbridge** bridge that can be pulled up to stop the enemy from entering a castle
slot long, thin hole
rampart *(usu. pl)* high wall of stone built around a castle
54 **pitch** *Pech*

COMPREHENSION ◀

1 Understanding the situation

a Based on what you know of the text's setting, draw a map.
On your map, you should label:
- the OrganInc Compound
- a Module
- bullet trains
- transport corridors
- the pleeblands

b Compare your map with a partner's.

ANALYSIS ◀

2 A story within a story

Read lines 48–61 again. Interpret the message of the short 'history' told by Jimmy's father.

▶ SF 19: Analysing narrative prose

3 Utopia or dystopia?

Analyse both utopian and dystopian elements in the text.

SUPPORT ▶ p. 205

BEYOND THE TEXT ◀

4 | YOU CHOOSE ▶ | Creative writing

▶ SF 37: Doing a creative writing task

a Write a text of about 200 words, describing the typical working day of a person living in the pleeblands.

b Imagine Jimmy breaks out of the Compound and spends an afternoon in the pleeblands. Write his diary entry for this day.

Watch over me

C1 Data collection and complacency

You are going to watch a video clip about free web services.

▶ SF 23: Analysing a film

1 Before viewing

a Discuss with a partner what the title of the clip leads you to expect about its content.

b Make a list of situations in which your data could be collected, and purposes it could be used for.

c Discuss whether this bothers you or not, and whether you would be prepared to do anything about it.

——— COMPREHENSION ◀

2 While viewing

Decide whether the sentences below are true or false. Correct the sentences that are false.

1 Sending emails via Gmail is a completely private activity.

2 The web service causes ads to be sent to your email address.

3 In 2005 there was a huge protest movement against data collection.

4 There is no real danger with this kind of data collection.

▶ SF 10: Working with closed test formats

🎬 **DVD**

driving main
party (here) group of people or organizations
complacency feeling of satisfaction with a situation, so that you do not think change is necessary
reassert sth. make other people recognize again your right to do sth.
crucial important
far-fetched *(adj)* hard to believe

3 Watching for detail

a Describe the goals of the 2005 initiative called 'The Attention Trust'.

b Explain why, according to the speaker, it should have been a 'no-brainer', but wasn't.

c Seth Goldstein says it is not right to say that people are 'perfectly happy' with the way our data is traded on the net. Explain his alternatives 'dumb happy' or 'naïve happy'.

——— ANALYSIS ◀

4 YOU CHOOSE ▶ Analysing techniques

a Explain how the video uses images to illustrate what is said by the speaker.

  OR

b Near the end of the video the image of sleepwalking is used both visually and *metaphorically. Explain both uses.

——— BEYOND THE TEXT ◀

5 From data collection to dystopia

a In the final section of the video clip, John Batelle mentions the dystopian novel *Nineteen Eighty-Four* in connection with data collection. Discuss how data collection could lead to a dystopian situation.

▶ SF 34: Argumentative writing

b Look at the following quotations from the *novel *The Circle* (cf. **B1**, pp. 62–63) and discuss how they can be linked to the video clip. Write a comment.

> 1 'I have a question, Mae. Do you behave better or worse when you're being watched?'
> 'Better. Without a doubt.'
> 'When you're alone, unwatched, unaccountable[1], what happens?'

> 2 *SECRETS ARE LIES*
> *SHARING IS CARING*
> *PRIVACY IS THEFT*

From: Dave Eggers, *The Circle*, 2013

[1]**unaccountable** not having to explain or give reasons for your actions to anyone

C2 Big Brother is watching you *George Orwell*

Nineteen Eighty-Four is a dystopian novel George Orwell published in 1949.
It is set in Oceania where 'Big Brother', the tyrannical ruler of the state, observes
everyone at all times with the help of the telescreen. The protagonist, Winston
Smith, secretly hates the government and dreams of rebellion against Big Brother.
He has started a secret love affair with his co-worker Julia, who is also against the
government, and he is afraid they will be found out.

He thought for a little while. 'Has it ever occurred to you,' he said, 'that the best thing for us to do would be simply to walk out of here before it's too late, and never see each other again?'

5 'Yes, dear, it has occurred to me, several times. But I'm not going to do it, all the same.'

'We've been lucky,' he said 'but it can't last much longer. You're young. You look normal and innocent. If you keep clear of people like me, you might stay alive for
10 another fifty years.'

'No. I've thought it all out. What you do, I'm going to do. And don't be too downhearted. I'm rather good at staying alive.'

'We may be together for another six months – a year –
15 there's no knowing. At the end we're certain to be apart. Do you realize how utterly alone we shall be? When once they get hold of us there will be nothing, literally nothing that either of us can do for the other. If I confess, they'll shoot you, and if I refuse to confess, they'll shoot you just the same. Nothing that I can do or say, or stop myself from saying, will put off
20 your death for as much as five minutes. Neither of us will even know whether the other is alive or dead. We shall be utterly without power of any kind. The one thing that matters is that we shouldn't betray one another, although even that can't make the slightest difference.'

'If you mean confessing,' she said, 'we shall do that, right enough. Everybody always
25 confesses. You can't help it. They torture you.'

'I don't mean confessing. Confession is not betrayal. What you say or do doesn't matter: only feelings matter. If they could make me stop loving you – that would be the real betrayal.'

She thought it over. 'They can't do that,' she said finally. 'It's the one thing they can't
30 do. They can make you say anything – ANYTHING – but they can't make you believe it. They can't get inside you.'

'No,' he said a little more hopefully, 'no; that's quite true. They can't get inside you. If you can FEEL that staying human is worth while, even when it can't have any result whatever, you've beaten them.'

35 He thought of the telescreen with its never-sleeping ear. They could spy upon you night and day, but if you kept your head you could still outwit them. With all their cleverness they had never mastered the secret of finding out what another human being was thinking. Perhaps that was less true when you were actually in their hands. One did not know what happened inside the Ministry of Love, but it was possible to
40 guess: tortures, drugs, delicate instruments that registered your nervous reactions, gradual wearing-down by sleeplessness and solitude and persistent questioning. Facts, at any rate, could not be kept hidden. They could be tracked down by enquiry,

1 **occur to sb.** come into sb.'s mind
9 **keep clear of sb.** stay away from sb.
12 **downhearted** sad
16 **utterly** completely
18 **confess (to sth.)** *(etwas) gestehen*
22 **betray sb.** give information about sb. to an enemy
25 **torture sb.** ['tɔːtʃə] hurt sb. to make them give you information
36 **outwit sb.** beat sb. by being cleverer than them
39 **Ministry of Love** in the novel, government ministry that uses fear to enforce loyalty to Big Brother
41 **gradual** slow
wear sb. down make sb. weaker
solitude state of being alone

43 **object** (here) aim; goal
46 **lay sth. bare** show sth. that
was a secret
utmost most extreme
48 **impregnable** impossible
to beat or change

they could be squeezed out of you by torture. But if the object was not to stay alive but to stay human, what difference did it ultimately make? They could not alter your feelings: for that matter you could not alter them yourself, even if you wanted to. They could lay bare in the utmost detail everything that you had done or said or thought; but the inner heart, whose workings were mysterious even to yourself, remained impregnable.

45

From: *Nineteen Eighty-Four*, 1949

COMPREHENSION ◀

1 Understanding the story
  a Describe the kind of society that Winston and Julia live in.
  b Point out what the two lovers are most worried about.

LANGUAGE AWARENESS ◀

2 Everyday English
Rewrite the following quotes from the text in everyday English.
1 'Yes, dear, it has occurred to me, several times.' (l. 5)
2 'We shall be utterly without power of any kind.' (l. 21)
3 'They could lay bare in the utmost detail everything that you had done or said or thought' (ll. 45–46)

ANALYSIS ◀

▶ SF 19: Analysing narrative prose

3 Interpreting key aspects
  a Interpret Winston's statement 'If you can FEEL that staying human is worth while [...] you've beaten them' (ll. 33–34).
  b Analyse the atmosphere of the extract by looking at the content of the dialogue and Winston's thoughts on the one hand, and the fact that this is a dialogue between lovers on the other hand.
    SUPPORT ▶ p. 205

BEYOND THE TEXT ◀

4 Room for hope?
  a 'With all their cleverness they had never mastered the secret of finding out what another human being was thinking' (ll. 36–38). Discuss whether this is true in the 21st century.
  b CHALLENGE ▶ Think of three steps that people your age can take to avoid a situation like the one in the text becoming reality in the future.

5 Other dystopian worlds
Look at the following quote said by Peeta in *The Hunger Games* (cf. pp. 58–61), then read lines 35–48 in the extract from *Nineteen Eighty Four*. Discuss similarities and differences between the worlds presented in *Nineteen Eighty Four* and *The Hunger Games*.

PEETA	I just keep wishing I could think of a way to show them that they don't own me. If I'm gonna die, I wanna still be me.
KATNISS	I just can't afford to think like that.

6 Big Brother in popular culture
Big Brother is the name of the fictional tyrannical ruler of Oceania. It is also the name of a famous reality TV show. Discuss why the TV producers might have chosen this name. Do you find the name appropriate? Justify your opinion.

A vision of the future

In this Chapter Task you will consider the texts you have read and tasks you have completed to write your own utopian or dystopian narrative.

1 Preparing your project

  a Choose whether you would like to work alone, with a partner or in a small group.

  b Decide which divisive issue in our society you are going to focus on. It can be an issue dealt with in the chapter, or something else you feel strongly about.

  c Create a mindmap with your chosen issue at the centre. Consider various aspects of the issue, e.g. areas of life that it affects, the opinions different groups of people might have about it, symbols that could be used to represent it, etc.

2 Considering genre and media

  a Decide whether your text will be a utopia or a dystopia or a mixture of both. Make notes on which genre would work best for your chosen issue and why.

  b Decide on the form of your text. It could be:

    ▪ an imaginary journey (p. 53)

    ▪ an *interior monologue (pp. 56–57)

    ▪ a description of a scene from a film (pp. 59–60) – including the presentation of different characters, film techniques and perhaps even a script

    ▪ an extract from a novel (pp. 62–63, 66–67)

  c Depending on which form you choose for your text, go back to the relevant pages in the chapter and look at the material again. Read/view it for analysis. Consider which aspects you could include in your text and what you would like to do differently.

▶ SF 37: Doing a creative writing task

3 Writing your text

  a Write an outline of your text. The following table might help you:

Issue	Setting	Characters	Plot

▶ SF 8: Structuring ideas

▶ SF 38: Writing a well-structured text

  b Write a rough draft. Ask a classmate to proofread your draft and give you feedback.

  c Make a neat copy of your text.

4 GALLERY WALK Presenting and evaluating a text

Present your finished text to the rest of the class, e.g. in a gallery walk, and evaluate your classmates' products. Take notes on your classmates' work, taking into account their content, which aspects you particularly liked and which aspects you think could be improved. Your teacher will give you an assessment sheet.

4 The Power of Words – from Shakespeare to Today

> Lackluster tennis tournament keeps fans away

> The suspect led the police on a wild goose chase

> Cruise ship returns to port a sorry sight

> Priest and pop star make strange bedfellows

> Referees urge fair play at World Cup

> 5 ways for shy people to break the ice

Download a list of chapter vocab here: 👆 **Webcode** context-10

Find an online dictionary here: 👆 **Webcode** context-52

▶ LP 1: Simple and progressive verb forms

1 Examining powerful language

a Work with a partner. Translate the headlines which each contain a phrase that was first used or coined by Shakespeare. Use a dictionary if necessary.

b Choose two of the phrases that you find particularly effective. Take turns explaining to each other what is so powerful about them that they are still being used in modern English.

2 Writing a *news story

Choose one of the headlines and write a short text about what you imagine is the story behind the headline. Write about 60 words.

3 Who was William Shakespeare?

Brainstorm in class what you know about Shakespeare and the time he lived in. Speculate why phrases that he coined became well-known.

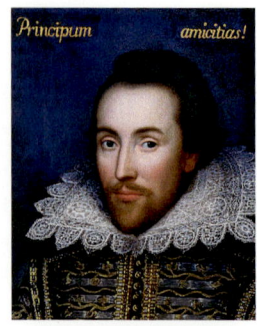

William Shakespeare, 'Cobbe Portrait'

▶ Fact File, p. 76

she wished she had shaped lips that kissed like Kim Kardashian

bigger boobs and Big Brother

de tongue fires a riddim dat shoots like shots

they become so dark and dense that I think they are bullets

Are words no more than waving, wavering flags?

surprised to hear a sudden silence explode in our ears

4 Thinking about poetic word power

a Read the lines above, which are taken from poems that you will find in this chapter. With a partner decide on the two that appeal to you most.

b With your partner, decide what it is about the phrases that suggest they come from a poem.

c Share your ideas with other couples who have chosen different phrases. Compare the different ways in which poetic words appealed to you.

CD1 09

*Listen to an audio version of the text
on the CD or download it here:*

Webcode context-11

▶ SF 1: Dealing with
    unknown words

The power of the spoken word

The importance of the spoken word in Shakespeare's time

In Shakespeare's time people went to the theatre to 'hear' a play. The stage
was equipped with only the most necessary props. The actors used
body language and gestures, but the visual aspect was not so important for the
overall dramatic impression. The most important element was the language,   5
the words spoken by the actors. Sometimes we even speak of word-scenery,
as the characters often describe the scenery for the audience.

Shakespeare included many scenes in his plays in which a character uses words to persuade other characters to do things
they might not want to originally do. Quite a few plays   10
rely on quick verbal exchange, in which characters reply to
each other in witty comments. Sometimes the word-fights are
playful, sometimes they contain an element of challenge and
sometimes they are cynical or evil. All of them demonstrate
Shakespeare's mastery of language, as well as his enjoyment   15
at creating these scenes.

Shakespeare's themes and language in our time

Since Shakespeare's time, the English language has developed considerably, while the themes of his plays have
remained relevant up to this day. That is why there is such a   20
wealth of adaptations of the plays both in writing and in films. Sometimes, it is
just the main theme that has been adapted, as in the musical *West Side Story*
(1957), which is based on Shakespeare's play *Romeo and Juliet*. Here, the
language has been changed to fit the setting of New York in the 1950s.

Occasionally there are filmed versions of his plays that keep Shakespeare's   25
language but are set in a different location. *William Shakespeare's Romeo and
Juliet* (1996), for example, is set in a fictitious modern American city called
'Verona Beach', complete with skyscrapers, large cars, and armed gangs –
and yet the characters speak in Shakespeare's iambic pentameters. The film
Richard III (1995) is set in a 1930s dictatorship. The popularity of these films   30
shows that Shakespeare's language is still understandable when accompanied
by images that we can relate to.

Poetry as drama

To this day, Shakespeare is not only remembered for his plays, but also for his
poetry. His cycle of 154 sonnets deals in different ways with love, the passing   35
of time, and death. While drama is no longer written in verse, poetry itself has
remained popular. Poets of every age have found new ways of exploring the
power of words to express feelings, attitudes and experiences in different types
of verse. Sometimes they return to writing traditional formats such as sonnets,
sometimes they write free verse that has no clear patterns either of rhyme or   40
rhythm. One tendency in the 21st century is to perform poetry to an audience,
thus lifting it off the page and making interaction between the poet and his or
her listeners possible. Performance poetry can be said to create a link between
Shakespeare's drama in verse and poetry of the 21st century.

▶ SF 3: Using a dictionary

1 Performance words

List words from the text that you could use when talking about

a what you can see

b what you can hear

during the performance in a theatre. Add short definitions to each word.

▶ LP 19: Collocations

2 Collocations

a Collocations are words that often 'go together'. Find as many collocations as possible in the boxes below. In some cases you may have to add an article, a pronoun or a preposition.

find	elements
contain	scenery
write	mastery
describe	verse
express	ways
perform	poetry
create	link
demonstrate	feelings

b Use at least four collocations to write a short text about a poem, play or song that you like.

3 Phrasal verbs

A phrasal verb consists of a verb and an adverb or preposition. Fill the gaps with the correct phrasal verbs. Look at the text again for help.

1 While Shakespeare's theatres had little scenery, today's theatres are … up-to-date video and sound projectors.

2 Many of Shakespeare's plays have been … the big screen.

3 Shakespeare is best … his plays and sonnets.

4 The novel, which … a romance between an Englishman and a Lithuanian immigrant, is … a seaside town in England.

5 The reason why Shakespeare is still popular today is because people can still … his ideas and characters.

6 The play, which is … an old legend, has been updated to a modern setting.

4 Word families

a Find the corresponding nouns to these verbs and adjectives. Look at the text for help or use a dictionary.

▶ SF 3: Using a dictionary
▶ LP 20: Word formation

Find an online dictionary here:

 Webcode context-52

1 be set in	4 adapt sth.	7 interact with sb./sth.
2 express sth.	5 popular	8 persuade sb. to do sth.
3 perform sth.	6 relevant	9 equip sb./sth. with sth.

b Write a sentence with each of the nouns.

5 Writing

Write an email to a friend telling him or her why you are (not) looking forward to seeing a Shakespeare play with your class. Include as many words and phrases from the text as possible.

Shakespeare's power of language

William Shakespeare
Ordinary people did not leave behind much documentation in the 16th century, which is why we have few documents
5 that mention Shakespeare. There is a lot of speculation about most of Shakespeare's life. We do know that he was born in Stratford-upon-Avon in 1564 and that he married Anne Hathaway in 1582, with
10 whom he had three children. In 1592 he was working as actor and playwright in London with a company of actors. He also published popular books of poetry. In 1599 he and other members of his company opened
15 The Globe, one of the largest and best theatres in London at that time. He wrote about 38 plays,

William Shakespeare, 'Chandos Portrait'

154 sonnets and two long poems, which together is often regarded as one of the greatest collections of literature created by one man. He moved back to Stratford 20 shortly before his death in 1616.

In Parts A and B there are excerpts from three of Shakespeare's plays. In groups of three, each choose one of the following: Macbeth, Richard III or The Taming of the Shrew. Search the internet for information about your play. Give a *synopsis about it to the others who then formulate two questions about the play. Answer your classmates' questions. Then swap roles.

A1 Lady Macbeth persuades her husband

In Shakespeare's play Macbeth, Macbeth has told his wife about prophecies he heard promising him he will become king of Scotland. When the present king, Duncan, honours them with a visit, they plan to murder him so that Macbeth can become his successor. In a *soliloquy immediately before the passage printed below, Macbeth conscience has warned him not to go ahead with the plan. His wife interrupts his thoughts at this point.

LADY MACBETH	He has almost supped: why have you left the chamber?
MACBETH	Hath he asked for me?
LADY MACBETH	Know you not he has?
MACBETH	We will proceed no further in this business:
	He hath honoured me of late; and I have bought 5
	Golden opinions from all sorts of people,
	Which would be worn now in their newest gloss,
	Not cast aside so soon.
LADY MACBETH	Was the hope drunk
	Wherein you dressed yourself? Hath it slept since? 10
	And wakes it now, to look so green and pale
	At what it did so freely? From this time
	Such I account thy love. Art thou afeard
	To be the same in thine own act and valour
	As thou art in desire? Wouldst thou have that 15
	Which thou esteem'st the ornament of life,
	And live a coward in thine own esteem,
	Letting 'I dare not' wait upon 'I would',
	Like the poor cat i' the adage?
MACBETH	Prithee, peace: 20
	I dare do all that may become a man;
	Who dares do more is none.

1 **supped** finished supper
5 **honoured me of late** showed me respect lately
7 **would be worn** should be enjoyed
8 **cast aside** thrown away
13 **Such I account thy love** I consider your love to be like that
14 **to be the same … as thou art in desire** to be as brave in what you do as in what you are wishing for
16 **esteem'st** *(v)* consider
17 **esteem** *(n)* great respect, admiration
18 **dare** be brave enough to do sth. **wait upon** be a servant to
19 **adage** ['ædɪdʒ] proverb, saying; (here) 'A cat likes to eat fish, but doesn't like to get its feet wet.'
20 **Prithee, peace** please be quiet

LADY MACBETH   What beast was't, then,
                That made you break this enterprise to me?
                When you durst do it, then you were a man;   25
                And, to be more than what you were, you would
                Be so much more the man. Nor time nor place
                Did then adhere, and yet you would make both:
                They have made themselves, and that their fitness now
                Does unmake you. I have given suck, and know   30
                How tender 'tis to love the babe that milks me:
                I would, while it was smiling in my face,
                Have plucked my nipple from his boneless gums,
                And dashed the brains out, had I so sworn as you
                Have done to this.   35
MACBETH   If we should fail?
LADY MACBETH   We fail!
                But screw your courage to the sticking-place,
                And we'll not fail. When Duncan is asleep -
                Whereto the rather shall his day's hard journey   40
                Soundly invite him – his two chamberlains
                Will I with wine and wassail so convince
                That memory, the warder of the brain,
                Shall be a fume, and the receipt of reason
                A limbeck only: when in swinish sleep   45
                Their drenched natures lie as in a death,
                What cannot you and I perform upon
                The unguarded Duncan? What not put upon
                His spongy officers, who shall bear the guilt
                Of our great quell?   50
MACBETH   Bring forth men-children only;
                For thy undaunted mettle should compose
                Nothing but males.

From: Macbeth, Act 1, Scene 7

25	**durst** *(past tense)* dared
27	**Nor time … adhere** neither the time nor the place were right then
28	**make both** force both to be right
29	**have made themselves** have offered themselves **fitness** suitability, being right for sth.
30	**give suck** breastfeed a baby
33	**plucked** pulled away **boneless gums** toothless mouth
38	**screw your courage to the sticking-place** get your courage up (image taken from the tuning of a violin: the player tightens each string until it produces the right note and then fixes it)
40	**Whereto … invite him** to which his long travels will lead him soon
41	**chamberlain** ['tʃeɪmbəlɪn] *Kammerdiener*
42	**wassail** ['wɒseɪl] ale, spiced beer
43	**warder** guard
44	**fume** alcoholic steam **receipt of reason** [rɪ'siːt] brain
45	**limbeck** *Destillierkolben*
46	**drenched** drunk
49	**spongy** ['spʌndʒɪ] like a sponge, soaked with liquid, (here) drunk **bear** take, stand
50	**quell** *(n)* killing, murder
52	**undaunted mettle** fearless character

◄ COMPREHENSION ◄

1 Understanding the conflict

  a An argument is taking place between Macbeth and Lady Macbeth. Collect keywords that underline the position of each character.

  b Write a short summary of each of the speeches in modern English.

  c State what Lady Macbeth is trying to persuade her husband to do.

◄ LANGUAGE AWARENESS ◄

2 Analysing ways of addressing

  a Study how Macbeth and Lady Macbeth address each other. Read the Fact File on the right and explain what their ways of addressing mean.

  b In one part of the dialogue, Lady Macbeth changes the form of address. Identify the change and discuss what may have caused it.

3 Rewriting Shakespeare's questions

Look at how Shakespeare formed questions. Instead of the modern use of the modal verb *do* he used a different form of question. Identify those questions and rewrite them in modern English.

■ FACT FILE

In **16th-century English** there were two forms of *you*: *thou* (object form: *thee*; possessive form: *thy*, *thine* = your), which was used similarly to German *du*.

The other form was *ye* or *you*. This was used as a term of respect or as the plural form (like the old German use of *Ihr*).

Verbs following *thou* ended in *-st*, e.g. *didst*, *camest*, *hast*. The second-person singular form of *be* was *art*: thou art = you are.

In Shakespeare's time, the third-person singular verb often ended in *-th*, e.g. *doth* (does), *hath* (has), *seemeth* (seems).

Part A

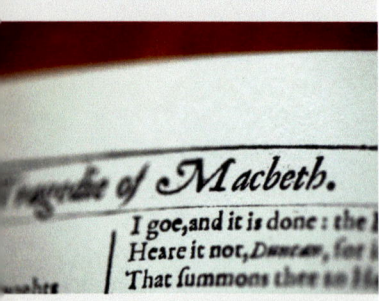

READING FOCUS ON SKILLS
Reading for analysis (drama extract)

Look at A1 again. Now you are going to analyse how the writer has made the content interesting by using the sound of the words, stylistic devices, metaphorical language and forms of characterization.

1 Reading aloud: The rhythm of the text
  a Read the text aloud to get a feeling for its *metre.
  b Read the Fact File on the left. Then count the syllables and the metric feet in ll. 1–22 of the extract from *Macbeth*.
  c Work with a partner. Read parts of the dialogue out loud again. Pay attention to the speakers completing the blank verse for each other.

▶ SF 17: Analysing stylistic devices
▶ SF 20: Analysing drama

2 Understanding *stylistic devices
  a Read Lady Macbeth's speeches and identify which form of punctuation appears a lot. Name the stylistic device and explain its purpose here.
  b Note down words that are repeated in the text and in which lines they occur. Describe the effect of their repetition.
  c Write a statement explaining what both stylistic devices tell you about the argumentation of both Macbeth and Lady Macbeth.

3 Analysing *images
When reading, you should always try to visualize what the words are telling you and which mental images are created.
  a Read ll. 4–6 again. Macbeth speaks about 'buying golden opinions' that he wants to 'wear in their newest gloss': Apparently he sees 'opinions' as new clothes. Explain what that tells you about his character.
  b Lady Macbeth responds by using imagery herself. Read ll. 9–12 and explain how she takes up her husband's image and expands it.
  c In l. 23 Lady Macbeth mentions a 'beast'. Explain what she is referring to.

4 Understanding *characterization
  a Lady Macbeth's passage from ll. 30–35 gives us a good idea of the kind of woman she is. Read the passage out loud. Explain the image she uses and what it tells you about her character.
  b Read the extract either aloud or in silence slowly and purposefully. Compare lengths, content and messages of the speakers' passages. Draw conclusions about the characters.
  c FREEZE-FRAME Work with a partner. Imagine how the actor and actress would perform the dialogue and create a freeze-frame. Get together with another pair. Present your freeze-frame and let them guess which moment you have chosen.
  d Write an analysis about the couple Macbeth and Lady Macbeth on the basis of the complete passage. Write at least 150 words.

> **■ FACT FILE**
>
> **Blank verse**
> The type of verse used most often by Shakespeare is called blank verse. It consists of iambic pentameters, which are five iambs. An iamb is an unstressed syllable followed by a stressed syllable, which sounds like 'dah DUM'. Blank verse is considered particularly close to normal English speech rhythm, which was probably what made it so popular in Shakespeare's time.
>
> *Note:*
> Shakespeare's rhythm is varied, lively and never monotonous, because his characters are saying important things. That is why not all lines in the excerpt can be spoken in the 'dah DUM' rhythm.

▶ SF 35: Writing a character profile

A2 Richard courts his enemy

In Richard III Richard, Duke of Gloucester, has killed his enemies King Henry VI and his son Edward Plantagenet. He wants to become king himself, and decides to marry Edward's widow Anne to strengthen his position. In this scene Richard approaches Anne as she accompanies the body of her father-in-law, Henry VI, to his burial place. Read the extract to see how Richard tries to persuade Lady Anne that he is courting her out of love. Try to visualize the scene, imagining how the two characters interact with each other.

■ **TROUBLE SPOT**

court (n) = Gericht, Hof
court (v) = umwerben, den Hof
machen

LADY ANNE	Didst thou not kill this king?	
GLOUCESTER	I grant ye.	
LADY ANNE	Dost grant me, hedgehog? then, God grant me too	
	Thou mayst be damned for that wicked deed!	
	O, he was gentle, mild, and virtuous!	5
GLOUCESTER	The fitter for the King of heaven, that hath him.	
LADY ANNE	He is in heaven, where thou shalt never come.	
GLOUCESTER	Let him thank me, that holp to send him thither;	
	For he was fitter for that place than earth.	
LADY ANNE	And thou unfit for any place but hell.	10
GLOUCESTER	Yes, one place else, if you will hear me name it.	
LADY ANNE	Some dungeon.	
GLOUCESTER	Your bed-chamber.	
LADY ANNE	Ill rest betide the chamber where thou liest!	
GLOUCESTER	So will it, madam till I lie with you.	15
LADY ANNE	I hope so.	
GLOUCESTER	I know so. But, gentle Lady Anne,	
	To leave this keen encounter of our wits,	
	And fall somewhat into a slower method,	
	Is not the causer of the timeless deaths	20
	Of these Plantagenets, Henry and Edward,	
	As blameful as the executioner?	
LADY ANNE	Thou art the cause, and most accursed effect.	
GLOUCESTER	Your beauty was the cause of that effect;	
	Your beauty: which did haunt me in my sleep	25
	To undertake the death of all the world,	
	So I might live one hour in your sweet bosom.	
LADY ANNE	If I thought that, I tell thee, homicide,	
	These nails should rend that beauty from my cheeks.	
GLOUCESTER	These eyes could never endure sweet beauty's wreck;	30
	You should not blemish it, if I stood by:	
	As all the world is cheered by the sun,	
	So I by that; it is my day, my life.	
LADY ANNE	Black night o'ershade thy day, and death thy life.	
GLOUCESTER	Curse not thyself, fair creature; thou art both.	35
LADY ANNE	I would I were, to be revenged on thee.	
GLOUCESTER	It is a quarrel most unnatural,	
	To be revenged on him that loveth you.	
LADY ANNE	It is a quarrel just and reasonable,	
	To be revenged on him that slew my husband.	40

King Richard III

2	**grant** admit, allow
6	**the fitter** the better
8	**holp** *(past tense)* helped
	thither there
12	**dungeon** ['dʌndʒən] dark underground prison
14	**Ill rest betide the chamber** may there be no peace and quiet to be had in the room
18	**keen encounter of our wits** our fierce argument
20	**timeless** too early
23	**accursed** damned
25	**haunt** follow, chase, stalk
29	**rend** rip, pull
30	**endure** tolerate
31	**blemish** ['blemɪʃ] ruin
40	**slew** *(past tense)* killed

GLOUCESTER	He that bereft thee, lady, of thy husband,	
	Did it to help thee to a better husband.	
LADY ANNE	His better doth not breathe upon the earth.	
GLOUCESTER	He lives that loves thee better than he could.	
LADY ANNE	Name him.	45
GLOUCESTER	Plantagenet.	
LADY ANNE	Why, that was he.	
GLOUCESTER	The selfsame name, but one of better nature.	
LADY ANNE	Where is he?	
GLOUCESTER	Here.	50

She spitteth at him.

	Why dost thou spit at me?	
LADY ANNE	Would it were mortal poison, for thy sake!	
GLOUCESTER	Never came poison from so sweet a place.	
LADY ANNE	Never hung poison on a fouler toad.	55
	Out of my sight! thou dost infect my eyes.	
GLOUCESTER	Thine eyes, sweet lady, have infected mine.	
LADY ANNE	Would they were basilisks', to strike thee dead!	
GLOUCESTER	I would they were, that I might die at once;	
	For now they kill me with a living death.	60
	Those eyes of thine from mine have drawn salt tears,	
	Shamed their aspect with store of childish drops: [...]	
	I never sued to friend nor enemy;	
	My tongue could never learn sweet smoothing word;	
	But now thy beauty is proposed my fee,	65
	My proud heart sues, and prompts my tongue to speak.	
	Teach not thy lips such scorn, for they were made	
	For kissing, lady, not for such contempt.	
	If thy revengeful heart cannot forgive,	
	Lo, here I lend thee this sharp-pointed sword;	70
	Which if thou please to hide in this true bosom.	

And let the soul forth that adoreth thee,
I lay it naked to the deadly stroke,
And humbly beg the death upon my knee.
Nay, do not pause; for I did kill King Henry, 75
But 'twas thy beauty that provoked me.
Nay, now dispatch; 'twas I that stabb'd young Edward,
But 'twas thy heavenly face that set me on.

Here she lets fall the sword. 80

Take up the sword again, or take up me.

From: *Richard III*, Act 1, Scene 2

The scene ends with Anne allowing Richard to place his ring on her finger and agreeing to meet him after the burial of Henry VI.

The opening of Richard III *in the First Folio of Shakespeare, 1623*

COMPREHENSION ◀

1 Understanding the content

a Outline the gist of the fight between Lady Anne and Gloucester.

b Describe Lady Anne's feelings for her dead husband and for Gloucester.

ANALYSIS ◀

2 A word fight

a Look closely at how one speaker takes up a particular word or concept from the other and changes it according to their own purposes. Make notes.

b Discuss your findings with a partner or in class.

3 Working with imagery

Work with a partner. Identify the *images each speaker uses. Explain them with the help of the annotations and from the context they are used in.

SUPPORT ▶ p. 206

4 Persuasive words and actions

a Note down words and phrases that Gloucester uses to change Lady Anne's feelings towards him.

b Examine if her reactions show the desired effect.

c Explain the effect of Gloucester offering Lady Anne his sword to kill him on the spot.

5 Understanding character

On the basis of your analysis, describe the speakers' characters.

SUPPORT ▶ p. 206

▶ SF35: Writing a character profile

LANGUAGE AWARENESS ◀

6 Forms of address

Look at the Fact File on p. 77 again. Analyse the use of *thou* and *you* forms as an indicator of the relationship of the speakers. Interpret their forms of addressing each other.

BEYOND THE TEXT ◀

7 Performing the scene

a Discuss how the characters could be presented on stage.

b In small groups, practise reading the dialogue out loud with appropriate *emphasis and gestures. Then perform your reading in front of the class.

Shakespeare's words updated

B1 My future wife

The following extract is taken from William Shakespeare's The Taming of the Shrew. *Petruchio has gone to Padua to find a wealthy wife. On hearing of the shrewish elder daughter of the wealthy Baptista Minola, who so far has driven any potential husband away with her sharp tongue, he decides that she is just the right woman for him. The following extract is from their very first meeting.*

shrew *widerspenstige, zänkische Frau*

PETRUCHIO	Good morrow, Kate; for that's your name, I hear.	
KATHARINA	Well have you heard, but something hard of hearing:	
	They call me Katharina that do talk of me.	
PETRUCHIO	You lie, in faith; for you are called plain Kate,	
	And bonny Kate and sometimes Kate the curst;	5
	But Kate, the prettiest Kate in Christendom	
	Kate of Kate Hall, my super-dainty Kate,	
	For dainties are all Kates, and therefore, Kate,	
	Take this of me, Kate of my consolation;	
	Hearing thy mildness praised in every town,	10
	Thy virtues spoke of, and thy beauty sounded,	
	Yet not so deeply as to thee belongs,	
	Myself am moved to woo thee for my wife.	
KATHARINA	Moved! In good time: let him that moved you hither	
	Remove you hence: I knew you at the first	15
	You were a moveable.	
PETRUCHIO	Why, what's a moveable?	
KATHARINA	A joined-stool.	
PETRUCHIO	Thou hast hit it: come, sit on me.	
KATHARINA	Asses are made to bear, and so are you.	20
PETRUCHIO	Women are made to bear, and so are you.	
KATHARINA	No such jade as you, if me you mean.	
PETRUCHIO	Alas! good Kate, I will not burden thee;	
	For, knowing thee to be but young and light –	
KATHARINA	Too light for such a swain as you to catch;	25
	And yet as heavy as my weight should be. […]	

She strikes him.

PETRUCHIO	I swear I'll cuff you, if you strike again.	
KATHARINA	So may you lose your arms:	
	If you strike me, you are no gentleman;	30
	And if no gentleman, why then no arms. […]	
PETRUCHIO	[…] 'Twas told me you were rough and coy and sullen,	
	And now I find report a very liar;	
	For thou are pleasant, gamesome, passing courteous,	
	But slow in speech, yet sweet as spring-time flowers:	35
	Thou canst not frown, thou canst not look askance,	
	Nor bite the lip, as angry wenches will,	
	Nor hast thou pleasure to be cross in talk,	
	But thou with mildness entertain'st thy wooers,	
	With gentle conference, soft and affable. […]	40

2 **something hard of hearing** you must be slightly deaf
5 **bonny** beautiful
curst *(participle)* cursed
7 **dainty** sweet
8 **dainties are all Kates** a pun on 'cate', an Elizabethan sweet
9 **consolation** *Trost*
11 **sounded** proclaimed, reported
13 **woo sb.** *jdn. umwerben*
14 **hither** to this place, here
15 **hence** away from here
18 **joined-stool** piece of furniture
20 **ass** donkey
bear *Lasten tragen; gebären*
22 **jade** worthless person
23 **Alas!** [ə'læs] expression of sadness, *Ach!*
25 **swain** lover, wooer (cf. l. 13)
28 **cuff sb.** hit sb.
29 **arms** *Wappen*
32 **coy** shy
sullen unfriendly
34 **gamesome** ['ɡeɪmsəm] playful
passing very, exceedingly
courteous ['kɜːtiəs] polite
36 **frown** [fraʊn] look displeased
askance [ə'skæns] *verächtlich*
37 **wench** girl
40 **conference** conversation
affable ['æfəble] likeable

Thus in plain terms: your father hath consented
That you shall be my wife; your dowry 'greed on;
And, will you, nill you, I will marry you.
Now, Kate, I am a husband for your turn;
For, by this light, whereby I see thy beauty,   45
Thy beauty, that doth make me like thee well,
Thou must be married to no man but me;
For I am he am born to tame you Kate,
And bring you from a wild Kate to a Kate
Conformable as other household Kates.   50
Here comes your father: never make denial;
I must and will have Katharina to my wife.

From: *The Taming of the Shrew*, Act 2, Scene 1

42 **dowry** ['daʊri] *Mitgift*
  'greed agreed
43 **will you, nill you** if you want or not
44 **for your turn** just right for you
50 **conformable** [kən'fɔːməbl] *angepasst, fügsam*
  household Kates wives by the name of Kate
51 **make denial** [dɪ'naɪəl] refuse

COMPREHENSION

1 **YOU CHOOSE** **Understanding the dialogue**

a Create a cartoon or a comic strip summarizing the scene. Draw 1–2 frames with speech bubbles and captions.

OR

b Write a short modern English version of the dialogue. Practise reading it with a partner, and then present it to the class.

▶ SF 37: Doing a creative writing task

ANALYSIS

2 Comparing dialogues

Compare the way Petruchio woos Katharina to the way Gloucester woos Anne (**A2**, pp. 79–81). Evaluate what each man reveals about himself and how effectively they each use words to achieve their aims.   **SUPPORT** ▶ p. 206

LANGUAGE AWARENESS

3 Playing with words

a Look at ll. 7–31 again. Describe the changes in meaning, grammar or form that occur to certain words.

b Translate those words into German. Explain why in some cases the word-play does not work and why in others it works the same as in English.

c Think of three more words that have at least two meanings (= homonyms). Write six appropriate sentences.

BEYOND THE TEXT

4 Modernizing the play

a Imagine the scene is going to be adapted for a modern film version. With a partner, discuss a suitable setting and which actors should take the leading roles. Consider in particular which elements from the original scene should be kept and which removed. Share your ideas in class.

b **CHALLENGE** Create a storyboard for the scene you are planning.

▶ SF 37: Doing a creative writing task

▶ DVD

quid *(BE sl)* British pound
clap eyes on sb. see sb. for the first time
trout *(infml)* unpleasant woman
chord *Akkord*
take the mick (out of sb.) *(BE infml)* make fun of sb.
certifiable lunatic [ˌsɜːtɪˈfaɪəbl ˈluːnətɪk] crazy person
bugger sth. up *(sl)* ruin sth.
put your cards on the table say what you really want
alluring *(adj)* attractive
arousing *(adj)* sexy
snarl make an angry noise when talking
lewd [luːd] sexually vulgar
obnoxious very annoying
plucky having courage and spirit

▶ SF 23: Analysing a film

'Modernizing Shakespeare'

VIEWING FOCUS ON SKILLS
Evaluating a modern Shakespeare adaptation

Kate in a Lift
The film sequence you are about to watch is from a BBC series in which Shakespeare plays were modernized. It represents the same scene from The Taming of the Shrew *that you have studied in* **B1***.*

1 Before viewing
Before watching the film excerpt, speculate which aspects might have been modernized. Look at your notes from **B1**, task **3** again.

2 Viewing without sound
You will watch the film extract without sound. Split the class in two groups, with one half doing task **a** and the other doing task **b**.
a Concentrate on the places shown in the scene. While viewing, make notes on them and the atmosphere they create. Explain why the director may have chosen them.
b Examine the body language and facial expressions of the two main characters. While viewing, make notes about what they tell you about their characters.
c Share your findings first with a partner, then report them to the class.

3 Viewing with sound
a Watch the film with sound. With your partner from task **2**, discuss if you get new information from the dialogue. List elements of the dialogue that surprised you.
b View the extract again and concentrate on the music. Describe how it is used, and to what effect.

4 Viewing for the final time
Before viewing the extract for the final time, look at ▶ SF 23 Analysing a film on p. 276. Then, in groups of four, examine the camera work. Two of you concentrate on the part in front of the flat, the other two on the part in the lift. Explain how the camera work affects you as a viewer. Share your findings in your group, then in class.

5 Evaluation
Evaluate how successful the director has been in adapting the material. Name the elements that were changed and the effect the scene has on you.
SUPPORT ▶ p. 207

B2 Responding to a sonnet

APPOINTMENT TASK
- Make an appointment card with the names of three partners.
- With your partners, discuss the statements on the right and make notes on your appointment card.
- Discuss your conclusions in class.

Now read the sonnets. Concentrate on the different images the words create in your mind.

1 *Love for someone does not change, even if the person you love changes.*
2 *Love can be between anyone, no matter what age, gender, race or religion.*
3 *Love is not a physical but a spiritual experience.*

Sonnet 116   *William Shakespeare*

Let me not to the marriage of true minds
Admit impediments. Love is not love
Which alters when it alteration finds,
Or bends with the remover to remove:
O no! It is an ever-fixèd mark   5
That looks on tempests and is never shaken;
It is the star to every wandering bark,
Whose worth's unknown, although his height be taken.
Love's not Time's fool, though rosy lips and cheeks
Within his bending sickle's compass come: 10
Love alters not with his brief hours and weeks,
But bears it out even to the edge of doom.
If this be error and upon me proved,
I never writ, nor no man ever loved.

1 **Let me not** May I never
2 **admit** accept
  impediment [ɪmˈpedɪmənt] *Hindernis*
3 **alter** [ˈɔːltə] change
4 **remover** person who goes away
5 **mark** landmark or star that helps a sailor to navigate
6 **tempest** storm
7 **wander** [ˈwɒndə] travel
  bark ship
10 **bending** curved
  sickle *Sichel*
  compass [ˈkʌmpəs] *Reichweite*
12 **bear sth. out** endure sth.
  edge of doom end of time
13 **upon** against
14 **writ** (have) written

In 1971, Northern Irish poet James Simmons (1933–2001) wrote a series of 'Marital Sonnets'. No. 4 reads like a modern response to Shakespeare's Sonnet 116.

Marital Sonnet 4   *James Simmons*

We murmured passionate language in that trance
when each was famished for the mutual kiss;
but we have altered, and it spoils all chance
of happiness, comparing that with this.
Displays of fireworks were put on by lust,   5
romantic symphonies, unholy wars:
now contraceptives, unworn, gather dust,
in which we once soared gleaming towards the stars.
In age's Leamington our joys last longer,
the libraries are good, the tea-rooms neat,   10
good arguments aren't broken off by anger,
new appetites are fed, we are replete.
Let's call this love, that alters when it finds
alteration, the marriage of two minds.

2 **famished** [ˈfæmɪʃd] very hungry
  mutual *gegenseitig*
7 **contraceptive** *Verhütungsmittel*
8 **soar** rise high
  gleam *(v)* shine
9 **Leamington** [ˈlemɪŋtən] a spa town in Warwickshire, England
12 **replete** [rɪˈpliːt] very full

From: *Poems 1956–1986*, 1986

▶ SF 21: Analysing poetry

Find a tool to make your poster here: 🖲 **Webcode** context-50

▶ SF 29: Writing a formal letter or email
▶ SF 34: Argumentative writing
▶ SF 37: Doing a creative writing task
▶ SF 38: Writing a well-structured text

COMPREHENSION ◀

1 Brief summaries

Summarize each poem's message in one sentence.

ANALYSIS ◀

2 GALLERY WALK Comparing the sonnets

Compare the two sonnets. Examine structure, development of the idea and style. Present your findings on posters and evaluate the posters in a gallery walk. SUPPORT ▶ p. 207

BEYOND THE TEXT ◀

3 Creative writing

Write a response to one of the sonnets. This can take the form of an email or a letter to a friend, a comment, or even a short poem. Refer to your notes from the pre-reading discussion.

📍 CULTURE SPOT

Shakespeare for the masses

WILL
POWER

1 Explain the wordplay on the T-shirt. Consider what wearing this T-shirt would mean to you.

2 What do objects like this tell you about Shakespeare's place in British culture?

3 Design a Shakespeare object. Choose a picture, pun, quote or slogan and present your idea to the class.

▶ SF 24: Giving a presentation

The powerful words of today's poets

C1 Performance poetry

Performance poetry

During the 1980s, the term 'performance poetry' came into popular usage to describe poetry written or
5 composed for performance before an audience rather than for print distribution. Before the invention of the printing press, all poetry was performed orally, and in many
10 cultures outside our Western traditions, oral poetry and storytelling are still more important than reading. In the West poetry has become a very individual form of
15 culture. With the rise of new media and technology, the interest in poetry on the page faded, but the spoken word remained important. Punk, reggae and hip hop all had an effect on how the spoken word 20 was perceived. Many contemporary poets took up these influences and started to 'perform' their poetry rather than just read it.

1 *State why you think oral poetry came into existence and what role it has played in society.*

2 *Do you prefer to listen to poetry or to read it? Give reasons for your answer.*

Benjamin Zephaniah

Dis poetry   *Benjamin Zephaniah*

Benjamin Zephaniah is well known in Britain for his oral renditions of his poems.

— COMPREHENSION ◀

1 First impressions
a Watch the performance. Make notes of your first impression and of what you hear. Exchange notes with a partner. ▶ LANGUAGE HELP
b Listen and watch again. Add to your notes.

2 A first attempt at understanding
Choose the sentences that correspond with how you understand the poem.
A The speaker is saying that his poetry is an essential part of his life.
B The speaker is saying that rhythm is all that matters.
C The speaker is saying that poetry needs to be written with love.
D The speaker is saying that poetry needs to be chanted.

3 Understanding the poem
Your teacher will give you the text. Read the poem.
a List the various descriptions of 'dis poetry' given in the poem.
b Sum up what his poetry means for the poet himself.

— ANALYSIS ◀

4 Looking at the language
Explain why the poet decided to spell some of the words as he did.

5 Looking at rhythm and rhyme
One of the keywords of the poem is 'riddim'. Analyse how the length of the lines and the *rhymes contribute to the *rhythm.

▶ ■ DVD

▶ SF 22: Listening

▶ SF 10: Working with closed test formats

■ LANGUAGE HELP
- He uses rhythmic gestures / body gestures / his hands to / while …
- He moves his hands along with the rhythm to …
- His vivid/lively facial expressions show/underline …
- He keeps his eyes closed/ open when/while …
- His slow/rapid speech / tone of voice is …

▶ SF 21: Analysing poetry

6 The meaning of the poem

With a partner, discuss the meaning of the last seven lines. Use your findings to write down your interpretation of the poem.

— BEYOND THE TEXT ◀

7 Reviewing a poetry performance

Watch the performance again. Pay special attention to the speaker's gestures. Then write a review for the English pages of your school magazine.
SUPPORT ▶ p. 207

► SF 32: Writing a review

Famous for what? *Hollie McNish*

Discuss what being famous means to you.
Then watch Hollie McNish perform her poem.

— COMPREHENSION ◀

1 Discussing your first reactions

Discuss your first impressions of the performance. Consider aspects like the poet herself, the manner of delivery, the type of poem, and the poem itself.

2 Understanding the poem

Describe the situation in the poem briefly and state what you think the message is.

3 Re-examining the message

Your teacher will give you the text. Read the poem and then look at your answer to task **2** again. If necessary, change your statement.

— ANALYSIS ◀

► SF 21: Analysing poetry

4 Analysing the style

Explain what makes this a poem. Examine the *rhythm, sound of words, *rhyme and *imagery.

— BEYOND THE TEXT ◀

 CD1 10
► SF 41: Mediation of written and oral texts

5 Mediation (German → English)

Imagine that an English friend sent you a link to Hollie McNish performing her poem. You want to show him or her that Germans do poetry performances too. You have come across the poetry performance that you can hear on the CD. Tell your friend what the subject of the poem is and how it is similar or different to the performance by Hollie McNish. Write about 150 words.

► SF 29: Writing a formal letter or email
► SF 37: Doing a creative writing task

6 YOU CHOOSE ▶ **Creative writing**

a Imagine you are a careers advisor at school. Write a letter to the girl addressed in Hollie McNish's poem.

 OR

b Imagine the person addressed in Hollie McNish's poem was a boy. What parts of the poem would have so be changed? Rewrite those lines using new phrases and ideas.

Hollie McNish

C2 The psychological power of words

All poets rely on the power of their words to make an impression on listeners and readers. On a different level, some poets write directly about the impact of words in our lives. The following two poems are examples – one by a British writer of Pakistani origin, the other by an American with a Chinese background.

- Before reading or listening, list situations in which the impact of words plays a decisive role.

The right word   *Imtiaz Dharker*

 CD1 11

Listen to Imtiaz Dharker reading her poem.

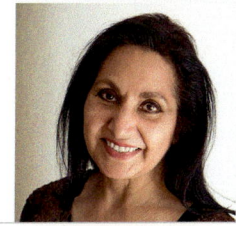

Imtiaz Dharker

——————————————————————— COMPREHENSION ◀

1 Giving an initial reaction
a Talk about your impression of the poem with a partner.
b Agree on one sentence that states the message of the poem.
c Now read the poem.

Outside the door,
lurking in the shadows,
is a terrorist.

Is that the wrong description?
Outside that door,   5
taking shelter in the shadows,
is a freedom fighter.

I haven't got this right.
Outside, waiting in the shadows,
is a hostile militant.   10

Are words no more
than waving, wavering flags?
Outside your door,
watchful in the shadows,
is a guerrilla warrior.   15

God help me.
Outside, defying every shadow,
stands a martyr.
I saw his face.

No words can help me now.   20
Just outside the door,
lost in shadows,
is a child who looks like mine.

One word for you.
Outside my door,   25
his hand too steady,
his eyes too hard
is a boy who looks like your son,
too.

I open the door.   30
Come in, I say.
Come in and eat with us.

The child steps in
and carefully, at my door,
takes off his shoes.   35

2 Understanding the general idea
a List the different descriptions of the people standing outside the speaker's door. **SUPPORT** ▶ p. 207
b Add *connotations that go with each description as well as the mental image it conveys. **SUPPORT** ▶ p. 207
c In one sentence, state the idea that the speaker is developing in the course of the poem.

——————————————————————— ANALYSIS ◀

3 Analysis and interpretation
Interpret the poem by analysing its structure and images. Evaluate whether the speaker gives an answer to her question about words being 'no more than waving, wavering flags' (ll. 11–12). Conclude your interpretation by considering whether she found 'the right word'.

2 **lurk** wait secretly, not wanting to be seen
12 **wave** *(v)* move a hand or a flag up and down, usually in greeting
waver *(v)* move in an unsteady or uncertain way
17 **defy sb./sth.** [dɪˈfaɪ] *jdm. / einer Sache trotzen, widerstehen*

▶ SF 17: Analysing stylistic devices
▶ SF 21: Analysing poetry

You should've stopped there *William Marr*

While reading, imagine the setting and context in which these lines are spoken. Try to 'see' what is going on here.

2 **uppercase** *(adj)* in capital letters
  bold *fett gedruckt*
4 **hiss** *zischen*
6 **scatter** move quickly into different directions
16 **shatter** fall to pieces suddenly
19 **crumble** fall to pieces slowly

first I see words coming out of your mouth
black words all UPPERCASE and bold
they become so dark and dense that I think they are bullets
wait a second they ARE bullets now all streaming hissing
smoking burning toward us — 5

we scatter and run for cover waiting for something
to happen but are surprised to hear a sudden silence
explode in our ears
I look up and find you just standing there
with your mouth wide open — 10
as if you are running out of ammunition
but from the expression on your twisted face
and out-stretched tongue there must still be
something inside that wants to come out

for a few seconds you remain in your frozen posture — 15
then right before our eyes your body shatters and breaks up
we slowly rise and gather around
trying to pick up the pieces but find they are so badly burned
that they crumble at a touch

you should've stopped there really — 20
before you opened your mouth

From: *In This 21st Century: New Poems from William Marr*

▶ SF 17: Analysing stylistic devices
▶ SF 21: Analysing poetry

▶ SF 34: Argumentative writing

COMPREHENSION ◀

1 Understanding the situation
Say in one sentence what kind of situation the poem deals with, including the relationship between the speaker and the person addressed.

ANALYSIS ◀

2 Analysing imagery
There are two main *images used in this poem. Analyse them and say what they have in common.

BEYOND THE TEXT ◀

3 Drawing on your personal experience, discuss whether you find the imagery appropriate.

4 YOU CHOOSE ▶ **Creative writing**

a Write a poem from the point of view of the person addressed.

OR

b Write a dramatic scene based on the poem. Add a few *stage directions to the dialogue. ▶ LANGUAGE HELP

'I can't wait to see the reviews in the newspaper to find out whether I like the movie or not.'

Writing a review

Reviews are written by critics to inform other people about the positive and negative aspects of a particular book, film, etc. But increasingly ordinary people write reviews on the internet not just about films and books, but also about general products.

For the task at hand, you are going to be the critic of a weekly magazine for young adults. You have been asked to hunt for some 'good stuff' in literature or film and write a review explaining to readers of your own age group why you like the material you have chosen.

When you have finished the task, your teacher will give you an assessment sheet.

1 Get hold of one of your literary favourites. This can be a novel, a short story, a play (that you have either read or watched on stage), a poem or a collection of poems, a song or a film. Take a fresh look at your chosen material and read/ view it for analysis.

2 Make an outline for your review and structure your material.

3 Write a catchy beginning for your review.

4 State what the text/film is about and what happens. Don't reveal anything that might ruin the pleasure for someone else (e.g. the ending).

5 Write the main body, which includes the reasons why you have chosen this particular book or film. Include quotes from the text/film that reveal the power of its language.

6 Write a suitable ending in which you recommend your item.

7 a GALLERY WALK When you are satisfied with your review, type a neat copy and present it in a gallery walk.

  b Move around and read all the reviews. Your teacher will give you an assessment sheet. Take a vote on which three should be printed.

- ▶ SF 19: Analysing narrative prose
- ▶ SF 20: Analysing drama
- ▶ SF 21: Analysing poetry
- ▶ SF 23: Analysing a film
- ▶ Focus on Skills: Reading for analysis (drama extract), p. 78
- ▶ SF 8: Structuring ideas
- ▶ SF 32: Writing a review

- ▶ SF 40: Proofreading

5

The UK – a Kingdom United?

BBC
Adele
roast
beer
pudding
neighbours

grumbling
GB **pride**
celebs
Queen
lawn

Kate Moss
cricket
peas

moan
loyalty
respect

Download a list of chapter vocab here: **Webcode** context-12

▶ SF 3: Using a dictionary

Find an online dictionary here: **Webcode** context-52

1 Getting to know the British
  a Choose four red words and four blue words from the flag. Explain them to a partner and say why you think they are part of 'Britishness'.
  b Choose four words you do not know and look them up in a monolingual dictionary. Guess why these words are considered typically British.
  c Find three words on the flag that you do not think are typically British. Compare your words with those chosen by a partner.

2 Looking at your own country
  What's typically German? Collect your ideas and make up a German flag in the same way as the British flag above. Present your German flag to your partner. Explain your choices and discuss the words that are different.

Prince George
benefits
rugby
fish & chips
Ascot
haggis
David Beckham
hypocrisy
Republic
booze
House of Lords
complain
fashion
newspaper
rain
lager
The Empire
Wales
values
James Bond
Marmite
music
monarchy
drink
football
Jason Statham
Giant's Causeway
Kate
humour culture
together
cuppa
Northern Ireland
weather manners
England
resilience posh
class
queuing
Commonwealth
integrity
tea
Shakespeare
pound sterling
NHS
rambling
bank holiday
Keira Knightley
Jamie Oliver
accents
Scotland
irony
Plymouth
cider
cynicism
Diamond Jubilee
traffic
prude
heritage
Downton Abbey
Westminster
Monty Python
Union
J. K. Rowling
multiculturalism
community
tolerance
xenophobia
Wimbledon

CD1 12

Listen to an audio version of the text on the CD or download it here:

Webcode context-13

Character of a country

A political state

The terms Great Britain, Britain, England and the UK are often mistakenly used as synonyms. Great Britain is the largest island of the British Isles (and also the largest island in Europe); England is a country on this island.
The United Kingdom (also called 'Britain') includes England, Scotland, Wales and Northern Ireland and is a state with a population of about 62 million people.   5
The Union Flag, also known as the Union Jack, has been the national flag of the United Kingdom since 1908 and represents the powerful community and strong individual identities of the different nations.   10
Characteristically, Scotland has always been seen as a separate nation and since the late 20th century, many Scots have wanted to be fully independent. However, in a 2014 referendum, 55% of the voting population voted to stay in the UK.
Even in the 21st century, the royal family remains a very important British   15
institution. Events like the opening ceremony of the 2012 Olympic Games (in which one scene showed the Queen jumping out of a helicopter with James Bond), the Queen's Diamond Jubilee, Prince William's marriage to Kate Middleton and the birth of Prince George all saw the British population celebrate the fresh and modern image portrayed by their monarchy.   20

Multiculturalism

As head of the British Empire, the UK was once a colonial superpower with territories in many countries, like India, Australia, New Zealand and small island nations like the Seychelles, Mauritius and the Maldives. Today there   25
is still a strong bond between many former states of the British Empire and most of these nations are members of the Commonwealth of Nations. Together, they work towards world peace, promotion of democracy worldwide, and ending racism, sexism, poverty, ignorance, and disease.   30
Partly due to its history, immigrants from all over the world have settled in the UK, shaping the culture and adding to the nation's diversity with their food, religions and music. The result is a very multicultural society with the aim that everyone, regardless of colour, race or culture, should feel at home.   35

An uncertain future

The UK plays a significant role in world politics as a member of the EU and has permanent representation on the UN Security Council and in NATO. Furthermore, the UK has one of the largest and most influential economies in the world.   40
However, the financial crisis of 2007–2008 did not leave the UK unaffected and has led to economic problems, increased unemployment, social inequality and poverty. Anti-immigration feeling has also increased in some parts of the population and politicians who oppose the EU and Britain's membership have become more and more popular.   45

▶ SF 2: Learning new words

1 Using your own knowledge
For each of the three parts of the text, try to think of one piece of information which is not mentioned. Write them down and compare your findings with a partner.

2 Words in use
a Find a <mark>highlighted</mark> expression from the text that describes or names the following:
1 the name of the national flag of the UK
2 a person who joins a team, a union or an organization
3 relatives of the monarch of the United Kingdom
4 something that connects people or things, keeping them firmly together
5 a country that governs many other countries
6 an institution made up of countries that were once under the leadership or control of the British crown
7 having a strong effect on somebody or something

b Give definitions or use examples to explain the following terms from the text:

1 multicultural society   5 former
2 referendum   6 diversity
3 image   7 crisis
4 shape   8 social inequality

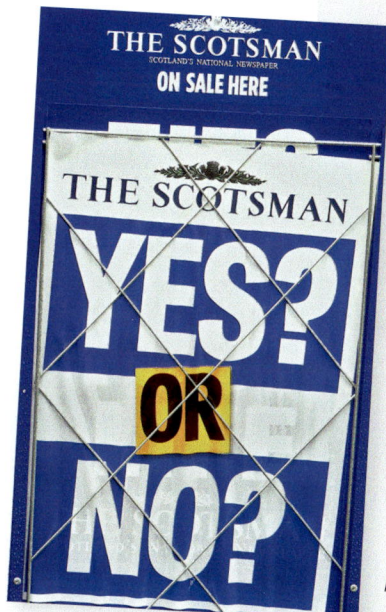

In the 2014 referendum, Scottish inhabitants voted either 'Yes' or 'No' over whether Scotland should leave the UK and become an independent country.

3 Phrases into English
In each of the following sentences, a useful phrase from the text is missing. Copy and complete the sentences. If you aren't sure how to translate the German words, look at the text again.
1 The royal family aims to *(ein frisches, modernes Erscheinungsbild vermitteln)*.
2 People with roots all over the world *(tragen zur Vielfalt der Nation bei)*.
3 Everyone should feel safe in the country they live in *(unabhängig von Hautfarbe, Rasse oder Kultur)*.
4 Events that began on Wall Street in New York *(haben das Vereinigte Königreich nicht unberührt gelassen)*.
5 Politicians *(die die EU ablehnen)* are gaining more popularity in some parts of the UK.

▶ LP 16: Avoiding Germanisms

◼ FACT FILE

Slogans should be easy to understand and be memorable. Good slogans play with language (e.g. rhyme or rhythm and puns) to make you think.

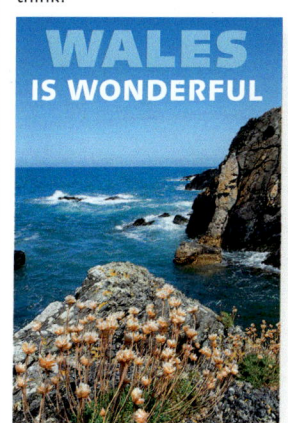

4 GALLERY WALK Writing
Create a slogan for an educational course on the UK's history and traditions, culture or politics. Write a short explanation for your slogan and use as many <mark>highlighted</mark> words from the text above as possible. Present your slogans in a gallery walk and decide on the best three.

A crowned nation

A1 Dangerous books   *Alan Bennett*

- In three sentences, state why you think reading is or isn't important. Share your answers in class.
- Discuss whether you think reading plays a part in a typical day in the Queen's life. What other duties might be on her agenda?

In the following extract from the novel The Uncommon Reader, *the Queen has developed an intense passion for literature. This starts to affect the way she carries out her public duties and what people think of her.*

One of the Queen's recurrent royal responsibilities was to open Parliament, an obligation she had never previously found particularly burdensome and actually rather enjoyed: to be driven down the Mall on a bright autumn morning even after fifty years was something of a treat. But not any more. She was dreading the two hours the whole thing was due to take, though fortunately they were in the coach, not the open   5

carriage, so she could take along her book. She'd got quite good at reading and waving, the trick being to keep the book below the level of the window and to keep focused on it and not on the crowds. The duke didn't like it one bit, of course, but goodness it   10
helped.

Which was all very well, except it was only when she was actually in the coach, with the procession drawn up in the palace forecourt and ready for the off, that, as she put on her glasses, she realised she'd   15
forgotten the book. And while the duke fumes in the corner and the postillions fidget, the horses shift and the harness clinks, Norman is rung on the mobile. The Guardsmen stand at ease and the procession waits. The officer in charge looks at his watch. Two minutes late. Knowing nothing displeases Her Majesty more and knowing nothing of the book, he does not look forward to the   20
repercussions that must inevitably follow. But here is Norman, skittering across the gravel with the book thoughtfully hidden in a shawl, and off they go.

Still, it is an ill-tempered royal couple that is driven down the Mall, the duke waving viciously from his side, the Queen listlessly from hers, and at some speed, too, as the procession tries to pick up the two minutes that have been lost.   25

At Westminster she popped the offending book behind a cushion in the carriage ready for the journey back, mindful as she sat on the throne and embarked on her speech of how tedious was the twaddle she was called on to deliver and that this was actually the only occasion when she got to read aloud to the nation. 'My government will do this ... my government will do that.' It was so barbarously phrased and wholly   30
devoid of style or interest that she felt it demeaned the very act of reading itself, with this year's performance even more garbled than usual as she, too, tried to pick up the missing couple of minutes.

It was with some relief that she got back into the coach and reached behind the cushion for her book. It was not there. Steadfastly waving as they rumbled along, she   35
surreptitiously felt behind the other cushions.

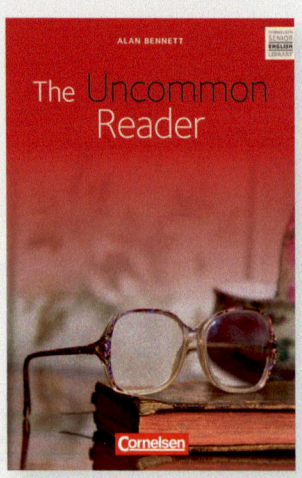

The Queen and the Duke of Edinburgh making a journey in the royal carriage

2 **burdensome** implying hard work
3 **the Mall** [mæl] road leading to Buckingham Palace
14 **draw up** position yourself
ready for the off ready to go
16 **fume** be very angry
17 **postillion** [pɒˈstɪlɪən] driver of a coach with horses
fidget [ˈfɪdʒɪt] make nervous movements
Norman fictional character in *The Uncommon Reader* who works as the Queen's servant
18 **stand at ease** relax *(military)*
21 **repercussion** [ˌriːpəˈkʌʃn] negative consequence
skitter run in a funny way
24 **vicious** [ˈvɪʃəs] angry
listless without energy or enthusiasm
28 **twaddle** [ˈtwɒdl] *(infml)* silly speech
30 **barbarous** very unpleasant
31 **devoid of sth.** without sth.
demean sth. make people have less respect for sth.
36 **surreptitious** [ˌsʌrəpˈtɪʃəs] subtle

'You're not sitting on it?'

'Sitting on what?'

'My book.'

40 'No, I am not. Some British Legion people here, and wheelchairs. Wave, for God's sake.'

When they arrived at the palace she had a word with Grant, the young footman in charge, who said that while ma'am had been in the Lords the sniffer dogs had been round and security had confiscated the book. He thought it had probably been 45 exploded.

'Exploded?' said the Queen. 'But it was Anita Brookner.'

The young man, who seemed remarkably undeferential, said security may have thought it was a device.

The Queen said: 'Yes. That is exactly what it is. A book is a device to ignite the 50 imagination.'

The footman said: 'Yes, ma'am.'

It was as if he was talking to his grandmother, and not for the first time the Queen was made unpleasantly aware of the hostility her reading seemed to arouse.

'Very well,' she said. 'Then you should inform security that I shall expect to find 55 another copy of the same book, vetted and explosive free, waiting on my desk tomorrow morning. And another thing. The carriage cushions are filthy. Look at my gloves.' Her Majesty departed.

'Fuck,' said the footman, fishing out the book from where he had been told to hide it down the front of his breeches. But of the lateness of the procession, to everyone's 60 surprise nothing was officially said.

From: *The Uncommon Reader*, 2008

40 **British Legion** [ˈliːdʒn] organization that helps ex-soldiers

44 **confiscate sth.** take sth. away

46 **Anita Brookner** (born 1928) British novelist and art historian

47 **undeferential** [ˌʌndɪfəˈrenʃl] showing no respect

49 **ignite sth.** *etwas entzünden*

55 **vet sth.** check sth.

59 **breeches** [ˈbrɪtʃɪz] (pl) *Reiterhose*

COMPREHENSION ◄

1 Identifying key points

a Point out how the Queen's reading habit interferes with her duties.

b Compare the Queen's day as shown in the passage to your initial ideas about a typical day in her life.

LANGUAGE AWARENESS ◄

2 Analysing direct speech

Analyse the language used in direct speech by the Queen, the duke and the footman. Assess its effect on your impression of their characters.

ANALYSIS ◄

3 Analysing humour

Analyse the *humour in this passage. Take into consideration how the *plot, certain aspects of the language and the *imagery contribute to the humorous effect.

BEYOND THE TEXT ◄

4 [YOU CHOOSE] ► Creative writing

a Imagine another situation (e.g. naming a ship / attending a pop-concert / being on a state visit) in which the Queen does not fulfil her duties because of her new hobby and write a similar passage. Try to include elements of *humour.

OR

b After the incident, the footman tells his wife about his encounter with the Queen. Write their dialogue and include the events that probably took place while the Queen was opening the Parliament.

[SUPPORT] ► p. 208

► SF 19: Analysing narrative prose

► LP 21: Writing about texts

► SF 37: Doing a creative writing task

► EE 4: Talking about sensitive issues

Find out more about the British royal family here:

 Webcode context-14

The Palace of Westminster, London

The British system of government

The head of state is the king or queen, who has many ceremonial functions and social duties but no real power. The monarch's duties include opening Parliament
5 and officially appointing the Prime Minister after his or her election.

The UK Parliament is known as the 'Mother of Parliaments' because it has served as a
10 model for many governments all over the world. It dates back to the year 1215, when a group of noblemen forced King John of England to respect certain
15 rights. Among these, set down in the Magna Carta, was their right to be consulted before the king could make them pay new taxes. Over the centuries, this group of noblemen evolved into today's Parliament.

Members of Parliament attending a session of Parliament in the House of Commons

20 The two houses of Parliament, the House of Lords and the House of Commons, meet in the Palace of Westminster. Thus journalists often refer to 'West-minster' when they mean Parliament, especially if they are talking about the House of Commons. There are
25 currently over 700 members of the House of Lords, but their power is limited. Although both houses of Parliament must, in theory, approve laws before they are submitted to the king or queen, the Lords can only delay a bill that has passed in the House of Commons.
30 Traditionally, a committee of the House of Lords was also the highest court in the land, but that function has been moved to the newly created Supreme Court.

Real power lies with the House of Commons, which is elected for up to five years (although the Prime
35 Minister can call a general election any time before that). Each Member of Parliament (MP) represents one of 650 constituencies (electoral districts) in the UK. In each constituency, the candidate with the most votes wins, and that person then sits in the Commons. In the

UK's so-called 'first-past-the-post' system, all other 40 votes are worthless. This effectively prevents smaller parties being elected to Parliament and can potentially lead to a majority in Parliament that does not always reflect the total number of votes. For example, in the 45 2005 general election, the Labour party won 55% of the seats in the House of Commons with just 35% of the votes.

Her Majesty's Government 50 consists of the Prime Minister (PM) and the Cabinet, which is made up of the MPs who run the different government departments. The most important ministers are the 55 Chancellor of the Exchequer, who is in charge of finance, the Foreign Secretary and the Home Secretary, who is responsible for the country's internal affairs. In the press, the Prime Minister's office is often referred to as 'Number 10', after its address at 10 Downing Street, 60 and the ministries are known as 'Whitehall', after the street in London where most of them are located.

1 *Describe the roles of the following people and groups to a partner using one sentence for each:*
   Partner A: the Prime Minister • the Cabinet
   Partner B: an MP • the monarch

2 *In a table, list what you now know about one of the houses of the UK Parliament. Present your list to your partner.*
   Partner A: The House of Lords
   Partner B: The House of Commons

3 *List differences and similarities to the German system of government.*

► The British System of Government, p. 342

FOCUS ON SKILLS

Listening for gist and detail

Listening is the key to successful oral communication. It requires focus, preparation and practice.

What do the British think of the royal family?

1 Before listening
You are going to hear two short interviews about people's opinions of the British monarchy. What might people say? Write 2–3 sentences.

2 Dealing with different accents
When listening to native English speakers, you will often hear people speak with different accents. When somebody's accent is difficult to understand, you should focus on words you can understand and use the context to figure out the rest of the sentence. As you listen, you will probably get used to the accent.
a Listen to a short excerpt of an interview. The interviewer and the interviewee have different accents. Try to write down exactly what both men say, then compare your answers with a partner.
b Discuss which man was easier to understand and why.

3 First listening: listening for gist
a Skim through the task below and note down keywords that you can listen out for. Compare your notes with a partner.
b Listen to the extract, then choose the right answers.
  1 The first interviewee …
     … considers the institution of the monarchy a brilliant idea.
     … isn't really sure what he thinks about the monarchy.
     … completely rejects the monarchy.
  2 The young couple …
     … think the royal family should be abolished.
     … have generally positive opinions about the royal family.
     … think the royal family is mainly a bad thing for the UK.

4 Second listening: listening for detail
Again, skim through the questions to find out what <u>specific</u> information you will have to listen out for.
a Listen to the first interview again. Are the sentences below true or false? Correct the false answers.
  1 The first interviewee understands why some people would like to have an elected president instead of a monarch.
  2 The Queen is his favourite member of the royal family.
  3 He was born during the Queen's reign.
  4 He does not think that Charles will become King.

FACT FILE

A regional accent is determined by where a speaker is from and where they live.
A social accent is often determined by a speaker's socioeconomic status, i.e. their level of education, how wealthy their family is, and their family's level of education. People from the same region can have different accents if they are from different socioeconomic groups.

🎧 **CD1** 13
▶ SF 22: Listening

🎧 **CD1** 14

Buckingham Palace, home of the Queen in London

b Listen to the second interview and finish the sentences.

1 The young woman says that the royal family does a lot of good for …

2 The young man mentions … as two examples of the stereotypical English image.

3 The young man says that the … has been lost.

4 The young man's favourite member of the royal family is …

5 The young man thinks that Kate has …

c Compare and discuss your results with a partner.

5 Evaluating the listening procedure

a Compare your initial expectations which you wrote for Task **1** with what you actually heard.

b Discuss the listening procedure with a partner. To what extent were your anticipations useful? Which tip or strategy was most helpful to you?

A2 Does Britain still need the monarchy?

COMPREHENSION

1 Listening for gist

Listen to part two of the podcast and decide which of the following statements best expresses the main ideas of the speakers.

a 1 The first interviewee would keep the monarchy, but doesn't like it very much.

2 The first interviewee thinks the media hate the royal family.

b 1 The second interviewee quite likes William and Harry.

2 The second interviewee thinks Australia should no longer be a member of the Commonwealth.

2 Listening for detail

Listen to the first interview again. Match the arguments given in the list below to those of the interviewee. There are more arguments than needed.

do a lot of charity • very expensive • outdated institution • symbol of Britain • attracts tourists • good role model • a tradition to keep • too many scandals • arrogant and snobby family • close to the people • loved by the media

BEYOND THE TEXT

3 Preparing for a discussion

a Look again at the arguments put forward by all of the speakers in both parts of the podcast. Divide their arguments into two columns: 'in favour of' and 'against' the monarchy.

b Together with a partner, add further arguments to your list.

4 Having a discussion

a In groups of 4–5, discuss whether the monarchy in Britain should be abolished. ▶ LANGUAGE HELP

b CHALLENGE ▶ Take notes of the different arguments raised during your discussion and present the three most convincing ones to the rest of the class.

🎧 **CD1** 15

▶ SF 22: Listening

▶ SF 10: Working with closed test formats

▶ SF 10: Working with closed test formats

■ LANGUAGE HELP

Stating your opinion:
- In my opinion … / The way I see it …
- As far as I'm concerned / If you ask me …
- I'm absolutely convinced that …

Agreeing:
- I couldn't agree with you more.
- Exactly! / Precisely! / Certainly! / Definitely!

Disagreeing:
- I'm not so sure, really.
- I'm not convinced that …
- I strongly disagree / I don't agree with you at all.

▶ SF 27: Having a discussion

The multicultural face of the UK

From Empire to Commonwealth
The British Empire was the largest colonial empire in the world covering nearly one fifth of the land worldwide
5 during the late 19th and early 20th centuries.

Since the 16th century, Britain had established colonies all over the world including settlement colonies like
10 Canada, Australia and New Zealand, trading colonies (e.g. India) as well as strategically important naval bases in the Mediterranean (e.g. Gibraltar). It was said that the sun never set on the
15 Empire, so great was its power and territory. However, the effects of a decolonization movement and two world wars led to the decline of the British Empire and the foundation of the Commonwealth of Nations. The Commonwealth
20 of Nations was founded in 1931 and is a voluntary association of 53 countries of the former British Empire.

Queen Victoria (1819–1901) ruled over almost a quarter of the world's population by the end of her reign.

The Head of the Commonwealth is the British monarch. The states are united by language (English), culture, history and in their values, such as 25 democracy, economic development, the rule of law and the guarantee of human rights.

The Commonwealth includes about two billion people, or 30% of the 30 world's population. Every four years, athletes from the member countries take part in the Commonwealth Games. These include classic Olympic sports as well as typical sports 35 played in Commonwealth countries (e.g. netball). The three key values of the Commonwealth Games movement are humanity, equality and destiny.

Explain and comment on the quote 'The sun never sets on the British Empire'.

B1 The British Empire report

The video you are about to watch presents the rise, dominance and fall of the British Empire.

1 Before viewing
Before you watch the video, speculate about how the filmmaker might deal with the subject of colonialism. Take into consideration the Fact File 'From Empire to Commonwealth'.

──────────────── ANALYSIS ◀

2 Viewing for the first time
Watch the video and describe it with two adjectives which you find most suitable: e.g. funny, informative, exaggerated, annoying, innovative, childish, surprising, etc. Explain your choices.

3 Examining how material is presented
a Watch the video for a second time. Examine the different methods that are used to present information. Consider how the events are visualized and supported by film excerpts, still pictures, sound effects and music.
b Compare your findings and discuss their effect on the viewer. To what extent do the presenter and the different material that is shown support the viewer's understanding of the Empire's history?

▶ SF 23: Analysing a film

▶️ **DVD**
peak highest point
leap big jump
shift sth. move sth.
spell trouble be a problem

Map of the world showing in red the extent of the British Empire in 1901

► SF37: Doing a creative
writing task

— BEYOND THE TEXT ◄

4 Beyond the video

    a List five important dates and events in German history. With a partner
        compare your lists and decide on the four most important events.

    b `CHALLENGE` ▶ Write the script for a video report aimed at an English
        audience in which you show and comment on important dates in German
        history. If you want to, you can use *irony and *humour or you can make it
        informative and objective.

B2 Between two cultures   *Mike Bartlett*

In the play Artefacts *by Mike Bartlett, Kelly is a teenage girl living in Great
Britain with her mother Susan. Her father left the family when Kelly was little to
live in his home country Iraq. In the following scenes, she meets her father
Ibrahim for the first time since he left.*

- Read the two extracts and imagine what the scenes would look like on a
stage.

Extract 1

IBRAHIM	Do you think we look alike?
KELLY	You and my uncle?
IBRAHIM	You and me.
KELLY	Uh ... No.
IBRAHIM	You're passionate.
KELLY	I'm English.
IBRAHIM	You are half Iraqi. You can have an Iraqi passport now.
KELLY	That's not much use.
IBRAHIM	Would you prefer it if I had been an American?
KELLY	No.
	Well, yeah. That would be better though, wouldn't it? Cos an American passport's worth loads. I could go there and work and stuff. But I told you I'm not going to go to Iraq, am I?

5

10

After a short pause when Kelly's mother Susan enters, Kelly continues.

KELLY	This afternoon when I was bored I looked in the mirror cos, apparently, I'm half Iraqi.
SUSAN	Are you sure you're both all right?
KELLY	But which bits?
SUSAN	Up here?
KELLY	Hips. Hands.
IBRAHIM	Kelly?
KELLY	I've got English legs. Iraqi breasts.
IBRAHIM	I wish we could've met earlier.
KELLY	But my stomach is slightly potted.
IBRAHIM	Kelly? [...]
KELLY	I have a little pot belly. Maybe this is the point they mix. The two countries. Where my genes got confused. This belly is not Iraqi or English. It's Engraqi. Iringlish. I like my belly. Yeah. [...] Am I what you expected?
IBRAHIM	I tried not to expect anything.

15

20

25

30

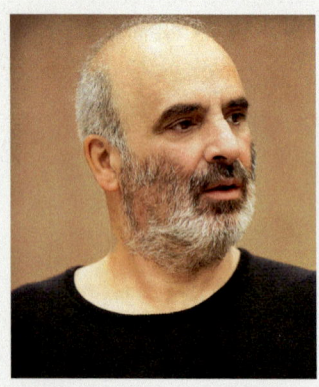

*Actor Peter Polycarpou played
the role of Ibrahim in* Artefacts
in 2008.

11 **cos** [kəz] *(infml)* because
24 **potted** (here) larger than usual

KELLY	But you did.
IBRAHIM	I imagined you might look like Kate Winslet.
KELLY	This isn't going very well, is it?
IBRAHIM	I don't know.
35 KELLY	Bit of a fucking disappointment for you.
IBRAHIM	No.
KELLY	If you were after –
IBRAHIM	You are better than Kate Winslet.
KELLY	What do you want?
40 IBRAHIM	You are you.
KELLY	Why are you here? Now, what do you *want*?
IBRAHIM	That we meet.
KELLY	Just that.
IBRAHIM	Yes.
45 KELLY	You don't want money?
IBRAHIM	I run the National Museum of Iraq. In Baghdad. A number of our artefacts were stolen. During the war. I was invited to come and give a lecture at the British Museum about the current state of our collection. That is where I have been today.
50 KELLY	So I'm not actually sure why you came at all.
IBRAHIM	It is expensive to fly here. I will probably never come back to Britain. So I thought it best we meet.

Extract 2

On her first visit to Iraq, Kelly meets her father's other family. One of Ibrahim's daughters has been kidnapped and Kelly asks her father about this incident.

IBRAHIM	Why? Why are you asking? Why do you want to know?
KELLY	I've got a right to know.
55 IBRAHIM	A right? You have no right to know about my family.
KELLY	She's my sister.
IBRAHIM	And I'm your father.
KELLY	Apparently.
IBRAHIM	You should trust me that I will do the right thing. But you don't. Do you? You think you know better. You have not been here a day yet. What makes you think you will know better than me?
60	
KELLY	Maybe I don't trust you. Not hard to work out why, is it? [...]
IBRAHIM	What makes you think what I am doing is a mistake?
KELLY	You are that kind of man.
65 IBRAHIM	Weak.
KELLY	Careless.
IBRAHIM	And why do you think I am *careless*? I will tell you.
KELLY	Yeah, all right then, tell me what I think.
IBRAHIM	You come here and you see this city and you see me and my normal house. You see how poor we are and we don't have things you have. And you see on your news how the country is fighting itself. And you think we are all careless. No, not just careless, you think we are stupid. So this is why you're asking what is going on, because you want to make sure that I am being civilised in what I am doing. That I am being intelligent – *reasonable* in how I am behaving. Because we Iraqis, you think, we tend to get things wrong all the time.
70	
75	

Actress Lizzie Watts performing in a production of Artefacts *at the Bush Theatre in London*

76 **tend to do sth.** do sth. regularly

⸱⸱⸱⸱▶

78 **mess sth. up** do sth. very badly

We allow our girls to be kidnapped.
We tend to mess things up.
That is really why you do not trust me.

KELLY   Cos I'm racist.   80

IBRAHIM   Because you are English. And you don't know any better. When you are
            a child in England you are still taught underneath that you should rule
            the world. How in the end Britain has always made the world better.

KELLY   You told me I'm half Iraqi.

IBRAHIM   I hoped you were.   85

KELLY   I am. Whether I like it or not. I can't choose.

IBRAHIM   Yes, you can. You can choose where you belong.

From: *Artefacts*, 2008

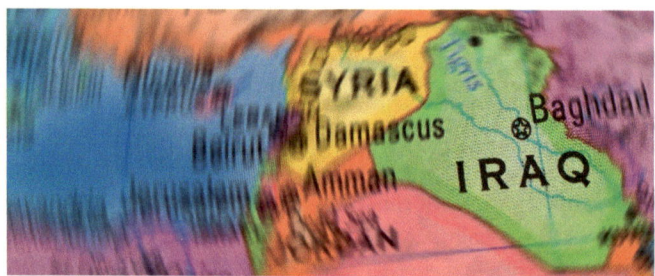

─── COMPREHENSION ◀

1 Looking for the main idea

  a Describe how Kelly tries to find out which culture she belongs to.

  b Point out which prejudices towards the Iraqi and English cultures are
discussed in the text.

▶ SF 20: Analysing drama

▶ LP 18: Writing about texts

─── ANALYSIS ◀

2 Analysing character relationships

Analyse the relationship between Kelly and her father Ibrahim. Reflect on
what they talk about and how they speak to each other.

SUPPORT ▶ p. 208

─────────────────────────────────── LANGUAGE AWARENESS ◀

3 Studying colloquial language

  a Read the explanation of colloquialism on the left and find examples of
colloquial language in the conversation between Kelly and Ibrahim.

  b Rewrite the examples you found in the text in formal English.

─────────────────────────────────────── BEYOND THE TEXT ◀

4 **YOU CHOOSE** ▶ **Creative writing**

a Write an email Kelly sends to her best friend in Britain after she has met her father in Iraq.	**b** Together with a partner, write a dialogue between Kelly's father Ibrahim and her mum Susan after the first meeting of father and daughter.

> ### FACT FILE
>
> In literature, **colloquialism** is the use of informal words and expressions in conversations to underline the speaker's social status, level of education, relationship with others, etc. The opposite of colloquialism is standard or formal English.
> Examples:
> **wanna**   *want to*
> **gonna**   *going to*
> **go nuts** *go insane*

▶ SF 37: Doing a creative
writing task

▶ SF 27: Having a discussion

5 Thinking about cultural identity

  a Together with a partner, discuss whether 'You can choose where you
belong' (l. 88). Who or what influences you in your choice? Think about
family, culture, education and list concrete examples for and against the
quote.

  b **CHALLENGE** ▶ Write a *comment on Ibrahim's idea that 'You can choose
where you belong.' (l. 88)

▶ LP 13: Placing emphasis
on key points

▶ SF 34: Argumentative writing

B3 The British and their tea

The British are famous for their love of tea. In the following podcast, you will get to know more about this tradition.

- Before listening, brainstorm in class what you know about the British tradition of drinking tea.

────────────────── COMPREHENSION ◀

1 Listening for gist

In one sentence, summarize what the podcast is about.

2 Listening for detail

a Complete the following statements about the history of tea.
1 The British made their first cup of tea sometime in the middle of the … century.
2 In the 19th century, tea became popular among … people.
3 Tea drinking has a much longer history in …, where people have drunk tea for thousands of years.
4 Nearly everyone in Britain puts … in their tea, and about a third of people add … to make the tea sweet.

b **CHALLENGE** ▶ While working on **2a**, take notes on how to make a nice cup of tea the British way.

3 Analysing style

How does the speaker of the podcast try to hold the audience's attention and entertain his listeners? **SUPPORT** ▶ p. 208

▶ SF 22: Listening

🎧 **CD1** 16

rich (here) dark; strong

┌─ ▮ TROUBLE SPOT ──────
drunk (v) = getrunken
drunk (adj) = betrunken
drunk (n) = Betrunkene/r
└─────────────────────

▶ EE 1: Eating in and out

▶ SF 17: Analysing stylistic devices

📍 CULTURE SPOT

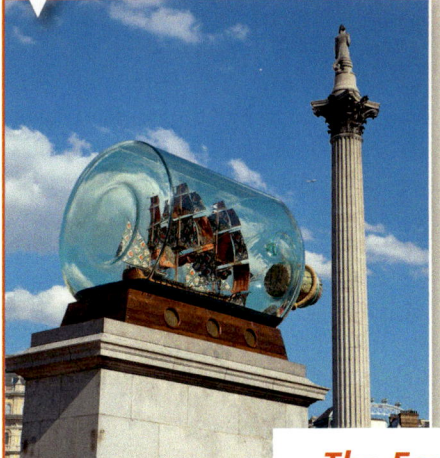

The Fourth Plinth is one of four pillars in Trafalgar Square in London, which was built in 1840. As there wasn't enough money to make a statue for it, it stood empty for 150 years. In 1999 a commission decided to display contemporary artworks on it and in 2010 the artwork Nelson's Ship in a Bottle *by Anglo-Nigerian artist sculptor Yinka Shonibare was unveiled.*

Yinka Shonibare

The Fourth Plinth

1 Comment on the idea to use the fourth plinth as a display for art.

2 Research other artworks that have been featured on the Fourth Plinth. Present the one you like best to the class. Give reasons. ▶ S5: Doing research

B4 Halal food festival

'Britishness' is influenced by the many different cultures found in the UK. One such influence is Britain's large Muslim population.

Haloodies at the Halal Food Festival in London

The first ever to be held in the UK and the world's largest, the Halal Food Festival is a three-day consumer food show dedicated to foodies who eat halal, or haloodies as they have been coined by festival events director Norman Khawaja. [...]

Visitors can look forward to over 100 exhibitors from across the globe showcasing the most innovative and delicious halal food and drink products, restaurants and street-food stalls. In addition, there is a cooking school and live demonstration kitchen featuring top chefs. [...]   5

Halal is an Arabic word meaning lawful or permissible. It not only covers food and drink but also all matters of daily life. Followers of Islam (Muslims) must follow a dietary requirement that does not permit pork or pork products or alcohol and only allows meat slaughtered in accordance to strict guidelines in the Qur'an. Halal food is not a cuisine or a style of cooking in its own right. Therefore any cuisine or style can become halal provided it is cooked using halal ingredients and prepared in a halal manner.   10

With a growing UK Muslim population currently standing at 2.7 million (Census 2011) with a £20.5 billion a year spending power and expected to rise to 5.5 million people by 2030 (Pew Report, The Future of the Global Muslim Population 2011) access to delicious halal food in the UK is becoming increasingly important. [...]   15   20

Improving the range, availability and quality of halal foods and restaurants drives the Halal Food Festival's founder Imran Kausar, who comments: 'The growing British Muslim middle classes have greater needs and demands from food producers, retailers and restaurateurs, and command significant spending power.'   25

From: HalalFocus, 2013

COMPREHENSION ◀

1 Finding key points
 a Explain the concept of halal.
 b Create an electronic flyer for the halal festival in which you inform the public about the key details of the event. ▶ LANGUAGE HELP

BEYOND THE TEXT ◀

2 YOU CHOOSE ▶ **Thinking about other food cultures**

a What other ideas for festivals to integrate different cultures can you think of? Choose one example and write an outline for an event similar to the text above.

OR

b Prepare a short oral presentation about similar food festivals in Germany.

B5 Eastern Europeans in the UK *Amelia Gentleman*

Many Polish migrants want to work in the UK, but success is not guaranteed.

The UK remains a promised land in popular Polish mythology. When someone returns from a stint working there, they are expected to come home driving an expensive car, with a suitcase full of savings. For some, like Michal Novak, 30, the return was triumphant. He came back after 14 years in Britain with enough money to buy a
5 smart flat in a good part of Warsaw, and the prospect of a good job in Poland, paying almost the same salary as he had received in London.

Even so, friends and colleagues were puzzled by his decision to return. 'People asked me "Why did you come back? It's so horrible here." As if it is a dogma that living in the UK is better. And it's not true,' he said.
10 Less triumphant will be the return of Lukasz Z, 24, and Adam B, 22, due to travel back by coach imminently, their fare paid for by the Polish charity Barka, that seeks out Poles sleeping rough in London, and encourages them to abandon their attempt to make it in the UK. It gives them tickets to get home and offers them somewhere to live once they arrive.
15 Adam has spent the past six months since he lost his factory job sleeping in parks, railway stations and squats, stealing food to survive. Lukasz has spent several chunks of the past year in Pentonville prison, sentenced for stealing and carrying a knife, after work as a painter and decorator dried up.

Neither man had been in trouble with the police at home, and neither has anything
20 positive to say about their time here.

Their stories illustrate the successes and failures of UK-Polish migration, a phenomenon that exploded on an unexpected scale with Poland's accession to the EU in 2004. [...]

Whilst the vast majority have found work in the building industry, or as carers,
25 cleaners or waitresses, not everyone has been happy. [...]

'I used to come across so many similar stories in London – of young Polish people with economics degrees working as waiters,' [Novak] said.

'Typically, they left Poland five years ago because they couldn't find any work here, but they fail to find anything proper there. So they got jobs much below what their
30 education has prepared them for, and they spent four or five years of their lives, working in a bar, not getting any experience. What can you do here after four years as a waiter in the UK?'

From: *The Guardian*, 6 April 2011

FACT FILE

Since the end of World War II, there has been a continual flow of **migrants from Poland** to the UK. After the fall of Communism in 1989 and the relaxing of travel restrictions within Europe, Polish immigration increased sharply. The expansion of the EU to include Poland in 2004 also paved the way for more Polish workers to relocate to the UK, as citizens from EU member states could work there legally. However, after 2007, Polish migration to the UK began to decrease as economic growth and less unemployment in Poland made it more attractive for Poles to stay in there for work.

2 **stint** *Arbeitsperiode*
8 **dogma** unquestioned belief
11 **imminent** ['– – –] happening very soon
16 **squat** [skwɒt] *(n) besetztes Haus*
chunk large part

COMPREHENSION ◄

1 Summarizing key parts of an article
Summarize the stories of Lukasz and Adam and present them to a partner.

► SF 31: Writing a summary

2 Mediation (English → German)
Write a blog entry in German about the successes and failures of immigrants in the UK, comparing the lives of the three Polish men portrayed in the article.

► SF 41: Mediation of written and oral texts

► LP 4: Present perfect and simple past

BEYOND THE TEXT ◄

3 YOU CHOOSE ► Writing

a Write a *comment on the idea of Britain as 'a promised land' (l. 1) for migrants.

 OR

b Write a letter from either Lukasz or Adam to friends or relatives in Poland, explaining what happened to them in the UK and why they are returning.

► SF 34: Argumentative writing
► LP 18: Writing about texts

Where do we go from here?

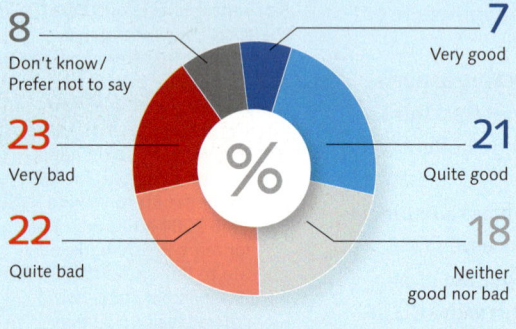

🎧 **CD1** 17
disillusionment [ˌdɪsɪˈluːʒnmənt]
state of no longer feeling enthusiasm
ensure sth. [ɪnˈʃʊə] make sure
that sth. happens

▶ SF 12: Analysing charts
and graphs
▶ SF 22: Listening

ON THE UK'S MEMBERSHIP OF THE EU

Thinking about the UK's membership of the European
Union, would you say that this is generally a good thing
or a bad thing?

8
Don't know/
Prefer not to say

7
Very good

23
Very bad

21
Quite good

22
Quite bad

18
Neither
good nor bad

Total: Bad thing **45%** **28%** **Total: Good thing**

Opinion Research carried out an online survey of 1,957 GB adults aged
18+ from 13 to 15 November 2012. Results have been weighted to
nationally representative criteria.

▶ SF 17: Analysing stylistic
devices

TROUBLE SPOT
eine Rede halten (l. 2) =
give / deliver / make a speech
Not: ~~hold a speech~~

C1 A referendum on the EU

• Before listening to a speech by British Prime Minister David Cameron about
the UK's membership in the EU, describe the chart below left.

COMPREHENSION ◀

1 Listening for gist
Which of these topics does David Cameron talk about?
1 reasons for the British to be sceptical about the EU
2 arguments why he wants a referendum right now
3 the right time for a referendum

2 Listening for detail
a Complete the sentences taken from Cameron's speech.
1 They resent the ... in our national life by what they
see as unnecessary rules and ...
2 But I don't believe that to make a ... at this moment
is the right way forward, either for Britain or for
Europe as a ...
3 And when the referendum comes let me say now
that if we can ... such an arrangement, I will ... for it
with all my heart and ...
b CHALLENGE ▶ Explain the reasons for the anti-EU
feeling mentioned by Cameron in your own words.

ANALYSIS ◀

3 Analysing style
Listen again. Analyse how Cameron tries to convince his
listeners of his views. Focus on language and content. Is
he successful? SUPPORT ▶ p. 209

C2 Merkel's speech in London

*In February 2014, Angela Merkel gave a speech in London to both Houses of
the British Parliament on the future of Europe. British expectations concerning her
speech were high – perhaps too high, as Merkel said herself at the beginning of
her address.*

BERLIN – Es ist eine Geste besonderer Wertschätzung für die Bundeskanzlerin: Erst
als dritte deutsche Politikerin nach Willy Brandt und Richard von Weizsäcker hielt
Angela Merkel an diesem Donnerstag eine Rede vor beiden Kammern des britischen
Parlaments. Die Regierungschefin selbst sprach zu Beginn ihres Auftritts von einer
„großen Ehre", die ihr zuteil werde. Die Einladung sei „Ausdruck der engen Verbun- 5
denheit zwischen unseren Ländern".

Die Kanzlerin erinnerte an ihren ersten Besuch in London im Frühjahr 1990. Mit
ihrem Mann sei sie durch den Hyde-Park zum dortigen Speakers Corner gegangen.
Dies sei gerade für sie als Ostdeutsche ein „Symbol der freien Rede" gewesen.
Merkel begann ihre Rede auf Englisch, wechselte erst nach einigen Minuten ins 10
Deutsche.

Die Kanzlerin wies selbst darauf hin, dass ihr Auftritt in der britischen Öffentlichkeit im Vorfeld mit hohen Erwartungen verbunden wurde. Die konservative Regierung um Premierminister David Cameron erhofft sich

15 Schützenhilfe von Deutschland in der Europapolitik. Cameron will im Rahmen von Vertragsreformen unter anderem die Arbeitnehmerfreizügigkeit innerhalb der EU begrenzen und die Arbeitszeitrichtlinie beschneiden. Bis 2017 will er das Volk über den Verbleib in der EU abstimmen lassen.

„Einige erwarten, dass meine Rede den Weg für eine fundamentale

20 Reform der europäischen Architektur ebnet, die alle angeblichen oder tatsächlichen britischen Wünsche zufriedenstellt", sagte Merkel. „Ich fürchte, ich muss Sie enttäuschen." Dies gelte aber auch für jene, die darauf setzten, dass sie den Briten in ihrer Rede klarmachen würde, dass man keinen Preis zahlen werde, um das Vereinigte Königreich in der EU zu halten. „Großbritannien

25 braucht seine europäische Berufung nicht zu beweisen", sagte die CDU-Politikerin und zitierte damit aus der Rede von Weizsäckers an gleicher Stelle im Jahr 1986.

Merkel blieb in ihrer Rede beim Grundsätzlichen. „Wir brauchen den Mut zur Veränderung, um die Erfolgsgeschichte der europäischen Einigung fort-

30 zusetzen", sagte die Kanzlerin. „Wir brauchen starke europäische Institutionen und starke Nationalstaaten." Das Subsidiaritätsprinzip müsse in Europa wieder mehr Beachtung finden, mahnte sie.

Gerade letzteren Satz werden die Briten gerne gehört haben. Großbritannien will bei einer EU-Reform über eine Rückverlagerung von Kompetenzen von europäischer

35 Ebene in die Nationalstaaten verhandeln. Merkel hatte zuletzt zwar ihre Bereitschaft dazu angedeutet – über das Ausmaß allerdings gehen die Vorstellungen weit auseinander. Das hatte Außenminister Frank-Walter Steinmeier (SPD) jüngst bei seinem Besuch in London klargemacht.

Merkel unterstrich denn auch die Grundwerte der EU, die nicht angetastet werden

40 dürften: der freie Handel, die Arbeitnehmerfreizügigkeit und ein „Europa ohne Grenzen". Zugleich betonte sie, dass sie Großbritanniens Platz in der EU sieht. Die EU brauche „ein starkes Vereinigtes Königreich mit einer starken Stimme in der Europäischen Union". Hintergrund ist die anhaltende britische Debatte über eine Renationalisierung und sogar einen Austritt des Landes aus der EU. „Unsere Vorstel-

45 lungen der künftigen Entwicklung der Europäischen Union mögen sich in Details immer wieder unterscheiden, aber wir, Deutschland und Großbritannien, teilen das Ziel einer starken, wettbewerbsfähigen Europäischen Union, die ihre Kräfte bündelt."

From: *Spiegel Online*, 27 February, 2014

Angela Merkel shakes David Cameron's hand in front of Number 10 Downing Street.

1 Mediation (German → English)

A Spanish follower of your blog wants to find out about Merkel's speech. Summarize chancellor Merkel's future visions regarding the EU in general and the position of Great Britain in the EU in English for him.

2 **Writing**

a Taking into account what you already know about Cameron's attitude towards the EU (from **C1**), write his reply to Merkel's speech.

b Write a dialogue between a critical journalist and Merkel that takes place directly after the speech.

▶ SF41: Mediation of written and oral texts

▶ LP4: Present perfect and simple past

▶ SF37: Doing a creative writing task

▶ SF34: Argumentative writing

▶ CC6: Talking about sensitive issues

▶ CC2: The language of politeness

Bastian Schweinsteiger at the 2014 World Cup Final

1 **dip into sth.** examine or read sth. casually or superficially
blogosphere ['blɒɡəsfɪə] the blogs on the internet
musing (usu. pl) thought
twitterati frequent users of the social media website Twitter
5 **cloak sth.** cover sth., hide sth.
begrudging (adj) missgünstig
6 **ruthless** having no pity, merciless
7 **inanimate** [ɪn'ænɪmət] not living
8 **by implication** as a consequence / effect
9 **resentful** [rɪ'zentfl] having or showing a feeling of anger
13 **at sb.'s expense** auf Kosten von jdm.
15 **root for sb.** applaud for / encourage sb.
Messrs ['mesəz] plural of Mr
19 **bonnet** Deckel, Haube
21 **R&D** research and development

► SF 31: Writing a summary

► SF 18: Analysing non-fiction

► SF 29: Writing a formal letter or email
► LP 11: Using the right register

C3 It's OK to like the Germans   *Stewart Wood*

Many Britons cheered for Germany in the 2014 World Cup final. But one journalist argues that there is a lot the Britons can learn from the Germans in the world outside the football stadiums.

Dip into the weekend papers, the blogosphere & the musings of the twitterati, and you'll see multiple variants on a similar sentiment: 'I can't quite believe it, and I never thought this would happen, but I find myself supporting Germany. Fancy that!'

Usually our praise for German football is similar to our praise for Germans in other spheres of life where they lead the world. We cloak it in begrudging virtues: 'efficient', 'clinical', 'ruthless'. Germans are applauded in the language we use to describe well-functioning inanimate objects, such as Mercedes cars, or Miele dishwashers. And characteristics of good cars and dishwashers are, by implication, characteristics of people that you admire in a slightly resentful way. 5

So we are impressed with Germany, but we don't have any particular affection for it or its people. We have respect for Germany, but we don't want to spend much time there. We applaud Germans' economic success, but we resent their dominance of the European Union. We make lots of jokes at their expense, but we say they have no sense of humour. 10

Maybe a day on which millions of Brits find themselves rooting for Messrs Müller, Hummels and Schweinsteiger is a good moment to challenge this approach to all things German. Because the truth is that there is much to like and admire about Germany. And – whisper it softly – there is a lot we can learn from them too. [...] 15

Take the state of Britain's economy. Underneath the bonnet of our recovery lies an economy characterised by low productivity, a poor record in technical skills, low levels of savings and investment and relatively weak performance in R&D. In the long run, we will simply not be able to compete internationally, or solve the cost of living crisis we face, without addressing these challenges. We cannot copy the German economy, or transplant the culture in which it is embedded. But we can learn much from the institutions and policies that have helped produce the most successful high-wage, high-skill economy of the modern era. [...] 20 25

Of course Germany has its share of problems, blind spots and policy failures too. And taking inspiration from German success does not mean wanting Britain to become Germany [...] But surely it is time for us as a country to take a collective deep breath, and tell ourselves: it's OK to like, admire and even learn lessons from Germany. And you never know: once we do, we may be on the long road to finally winning another World Cup. 30

From: *The Guardian*, 13 July 2014

COMPREHENSION ◄

1 Summarizing
Summarize the writer's main points concerning Britons' relationship to Germany. **SUPPORT** ▶ p. 209

ANALYSIS ◄

2 Analysing key vocabulary
Analyse the three 'begrudging virtues' in ll. 5–6 and explain what they tell us about how some British view German people.

BEYOND THE TEXT ◄

3 YOU CHOOSE ▶ **Responding to the article**

a Write an email to the *Guardian*'s editor in response to this article. **OR**   **b** Write an article on what Germany can learn from Britain.

A podcast on British culture

In this Chapter Task you will listen to a report on a British TV show and use what you learn to create your own podcast on an aspect of British culture.

> ■ **FACT FILE**
>
> **Downton Abbey** is a well-known and popular British TV series that is broadcast by ITV in the UK and PBS in the USA. The period drama series, set in Yorkshire, England, follows the wealthy Crawley family through life's events as they are impacted by history. Some of the major 5
> historical events include the sinking of the Titanic, World War I and the Spanish influenza pandemic. Julian Fellowes is the creator, executive producer and writer of this series that is co-produced by Carnival Films and Masterpiece. *Downton Abbey* has won several awards, 10
> including a Golden Globe and a Primetime Emmy.

1 Understanding an example podcast
  a Read the Fact File and look at the picture. Collect ideas about the setting and the characters of the series.
  b Listen to the podcast and complete the sentence: In the interview …
    1 … the executive producer summarizes the plot of *Downton Abbey* for those who do not know the series.
    2 … *Downton Abbey's* success in the UK and worldwide is mentioned.
    3 … the executive producer announces the final season of the series and gives hints about its ending.
  c Listen again. Which statements are true? Correct the wrong statements.
    1 *Downton Abbey* is set around the time of the Second World War.
    2 *Downton Abbey* is a uniquely English *genre that cannot be produced anywhere other than in Great Britain.
    3 *Downton Abbey* portrays the class system and shows how aristocrats lived in a very contemporary way.
    4 The fourth series and the Christmas special have to be cancelled since many key stars are leaving the series for Hollywood.

2 Thinking about podcasts
Collect ideas about what makes a podcast interesting.

3 Creating a podcast
Go back to the flag on the Lead-in pages (pp. 92–93). Choose a topic connected to the UK and discuss it in your own short podcast, between three and four minutes long. Organize your work, make an outline, write your script, practise and record it.

4 Evaluating a podcast
Present your podcast to the class. While listening to your classmates' podcasts, take notes on their content as well as their strengths and weaknesses. Give feedback, praising the aspects that you liked and giving clear, constructive advice for the aspects your classmates could improve. Your teacher will give you an assessment sheet.

 CD1 18

expressly definitely
reverential [ˌrevəˈrenʃl] very serious
life blood sth. that is necessary for success and survival

▶ SF 22: Listening

▶ SF 6: Doing project work
▶ SF 8: Structuring ideas
▶ LP 13: Placing emphasis on key points

Find a recording tool here:
 Webcode context-55

6 India – a Kaleidoscope

- India is the largest democracy, the 2nd most populous country and the 9th largest economy in the world.

- Four world religions originated in the Indian subcontinent: Hinduism, Buddhism, Jainism and Sikhism.

- 50 % of all Indians are below the age of 25.

Download a list of chapter vocab here: **Webcode** context-15

▶ SF 11: Analysing pictures

1 A first glimpse of India: photos and facts
Work with a partner. Choose one picture and speculate about the people you see and where and when the photo might have been taken. Link your photo to the facts about India. Present your picture in class, saying what you find most interesting and surprising.

2 Presenting India
Form groups. Imagine you are going to produce a short video clip about India for a multicultural festival at your school. Brainstorm ideas about what your audience might want to know about India, and discuss how you would present them in your clip. Share your ideas in class. Use them when you work on the Chapter Task (cf. p. 131).

C

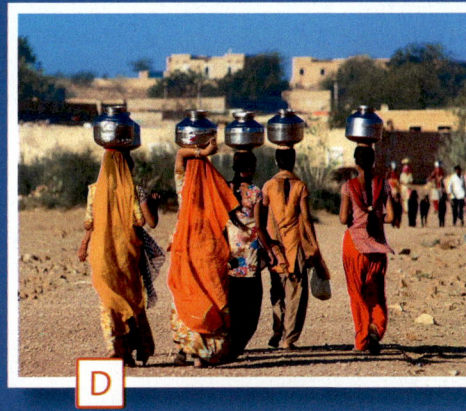

D

- The literacy rate in India is 65% among women and 82% among men.

- India is about 31% urban (as compared to 82.4% in the USA and 73% in Germany).

- Mumbai (21 million), Delhi (16 million) and Kolkata (14 million) are among the world's biggest metropolitan areas.

literacy ['lɪtərəsi] ability to read and write

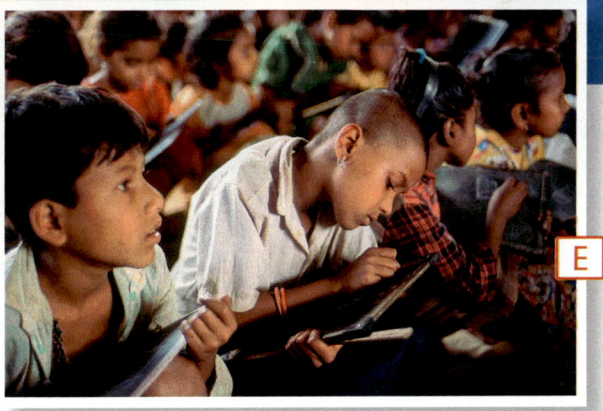

E

PREVIEW

In this chapter you will learn about India as a modern society and about its history. You will gain an insight into India's development from a former British colony into an independent nation and learn about Indian communities abroad.

Main topics

Focus on Skills: LISTENING and VIEWING

Chapter Task: Putting together a multi-media presentation about India for a multicultural festival at your school

CD2 02

Listen to an audio version of the text on the CD or download it here:

Webcode context-16

TROUBLE SPOT

Hindi = one of the official languages spoken in India
Hindu (l. 27) = a person whose religion is Hinduism

In 2001, Shahrukh Khan starred as Ashoka in the Bollywood blockbuster movie of the same name.

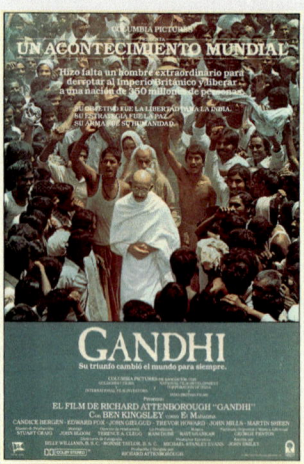

The 1982 biopic Gandhi *retells Gandhi's life from his time in South Africa to his assassination. The movie won eight Oscars.*

India then and now

India before the arrival of the Europeans

Mark Twain once referred to India as 'the cradle of the human race'. Indeed, India can look back on a long history. As early as 2500 BC large cities emerged along the Indus River. This civilization traded with Mesopotamia and Egypt and developed a distinctive culture, from which Hinduism emerged. The Mauryan   5
Empire, the first and largest empire on the Indian subcontinent, reached its peak in the 3rd century BC. Under its ruler Ashoka, Buddhism spread through-out the region. Arts and science flourished again in the 4th century AD during the Golden Age of the Gupta emperors. The concepts of zero and infinity are believed to have been developed by Indian mathematicians during this era.   10
In the 12th century AD Islamic invaders conquered northern India. Islamic rule reached its zenith during the Mughal period, which began in 1526 and led to the unification of large parts of India. It was during the Mughal era that many magnificent buildings such as the Taj Mahal were built.

India and the British Empire   15

When European trading companies arrived in India in the early 17th century to gain access to the country's wealth, the decline of the Mughal empire was accelerated. A century later, the British East India Company had become the dominant force in the subcontinent. After a massive revolt against the British in 1857 the last Mughal emperor was deposed and the British Crown took over   20
control, turning India into the largest and most profitable colony of its empire, its 'Jewel in the Crown'. British rule in India, also known as 'the Raj', lasted until 1947. During this era, the British modernized the country, but mis-management, food shortages and diseases also led to the deaths of millions of people and resentment against the colonial power. The Indian struggle for   25
independence, led by Gandhi and Nehru, culminated in 1947, when the former colony was divided into two separate countries, Hindu-dominated India and Muslim-dominated Pakistan. After Partition widespread displacement of Hindus and Muslims and sectarian violence between the two groups followed. To this day, the relationship between India and Pakistan remains tense.   30

India today

India is often described as a land of contrasts and paradoxes. It is home to ten percent of the world's millionaires, but also to one third of the world's poor. It is the world's largest democracy, but millions of its citizens are still illiterate. India is the largest country in southern Asia, yet it is densely populated with a   35
population exceeding 1.2 billion people, half of them under the age of 25. India is also one of the world's most promising new markets, but the benefits of economic growth have not yet reached all Indians. In fact, India's growth poses many new challenges. India will need to feed, house and educate the next generation of Indians, who will both contribute to and benefit from the   40
country's success. In the next two decades, India will see a massive migration from rural areas to the cities. The demand for energy will increase as future city dwellers will need electricity, water and mass transit. Today 400 million Indians are not connected to the electricity grid. The Indian government aims to increase power generation by 700% in the next 25 years. Will the new India   45
manage to meet these challenges successfully?

► SF 2: Learning new words

1 Paraphrasing key terms

Paraphrase the following key terms, which are used frequently when talking about India:

1 Indian subcontinent
2 colonial power
3 the Jewel in the Crown
4 the Raj
5 Independence
6 Partition

2 Words in use

Find the <mark>highlighted</mark> words in the text to match the definitions:

1 the act of joining parts of a country together
2 a situation when people do not have enough to eat
3 the act of forcing people to leave the area where they live
4 a violent confrontation between different groups in society
5 increase in business activities
6 movement of a large number of people

3 Prepositions

► LP 19: Collocations

Complete the following sentences about India with the correct prepositions. Look at the text if necessary:

1 Gandhi united millions of Indians in their struggle … independence.
2 India is home … about 1.56 million millionaires.
3 There is great demand … highly-skilled IT professionals.
4 Indian citizens have started to show growing resentment … inequality.

4 Verbs and nouns

► LP 19: Collocations

a Many verbs in English have a tendency to form partnerships with nouns (as in *make a decision* or *find a solution*). These are called 'collocations'. Scan the text for the noun *challenge*: which verbs does *challenge* collocate with?

b Search for more examples of verbs collocating with *challenge* using a monolingual dictionary or a corpus, e.g. the British National Corpus (BNC). Illustrate each collocation with an example sentence.

Find an online dictionary here:
 Webcode context-52

c Do the same for the nouns *access* and *control*.

5 Images of India

► SF 38: Writing a
well-structured text

India has been described as 'the cradle of the human race' and as 'a land of contrasts and paradoxes'. Write two paragraphs in which you explain the two images. Choose appropriate vocabulary from the text and the tasks above.

India's past: echoes and reflections

A1 India's UNESCO World Heritage sites

The following WebQuest will take you on a virtual journey across India through time and space.

Qutb Minar

Mountain Railways of India

Sanchi

Taj Mahal

Ellora Caves

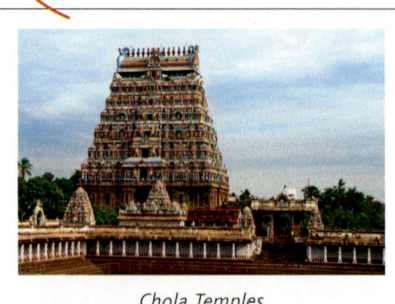

Chola Temples

▶ SF 5: Doing research

▶ SF 24: Giving a presentation

A WebQuest

a Form six groups. Each group works on one site. Go to the UNESCO World Heritage website and find information, videos, etc. there about the history and cultural significance of your site. Present your findings in class, explaining what makes them places of outstanding universal value.

b Together create a timeline of Indian history based on the information you have collected.

A2 Colonizers and colonized

To feel that somewhere among those millions you have left a little justice or happiness or prosperity, a sense of manliness or moral dignity, a spring of patriotism, a dawn of intellectual enlightenment
5 or a stirring of duty where it did not before exist – that is enough, that is the Englishman's justification in India.

Lord Curzon, Viceroy of India from 1899 to 1905, in his farewell speech on leaving India

— ANALYSIS ◀

Comparing a quote and photos
Study the photos and the quote carefully. Then prepare an oral statement in which you explain what they tell you about the relationship between the British and the Indians during the British Raj. **SUPPORT** ▶ p. 210

A3 The British Empire from an Indian perspective

Gurcharan Das

In this text you will learn about the impact of the British Empire from an Indian perspective. Certain parts of the text have been left out (cf. gap A, etc.) – don't worry about them on your first reading.

[A] Britain gave us democracy, the rule of law, an independent judiciary and a free press. It built railways, canals, and harbors, but it could not bring about an industrial revolution. It could not raise economic growth or lift people out of poverty. It could not avert famines. The truth is the Raj was economically incompetent. It just did not
5 know how to 'develop' a country. Had it known it, Britain could have gained much from having a larger market for its manufactures. It introduced modern education and helped create a small middle class, but it did not educate the mass of the people. This was its other failure and linked to the first, for development is not possible without mass literacy.

10 [B] Had India remained united, billions could have been saved in defense expenditures and invested instead in improving the lives of ordinary people in both countries. Whether an undivided India could have survived the Muslim-Hindu animosity is another counterfactual of history.

[C] Many Indians despair over the divisiveness of caste and would prefer to wish it
15 away. However, the hold of the Indian way of life is also a bulwark against the onslaught of the global culture. The British gave us the English language, which allowed us to converse with our compatriots in a country with 16 official languages. However, English also divided us into two nations – the 10 percent elite who learned English and shut out the 90 percent who did not. Knowing English today,
20 though, gives Indians a competitive advantage in the global economy and is an important factor in our nascent success in the information economy.

[D] In school we had learned that the Indian subcontinent was a triangle with the Himalayas, the Arabian Sea, and the Bay of Bengal as its sides. The Himalayas ran from east to west and cut off the cold winds from the north. This allowed agriculture

4 **dawn** time of day when light first appears
enlightenment process of understanding sth.
5 **stirring of sth.** ['stɜːrɪŋ] beginning of sth.
viceroy ['vaɪsrɔɪ] person representing the British monarch in India

▶ SF 11: Analysing pictures

1 **judiciary** [dʒuːˈdɪʃəri] *Gerichtsbarkeit*
4 **avert sth.** [əˈvɜːt] prevent sth.
famine ['fæmɪn] long period of time without food
6 **manufactures** (here) goods made in large numbers
10 **expenditure** [ɪkˈspendɪtʃə] amount of money spent
12 **animosity** [ˌænɪˈmɒsəti] strong feeling of hatred
13 **counterfactual** sth. that has not happened but might have under different conditions
14 **divisiveness** [dɪˈvaɪsɪvnɪs] force that splits people into different groups
15 **bulwark** ['bʊlwək] *(fml)* person or thing that protects or defends sth.
17 **16 official languages** 23 languages are now recognized for official use at state level
21 **nascent** ['neɪsənt] beginning to exist

27 **Aryans** [ˈeəriənz] ancient race that moved into India from Central Asia around 1500 BC
Mughals [ˈmuːgaːlz] Muslim dynasty that conquered northern India in the 16th century
31 **infuriating** (adj) making you extremely angry

to prosper and created wealth, but it also attracted barbarian invaders from the north. 25
It gave us a warm climate so that no one who came wanted to leave. First came the
Aryans, then the Turks, the Afghans, and the Mughals. They came, they stayed, and
they merged and became Indian. To accommodate them we merely created a new sub-
caste each time and they became part of our diversity. The British did not. But now
that they have been gone for more than fifty years, our confidence is restored, espe- 30
cially among the young. Our infuriating diversity may also be of some value. Because
we have always learned to live with pluralism, it is possible that we might be better
prepared to negotiate the diversity of the global economy.

From: *India Unbound*, 2001

▶ SF 10: Working with closed test formats

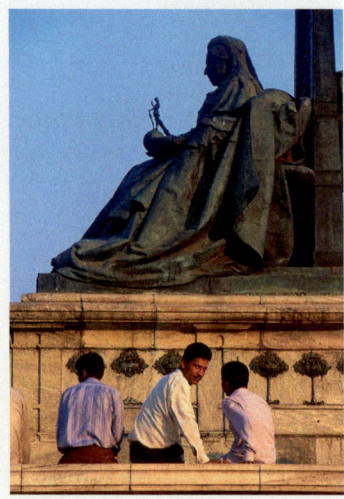

Statue of Queen Victoria in Kolkata

▶ SF 41: Mediation of written and oral texts

▶ SF 9: Paraphrasing

COMPREHENSION ◀

1 Filling in the gaps
Four passages from the text above have been omitted. For each of the four
gaps (A, B, C, D) select the most appropriate passage from the list below.
Note that there are six passages to choose from. Compare with a partner.
1 Although Indians gloss over it, the British Raj was the most important
  event in the making of modern India – for better and for worse.
2 As a subdivisional officer, my father was an important official of the
  British Raj.
3 The British gave us a hundred years of peace – the so-called Pax Britannica
  – but they also consciously pursued a divide-and-rule policy which made
  Hindus and Muslims conscious of their separate identities. This led to a
  tragic division of the country.
4 The British were different from our other invaders. They did not merge
  with us and remained aloof* to the end. This shook our self-confidence.

*aloof distant, impersonal

5 The Raj gave us modern values and institutions, but it did not interfere
  with our ancient traditions and our religion. India has therefore preserved
  its spiritual heritage and the old way of life continues.
6 Western education provided the stimulus for the most dramatic change
  in the minds of Indians in a thousand years.

2 Aspects of British rule
List the positive and the negative aspects mentioned by Gurcharan Das
about British rule in India.

3 Mediation (English ➔ German)
In your History class, you are discussing the legacy of colonialism. You have
read this text and offer to summarize the main points raised in the text in
German. Make notes and practise your talk.

ANALYSIS ◀

4 A critical view of British rule in India
Work with a partner. Explain the following quotes from the text and point
out what they tell you about the legacy of the British Raj.
1 'The Raj was economically incompetent.' (l. 4)
2 'Had India remained united, billions could have been saved in defense
  expenditures.' (ll. 10–11)
3 'English … divided us into two nations.' (l. 18)
4 'Our infuriating diversity may … be of some value.' (l. 32)

BEYOND THE TEXT ◀

5 **CHALLENGE** ▶ **The legacy of the Raj**

Discuss whether the British Raj was beneficial for India, both during the time of the Raj itself and following Independence. Justify your opinion by referring to the texts you have examined. **SUPPORT** ▶ p. 210

A4 Gandhi remembered   *Chetan Bhagat*

- **3–2–1 BRAINSTORMING** Write down three things you know about Mahatma Gandhi, two reasons why he is considered very important today, and one question you have about him. In class, share your ideas and create a mind map about Gandhi.

Find a mindmapping tool here:
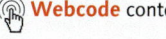 **Webcode** context-53

■ FACT FILE

Gandhi and India's struggle for independence

Mohandas Karamchand Gandhi was born in Porbandar in Gujarat in 1869 to Hindu parents. At the age of 19, he was sent to London to become a barrister.

He returned to India in 1891 to practice law. Two years later, he moved to
5 Durban, South Africa, where he accepted a job at an Indian law firm.

Gandhi was shocked at the way Indians were treated there. He became actively involved in fighting for their rights and developed his philosophy of non-violence, *satyagraha* ('devotion to truth'). After 20 years of fighting for the rights of Indians and Africans, Gandhi returned to India in 1915.
10 Gandhi continued his fight against colonial rule in India by organizing peaceful protests.

Millions of Indians followed him. His campaigns for independence ultimately led the British to withdraw from India in 1947.

But independence from British rule came at a price: the Partition of the sub-
15 continent. In 1948 Gandhi, who had been opposed to Partition, was shot by a young Hindu fanatic who was angry at him for his tolerance towards Muslims.

Gandhi's philosophy of non-violent resistance has inspired millions of people around the world, and even today the Mahatma ('Great Soul') is admired for his courage, will-power, strength and determination in fighting for a just cause.

1 *Add more details to your mind map.*
2 *Use the mind map to give a one-minute speech about Gandhi.*

India celebrates Independence Day.

■ TROUBLE SPOT

fanatic (l. 16) = noun (person who is extremely enthusiastic about sth.)
fanatical = adjective (enthusiastic)

In 2012, Chetan Bhagat, one of the most popular Indian novelists writing in English today, wrote the following fictional letter to Gandhi.

Dear Gandhiji,

You left us more than sixty years ago. If you were still around, you would have been more than 140 years old. However, we have not forgotten you. You are on every bank-note and most stamps. There are many statues of you. Prestigious roads in almost
5 every city are named after you. Our politicians try to model themselves on you. They wear the fabric you promoted, they quote you at every instance, they've got a photo-graph of you in their offices and some even eat and live like you. There are books, TV programmes and movies about you. Seriously, you'd be impressed at how much we still adore you. However, there are things that won't make you feel proud. The India
10 you spent all your life making free is far from free. True, the white guys are gone. But there are still millions of poor people. After sixty-plus years, we are still among the poorest nations on earth. This lack of money leads to a lot of problems in healthcare, infrastructure and education. Many children still don't go to a good school. Those who

1 **Gandhiji** in many Indian languages '-ji' can be added to names to show respect

■ TROUBLE SPOT

fabric ['fæbrɪk] (l. 6) = material from which clothes are made
Fabrik = company, firm

■ TROUBLE SPOT

programme (l. 8) = sth. that people watch on TV or listen to on the radio
Fernsehprogramm, -kanal = TV channel

Election campaign in India

do don't get into good colleges. And those who go to college don't get good jobs. We need to get rich, and fast. Not only to make more schools and colleges, but also because most Indian problems are linked to the lack of money. Yet, it is considered un-Indian to think that way. The young generation, which thinks like that, is considered materialistic and greedy. The older generation takes the moral high ground – slowness in work is termed patience, non-stop discussion and no action is called careful consider-ation and lack of improvement in stand-ards of living is countered with claims about the need to live with austerity. And yes, in many cases, politicians who speak like this claim to be your fans.

The younger generation wishes you could come down for one day and clarify these points. Is progress un-Indian? Is change bad? Is a desire to see my country as rich as some other nations materialistic? Is getting things done fast impatience? If you blessed our purpose of building a developed India, the job would become so much easier.

The young generation needs you down here for something else, too. We have a new battle here just like the one you fought with the British. The enemy is not as clear as it was in your case – the white people. Our enemy is the old school of thought, or rather, the people who defend the old school of thought. They do this in the name of antique Indian policies, culture and values. You could help identify this enemy more clearly. Many people who are at the helm of affairs now have served India for decades, maybe with good intentions.

But obviously they don't want to accept they screwed up. We wish they would, though, and we'd have a national day of shame. It won't be easy, but from there we could make a new beginning. But they won't, for they are in power. And to defend themselves and their ways, they don't mind crushing the aspirations, ideas and talent of an entire generation.

Yes, there is a lot of talk of India being a young nation and about youth power. How-ever, youth power is the biggest myth going around India right now. Of course, the youth has spending power – we can buy enough SIM cards, sneakers and fizzy drinks to keep many MNCs in business. But we do not have the power to change things. Can the youth get a new college set up? Can the youth ask the government to provide tax incentives to MNCs to relocate jobs to smaller towns? No way. We are wooed, used, but seldom heard. If you came down, you could unite us. You used religious festivals as social events and propagated your cause. You understood that people need enter-tainment to bind them. Perhaps we could integrate colleges in the same way, link all colleges maybe for their annual festivals and the message of change could be channelled through them. We have amazing technology such as the Internet now. You would use it so well. If the youth unites, there could actually be youth power.

With our purpose blessed, enemy identified and youth united, we could take the first steps towards the new Indian revolution. After all, China had one and only after that did they get on the path of true progress.

15
20
25
30
35
40
45
50
55
60

19 **lack of sth.** state of not having sth.
23 **greedy** wanting more money
take the moral high ground claim that your arguments are morally better than other people's arguments
29 **austerity** [ɒsˈterəti] situation when people do not have a lot of money
42 **at the helm of sth.** in charge of sth.
44 **screw up** (infml) do sth. badly
52 **MNC = multinational company** company operating all over the world
53 **tax incentive** [ˌɪnˈsentɪv] *Steuer-anreiz*
54 **woo sb.** try to get sb.'s support
56 **propagate your cause** [ˈprɒpəgeɪt] spread your ideas

But if it is not feasible for you to come back, we'll have to try to bring about change
65 ourselves. If we can be inspired to do that, we can say we have not forgotten you and
understand the meaning of your birthday. We hope you had a good one up there!
Lots of love, The Younger Generation

64 **feasible** that can be achieved

'Letter to Bapu from Generation Next on His Birthday', *What Young India Wants*, 2012

COMPREHENSION

1 True/false statements

Write six true/false statements on a piece of
paper. Swap your statements with a partner.
Check your partner's statements, correct the
false ones and check each other's solutions.

2 Finishing sentences

Finish the sentences with ideas from the text.
1 If Gandhi lived in India today, he would be
shocked to hear that …
2 Young Indians need Gandhi to …
3 Gandhi's message to young Indians would
be …

▶ SF 10: Working
with closed test
formats

LANGUAGE AWARENESS ◀

3 Informal style

Chetan Bhagat often uses informal language in his letter.
a Put the following examples of informal English into formal English:
1 'If you were still around.' (l. 1)
2 'True, the white guys are gone.' (l. 10)
3 'But obviously they don't want to accept they screwed up.' (l. 44)
4 'No way.' (l. 54)
b Scan the letter for at least three more examples of informal style
and put them into formal style.
c Explain why Bhagat uses informal diction in this text.

▶ LP 11: Using the right register

BEYOND THE TEXT ◀

4 YOU CHOOSE ▶ Youth empowerment

Choose one of the following writing tasks. ▶ LANGUAGE HELP

a An Indian newspaper has asked young
people to write about their Indian dream
and contribute a text for their online blog.
Imagine you are a teenager growing up in
India. Write a blog entry. Use ideas for
your blog from Bhagat's letter. You could
start like this: 'I dream of an India that …,
a country that stands up to …, an India
Mahatma Gandhi would be proud of …'

 OR

b '[Young people] do
not have the power
to change things.'
(l. 50) Comment on
this statement with
reference to the
community *you*
live in.

LANGUAGE HELP
• What I would like to see is …
• If we put all our efforts together …
• We have the potential to …
• One major obstacle is …
• If we want to see improvements, we have to …
• Our main contribution could be …

▶ SF 37: Doing a creative
writing task
▶ SF 38: Writing a well-
structured text

🎧 **CD2** 03

Ela Gandhi

▶ SF 22: Listening

Nelson Mandela (1918–2013) was a civil rights activist in South Africa who fought against apartheid. Inspired by Gandhi, he became a leader of the African National Congress (ANC) and was sent to prison after protesting against racial inequality. When he was released in 1990 after 27 years in prison, he continued his fight – and succeeded. In the 1994 presidential elections all races were finally allowed to vote, and Nelson Mandela won the election and became president. Like Gandhi, Mandela is regarded as a role model of tolerance and reconciliation around the world today.

🟥 LISTENING **FOCUS ON SKILLS**

Listening to a radio interview

In this section you are going to focus on how to listen to a radio interview. Ela Gandhi, Mahatma Gandhi's granddaughter, is a peace activist and politician. She grew up in Durban, South Africa, and knew both Mahatma Gandhi and Nelson Mandela personally. You are going to listen to part of a radio interview with her.

1 Before listening

Sometimes you may have an idea what a radio report or an interview you are about to listen to might be about. In this case it is useful to collect some words that you might expect to hear. This will make it easier to understand the interview.

Before you listen to the interview with Ela Gandhi, read the Fact File below left and brainstorm what an interview with someone who knew both Gandhi and Mandela might be about. Make a list of keywords you expect to hear.

2 Listening for gist

Listen to the interview for the first time to get the gist. Before you do, read the task below carefully so you know what information to listen out for.

> What is Ela Gandhi speaking about? Choose the correct answers:
> Ela Gandhi is speaking about:
> 1 Her childhood memories in South Africa.
> 2 Nelson Mandela's visit to India.
> 3 Similarities between Mahatma Gandhi and Nelson Mandela.
> 4 The situation in South Africa when Mandela was released from prison.
> 5 The political situation in South Africa after Nelson Mandela's death.

3 Listening for detail

Listen to the interview again and pay attention to details. In the task below you will be asked to complete sentences while listening. When doing a task like this, you are usually not expected to write down exactly what you have heard. You may use your own words to show that you have understood that particular part of the text.

> Listen again and complete the sentences:
> 1 Gandhi and Mandela were capable of inspiring people because …
> 2 Both Gandhi's and Mandela's ideal was to …
> 3 When Mandela visited Gandhi's home in India, he refused to … because …
> 4 The fact that Nelson Mandela invited the man who had demanded the death penalty for him symbolizes …
> 5 When Mandela was released from prison, South Africans hoped that … despite the fact that … .

Tales from modern India

B1 Urbanization in India: the big picture

net new employment *Nettoneu-beschäftigung (= Differenz aus der Anzahl neu geschaffener Arbeits-plätze und der Anzahl beendeter Arbeitsverhältnisse)*
residential space area consisting of houses rather than offices

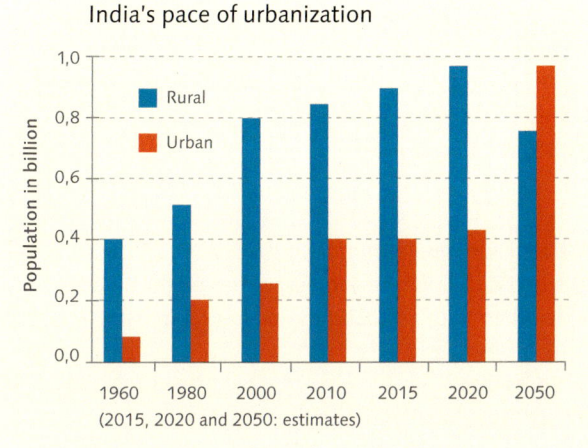

India's pace of urbanization

- Rural
- Urban

Population in billion

1960 1980 2000 2010 2015 2020 2050
(2015, 2020 and 2050: estimates)

FACT FILE

India in 2030
- **590 million** people will live in cities, nearly twice the population of the USA today.
- **70%** of net new employment will be generated in cities.
- **91 million** urban households will be middle-class, up from **22 million** today.
- **68** cities will have a population of 1 million plus, up from **42** today; Europe has 35 today.
- **700–900 million m²** of commercial and residential space will be built – or a new Chicago every year.
- **2.5 billion m²** of roads will be built, 20 times the amount added in the past decade.
- **7,400 km** of metros and subways will be constructed – 20 times the capacity added in the past decade.

From: Equitymaster, 10 October 2012

COMPREHENSION ◀

1 Indian urbanization
Use the bar chart above to describe the process of urbanization in India.
SUPPORT ▶ p. 210

▶ SF 12: Analysing charts and graphs

ANALYSIS ◀

2 Key figures
Work with a partner and analyse the consequences of urbanization for the future of India. One partner focuses on the opportunities that urbanization provides, one on the dangers. Use the key figures provided in the Fact File as a starting point. Exchange your ideas with each other afterwards and discuss them.

B2 Life in a megacity

Kolkata is one of the fastest-growing megacities in the world. The poster on the right is of the documentary film The Revolutionary Optimists *(2013), which follows several young children growing up in Kolkata.*

ANALYSIS ◀

1 The poster
Study the poster. Speculate about the girl: who is she, what may she be doing? Use the data and facts from **B1**.

BEYOND THE TEXT ◀

2 Creative writing
Use your ideas to write down what the girl may be saying.

HOW FAR WOULD YOU GO TO CHANGE YOUR WORLD?

THE**REVOLUTIONARY**OPTIMISTS

▶ SF 11: Analysing pictures
▶ SF 37: Doing a creative writing task

DVD

feature film main film with a story

▶ SF 23: Analysing a film

VIEWING **FOCUS ON SKILLS**

Watching a film trailer

In the previous section you examined a poster. Now you are going to watch the trailer for the documentary film The Revolutionary Optimists *(2013). A film trailer is a short film advertising a feature film or documentary. A trailer introduces audiences to the film it advertises and tries to get them interested in watching the whole film. Trailers use various techniques to create interest and grab the viewers' attention. When dealing with a film trailer you should therefore pay special attention not only to the story of the film and the actors, but also to camera work, visual elements, sound and music.*

1 Before viewing
Before you watch the trailer for *The Revolutionary Optimists*, speculate about what you expect to see in it and how the subject matter might be presented. Use the notes you made when you discussed the poster (cf. p. 123).

2 While viewing: first impressions
 a While watching the first time, take notes on the following aspects:
 • *characters and *setting (who do you see? where are they?)
 • actions (what are people doing in the film?)
 Share your findings.
 b What would you say the documentary film is about?

3 While viewing: camera work
 a Watch the trailer again, this time without sound so that you can concentrate on the camera work. Choose the correct answers:

1 The field size predominantly used in the trailer is			
a long shots	b full shots	c medium shots	d close-ups

2 The camera angle predominantly used in the trailer is		
a high angle	b low angle	c eye level

3 The type of camera movement predominantly used in the trailer is			
a zooming	b tilting	c tracking	d panning

 b Explain the function of each of these techniques in this trailer.

4 Analysing the voice-over
Watch the trailer a third time, this time with sound. Concentrate on the intertitles and the voice-over. Make notes on the information they provide and explain how they contribute to the trailer.

5 Evaluating the trailer
Look through your findings in tasks **1–4** and discuss whether the trailer is successful in creating interest in the film.

B3 Celebrating Indian culture

*Sanjeev Bhaskar is a well-known British comedian and broadcaster. In 2007
he made a four-part television series for the BBC, India with Sanjeev Bhaskar,
in which he travelled back to the country of his ancestors.*

─────────────────────────────────── BEFORE VIEWING ◀

1 PLACEMAT The importance of Holi
On 15 March 2014, the President of India, Shri Pranab Mukherjee, published
the following message on the occasion of one of the most important festivals
celebrated in India, Holi:

> On the happy occasion of Holi, I extend my greetings and good wishes to all my
> fellow citizens. As spring arrives, this festival of colours brings with it a joyous
> celebration of the rejuvenation of nature and ushers in renewed faith in peaceful
> co-existence. Holi not only brings joy and gaiety in our lives but also provides an
> opportunity to strengthen the bonds of friendship and brotherhood among
> people of all faiths. May this festival reinforce the multi-coloured hues of our
> extraordinary heritage and bring peace and prosperity to our Motherland.
>
> From: the website of the President of India, 16 March 2014

Why are religious festivals important to people around the world? Generate
ideas in a placemat activity. Include ideas from President Mukherjee's
message to the Indian people.

▶ CC 1: Cultural awareness

─────────────────────────────────── COMPREHENSION ◀

2 First viewing: no sound
You are going to watch a scene from *India with Sanjeev Bhaskar* showing
Bhaskar celebrating Holi. Watch the clip without sound first and take notes
on how Holi is celebrated.

 DVD

▶ SF 23: Analysing a film

3 Second viewing: with sound
Watch the clip again, now with sound, and take notes on how Bhaskar
explains the importance of Holi today.

─────────────────────────────────── ANALYSIS ◀

4 Third viewing: analysing camera work and sound
Watch the clip for a third time and analyse how the camera work and the
soundtrack contribute to creating Bhaskar's perspective of Holi.

─────────────────────────────────── BEYOND THE TEXT ◀

5 The meaning of Holi
Research the religious side of Holi and explain its origins and meaning.

▶ SF 5: Doing research

6 Mediation (German ➔ English)
Holi has become a global phenomenon in recent years. It is even celebrated
in Germany today. An Indian friend of yours wants to know why. You have
come across the following interview with Maxim Derenko (cf. p. 126), who
started organizing Holi festivals in Germany in 2011. Based on this interview,
write an email to your friend answering his question. SUPPORT ▶ p. 210

▶ SF 41: Mediation of written
and oral texts

Wie kam die Idee, das indische Holi-Festival in Deutschland zu veranstalten?
Mein Kollege und Mitveranstalter, Jasper Hellmann, war 2011 in Indien auf Durch-
reise. Er war beim ursprünglichen Holi-Festival selbst vor Ort und war total begeis-
tert davon. Bei seiner Rückkehr steckte er mich und Max Riedel, den dritten Mann
im Bunde, mit der Idee an, ein Holi-Festival in Deutschland zu veranstalten. 5

*In Indien ist das Holi-Fest ein hinduistisches Frühlingsfest. Wie kommt es, dass es trotz
fehlenden traditionellen Hintergrunds in Deutschland so gut aufgenommen wird?*
Die Reaktionen und Erfahrungen aus dem letzten Jahr haben gezeigt, dass die
Kernelemente des Holi-Festes [...] bei den Leuten gut ankommen. Bei dieser Fest-
lichkeit steht die Gleichheit aller Menschen im Vordergrund, denn in Indien werden 10
die sogenannten Kasten aufgehoben. In Deutschland gibt es zwar keine Kasten, jedoch soziale Unterschiede. Des Weiteren wird Toleranz und gegenseitiger Respekt
großgeschrieben. Die vielen bunten Farben spielen einen weiteren Faktor beim Festival. Die Symbolik für die Gleichheit und die Besonderheit dieses Festivals sind die
Farben, diese sollen alle Menschen gleich (bunt) machen. 15

Habt ihr mit dem Erfolg der ersten Holi-Festivals im letzten Jahr gerechnet?
Wir haben natürlich nicht mit einem so durchschlagenden Erfolg gerechnet. Eigentlich war die Idee ein kleines Open-Air-Festival für einige Leute zu machen, in diesem
Bereich haben wir auch schon Erfahrungen in Berlin gesammelt. Ein solches Festival gab es zuvor noch nie in Deutschland. [...] 20

Wird sich das Holi-Festival etablieren können oder handelt es um einen aktuellen Trend?
Die Resonanz des letzten Jahres hat gezeigt, dass der Hype ungebrochen ist und die
Nachfrage immer noch sehr hoch ist. Wir haben unsere Tour für dieses Jahr durch-
geplant und waren innerhalb weniger Stunden in fast allen Städten ausverkauft.

From: 'Holi Festivals – der neue Trend?!', *ARTikel*, 1 July 2013

📍 CULTURE SPOT

'[Indian truck art is] an art form that makes
journeys through the dusty highways of India
incredible in more ways than one. With a kaleidoscope of bright paints, motifs, typography
and some unique couplets, these Indian trucks
take you on a rather colourful journey of
diverse cultures and beliefs of the country.'

From: the website of Horn Please, 2012

Indian truck art

1 Describe the trucks in the photos.

2 Explain how Indian truck art relates to what you have
learned about India in this chapter so far.

Indians abroad

C1 The Indian diaspora

1 BRAINSTORMING **Moving to foreign countries**
Work in pairs and brainstorm possible reasons why people move to foreign countries today.

2 Locating the Indian diaspora
The word *diaspora* describes communities of people who live outside their country of origin. India has the second largest diaspora comprising around 30 million ethnic Indians living in more than 100 countries.

  a Work in pairs. Each pair focuses on one of the regions or countries on the right. Research the history, size and role of the Indian diaspora in the area you are dealing with and make a poster summarizing your findings.
    SUPPORT ▶ p.211

  b GALLERY WALK Present your posters in a gallery walk activity.

Countries/regions
- United Kingdom
- United States
- Canada
- The Middle East (UAE, Saudi Arabia, Oman, Kuwait)
- South Africa
- East Africa (Tanzania, Kenya)
- South-East Asia (Malaysia, Singapore)
- South America and the Caribbean (Guyana, Suriname, Trinidad)
- Pacific Islands (Fiji)
- Indian Ocean Islands (Mauritius, Reunion)

Find a map showing the regions here:
🖐 **Webcode** context–17

Find a tool to make your poster here: 🖐 **Webcode** context-50

C2 A taste of the Indian diaspora   *Michelle Warwicker*

When it comes to food, the Indians of the diaspora have not only absorbed influences from the countries they live in but have also influenced the cuisine of their new countries.

Bunny chow has nothing to do with rabbits. [...] It is made with a half or a quarter loaf of bread, hollowed out and filled with steaming curry cooked with meat or beans. A traditional bunny chow (or simply 'bunny' if you are in Durban in South Africa where the dish originated) is made with mutton,
5 chicken, mince, lamb or kidney beans. The loaf is crusty enough to hold the saucy filling in a parcel, and the bread from the centre is placed on top to keep the curry warm and provide diners with something to scoop with. Cheap, tasty and filling, bunny chow is one of the most popular takeaway meals in its home city. It is sold in small
10 diners and takeaway kiosks and is rarely even served with a fork. [...]

  Durban is home to a very large population of people of Indian ethnic origin, and the dish fuses Indian and African influences. Bunny chow may owe its origins to the Indian immigrants who arrived in South Africa in the second half of the 19th century to be put
15 to work on sugar plantations. One theory is that they began to use a sturdy bread loaf so they could transport curry to the plantations to eat during the day. Today bunny chow has spread to other South African cities, but the original and for many people the best is still found in Durban.

From: 'What is bunny chow?', BBC, 20 January 2014

1 **chow** [tʃaʊ] *(sl)* food

Bunny chow

─────────────────── COMPREHENSION ◀

1 Thinking about food and culture
Outline how bunny chow reflects the Indian diaspora experience.

▶ EE 1: Eating in and out

─────────────────── BEYOND THE TEXT ◀

2 Fusion cuisine
Discuss to what extent fusion food is an integral part of modern society.

C3 **English lessons**   *Shauna Singh Baldwin*

Shauna Singh Baldwin is an Indo-Canadian author. Born in Montreal, she grew up in Delhi and went to the USA to study. The following short story is about an Indian woman who has moved to the USA.

I told Tony – that is what he likes me to call him in America – I told Tony I will take English lessons till my green card comes. Valerie says there are English teachers who will teach me for free and she will find a good one who will come to the apartment so that I do not have to go outside. Tony says OK, and then he leaves for work at the card-board factory.   5

I pick up the breakfast dishes and Suryavir's toys. No one can say his name here – I will tell them at the school to call him Johnny, like Tony's Johnny Walker whisky.

The phone rings and my heart starts to pound – *dharak dharak*. Our answering machine message has Valerie's voice, and I follow the words with her accent.

'We're naat here right naow, but if you leeev a mehsej, weell get right baak to you.'   10
But it is only Valerie herself. 'Pick up the phone, Kanwaljit. I want to know if you're home so I can drop the kids off for the day.'

'Hello,' I say. 'I am here. You come.'

Valerie is a nice person, but you cannot be too careful. Tony says we cannot meet anyone from India till my green card comes, so Valerie is the only one who sees me.   15
I call her Grocery Store Valerie to myself, because she answered my card in the grocery store, and now I babysit her two strong and unruly boys. What farmers they would have made in Punjab. My son is not so strong. More than two years of women's company. I spoilt him while we were waiting for Tony to get his citizenship, but what was I to do? If I had disciplined him, Tony's parents would have been   20
angry – he is their only grandson.

Valerie's boys don't listen to love or scolding. But they go to school, and Valerie says it is the law. I have to send Suryavir to school. So I went there with her to register him and on the form I wrote the address I had memorized from Valerie's cheques, not ours. Still, Tony was worried in case anyone who might report us saw me. He makes   25
me dress in pants so that I look Mexican, and says it is only a short while now. I hope so.

But first I will learn English. It's not that I don't understand it, but it has too many words. Get it. Put it. I am stuffed. Pick up your stuff. On the other hand. Hand it to you. I learned English in school, passed my matriculation examination, too. We   30
learned whole passages of translation by heart – I had a good memory. Now Tony says I must speak English to pass my immigration interview and to memorize my amnesty story.

A knock. Someone is standing far away from the peephole – why are they doing that? Oh, it's Valerie; she was bending down to tie a shoelace for little Mark.   35

'Hello, hello. Come in. How are you?'

Valerie has found an English teacher who will come to the apartment and teach me for free. But Tony and I are afraid. This English teacher is from India and we didn't want to meet any people from India.

Valerie said she told the teacher I am Tony's girlfriend and that Suryavir is our son.   40
She said the English teacher was surprised. Indian couples do not usually live to-gether, she told Valerie. Tony says to tell Valerie we don't need this teacher. But I took her phone number to please Valerie. I may call her just to speak in Punjabi for a while.

I told Valerie I will change my name. I asked her to call me Kelly. No one here can say Kanwaljit. And Kanwaljit is left far away in Amritsar before the fire.   45

2 **green card** ['--] document that allows sb. to work legally in the USA

7 **Johnny Walker whisky** US brand of whisky

18 **Punjab** [pʌnˈdʒɑːb] region in north-western India, largely populated by Sikhs

22 **scold sb.** speak angrily to sb. who has misbehaved

29 **stuffed** *(adj)* full from eating

30 **matriculation examination** exam taken in the final year of school

Some nights I lie next to Tony, here in America where I live like a worm avoiding the sunlight, and I wonder if he knows. And is it only because it was his brother that he does not sense that another man's body has come between us, or is it that he cannot remember the fire we felt in those early days? We only had three weeks in which
50 Suryavir was made. Then he was gone.

If I had been able to return to my parents until he told me to come to America, I would not have been so weak. But to do so would have smelled of disgrace, and I am not shameless. Nor was it a matter of a month or two. Tony told me after six months, when I was becoming big with his son; it would take him two more years.

55 I tell myself it is not only another man's body that invades our bed, but another woman's too. And yet, that is different. I hear her tearful voice on our answering machine. Her anger follows us from city to city – Fremont, Dallas, Houston, Miami, New York, Chicago – threatening to report us to Immigration. He lived with her for two years, shared her bed, paid her our life savings for a marriage certificate. I will ask
60 the English teacher how to say, 'Is not two years of our life enough? Is not my worm existence, my unacknowledged wifehood, enough for you? Enough that I call myself his girlfriend, my son his bastard?'

But she does not have form, no substance in our bed, I cannot imagine him with her black body – and if I can, what of it? Many men pay prostitutes. This one's price
65 was higher and she lasted longer. And he got his green card after two years. Thus am I here.

The other man in bed with us – he has form. He looks like Tony, only younger. And he still laughs at me, waving pictures of Tony with her. Telling me Tony left me for an untouchable, a *hubshi*. Threatening to tell my parents if I would not open my legs to
70 him.

I did. *Rubba-merey*, I did.

I thought some force would come upon us then and tear him from my flesh before the act was done. Save me, as the virtue of Dropadi was saved. And it did. Too late for virtue but soon enough for vengeance.

75 The police came looking for him. Oh, not for my protection – no. They were rounding up all Sikh boys between the ages of fifteen and twenty-five for 'questioning'. Tony's parents knew what was in store and they hid him in the servant's quarter, a concrete room on the flat roof of the house.

They told the police he was with Tony in America. That made them angry. One
80 sinewy fellow with a whisky smell took a can of gasoline and slowly, as we marched from the rooms around, and as Suryavir's eyes grew larger, poured it in a steady dribble all round the centre courtyard. They all walked to the door and, almost as an afterthought, the sinewy policeman threw a lit match and the world exploded from silence into horror.

85 I took no chances. I gave Suryavir to Tony's mother and then climbed out of the back window. His father was blinded by tears and I pushed him after them. Then I ran up the narrow steep staircase to the servant's quarter on the roofs.

And I locked it.

And ran back through lung-searing smoke and purifying flame. I was given venge-
90 ance, and I took it as my due. But still he comes between us – the half-dead only half a world away.

I called the English teacher today. She speaks Punjabi with a city accent. I will have to ask Tony, but I think it will be, like Americans say, 'fine, fine' for her to come and teach me.

■ **FACT FILE**

The Sikhs
Since the formation of India, many Sikhs (l. 76) have demanded a separate Sikh state in Punjab. During the 1980s militancy reached a peak, leading to an attack by Indian forces on the Golden Temple of Amritsar, Punjab (l. 45) – the Sikhs' holiest temple – and the subsequent assassination of the prime minister, Indira Gandhi.

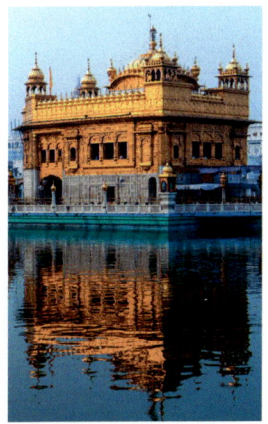

The Golden Temple of Amritsar

---

52 **disgrace** loss of respect
61 **unacknowledged** (*adj*) not publicly recognized
69 **hubshi** (here) black (originally Punjabi/Hindi for 'Ethiopian')
71 **rubba-merey** (Punjabi/Hindi) oh my God
73 **Dropadi** popular heroine in Hindu mythology who is regarded as a role model of virtue, bravery and resilience
74 **vengeance** ['vendʒəns] revenge
80 **sinewy** ['sɪnjuːi] having a thin body
89 **searing** (*adj*) so strong that it burns you
89 **purify sth.** make sth. pure

Her family on her father's side is from Rajasansi, just outside Amritsar. And she is married to a white guy so she is probably not part of the Gurdwara congregation; they have all heard of Tony's Green-Card Wife. (These matters travel faster than aeroplanes fly between cities.) I will tell Tony I will take English lessons, and that she will be my teacher. 95

Tony was finishing breakfast when Mrs Keogh, the English teacher, arrived. She knocked and I let her in. Then I asked her to sit down, offered her some tea and listened while she and Tony spoke English. 100

'Thank you very much. My girlfriend is just new from India. As soon as her green card comes we will be getting married, so till then I think English lessons will help her pass the time.' 105

The English teacher did not remark on 'my girlfriend'. Good. Not a prying woman. She said, 'I am glad to help you and your fiancée.'

Tony continued, 'I will not like it if you teach her more than I know. But just enough for her to get a good-paying job at Dunkin' Donuts or maybe the Holiday Inn. She will learn quickly but you must not teach her too many American ideas.' 110

The English teacher smiled at me.

Tomorrow, I will ask her where I can learn how to drive.

From: *English Lessons, and Other Stories*, 1996

96 **Gurdwara** building in which Sikhs worship
100 **Keogh** ['kiːəʊ]
106 **pry** try to find out things about other people's private lives
109 **Holiday Inn** US hotel chain

COMPREHENSION ◀

1 Characters and plot
  a Read up to l. 45 and collect facts about the narrator, her husband, her son and Valerie.
  b Read on up to l. 91 and summarize what the narrator's dark secret is.
  c Read the last part of the story and point out the meaning of the English lessons for the narrator and for her husband.

ANALYSIS ◀

▶ SF 19: Analysing narrative prose

2 The protagonist's identity
  a Work with a partner and examine the different facets of Kanwaljit's identity. Consider the following aspects: her personality, family, friends, relationships, cultural background, feelings and thoughts, language. Use visual aids to present your findings.

▶ SF 5: Doing research

  b CHALLENGE ▶ Compare Kanwaljit's and Tony's migrant experiences. Consider their hopes for and expectations of living in the USA.

LANGUAGE AWARENESS ◀

▶ LP 2: Present tense or future?
▶ LP 3: Simple present and present perfect
▶ LP 4: Present perfect and simple past

3 The use of tenses
Oral and written storytelling is traditionally done in the past tense. This story also uses the present tense and the future for narration. Analyse the use and functions of the different narrative tenses in the story.
SUPPORT ▶ p. 211

BEYOND THE TEXT ◀

▶ SF 37: Doing a creative writing task

4 Writing a letter about your life
Imagine you are Kanwaljit in three years' time. Write a letter to your parents in which you tell them about your new life.

▶ SF 6: Doing project work
▶ SF 24: Giving a presentation

Presenting India

After working on this chapter, gather ideas for a multimedia presentation on the topic 'India – a kaleidoscope' for a multicultural festival at your school.

1 Form groups. Each group picks one topic. You could include some of the following aspects in your presentation:
Germans in India – the Indian diaspora in Germany – the global importance of India in the 21st century – Indian festivals – Indian foods – Indian classical and popular music – Indian literature – Indian movies – reasons to visit India – traces of India in your community (e.g. food, music, clothes) – ways to promote intercultural relations between India and Germany (e.g. exchange programmes, business cooperation, etc.)

2 Think about interesting ways of presenting *your* topic, e.g. interviews, slide shows, showing a film, making your own film, or reading out poetry or stories you like. Use ideas from this unit and choose at least one audio file (e.g. a radio interview or report) or video clip (e.g. an excerpt from a feature film or documentary, a trailer, song) for your presentation.

3 Prepare your presentation. Make sure work is distributed equally among the group and agree on a project schedule.

4 On the day of your presentation, come prepared and give your presentation.

5 With the use of an assessment sheet, which your teacher will give you, evaluate the work of the different groups.

India

ভারত

భారత

ভারত

India – a Kaleidoscope   **Chapter 6**   131

7 The USA – Still the Promised Land ?

A

B

C

Download a list of chapter vocab here: 👆 **Webcode** context-18

Download a detailed timeline as well as further information and tasks based on the pictures: 👆 **Webcode** context-19

1 GROUP PUZZLE **The American experience**

a Form six groups. Give each group a letter A–F.
In your group, talk about the picture that matches your letter: What situation does it show? What do you know about this episode in US history? Share your knowledge.

b Use the webcode to access further information on the story behind your picture. Share the new information in your group.

c Form new groups of at least six members each; all six letters must be represented in each group. Tell each other about your pictures. Discuss what makes them part of the American experience.

Timeline of American history

1775–1783   1789   1861–1865   1890

1607 1620   4 July 1776   1803

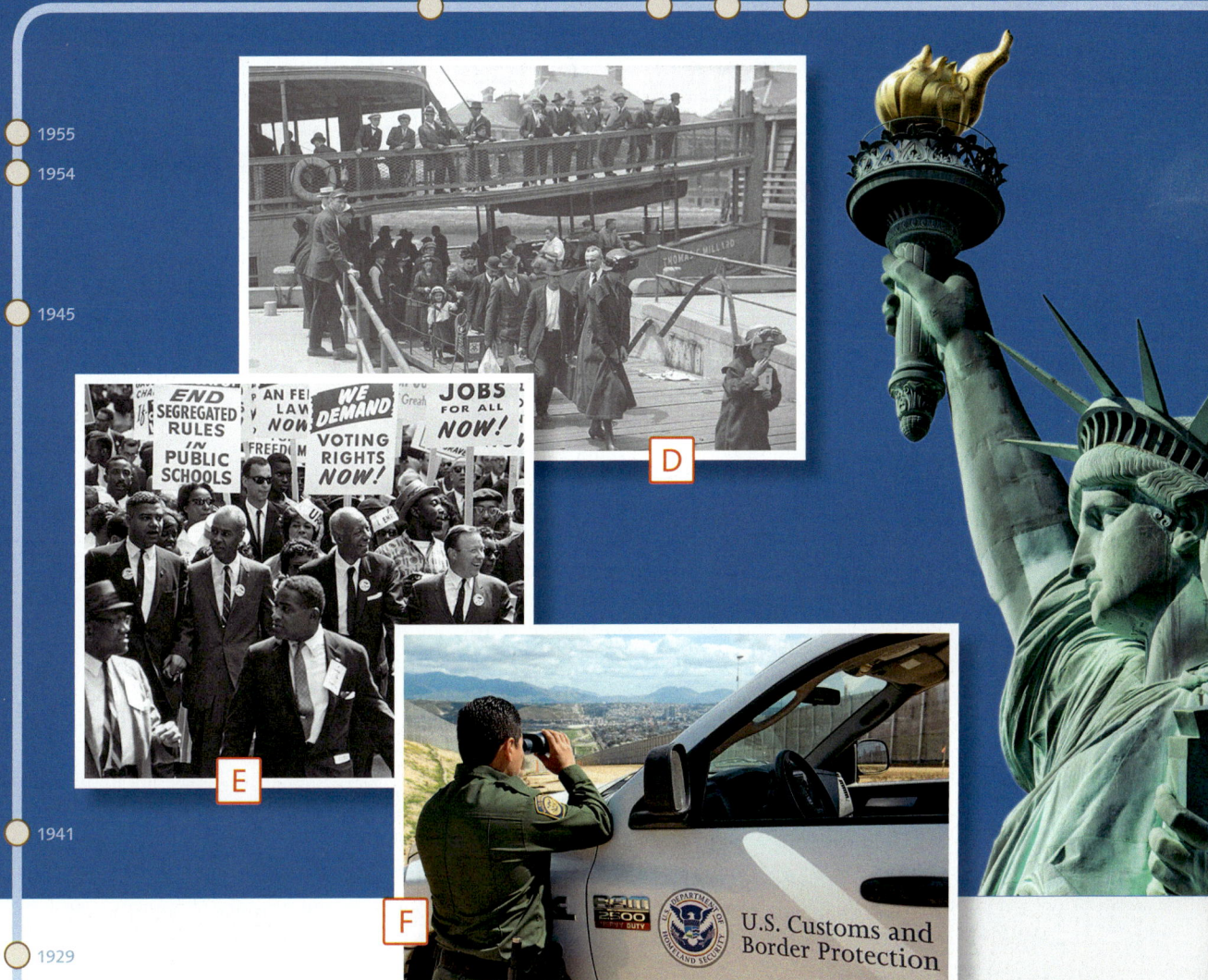

1989–1991   2001   2006   2008

1955
1954

1945

1941

1929

D

E

F

U.S. Customs and
Border Protection

2 Putting yourself in the picture

a Choose one person from any of the six pictures.
Write an *interior monologue for your person: How (or why) did you
get into your present situation? How do you imagine your future?

b Form groups of 4–5. Read your monologues to each other. The
listeners try to guess which person you have chosen.

c Discuss the different motives of the people you have talked about,
and how they are connected with the idea of America as 'the
Promised Land'.

1919
1917

> **■ TROUBLE SPOT**
>
> *The term 'America' is often used
> to refer to the USA (rather than
> the entire American continent).
> Strictly speaking this is not
> correct. If you do use the term,
> make sure the meaning is made
> clear by the context.*

PREVIEW

In this chapter you will examine the image of the USA at home and abroad and learn more about some of
the challenges facing the United States today.

Main topics

Focus on Skills: SPEAKING

Chapter Task: Giving a speech in which you
explain why you would like to be given the

CD2 04

Listen to an audio version of the text on the CD or download it here:

Webcode context-21

A country like no other

A nation founded on principle

Most nations are held together by a common history, language and culture. The USA is different: it is a nation united solely by the shared values of equality, democracy, and individual freedom. The Founding Fathers, inspired by the ideas of the Enlightenment, created a self-governing republic without social barriers. 5
The crowned heads of Europe expected the young nation to collapse in chaos; instead, it grew and prospered, ultimately rising to the status of a world power.

Land of opportunity

While the promise of freedom from religious and political persecution played and continues to play a 10
major role in attracting immigrants to America's shores, it became clearer as the United States expanded westward that the continent also held vast stores of natural resources. In the first half of the 19th century, it was mainly the availability of cheap farmland that drew 15
millions to try their luck in the New World; later, huge supplies of coal and iron ore powered the growth of industry, attracting further waves of immigration. The economic vitality of the young nation gave rise to the material side of the American dream, expressed in 20
slogans like 'from rags to riches' or 'the sky's the limit'. In a country so rich in opportunity, success was believed to lie in the hands of the individual. A culture arose that honoured personal material success; as long as upward mobility guaranteed equality of opportunity 25
for all, the majority felt that the self-made millionaire had a right to his wealth.

'Remember, gentlemen, we aren't here just to draft a constitution. We're here to draft the best damned constitution in the world.'

The American century – and beyond

The 20th century saw the United States rise to a position of economic and military leadership in the world. America viewed itself as a beacon of 30
democracy, which it strove to export to other countries. With the collapse of the Soviet Union and the end of the Cold War (1989), the USA was seemingly the only superpower left standing. Yet since the turn of the century, the USA has increasingly been forced to cope with doubts and difficulties. The attacks of 11 September 2001 left Americans with a deep-seated feeling of insecurity. The 35
official response – two undeclared wars and an unprecedented expansion of surveillance operations – cost the USA sympathy abroad and contributed to the heavy debt burden. Economic turmoil, the massive loss of jobs in the manufacturing sector, a housing crisis that cost millions their home, and a widening gap between rich and poor that undermines the equality of 40
opportunity – all of these factors cause Americans today to wonder if the American dream still holds true for their generation. It remains to be seen if this extraordinary nation, which has in the past so often demonstrated its ability to reinvent itself, will once more rise to the challenges of a new era.

> **■ TROUBLE SPOT**
>
> **the USA** (l. 32) + *singular verb*
> **The USA is/was/has …**

A country like no other

▶ SF 2: Learning new words

1 Words in use

Replace the underlined words with highlighted expressions from the text:

1 In the 20th century the United States became the most powerful country in the world.
2 Americans believe in giving everyone the same chance in life.
3 We don't know yet if the USA will remain the leading world power.
4 The availability of cheap land was an important factor attracting Europe's rural poor to America's shores.
5 The growing difference between rich and poor is without parallel.

2 Collocations with prepositions

▶ LP 19: Collocations

a Complete the underlined collocations with the correct prepositions. If you need help, look at the text again:
1 By 1900, the USA had risen *to* the status of a major industrial country.
2 The United States of America became known as the land of promise, a country rich *in* opportunity.
3 Hundreds of different ethnic groups have all contributed *to* American culture.
4 Stories of successful immigrants gave rise *to* the saying that in America the streets were paved with gold.
5 For many European Jews, freedom *from* persecution made the USA the new Promised Land.
6 The American dream didn't hold true *for* everyone; African Americans and Native Americans, for example, were long excluded.
b Find four more collocations with prepositions in the text and write a quiz for your partner. Then do the quiz your partner gives you.

3 Connotation

Most people react positively to the word *freedom* and negatively to *slavery*. This emotional aspect of language is called *connotation.
a Sort the words in the list on the right into two groups (positive/negative connotation). Compare results with your partner.
b Together, find three more words from the text for each of the two groups.

values • persecution • doubts • prosper • opportunity • insecurity • undermine • equality

4 General terms ('Oberbegriffe')

a Find general terms to describe each of the five (groups of) examples. Choose the terms from the highlighted expressions in the text.
1 George Washington and Benjamin Franklin
→ **general term:** *the Founding Fathers*
2 coal, oil, water, farmland → **general term:** …
3 Free public schools are available to everyone. → …
4 A factory worker rises to become the director of a large firm. → …
5 Only landowners are allowed to vote. → …
b Choose three more general terms from the highlighted words in the text. Write an example illustrating each of them. Swap examples with a partner and find the correct terms from the text.

5 Your view

The USA – still 'a beacon of democracy' (ll. 30-31) for the rest of the world? State your opinion in a short text (ca. 200 words).

▶ LP 14: Linking words and phrases

Pulitzer Prize-winning journalist Liz Balmaseda

■ **FACT FILE**

Pulitzer Prize
The Pulitzer Prizes were established in 1917 by the US publisher Joseph Pulitzer. They are awarded annually in the fields of journalism, literature and musical composition.

The American dream

A1 ¡Viva América! *Liz Balmaseda*

Liz Balmaseda (born 1959) is a Cuban-American journalist who has worked for various Miami newspapers as well as for Newsweek and NBC News. She won Pulitzer Prizes for journalism in 1993 and 2001. Balmaseda contributed this text to an online collection of immigrant stories.

I grew up in America's most Cuban city – Hialeah, Florida. The municipality's tagline, 'The City of Progress', far more often was quoted in Spanish. The cheering section at local football games brought conga drums. The Catholic saint statues that often adorned front lawns concealed Afro-Cuban alter egos. And the 'fries' at fast-food drive-thru joints were made of yuca. 5

But the city was fiercely American, just as my parents were fiercely American. Having fled Cuba shortly after its Communist regime took hold of the island, they brought me to Florida when I was 10 months old and raised me to cherish the American dream. Cuba lingered only in the flavor notes of my mother's cooking, the rhythms on our stereo, and the bottomless sense of yearning for loved ones stranded 10 on the island. The rest of it was all-American: The stray threads I pulled off my mother's clothes when she returned each night after a grueling day at her clothing factory job. The snazzy ties my dad wore to work as a car salesman. His religious attention to Election Day, when he'd leap out of bed to cast his vote. The pride I sensed in my parents after I brought home the miniature trophy that declared me the winner 15 of the first-grade spelling bee, in the year I learned to speak English.

I could say it was by magic that a loving and supportive community emerged around our family. But that village force of good neighbors, church friends, American-born school teachers who took the initiative to visit our home and offer a word of praise and encouragement – that doesn't happen by magic. It happens in response to a life 20 embraced, a life that is often turbulent, painful and imperfect. This is what I learned from my mother, may she rest in peace. This is what I continue to learn from my father. At 84, he is stricken with Parkinson's. Last Election Day, I sat with him at the polling place and, at his direction, filled out the ballot. I watched as he slipped the ballot into the box and gave the poll worker a smile of great accomplishment. It's an 25 image I'll carry with me always.

My Cuba is now buried in a Miami cemetery. But my America resounds in all its glory, like a hundred conga drums playing beneath Friday night lights in Hialeah.

From: *The Huffington Post*, 19 July 2013

1 **municipality** [mjuːˌnɪsɪˈpæləti] town
  tagline motto, slogan
3 **conga drum** kind of African drum
4 **adorn sth.** *etwas schmücken*
  conceal sth. hide sth.
  alter ego [ˌæltər ˈiːɡəʊ] alternate identity
5 **joint** *(infml)* small restaurant
  yuca *(Spanish) Cassava (Wurzel der Maniokpflanze)*
6 **fiercely** passionately, intensely
8 **cherish sth.** love sth.
9 **linger** [ˈlɪŋɡə] remain
10 **yearning** [ˈjɜːnɪŋ] *(fml)* feeling of wanting sth. badly
11 **stray threads** *einzelne Fäden*
12 **grueling** *(AE)* = *(BE)* **gruelling** very hard
13 **snazzy** *(infml)* showy
  religious (here) taking sth. very seriously
14 **leap** *(v)* jump
16 **spelling bee** spelling contest
17 **supportive** offering support
  emerge come into existence
21 **embrace sb.** take sb. into your arms
23 **be stricken with sth.** *an etwas erkrankt sein*
24 **polling place** place where voters can cast their vote in an election
25 **accomplishment** [əˈkʌmplɪʃmənt] feeling of having achieved sth.
27 **resound** [rɪˈzaʊnd] *ertönen*

Hialeah City Hall

COMPREHENSION ◀

1 First reactions

Talk about your reactions to the text. Why do you think Balmaseda chose to submit her family's story to the immigrants website?

ANALYSIS ◀

2 From Havana to Hialeah

Balmaseda uses many *images to describe life in Hialeah. Find some examples and explain why they are important to her.

LANGUAGE AWARENESS ◀

3 Words that convey emotion

a Collect words from the text that express the author's (or someone else's) feelings (e.g., 'fiercely', l.6). Examine how they influence the effect of the text.

b The following text sounds bland because it lacks words that convey feelings. Rewrite it to give it more emotional impact. ▶ LANGUAGE HELP

My father thought that his life would change for the worse if Castro came to power in Cuba. He applied to the US Embassy in Havana for an immigration permit. He waited three months. Then a letter arrived saying we could leave for the USA. My parents packed their belongings and said goodbye to their friends and relatives in Cuba. On March 11th, 1958, on board a small passenger ship bound for Miami, they had their first glimpse of the US mainland.

SUPPORT ▶ p.212

> **LANGUAGE HELP**
> - anxious
> - be ~ to do sth.
> - excited
> - fear *(n, v)*
> - hope *(n, v)*
> - nervous
> - overjoyed
> - relieved
> - sad
> - tearful
> - thrilled
> - with a feeling of ~
> - with trembling hands

BEYOND THE TEXT ◀

4 GROUP INTERVIEW One family's American dream

a Form groups of four. One of you is Liz Balmaseda, another is her father, and the third member is her mother. The fourth member of the group is a journalist who is interviewing the family on the subject 'Our American dream'. Prepare your roles using the role cards that your teacher will give you. Then carry out the interview.

b Summarize the aspects of the American dream that were named in your group and present them to the rest of the class.

▶ SF 26: Taking part in an interview

A2 Reinventing the American dream *June Sochen*

- Speculate on the title of the following text. Why might the author, a former professor of history, think that the American dream needs reinventing?

Certain parts of the text have been left out (cf. gap 1, etc.) – don't worry about them on your first reading.

Given the uncertain economic conditions, a contentious presidential campaign and the high cost of a college education, it is difficult to know how the traditional definition of the Dream can be applied for the younger generation. [1] Answering the question looking backward is easier than looking forward.

5   For the generation that fought to free the American colonies from Great Britain, it meant freedom of religion and speech and the liberty to pursue your own path. Contrary to the experience of most people across the Atlantic in the 1700s, Americans looked to a bright future. Children benefited from public school education, hardworking parents, and seemingly endless land to be purchased and cultivated.

1 **contentious** full of conflict
8 **benefit** ['benɪfɪt] *(v) profitieren*
9 **purchase sth.** ['pɜːtʃəs] *(fml)* buy sth.

If things were not favorable for you in Boston, you could pack your belongings, hitch your wagon, and take your family to the West. [...] 10

The popular press and penny novels heralded the 'rags to riches' stories of ordinary Americans. This country could fulfill both the ideals and the material aspirations of all newcomers, or so the rhetoric promised. For much of the 19th Century, upward mobility became a constant theme in all political pronouncements, sermons, and business proposals. If you worked hard, you could achieve the American Dream of more education than your parents, greater economic success than your parents, and a larger home than your parents. 15

There were enough measurable examples of success to make most Americans believe that the American Dream was attainable for them. [2] Though the Civil War surely set back the hopes and plans of a generation, the post-war generation looked forward to a brighter future. 20

The 20th Century, though promising much of the same, had more obstacles in its path. Two world wars, the worst depression in American history, the Cold War, Korea and Vietnam all slowed down the belief, and the actuality, of inevitable progress toward everyone's fulfillment of the American Dream. Indeed, the seeming certainty that each generation would do better than the last one, has been dashed in recent years. 25

The 21st Century started with a new threat: September 11, 2001 and the attack on the World Trade Center. [3] The dot.com bubble burst early in the century followed by the Great Recession of 2007; though the recession is formally over, it has left us five years later with high unemployment and great uncertainty about the future. 30

The divide between the generations is dramatic. [4] Recent college graduates find their career hopes unrealized in the current job market. Wages have stagnated in the last 30 years with manufacturing and service industries going overseas. 35

Only a small segment of the economy – the banks and insurance companies, for example – seem[s] to be thriving.

[5] This country remains a desirable destination for immigrants from all over the world. Just as new immigrants believe in the American Dream, most Americans, according to the polls, also appreciate the multiple benefits offered by this country and have no desire to live elsewhere. The current economic troubles are seen as challenges to overcome, not as insuperable obstacles. Home ownership remains a goal as does job security. 40

Despite our troubles, the original meaning of the Dream, the ideological portion, remains vibrant while the material promises are harder to obtain. The freedoms enjoyed in this country cannot be taken for granted as there are still many places on the globe where repression describes daily life for many people. Though surely the material aspect of the Dream continues to be a goal – a home [...], a yearly vacation, and a job that pays all the bills – preserving the ideals of the American Dream is more important than ever before. 45 50

From: *Naples Daily News*, 8 August 2012

---

10 favorable (AE) = (BE) **favourable** *günstig*
11 hitch your wagon (here) attach your wagon to horses
12 herald sth. ['herəld] (v, fml) call attention to sth.
14 rhetoric ['retərɪk] (fml) (here) speech-making
15 pronouncement public statement
16 proposal plan, idea
20 attainable within reach
21 set sth. back etwas zurückwerfen
23 obstacle ['ɒbstəkl] sth. that is in the way
26 inevitable [ɪn'evitəbl] unvermeidlich
28 dash sth. destroy sth.
30 dot.com bubble period from ca. 1997–2000, when the value of internet start-ups rose sharply and then collapsed
33 divide (n) gap
38 desirable [dɪ'zaɪərəbl] attractive
40 appreciate sth. [ə'priːʃieɪt] know the value of sth.
benefit (n) advantage
42 insuperable [ɪn'suːpərəbl] (fml) unüberwindlich
45 vibrant ['vaɪbrənt] alive
46 take sth. for granted etwas als selbstverständlich ansehen
47 repression Unterdrückung

▶ SF 10: Working with closed test formats

  COMPREHENSION ◀

1 Filling in the gaps

  a Five sentences have been removed from the text; the gaps are marked and numbered. Choose the right sentence for each gap from sentences A–G below (there are two sentences that don't belong to the text):

    A Workers over 50 who lost their jobs may never recover the earnings and positions they once had.

B But the American Dream continues to live.

C In particular, African Americans and many women felt excluded from the Dream.

D There was little government on any level to help or hinder individual accomplishment.

E Americans have always believed in the power of the individual to shape his or her own life.

F Indeed, all future generations may have to reinterpret the Dream.

G International terrorism became a new concern.

b Compare solutions with your partner and discuss points where you differ.

2 The main idea

Sum up the main reasons Sochen gives why the American dream needs to be reinvented. Compare her reasons with the ideas your class had before reading the text.

──────────────────────────────── **ANALYSIS** ◀

3 Exploring the American dream

a Form small groups. Each group will need a blank poster. Your task is to present the information on the American dream contained in the text in the form of a clearly structured mind map. Follow these steps:

1 Divide the subtopics from the list on the right among the members of your group. Each member makes notes on their subtopic.

2 Pool your results and create a mind map that presents your information in a clearly structured form.

b Display your posters on the walls of your classroom. Compare the mind maps created by your classmates and discuss their pros and cons.

──────────────────────── **BEYOND THE TEXT** ◀

4 YOU CHOOSE ▶ Comparing interpretations

a Reread **A1** (¡Viva América!) in the light of what you have learned about the American dream. Then write a comment of ca. 200 words on the topic: 'The Balmasedas – an American dream come true'.

 OR

b Write a comment relating June Sochen's views on the American dream (**A2**) to the cartoon below.

Find a mindmapping tool here:

 Webcode context-53

────────────────────

• *political ideals*
• *economic opportunity*
• *upward mobility*
• *threats to the dream*
• *state of the dream today*

▶ SF 34: Argumentative writing
▶ SF 13: Analysing cartoons
▶ SF 18: Analysing non-fiction

CULTURE SPOT

Flag (1954)

is a painting by the American artist Jasper Johns (born 1930). It is on display at the Museum of Modern Art in Manhattan, New York City.

▶ CC 1: Cultural awareness

🎧 **CD2** 05

1 Describe your reaction to the work of art above. Would you react the same way to a painting of the German flag in a German art museum? Explain.

2 Listen to a recording of two US teenagers talking about the picture. How do their views influence your reaction to the painting?

3 The photo on the right shows a small section of the painting in detail. Describe what you can recognize in the painting, and discuss why you think the artist chose this technique.

4 Jasper Johns's 'Flag': a statement on the American dream? Discuss.

For another work of art based on the Stars and Stripes, see p. 15.

Dealing with diversity

■ FACT FILE

Ethnic neighbourhoods

Because of its history, the USA is a racially and ethnically diverse nation. With immigrants pouring in from
all over the world, it was only natural that new-
5 comers to America's shores flocked to neighbourhoods where they could speak their own language
and live their culture. They often had networks of
friends and relatives from the Old World who helped
them find work and a place to live. By 1900, Polish,
10 Irish, Italian, German, Jewish and Asian quarters had
arisen in virtually every city in the US.

Although **ghetto** is technically just another word for
'ethnic neighbourhood', in the USA it is used mainly
for the – usually undesirable – quarters of a city in

which African Americans formerly were forced to live. 15
Black families wishing to move to a better part of
town found that no landlord would rent them an
apartment and no bank would give them credit to
buy a house. White homeowners feared that the
appearance of black faces in their street would send 20
property values into a downward spiral. It was only
after the Civil Rights Act of 1968 prohibited discrimination in housing that the situation of African American families slowly began to improve.

*List the 'push and pull factors' that lead to the creation
of ethnic neighbourhoods. Do they exist in Germany
too?*

B1 The new neighbours   Bruce Norris

September 1959. *Karl comes to visit his neighbours Russ and Bev,
who have just sold their inner-city house (where the scene takes place)
and bought a new one in the suburbs. Jim is a young clergyman who
has come to talk to Russ. Ted Driscoll is the real estate agent who has
sold the house for Russ and his wife. Betsy is Karl's wife.*

- While you are reading the dialogue, form a mental image of the
  situation, i.e. the characters and what they may be doing while
  they are speaking.

*Stuart McQuarrie (Russ) and
Sophie Thompson (Bev) in a
performance of* Clybourne Park

KARL [...] I take it, Russ, you're
aware that the Community
Association meets the first
Tuesday of each month? And
5 as I'm sure you know, Don
Skinner is part of the steering
committee. And somehow it
came to Don's attention at
this late juncture that Ted
10 Driscoll had found a buyer for
this house and I have to say it
did come as something of a
shock when Don told us what
sort of people they were.
15 RUSS What sort of people are they?
(*Beat. Karl stares at Russ.*)
KARL Well. (*Chuckles.*) Uhh ... Huh.
I suppose I'm forced to
consider the possibility that
20 you actually don't *know*.

RUSS Don't know *what*?
KARL Well, I mean. That
they're colored.
RUSS Who are?
KARL The family. It's a colored   25
family.
(*Pause.*)
So: I contacted the family –
JIM Wait wait wait.
KARL (*To Russ.*)   30
You're saying Ted never
bothered to tell you?
RUSS We, uhh ... sort of gave Ted
free rein on the –
JIM I don't think you're right on   35
this one, Karl.
KARL Oh, but I am. Oh, I've spoken
with the family.
RUSS Bev?
JIM On the *telephone*?   40

▸

real estate agent *Immobilien-
makler/in*
1 **I take it** *(infml)* I assume
6 **steering committee** [kə'mɪti]
Steuerungskomitee
9 **juncture** ['jʌŋktʃə] *(fml)*
moment in time
16 **beat** *(n)* brief pause
17 **chuckle** laugh briefly and quietly
25 **colored** *(AE)* = *(BE)* **coloured**
*(used for black people until the
late 1950s, now an old-fashioned
or offensive word)*
32 **bother to do sth.** ['bɒðə]
think it necessary to do sth.
33 **give sb. free rein (on sth.)** [reɪn]
*jdm. freie Hand geben (in einer
Sache)*

KARL Oh, no. As a matter of fact, Betsy and I've just come directly from … *(Beat, for effect.)* well, from *Hamilton Park.*

BEV *(To Russ.)* What is it?

45 RUSS C'mere a second.

KARL Now, Russ. You know as well as I do that this is a progressive community.

BEV *(To Russ as she joins them.)* What's he talking about?

50 KARL If you take the case of Gelman's grocery: That's a fine example of how we've all embraced a different way of thinking –

RUSS Slow down a second. Bev, get Ted Driscoll on the phone.

55 BEV *(To Russ.)* What for?

RUSS Karl says. Karl is *claiming* –

KARL Russ, I have met *personally* with the family, and –

60 BEV What family?

RUSS He claims this family. The family to whom Ted sold the house.

KARL It's a colored family. *(Jim shakes his head.)*

65 JIM *(To Karl.)* Sorry, don't we say *Negro*, now?

KARL *(Irritated.)* I *say* Negro. –

JIM *(Overlapping.)* Well, it's only common courtesy, and I'm –

70 KARL *(Continuous.)* – I say them *inter-changeably* –

JIM *(Overlapping.)* – not trying to tell you how to conduct your business.

KARL *(Continuous.)* – and of course I said

75 *Negro* to them – No I think we both know what you're doing.

JIM And furthermore, I don't think Ted would pull a stunt like that.

KARL Yes. We all admire Ted. But I don't

80 think any of us would accuse him of putting the community's interests ahead of his own. […]

BEV Waitwaitwait. Karl, are you *sure?*

KARL I was sitting with them not two

85 hours ago.

BEV But isn't it possible that they're … I don't know, *Mediterranean,* or – ?

KARL Bev, they are *one hundred percent.* And I don't know how much time

90 any of you have spent in Hamilton Park, but Betsy was waiting in the car and I can tell you, there are some *unsavory* characters. […] Now, some would say change is

95 inevitable. And I can support that, if it's change for the better. But I'll tell you what I *can't* support, and that's disregarding the needs of the people who *live* in a community.

BEV But don't they have needs, too? 100

KARL Don't who?

BEV The family.

KARL Which family?

BEV The ones who –

KARL The *purchasers?* 105

BEV I mean, in, in, in, in *principle,* don't we *all* deserve to – shouldn't we *all* have the opportunity to, to, to –

KARL *(Chuckles with amazement, shakes his head.)* Well, *Bev.* 110

JIM In *principle,* no question.

KARL But you can't *live* in a principle, can you? Gotta live in a *house.*

BEV And so do they.

KARL Not in *this* house, they don't. 115

JIM But here's the real question:

KARL And what happened to *love thy neighbor?* If we're being so principled.

BEV They would *become* our neighbors. 120

KARL And what about the neighbors you already *have,* Bev?

BEV I care about them, too!

KARL Well, I'm afraid you can't have it both ways. 125

RUSS Okay. Assuming –

BEV Wait. Why not? […]

JIM But the key question is this:

BEV No. Why *not* have it both ways?

KARL Darling, I came to talk to Russ. […] 130

BEV Why not, if it would *benefit* someone?

JIM But *would* they benefit?

BEV If we could make them our *neighbors.*

KARL But they won't be *your* neighbors, Bev. *You're* the ones moving *away!* 135

From: *Clybourne Park,* 2010 – Act One

► SF 10: Working with closed test formats

COMPREHENSION ◄

1 The topic

Sum up the main topic of the conversation in one sentence.

2 True or false?

Check each of the following statements. If you think the statement is true, point to evidence in the dialogue. If you think it is false, correct it.

1 A black family has bought Ted Driscoll's house.
2 Karl has just phoned the people who bought the house.
3 Russ didn't know that the house had been sold to African Americans.
4 Karl is upset about a black family moving into the neighbourhood.
5 Karl thinks that Hamilton Park is a progressive community.
6 Bev believes that everyone should be given a chance.

ANALYSIS ◄

3 Working with a *dramatic text

🎧 **CD2** 06
► SF 22: Listening

a In groups of four, each of you chooses one of the four roles in the scene. Listen to a recording of the text and concentrate on 'your' character while listening. Try and imagine what your character is doing, and where he/she is standing, etc.

b 'Playback': In your group, decide where you want to stand while you are playing your roles. Then practise playing your part in pantomime while the recording is on.

4 Examining the *characters

Copy and complete the table. For the second column, choose phrases from the box on the right, or make up your own. ► **LANGUAGE HELP**

	Behaviour/character traits	Evidence from text (line numbers)
Karl		
Russ		
Bev		
Jim		

■ LANGUAGE HELP

- naïve
- shocked
- angry
- hypocritical
- idealistic
- wants to appear liberal
- self-confident
- tries to mediate
- embarrassed
- bossy

5 The dramatic conflict

► SF 20: Analysing drama

At the heart of every drama is a conflict that is usually embodied by two of the characters. Choose the two characters that you think most clearly embody conflict in this scene. Contrast their points of view in a text of 100–150 words.

BEYOND THE TEXT ◄

6 The other side of the coin SUPPORT ► p. 212

► SF 37: Doing a creative writing task

Form groups of four. Two of you are Bev and Russ, the other two are the African American couple who have bought the house in Clybourne Street. Imagine that after Karl has left, the black couple come to look at the house. How would Russ and Bev behave? How might the black couple explain their wish to move to an all-white neighbourhood? Discuss the issues at hand, then prepare role cards for your parts. Practise the scene, then perform it for your class.

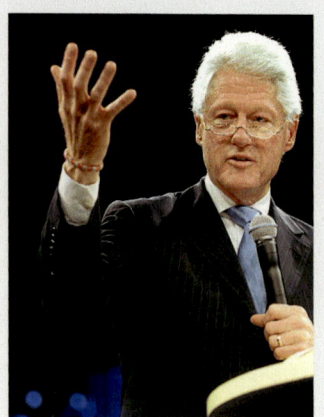

*Bill Clinton,
42nd President of the USA*

2 **strengthen sth.** make sth.
stronger
7 **ensure** make sure *(sicherstellen)*
8 **the brass ring** *(AE, infml)* the
opportunity to be successful
14 **industrious** [ɪnˈdʌstriəs] hardworking
15 **heritage** [ˈherɪtɪdʒ] cultural
tradition
26 **magnitude** *Größenordnung*
29 **unequivocally** [ˌʌnɪˈkwɪvəkli]
unmissverständlich
30 **revitalize sth.** [ˌriːˈvaɪtəlaɪz] give
sth. new life
32 **energize sth.** [ˈenədʒaɪz] give
sth. energy
35 **descendant** [dɪˈsendənt]
Nachkomme
36 **Ellis Island** N.Y. centre for new
immigrants, 1892–1954
38 **faith** religion

New York doorbell nameplate

B2 The changing face of America   *William J. Clinton*

*Looking back on history of the USA at the end of the 20th century, Clinton,
President of the United States from 1993–2001, points out how the lessons of
the past can help the United States cope with the challenges of the future. His
message still sounds true in the second decade of the 21st century. Clinton made
the *speech from which this excerpt is taken to graduating students at Portland
State University.*

Today I want to talk to you about what may be the most important subject of all, how
we can strengthen the bonds of our national community as we grow more racially and
ethnically diverse. [...]

The driving force behind our increasing diversity is a new, large wave of immigration.
It is changing the face of America. And while most of the changes are good, they do   5
present challenges which demand more, both from new immigrants and from our
citizens. Citizens share a responsibility to welcome new immigrants, to ensure that
they strengthen our Nation, to give them their chance at the brass ring. In turn, new
immigrants have a responsibility to learn, to work, to contribute to America. If both
citizens and immigrants do their part, we will grow ever stronger in the new global   10
information economy.

More than any other nation on Earth, America has constantly drawn strength and
spirit from wave after wave of immigrants. In each generation, they have proved to be
the most restless, the most adventurous, the most innovative, the most industrious
of people. Bearing different memories, honoring different heritages, they have   15
strengthened our economy, enriched our culture, renewed our promise of freedom
and opportunity for all. [...]

But now we are being tested again by a new wave of immigration larger than any in a
century, far more diverse than any in our history. Each year, nearly a million people
come legally to America. Today, nearly one in ten people in America was born in   20
another country; one in five schoolchildren are from immigrant families. Today,
largely because of immigration, there is no majority race in Hawaii or Houston or
New York City. Within five years, there will be no majority race in our largest State,
California. In a little more than 50 years, there will be no majority race in the United
States. No other nation in history has gone through demographic change of this   25
magnitude in so short a time.

What do the changes mean? They can either strengthen and unite us, or they can
weaken and divide us. We must decide.

Let me state my view unequivocally. I believe new immigrants are good for America.
They are revitalizing our cities. They are building our new economy. They are   30
strengthening our ties to the global economy, just as earlier waves of immigrants
settled the new frontier and powered the Industrial Revolution. They are energizing
our culture and broadening our vision of the world. They are renewing our most basic
values and reminding us all of what it truly means to be an American. [...]

My fellow Americans, we descendants of those who passed through the portals of   35
Ellis Island must not lock the door behind us. Americans whose parents were denied
the rights of citizenship simply because of the color of their skin must not deny those
rights to others because of the country of their birth or the nature of their faith.

We should treat new immigrants as we would have wanted our own grandparents to
40 be treated. We should share our country with them, not shun them or shut them out.
But mark my words, unless we handle this well, immigration of this sweep and scope
could threaten the bonds of our Union.

Around the world, we see what can happen when people who live on the same land
put race and ethnicity before country and humanity. If America is to remain the
45 world's most diverse democracy, if immigration is to strengthen America as it has
throughout our history, then we must say to one another: Whether your ancestors
came here in slave ships or on the Mayflower, whether they landed on Ellis Island or
at Los Angeles International Airport, or have been here for thousands of years, if you
believe in the Declaration of Independence and the Constitution, if you accept the
50 responsibilities as well as the rights embedded in them, then you are an American.
Only that belief can keep us one America in the 21st century.

From: 'Commencement Address at Portland State University', 13 June 1998

COMPREHENSION ◀

1 Clinton's message
Summarize Clinton's position on diversity in no more than four sentences.

LANGUAGE AWARENESS ◀

2 Political vocabulary
  a Clinton's speech contains many words and phrases related to the idea of a
country and the people who live in it, e.g. *our national community* (l. 2).
Collect more examples from the text.
  b Compare lists with a partner and add any words or phrases that are missing
from your list.
  c Examine the connotations of the words and phrases.
  d YOU CHOOSE

Arrange the terms you have
found in the form of a mind map. Use at least five of the terms you
have found in sentences of your
own.

■ **TROUBLE SPOT**

treat sb. (l. 40) = *jdn. behan-deln (auch als Arzt/Ärztin)*
deal with a topic = *ein Thema behandeln*
handle a situation/problem (l. 41) = *mit einer Situation / einem Problem o. Ä. umgehen, zurechtkommen*

40 **shun sb.** avoid sb.
41 **sweep, scope** *Größenordnung*
44 **ethnicity** [eθ'nɪsəti] *ethnische Zugehörigkeit*

Find a mindmapping tool here:
 Webcode context-53

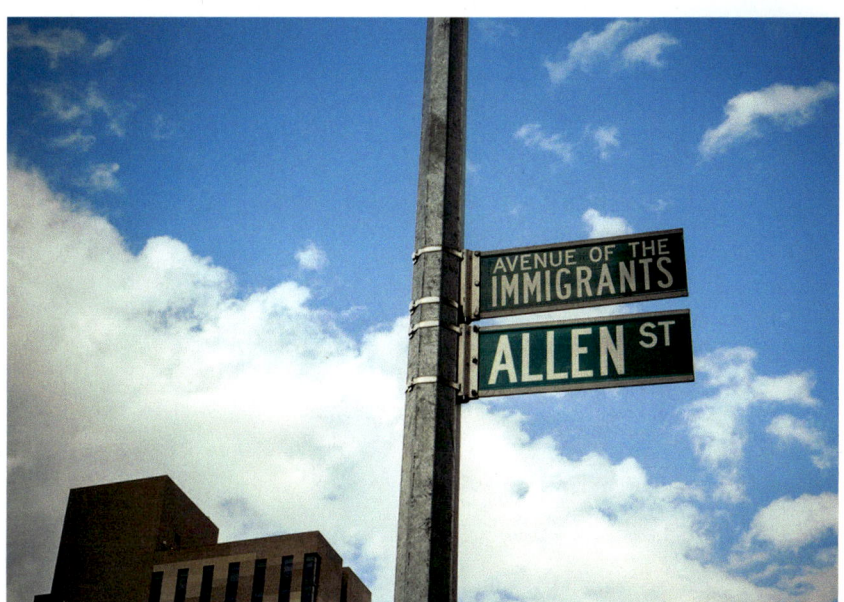

New York street sign

SPEAKING FOCUS ON SKILLS

Speaking in front of an audience

Before you speak in front of an audience, you should consider how to make your speech more effective. Analysing a professional speech is a good way to examine *stylistic devices and their effect.

Analysing a speech

1 Analysing the structure

a Identify the following parts of Clinton's speech (pp. 144–145) by putting them in the correct order and giving line numbers:

1 Statement of the main topic
2 Appeal to the audience to be fair in dealing with the consequences
3 Appeal to the audience to make a commitment
4 Description of historical developments
5 Statement of the challenge
6 Description of the present situation
7 Statement of opinion

b Examine how Clinton links the parts of his speech to make it easier for his listeners to follow his ideas. List the different ways of linking ideas for your own later use.

2 Analysing the *stylistic devices

a Examine the language of the speech. Point out passages where Clinton

- catches his listeners' attention
- emphasizes his message
- creates a feeling of unity with his audience
- reveals a positive or negative attitude to his topic
- appeals to his listeners' sense of fairness.

Make notes on your findings (including line numbers).

b Compare notes with your partner. Analyse your examples and explain the techniques used. The terms you may need are in the list on the left.

c Team up with another pair and give Clinton's speech an 'effectiveness rating' (on a scale from 1 to 6).

Preparing your own speech

1 Choosing a topic

Choose one of the following topics to prepare and deliver your own speech modelled on the one you have just analysed:

- *Living together in our multicultural school*
- *The world is changing – let's change with it!*
- *The challenges of freedom in a diverse society*

2 Collecting and organizing ideas

a Brainstorm what ideas/associations/aspects of your topic come into your head.

b Sort the ideas, keeping in mind that your speech will need a clear structure.

c Prepare an outline that includes suitable linking phrases and signpost words, e.g. 'for one thing …', 'In addition …', 'above all …'.

*alliteration • *anaphora [ə'næfərə] • comparative/ superlative • *connotation • *contrast • *direct address • *enumeration • *emphasis • *metaphor • *parallelism • personal pronoun • *repetition • *rhetorical question • *simile • *wordplay

▶ SF 8: Structuring ideas
▶ LP 14: Linking words and phrases

3 Writing a first draft

a Decide on a good opening sentence. Choose from the following list, or phrase your own:

- *Today I would like to talk to you about what we can do to make life easier for all of us at this school.*
- *Last night I went to a multicultural community event, and that gave me the idea of talking to you about how our world is changing and what we can do to change our attitudes.*
- *The other day I saw a sign that said 'Freedom is never free', and I started thinking about the price of freedom in our democracy. Today I would like to tell you my thoughts on this subject.*

▶ SF 25: Giving a speech

b Remember to use stylistic devices like those you identified in Clinton's speech in order to

- catch your listeners' attention: *Do you know how many nations are represented by the students at our school?*
- emphasize your message: *Cheap air travel, the internet, the end of the Cold War – all of these developments have made our world smaller and more connected than it has ever been before.*
- create a feeling of unity with your audience: *Together, we can find a solution.*
- convey a positive or negative attitude: *Tolerance and respect lead to understanding and cooperation; intolerance and distrust to conflict and violence.*
- appeal to your listeners' sense of fairness: *Imagine how you would feel if this happened to you.*

▶ LP 13: Placing emphasis on key points

c Take special care with your closing sentence(s), because this is what will stick in your listeners' minds.

4 Revising your draft

Read your draft aloud to a partner to test its effect as a spoken text. Mark the passages that don't 'work' and note what changes you want to make. Then write a revised version, always keeping in mind that it is a speech with which you want to make an impact on your listeners.

Rehearsing and delivering your speech

1 Decide how you want to deliver your speech, and take the necessary precautions to ensure you don't get mixed up and can be seen and understood clearly:

Method	Position
Speaking freely from notes on index cards	Standing in front of the class
Reading aloud from a manuscript	Sitting at a desk in front of the class

2 Practise your speech until you feel comfortable with it. You can make a recording of the speech and then listen to yourself speaking to get an 'outside impression'. Practise speaking in front of a full-length mirror to monitor your eye contact and body language. Refer to the Skills File (p. 280) for additional tips on how to deliver a speech.

Find a tool to improve your speaking skills here:
 Webcode context-51

Find a recording tool here:
 Webcode context-55

▶ SF22: Listening

Barack Obama, 44th President of the USA

🎧 **CD2** 07

premise ['premɪs] assumption (*cf. German Prämisse*)
land-grant college college funded with money from the sale of state-owned land
bust (*v*) break up
Medicare, Medicaid state-supported healthcare programs
New Deal, War on Poverty, Great Society slogans of social policy under (F. D.) Roosevelt and Johnson
prosperity [prɒ'sperəti] *Wohlstand*
confine sb. to sth. limit sb. to sth.
blue-collar job factory job
debt [det] money you owe sb.
consistently [kən'sɪstəntli] regularly
unravel [ʌn'rævl] fall apart
automate ['ɔːtəmeɪt] become automated
leverage [*AE:* 'levərɪdʒ, *BE:* 'liːvərɪdʒ] negotiating power
begrudge sth. *etwas missgönnen*
aspire to sth. strive to reach sth.
handsomely ['hænsəmli] generously
offend sb. upset sb.

Equality and inequality

C1 The danger to the dream   *Barack Obama*

The extract you are about to hear is taken from a speech made by President Barack Obama on 4 December 2013.

—————————————————————————————— COMPREHENSION ◀

1 Listening for gist
After listening to the excerpt once, decide which of the following statements best summarizes the main idea:
1 America has always rewarded success.
2 The present imbalance between poor and rich threatens the American dream.
3 The task of the government is to ensure that everyone has a fair share of the United States' wealth.

2 Listening for detail
▸ YOU CHOOSE ▸ Together with your partner, choose either task **a** or task **b** before listening to the speech a second time.

a Looking backward
1 Obama begins by pointing to four former presidents: Abraham Lincoln, Theodor ('Teddy') Roosevelt, Franklin D. Roosevelt ('FDR'), and Lyndon B. Johnson ('LBJ'). Take notes on each of them while listening.
2 Compare notes with your partner. Together, decide what these presidents had in common and why Obama mentions them.
3 Link up with a pair that chose task **b**. Tell each other what you have learned.

OR

b Then and now
1 Take notes on the following points:
· the American attitude to success
· upward mobility
· factors that limited upward mobility in the past
· the threat to upward mobility in the present.
2 Compare notes with your partner. Make any necessary additions or corrections.
3 Link up with a pair that chose task **a**. Tell each other what you have learned.

—————————————————————————————— BEYOND THE TEXT ◀

3 More success stories
Choose one American person who you regard as a success story. Research this person's *biography and report back to your class.

> *Steve Jobs*   *Steven Spielberg*   *Henry Ford*
>
> *Bill Gates*   *Lady Gaga*
>
> *Oprah Winfrey*   *Hillary Clinton*   *...*

C2　How to become homeless

You are going to watch an excerpt from the 2009 documentary Capitalism: A
Love Story. *In it, film-maker Michael Moore explains how millions of Americans
lost their homes following the financial crisis of 2008.*

▶ DVD

> ### FACT FILE
>
> **Home ownership**
> Since only few people can afford to
> pay cash for a house, the usual
> procedure is to borrow the money
> 5　you need from a bank. The so-
> called **mortgage** [ˈmɔːɡɪdʒ] (a kind
> of loan) can have either a fixed
> **interest rate** (e.g., for a 10-year
>
> period) or a floating rate that varies
> with the money market. If the　10
> borrower cannot pay the monthly
> rate, the bank **forecloses**, meaning
> it cancels the mortgage and tries to
> sell the house to get its money
> back. In a **boom market**, this is　15
> usually no problem, but if housing
> prices fall, the bank can
> be left with a loss.
>
>
>
> *Make sure you understand
> the four terms **in bold
> print**. Then shut your
> book. Together with your
> partner, take turns asking
> each other to explain each
> of the terms in bold.*

hunky-dory *(infml)* state in which
everyone is happy
tap sth. *etwas anzapfen*
home equity [ˈekwəti] net value
of your house
refinance your home pay back
old loans by taking out new ones
scam dishonest plan for making
money
down payment *Anzahlung*
approved [əˈpruːvd] accepted (as
customers)
demeanor *(AE)* = *(BE)* **demeanour**
way sb. looks or behaves
pitch sales talk
subprime used to describe loans
to people who are considered bad
risks
on disability receiving disability
payments *(Erwerbsunfähigkeits-
rente)*
foreclosure notice letter stating
that your mortgage has been
cancelled

COMPREHENSION ◀

1　Writing conference: first reactions (first viewing)
Form small groups. Write down your first reaction to the video. Then
pass your paper to the right. Add comments to the papers you are given.

2　Understanding the background
Copy and complete the following text using words from the list on the right:

US *homeowners* were persuaded to … from banks to finance … The new …
had a … interest rate. When the interest rate …, many … were unable to
pay the … rates. They lost the … of their houses and were forced to … .

ANALYSIS ◀

3　Film technique (second viewing)
While watching the film for the second time, make notes on the effect it has
on you. Fill in the missing information on the worksheet that your teacher
will give you.

BEYOND THE TEXT ◀

4　Discuss how effective the film is at helping people to understand the housing
crisis.

5　YOU CHOOSE ▶　Michael Moore: an American institution

a　Research Moore's
career and report
back to your class.

OR

b　Read a few online reviews of *Capitalism:
A Love Story* and report back to your class:
What did the critics praise or criticize about
the film?

*borrow money •
consumer spending •
floating • homeowners •
monthly • mortgages •
move out • owners •
ownership • rose*

▶ SF 23: Analysing a film

Film-maker Michael Moore

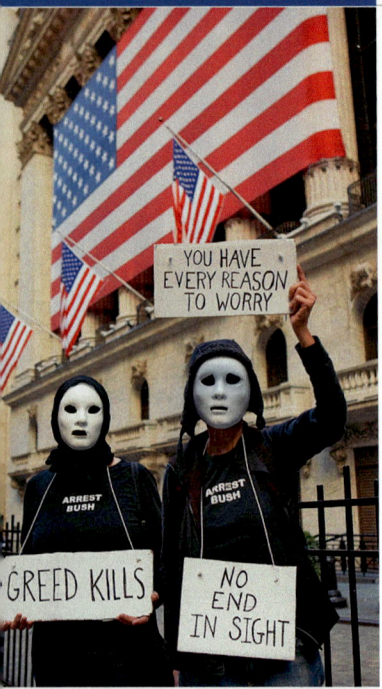

*Anti-bank bailout protests
on Wall Street in 2008*

C3 A politics lesson   *Todd Strasser*

In Todd Strasser's 2014 novel No Place, *the narrator Dan Halprin, a popular
high-school athlete in his final year, is forced to move in with relatives when both
his parents lose their jobs. For some weeks, a student activist has been trying to
recruit him for a protest march on Washington.*

One day the following week I was leaving the cafeteria with Noah and some friends
from the team, talking and laughing when the ratty-haired kid at the table in the hall
called out, 'Hey, Dan, ready to sign up?'

I felt myself tense. All my friends, plus a couple of kids at the sign-up table, were
watching and listening. 'Why do you ask?' 'Seems like a good time,' he said. 5

Had he heard that we'd lost our home? Did he think that would make me more
sympathetic to his cause? 'Why's that?' I gave him a hard look.

Some kids will back down when you give them that look, but this kid kept his eyes
steadily on mine. 'Just figured for once I had your undivided attention.'

It took a second to realize that for the past few weeks I'd been with Talia every time 10
I'd passed him, and he probably remembered that time she'd pulled me away before
he had a chance to lay out his spiel. But Talia wasn't feeling well and had stayed home
that day. Still, it had to take guts to stand up in front of senior athletes and call one
out. I looked at the posters on the wall behind him.

> **400 Americans have more than half the wealth in
> this country.** 15
>
> **Why is it easier to believe that
> 150,000,000 Americans are being LAZY rather than
> that 400 Americans are being GREEDY?**
>
> **STOP THE WAR ON THE POOR!** 20
>
> **Bail out schools, not banks!**

'People are suffering,' the kid said. 'They can't find work, or get a decent education.
You think it's fair that someone dies because he can't pay for adequate medical care
while someone else with the same disease lives because he can?'

My friends started to drift away. Meanwhile, I thought of Meg's family living in 25
Dignityville because her mom and brother had to spend practically everything they
earned on medicine for Mr. Fine. I used to think that life was like sports: Things were
rarely fair. The other team cheated. Your best player got hurt. You threw a perfect
strike and the ump called it a ball.

But that's a game, not life. 30

In sports people don't die because they can't afford medicine.

*They don't become homeless because a company goes out of business or moves jobs
overseas.*

I gestured at the posters. 'You really think marching's gonna make a difference?'

The ratty-haired kid looked surprised. 'You don't think protests changed the war in 35
Vietnam or segregation in the South?'

Glossary

4 **tense** (v) become tense
7 **be sympathetic to sth.** [ˌsɪmpəˈθetɪk] *einer Sache gegenüber aufgeschlossen sein*
cause *Sache, Anliegen*
9 **figure** [AE: ˈfɪɡjɔr, BE: ˈfɪɡə] (v) (infml) think, believe
10 **Talia** Dan's girlfriend
12 **lay out a spiel** (infml) make a speech
13 **guts** (infml) courage
call sb. out *jdn. namentlich ansprechen*
21 **bail sb. out** rescue sb. from a difficult situation

■ TROUBLE SPOT

decent [ˈdiːsnt] (l.22) = *anständig*
But: *dezent* =
1. subdued, soft *(colours, music, etc.)*;
2. tactful, discreet *(behaviour)*

25 **Meg Fine** girl in Dan's class. Her father has cancer.
26 **Dignityville** name of tent city for the homeless in Dan's town
28 **You threw a perfect strike and the ump called it a ball.** The ball you threw was in the valid zone but the umpire *(Schieds-richter/in)* said it wasn't.

I couldn't say. We may have studied those events in school, but those old protest movements were about as real to me as trigonometry. You learned what you needed to ace the test. And not for an instant did it feel like it had any actual meaning in your
40 life.

'If we don't do something, it's only going to get worse,' the kid said. 'And it's not the kind of thing one person can do. Marches show strength. They tell politicians that we have the numbers and the votes to change elections.'

I was more than three years away from being able to drink legally, but only months
45 from being able to vote. Sure, voting may have been way more important, but given the choice, I would have switched those two age requirements in a heartbeat.

The kid was still waiting for me to respond.

'Can I ask you something personal?' I said. 'Why do you care? You homeless or something?'

50 The kid gave me a long, curious look, then said, 'No, I care ... because I'm *not* homeless.'

From: No Place, 2014

COMPREHENSION ◀

1 Mediation (English ➜ German)
Tell your parents/little brother/sister at the dinner table in two German sentences what the novel extract is about.

▶ SF 41: Mediation of written and oral texts

2 Interviews
Write five interview questions for Dan Halprin based on the text you have just read. Ask your partner your questions, then answer your partner's questions. Discuss any points on which you differ.

▶ SF 26: Taking part in an interview

ANALYSIS ◀

3 Dan's political development
Point to examples from the text that show how Dan's interest in politics and political action is changing. Examine the factors that influence him.

LANGUAGE AWARENESS ◀

4 Uses of the progressive form
a Collect examples of the past progressive from the extract. Compare lists with your partner. Together, formulate a rule explaining when the past progressive is used.
b In the following text, no progressive forms have been used. Rewrite the text, deciding which verbs should be put in the past progressive:
When Mr Purcellen arrived home that evening, I sat next to Talia on the front porch. It was a warm evening; the moon shone behind the trees, and a soft wind blew. Mr Purcellen got out of the old pickup he always drove to work. He walked across the dark lawn and stopped about ten yards from the house. I think he watched us, but I couldn't guess what he thought.
c CHALLENGE ▶ Examine the text on the poster (in the middle of the opposite page). The second sentence uses a progressive form of the verb *be* twice. Explain how this form differs in meaning from the simple form of the verb.

▶ LP 1: Simple and progressive verb forms
▶ SF 4: Using a grammar book

BEYOND THE TEXT ◀

5 YOU CHOOSE ▶ Creative writing

a Retell the episode described in the extract from the point of view of the student activist. **OR** b Write a continuation of the extract, in which Dan decides whether he wants to sign up for the protest march.

▶ SF 37: Doing a creative writing task

39 **ace a test** get a good mark on a test

━ **TROUBLE SPOT** ━
actual ['æktʃuəl] (l. 39) = *real, concrete*
But: *aktuell* = ***current, topical***

The USA – Still the Promised Land? Chapter 7

151

The Unites States' place in the world

D1 Facts and figures

	USA	China	Germany	Brazil	Russia	India
1 GDP	16,244,600	8,277,103	3,428,131	2,252,664	2,014,775	1,841,710
2 Military spending	682,478	166,107	45,785	43,576	90,749	46,125
3 Balance of trade	−784,775	155,142	219,938	19,169	198,760	−154,401

All figures are in millions of US dollars and are from 2012, except (3), which contains data from 2011.

> ■ **FACT FILE**
>
> **GDP** (**Gross** [grəʊs] **Domestic Product**) is defined as the total value of goods and services produced in a country. The **balance of trade** is the difference between the total value of exports from a country and imports into the same country. A negative balance (**deficit** ['defɪsɪt]; opposite: **surplus** ['sɜːpləs]) means the country imports more than it exports.

► SF 12: Analysing charts and graphs

COMPREHENSION ◄

1 Understanding the figures
  a Write eight sentences comparing the figures in the table. **SUPPORT** ▶ p. 212
  b Compare sentences with your partner. Check each other's information to make sure you have both got the facts right.

BEYOND THE TEXT ◄

2 The facts behind the figures
  Link up with another pair and discuss what influence the facts from the table above could have on the balance of power in the world.

🎧 **CD2** 08

► SF 41: Mediation of written and oral texts

D2 The German view   *Michael Hochgeschwender*

In the podcast you are about to hear, historian Michael Hochgeschwender is asked if the USA is still the leading world power. When you mention this interview to your American e-pal, she wants to know what the professor says about the USA's status in the world. You will hear the interview twice.

► SF 22: Listening

COMPREHENSION ◄

1 While listening
  Listen to what Hochgeschwender says about the position of the USA in the world. Take notes on the following aspects:
  • what the historian says about the world status of the United States,
  • his reasons for his opinion,
  • his views on the future development of the United States' role.

2 After listening
  Compare notes with your partner.

BEYOND THE TEXT ◄

► SF 41: Mediation of written and oral texts
► CC 6: Talking about sensitive issues

3 Mediation (German → English)
  a Use your notes to write an email of about 150 words explaining Hochgeschwender's position to your e-pal.
  b **CHALLENGE** ▶ Add a further paragraph to your email from **a** in which you comment on the historian's views and ask your American e-pal for her opinion.

D3 Better than its reputation *Anne Applebaum*

The 20th century is sometimes called 'the American century'. Collect reasons why this might be. How do you think historians will refer to the present century?

LONDON – In Beijing a few months ago, I met a young Filipina journalist who did video interviews for a Chinese website. She seemed clever and competent. She spoke perfect American English, which she learned growing up near a U.S. base. She was very pleased to be in China: Her job in Beijing was interesting, well-paid, and gave
5 her a future. I asked whether she thought her career might take her to the United States. She shrugged. She would never get a visa, let alone a job. Not worth trying.

At the time, I thought this conversation rather ominous. It seemed another reminder that the American dream is looking rather tarnished these days, and not only to Americans. To much of the outside world, the United States appears unprom-
10 ising and unwelcoming, especially compared with the largest economy in East Asia, the new land of opportunity. We are growing far more slowly than China. Our middle class is downwardly mobile. U.S. news organizations are not scouring the world for talent, whereas China's apparently are. [...]

And yet, when a disaster unfolds and resources
15 have to be rapidly mobilized, it's as if nothing has changed. One of the largest typhoons on record hit the Philippines last week. The extent of the damage isn't yet known. But the American response is already larger – by a factor of hundreds
20 – than that of the largest economy in East Asia. The United States is sending an aircraft carrier to the worst-hit regions and has promised $20 million in emergency aid. Millions more will be raised by U.S. charities. The British are sending a
25 warship and $16 million. Even the Vatican has promised $4 million. And the government of China, the new land of opportunity? $100,000.

There are politics behind China's stinginess. China has recently made claims on Philippine territory, citing historical documents
30 that date to the fifth century. The Philippine government has responded with anger, a lawsuit, and an invitation to the U.S. Navy to reopen some bases closed in the 1990s. There are also politics behind American generosity, which partly reflects the renewed warmth and military cooperation between Washington and Manila.

But these differing responses to the typhoon also signify a different set of attitudes
35 to power, and not just to 'soft power': Americans, like Europeans, have long believed that strength and wealth entail responsibility. That's why two American ex-presidents voluntarily coordinated the international response to the 2004 tsunami, even though Indonesia was not the site of a U.S. naval base. That's why massive amounts of U.S. aid went to victims of the 2005 earthquake in Kashmir, even though relations between
40 the United States and Pakistan were deteriorating at the time.

That's also why an American president who is actively uninterested in engaging with the Syrian conflict has pledged more than $1 billion in humanitarian aid to Syrian refugees, accounting for nearly 30 percent of all such aid; European contributions as a whole make up a good percentage of the rest. China's contribution, mean-
45 while, comes to $3 million, less than that of Luxembourg. China plays an enormous political role in Syria – the Chinese veto has helped keep the United Nations firmly

Members of the US and Philippine army unload US aid as part of relief efforts after Typhoon Haiyan

6 **let alone** *geschweige denn*
7 **ominous** ['ɒmɪnəs] suggesting that sth. bad is going to happen
8 **tarnished** (here) no longer attractive
12 **scour sth.** ['skaʊə] search sth. intensely
14 **unfold** (here) happen
16 **on record** [BE: 'rekɔːd, AE: 'rekərd] *seit Menschengedenken*
17 **extent** *Ausmaß*
21 **aircraft carrier** *Flugzeugträger*
24 **charity** organization that helps people in need
28 **stinginess** ['stɪndʒɪnəs] *Geiz*
31 **lawsuit** *(juristische) Klage*
36 **entail sth.** have sth. as a consequence
41 **deteriorate** [dɪ'tɪəriəreɪt] become worse
42 **engage with sth.** get involved in sth.
43 **pledge sth.** promise to give sth.
44 **account for sth.** *etwas ausmachen*

47 **sidelined** unable to take action
obligated ['ɒblɪgeɪtɪd]
verpflichtet
50 **counter sth.** deal with the
effects of sth.
facilitate sth. [fə'sɪlɪteɪt] *(fml)*
make sth. easier
52 **for its own sake** *als Selbstzweck*
56 **elaborate** [ɪ'læbərət] long and
complex
58 **wane** become less
59 **taper off** become less

sidelined there – but clearly does not feel obligated to help those affected by its decisions.

The Chinese do give development aid, but differently: not in response to tragedies, not to counter disaster, but to facilitate the export of raw materials to China. There is 50 merit to some of China's efforts, especially in Africa. But the Chinese state is not, for the most part, interested in generosity for its own sake. Nor do many Chinese billionaires believe that new wealth brings new obligations. Several of them refused even to meet Bill Gates a few years ago, apparently because they were afraid he might ask them to give away some of their money. 55

All of which is not an elaborate excuse for messy American foreign policy, or the still-weak American economy, or the indecisive American president. It's just a little reminder: U.S. strength may be waning, U.S. status may be fading, and U.S. attraction for talented foreigners may soon taper off. But there will be reasons to be sorry if America isn't a superpower anymore, perhaps more than America's critics think. 60

From: 'Why America's critics will miss the U.S. superpower',
Slate (magazine), 13 November 2013

COMPREHENSION ◀

1 Summarizing the text
Summarize the *author's views on the United States' role in the world in no more than four sentences.

2 Collecting information
a Copy and complete the table with information from the text:

	China	USA
strong points		
weak points		

b Compare tables with your partner; add any missing information.

ANALYSIS ◀

▶ SF 18: Analysing non-fiction

▶ LP 13: Placing emphasis on key points

3 The author's bias
a Examine the author's position: Whose side is she on? Give examples from the text that illustrate her position (selection of facts, word choice, use of emphasis, juxtaposition, sentence structure, etc.). **SUPPORT** ▶ p. 213
b Use your results from tasks 1–3 to analyse the author's strategy: How does she structure her arguments and what *stylistic devices does the use?

LANGUAGE AWARENESS ◀

▶ LP 20: Word formation

▶ SF 3: Using a dictionary

Find an online dictionary here:
 Webcode context-52

4 Word formation
a Form eight word pairs (either 'noun – adjective' or 'noun – verb') using words from the text. Example: *generosity – generous; contribution – contribute*. Consult a monolingual dictionary if necessary.
b Use the words that don't appear in the text in sentences of your own.

BEYOND THE TEXT ◀

▶ LP 2: Present tense or future?

5 WRITING CONFERENCE The next ten years
Form small groups. Write down your ideas on the topic: Will the USA still play a major role in the world ten years from now? Share your ideas with your group, and discuss the reasons for your opinions.

Giving a speech on why you would like to visit the USA

Imagine you discover this advert on the internet:

The Chance of a Lifetime!

The German-American Friendship Organization is offering ten stipends for German teenagers aged 18 or older. Winners will spend three months in the United States, living with American families, visiting schools, businesses and places of interest, talking to politicians, business people, and just plain Americans of all ages.

To apply to our program, send us a video of not more than five minutes in which you make a speech on the subject: 'Why I want to learn more about the United States of America.'

Excited at the prospect of an all-expenses-paid stay in the USA, you decide to apply.

1 Getting started

Collect your ideas using a suitable method: What do you find fascinating, irritating, or intriguing about the USA and about Americans? What kinds of people would you like to talk to? What questions would you ask them?

▶ SF 25: Giving a speech

2 Writing your speech

a Organize your ideas in the form of an outline. Use the outline to write a first draft.

b Read your drafts aloud in small groups and discuss them, suggesting improvements where needed.

c Prepare a revised version. Make sure it does not take longer than five minutes. Practise reading your speech in front of a friend or a mirror until you feel confident with it. Then make a video of yourself delivering your speech.

Find a tool to improve your speaking skills here:
 Webcode context-51

Find a tool to create your video here: **Webcode** context-54

3 Evaluation

Form small groups. In your group, let the others watch your video (or you can deliver it 'live'). The others give you feedback. They fill in assessment sheets given out by your teacher.

8 Beyond the Nation – Europe and a Globalized World

A

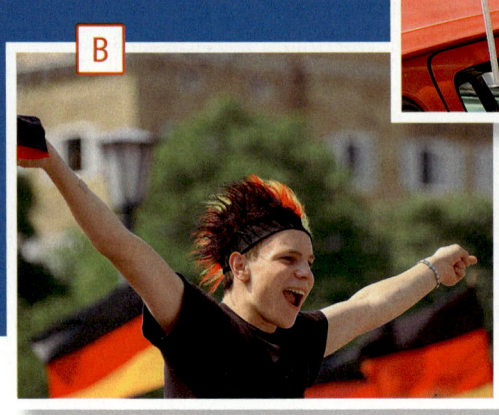

B

C

Download a list of chapter vocab here: **Webcode** context-22

▶ CC 1: Cultural awareness

▶ SF 41: Mediation of written and oral texts
▶ SF 24: Giving a presentation

1 Displaying one's national identity
During great sports events, above all soccer world championships, people often display their national identity and patriotism by carrying flags or singing their national anthem.

a THINK Describe your attitude to this behaviour, referring to the pictures above and your own experience.

b PAIR Compare and discuss your ideas with a partner.

c SHARE Present your most interesting findings to the class.

2 YOU CHOOSE ▶ **Researching flags and anthems**

a Use German sources to find out about the history of the German flag and the national anthem. Prepare a short presentation for English-speaking visitors to your school.

OR

b Choose a country and do some research into the history of its anthem and flag. Present your findings to the class.

3 Understanding national symbols
Define the function of national symbols such as flags and anthems.

4 Finding out about international institutions

   a Find out about the roles of the following institutions: UN, UNESCO, WHO, Commonwealth, EU. Describe and explain their logos.

   b Say why institutions that cut across national boundaries might be necessary.

5 Thinking about your sense of identity

   a Complete this sentence: 'I rather see myself as (1) a German or other national citizen, (2) a European, (3) a cosmopolitan citizen, (4) none of the above.' Say why.

   b Find out how the majority of your class see themselves and why.

CD2 09

Listen to an audio version of the text on the CD or download it here:
Webcode context-23

> **TROUBLE SPOT**
>
> Preis = **prize** (award given to sb. for an achievement)
> Preis = **price** (the money you have to pay for sth.)

Globalization: Europe, the world

European integration as a model?

Political experts say that the power of nation states has been declining and that today the most important decisions are taken on an international level. The European Union, which connects independent nation states, is a good example. The two principal purposes of the European Union (and of its predecessors) are to secure peace and promote economic growth. In 2012, the European Union was awarded the Nobel Peace Prize for overcoming the hostility among European countries after the Second World War and for advancing reconciliation and peace. At the moment of the award, however, Europe was and still is challenged by a monetary crisis, which forced many member states to make massive cuts in their budgets. As a result, unemployment rates increased and many young people, especially those from Spain or Greece were forced to leave their countries and find occupation elsewhere. 5

10

Chances and risks of globalization

GLOBALIZATION MEANS WHEN YOUR EMAIL ACCOUNT IS FULL WITH SPAM FROM COUNTRIES YOU'VE NEVER HEARD OF...

Globalization can be described as a process in which barriers, especially trade barriers, between nations are removed. This process accelerated when modern communication technologies came into play and transport costs decreased. It made international collaboration and competition possible: Companies in the developed countries were able to outsource their production and services to countries whose labour force was prepared to work for significantly lower wages. 15

20

This international division of labour may have freed many people in the developing countries from extreme poverty; however, many of them have to work under poor working conditions with low safety standards. In the traditional industrialized countries, globalization has resulted in redundancies in the domestic workforce. 25

The threats and opportunities of globalization can be illustrated well through the example of international sports. Top soccer clubs pay enormous sums for the best players from all over the world, allowing for extraordinary labour mobility. Yet, only the richest clubs can participate in this 'leg-drain' and if players are frequently being bought and sold they may feel uprooted and unable to develop a sound sense of identity. 30

English as a global language 35

The cultural impact of globalization is illustrated most clearly by the role of English as a global language. Today, English is not only the native language of more than 360 million speakers worldwide, but it is also used as a lingua franca between non-native speakers of English in international business, science and technology, and popular culture. On the one hand, this makes international communication easier, but on the other hand, it threatens local languages and thus cultural and linguistic diversity. 40

▶ SF 2: Learning new words

Find an online thesaurus here:
 Webcode context-52

1 Words in use: synonyms

Find a highlighted word or expression that means the same as …
1 the aim or function of something.
2 the percentage of people in a country without a job.
3 the readiness of people to work in different places.
4 not feel at home anywhere.
5 give a job to external workers, often in another country.
6 language spoken all over the world.

2 Word formation

For each gap in the sentences below choose a suitable word from the list
on the right, turn it into the required word class (e.g. a verb into a noun)
and adjust its grammatical form if necessary (e.g. the plural form).
1 Some European countries had an extremely … relationship for centuries.
2 With the Treaty of Friendship (1963) France and Germany were
officially …
3 In our times of globalization, individuals world-wide have to … and …
4 Since the EU was …, lasting peace has been one of its aims.
5 Today, the EU is facing great …

*collaboration •
competition • challenge •
foundation • hostility •
reconciliation*

▶ LP 20: Word formation

3 Activating your vocabulary

Translate the following passage. The underlined words and phrases are
taken from the text, but you should try to translate them without looking at
the text again. Paraphrase if you do not know the exact word or expression.
Revise your version with the help of the text and a dictionary.

▶ SF 9: Paraphrasing
▶ SF 3: Using a dictionary

Find an online dictionary here:
 Webcode context-52

Globalisierung ist ein Prozess voller Chancen und Risiken. Kritiker
befürchten, dass sie Arbeitsplätze in den traditionellen Industrieländern
gefährdet und Arbeiter in den Entwicklungsländern ausbeutet, die oft
unter sehr schlechten Arbeitsbedingungen arbeiten müssen. Befürworter
der Globalisierung glauben, dass sie extreme Armut in vielen Ländern
besiegen kann. Der Abbau von Handelsschranken sei von Vorteil für alle.

▶ LP 16: Avoiding Germanisms

4 Mediation (English → German)

You are asked to briefly inform your politics course in German on the future
of nation states as described in this text. Prepare and give a short oral
presentation. Make visual aids if necessary.

▶ SF 41: Mediation of written
and oral texts
▶ SF 7: Making visual aids
▶ SF 24: Giving a presentation

European integration as a model?

A1 A great achievement of the past   *Herman Van Rompuy*

Since 1901 the Nobel Peace Prize has been awarded annually (with few exceptions) to individuals and institutions who have sought to establish or keep peace. During the award ceremony, the winner is required to give the Nobel Lecture, a lecture on a subject related to the topic of the prize. When in 2012 the European Union was awarded the prize, the Nobel Lecture was given by Herman Van Rompuy, President of the European Council, and José Manuel Barroso, President of the European Commission.

1 Before listening
Look at the picture below and describe the setting and the general atmosphere of the ceremony.

▶ SF 11: Analysing pictures
▶ SF 22: Listening
▶ SF 10: Working with closed test formats

🎧 **CD2** 10, 11, 12, 13

Herodotus [həˈrɒdətəs] (ca. 484–425 BC) Greek historian
Winston Churchill (1874–1965) British Prime Minister (1940–1945 and 1951–1955)
founder person who starts an institution or organization
ceasefire [ˈsiːsfaɪə] time when enemies stop fighting
reconciliation [ˌrekənsɪliˈeɪʃn] situation where two people or groups become friendly again after a disagreement
Konrad Adenauer (1876–1967) first post-war Chancellor of West Germany (1949–1963)
Treaty of Rome founding document of the European Economic Community from 1957
Willy Brandt (1913–1992) West German Chancellor (1969–1974)
Gdansk Danzig, Polish seaport
François Mitterand (1916–1996) French President (1981–1995)
Helmut Kohl (born 1930) West German Chancellor (1982–1998)
Tallin, Riga, Vilnius capitals of the Baltic states Estonia, Latvia and Lithuania, respectively
Jean Monnet (1888–1979) French diplomat, considered to be one of the founding fathers of the European Union
perpetual [pəˈpetʃuəl] continuing for a long period of time with no interruption
Srebrenica town in Bosnia, site of a massacre during the Balkan War (1995)
Abraham Lincoln [ˈlɪŋkən] (1809–1865) President of the United States (1861–1865)

COMPREHENSION ◀

2 Listening for gist
Listen to the audio file, which contains Van Rompuy's part of the Nobel Lecture. From the following statements choose the one that best describes the speaker's message.
1 Peacekeeping is Europe's ongoing goal.
2 Lasting peace has been established in Europe.
3 Current challenges are threatening to seriously destabilize the EU.

3 Listening for detail: part 1
Listen to the first part of the speech, then decide whether the following statements are true or false according to the speaker.
1 The Nobel Prize belongs to Europe's political elite, who united Europe after World War II.
2 War used to be a constant feature of European history.
3 Van Rompuy still has wartime memories of his own.
4 Europe would not have gained peace without the European Union.
5 Konrad Adenauer was awarded a French medal in 1951.

4 Listening for detail: part 2

Say which historical events depicted in the photos are mentioned by Rompuy. Give the photos headings.

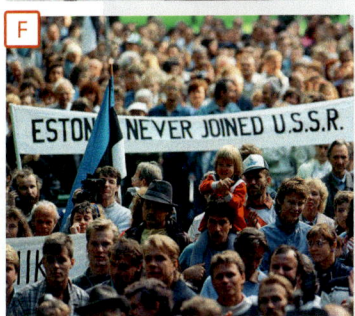

5 Listening for detail: part 3

Choose the correct statement.

a Rompuy mentions the example of Srebrenica to prove that …
1 … there is no European post-war generation.
2 … there was war in Europe not very long ago.
3 … Soviet rule in Eastern Europe was responsible for massacres.

b According to the speaker, the economic crisis …
1 … does not put the European Union to the test.
2 … mainly affects young academics.
3 … reduces the feeling of solidarity.

—————————————————— LANGUAGE AWARENESS ◀

6 A non-native accent

a Listen to the speech once more and examine Van Rompuy's English. Identify elements that show that English is not his native tongue.

▶ LANGUAGE HELP

b Do you think it's a disadvantage to speak with an accent? Say why or why not.

—————————————————— BEYOND THE TEXT ◀

7 YOU CHOOSE ▶ Research on the EU

Do some research on one of the topics below, then present your results:

a Describe the status of English in the European institutions. Discuss whether the use of other languages, e.g. German, should be promoted within European institutions.

 OR

b Outline the events that led to European unification and describe their context and consequences. Add more 'historical moments' that helped to unite Europe.

LANGUAGE HELP
- pronounce … as … / say … instead of …
- not pronounce … properly
- use voiceless/voiced consonants
- long/short vowel / diphthong

▶ SF 24: Giving a presentation

A2 Young, educated – and leaving the country

Liz Alderman

The following extract from an article illustrates the consequences of the European financial crisis for individuals.

Soon after her 23rd birthday four years ago, Melissa Abadía made a wrenching decision: She would leave her close-knit family in Spain, where the grinding fallout from the 2008 financial crisis had made securing a good job impossible, and move to the Netherlands, where employers were still hiring.

'When I got on the plane, I was crying,' Ms. Abadía, a bright, ebullient woman, 5 recalled. 'But I had to decide: Should I fight for something back home that makes no sense, or get out of there and make a life for myself?'

Despite five years of training in nursing in her hometown, Castellón de la Plana, in eastern Spain, she now works in a windowless stockroom in Amsterdam organizing purses, socks and other accessories at a clothing store. 10

It is a sign of the plight of her generation that simply having a job and a measure of independence makes her one of the lucky ones – never mind homesickness, dashed dreams of a very different career and a gradual acceptance that her life will probably never be the one she expected to live.

'Of course, I hate the fact that I have to do this,' she said, speaking in somber tones. 15 'Leaving your country should be a decision, not an obligation.'

Finding only unpaid nursing internships and a temporary nightclub job in Spain, Ms. Abadía scoured the Internet for work in Europe's more prosperous north. She quickly found employment as an au pair in Amsterdam.

For the first time, she experienced the shock of being an immigrant. Having arrived 20 in Amsterdam as part of an influx of young Spanish, Greek, Italian and Portuguese men and women all searching for any employment, 'I now know what it's like to be seen as someone who's coming to steal jobs,' she said.

She soon found better-paying work at the clothing shop, near the Royal Palace. The store was crowded with at least 10 other young Spaniards who had migrated for 25 employment.

She spent two years bouncing between short-term contracts, which employers have sharply increased during the crisis to cut costs and avoid the expensive labor protections granted to permanent employees.

In some countries, especially those with the highest youth unemployment rates, 30 short-term contracts are nothing more than opportunities for employers to take advantage of the weak labor market.

But when used by employers as intended – to give experience to young people who otherwise could not get a start – they can lead to steady work. That was the case with Ms. Abadía, whose employer eventually turned her temporary job into a permanent 35 contract with benefits overseeing the store's biggest stockroom.

On one level, having even that kind of employment is a victory in today's Europe. Her salary of €1,200 a month (about $1,600) was nearly twice what she could have expected to make in Spain.

'The day I signed a permanent contract was the best day of my life,' she said one 40 recent weeknight, beaming as she sipped a Coke at a bustling pub.

'It is almost impossible to get one now in Spain,' she said. 'Here, they trust me, a Spanish girl, and give me responsibilities. I can pay my rent, save money and be independent. I'm even writing a book.'

Working in a clothes shop

1 **wrench** *(adj)* very difficult and painful
2 **grinding** ['graɪndɪŋ] *(adj)* never ending or improving
fallout ['– –] (here) long-term consequences of a disaster
5 **ebullient** [ɪ'bʌlɪənt] *(fml)* full of energy
9 **stockroom** room where goods are kept in a shop
11 **plight** difficult and sad situation
15 **somber** *(AE)* = *(BE)* **sombre** serious and a little sad
16 **obligation** *Pflicht*
17 **internship** ['– – –] temporary job, often for little or no pay, especially done by newcomers to a job
27 **bounce between jobs** move from one job to another
contract ['– –] formal document containing an agreement, e.g. between employer and employee
36 **benefits** ['benɪfɪts] advantages given to an employee in addition to their salary (e.g. sick pay, health insurance)
oversee sb./sth. (here) be the manager of sth.
41 **beam** *(v)* smile broadly

45 But because of her work hours, she still does not qualify for the Netherlands' monthly minimum wage of €1,477 (about $2,000), and her new career was a long way from where she had always hoped to end up.

Discussing the path that had brought her to this point, Ms. Abadía became suddenly pensive. Adjusting to a life far from home in a job beneath her skills has been harder 50 than she imagined.

'I gave up the thought of working as a nurse long ago,' she said. 'With this job, I'm so tired sometimes that I can't move. I don't know what a weekend is anymore.'

Above all, Ms. Abadía still yearns for Spain. [...]

'Recently, I heard criticism that people like us are running away,' Ms. Abadía said. 55 'We didn't run away. We left because the economic situation and the politicians pushed us.'

'If they don't fix things, they are going to lose a couple generations of smart, young people,' Ms. Abadía added as her friends nodded in agreement. 'And then what will happen to the country that's left behind?'

60 That question is weighing on European leaders. An estimated 100,000 university graduates have left Spain, and hundreds of thousands more from Europe's crisis-hit countries have gone to Germany, Britain, and the Nordic states for jobs in engineering, science and medicine. Many others have gone farther afield to Australia, Canada and the United States.

65 The current migration 'is mostly the skilled part of the population,' said Massimiliano Mascherini, a research manager at Eurofound, a European Union research agency. 'It is alarming for the countries that young people are leaving, and it should be a big source of concern for their governments.'

From: *The New York Times*, 15 November 2013

COMPREHENSION ◄

1 Understanding Melissa Abadía's situation
Point out why Melissa Abadía left Spain, how her working life developed in Amsterdam and which consequences youth unemployment in Europe has in general.

LANGUAGE AWARENESS ◄

2 Transforming direct into indirect speech
  a Choose two quotations by Melissa Abadía and turn them into indirect speech.
  b Explain what changes you have to make when turning direct into indirect speech. What role does the introductory verb play?

ANALYSIS ◄

3 Examining the use of direct and indirect speech
  a Go back to your results from task **2** and compare the effect of direct speech and indirect speech respectively.
  b Analyse the effect the writer achieves by using many direct quotations.
  c CHALLENGE ▶ Explain why direct statements are used frequently in reports and feature articles.

BEYOND THE TEXT ◄

4 Creative writing SUPPORT ▶ p. 214
Form groups of four. Each select one important moment of Melissa Abadía's immigrant experience and write a diary entry. Read out your entries to your group and join your texts to form one coherent diary entry.

TROUBLE SPOT
career (l. 46)
= beruflicher Werdegang
= erfolgreiche Karriere

49 **pensive** thinking deeply, worrying about sth.
49 **beneath sb./sth.** lower than sb./sth., not good enough for sb./sth.
60 **weigh on sb.** make sb. worried
63 **farther afield** far way from home

▶ LP 4: Present perfect and simple past

▶ SF 18: Analysing non-fiction

▶ SF 37: Doing a creative writing task

A3 Hunting for personnel   *Sascha Schmierer*

In some European countries many young people face the problem of unemployment. In others, employers in some areas have great difficulty filling their job vacancies. Read this text from a German newspaper about a way to solve both problems.

Es steht nicht zu befürchten, dass die Krankenschwestern im Ludwigsburger Klinikum ihre Patienten beim Weckruf am Morgen künftig mit einem fröhlichen „Buenos Días" begrüßen. Und das Küchenteam wird statt leckerer Tapas wohl auch weiterhin salzarm zubereitete Krankenhauskost servieren. Dennoch bricht für den Klinikenverbund Ludwigsburg-Bietigheim nächsten Mittwoch eine „spanische Ära" an.   5

Pünktlich um 9.30 Uhr wird die Medizindirektorin Andrea Grebe im Konferenzraum an der Erlachhofstraße mehr als 30 neue Pflegekräfte von der Iberischen Halbinsel begrüßen. Nach einem ambitionierten Sprachkurs sollen die hoch qualifizierten neuen Mitarbeiter den eklatanten Personalmangel in der Intensivmedizin in den   10 drei Häusern in Ludwigsburg, Bietigheim und Neuenbürg beheben – olé im OP sozusagen.

„Fachkräfte für Intensivstationen und den OP-Bereich sind in Deutschland fast nicht zu finden, der Markt ist leergefegt", erklärt der Kliniken-Sprecher Alexander   15 Tsongas den für ein schwäbisches Spital bisher noch eher ungewöhnlichen Schritt. Weil bei der Suche nach qualifiziertem Personal allerdings weder regionale Berufsmessen noch die Werbeaktionen in angrenzenden Bundesländern erfolgreich waren, wichen die Stellenbesetzer des   20 Kliniken-Verbunds nach Südeuropa aus.

Auf die in Spanien geschalteten Anzeigen für OP-Pflegekräfte meldeten sich binnen weniger Tage zahlreiche Bewerber, mit 60 Kandidaten führten die Personalchefs ein Vorstellungsgespräch.   25

Ergebnis ist, dass bereits nächste Woche mehr als 30 spanische Pflegekräfte ihren Dienst in Ludwigsburg antreten. Bevor die neuen Mitarbeiter – bis auf wenige Ausnahmen handelt es sich um junge Frauen – auf die Tochterkliniken verteilt werden, steht ein je nach Vorkenntnissen zwischen vier und sechs Monaten   30 dauernder Intensivsprachkurs auf dem Lehrplan. Parallel zum Deutschlernen sind Arbeitspraktika in den Krankenhäusern vorgesehen. Für das erste halbe Jahr sind die neuen Pflegekräfte mit einem Praktikantenvertrag ausgestattet. Nach der Probezeit winkt ein unbefristeter Arbeitsvertrag – schließlich hofft die Chefetage des Kliniken-Verbunds, dass die neuen Mitarbeiter aus dem Süden im kalten Deutschland nicht   35 gleich das Weite suchen.

From: *Stuttgarter Nachrichten*, 12 October 2012

Comparing situations
Compare the information presented in the article with Melissa Abadía's situation (cf. p. 162).

▶ LP 6: Infinitive or gerund after certain nouns

■ **TROUBLE SPOT**

jdn. / etwas pflegen
= (a sick person) *nurse sb. / care for sb.*
= (an animal) *look after sth.*
= (a garden, a plant) *tend sth.*

MEDIATION FOCUS ON SKILLS

Mediating texts in oral communication

*Imagine the following situation: On a trip to Amsterdam you meet Melissa Abadía (cf. **A2**, p. 162) in a pub and she tells you her story in English. You remember the article about job vacancies in Germany (cf. **A3**, p. 164) and decide to tell her about it.*

▶ SF 41: Mediation of written and oral texts

1 Choosing the relevant information

a Examine the situation closely, then look at the following keywords from text **A3**. Which of them do you think would be relevant to Abadía?

> **TROUBLE SPOT**
> *information* (sing)
> Not: ~~informations~~

1 Um 9.30 werden die neuen Pflegekräfte in Ludwigsburg begrüßt.	4 In Deutschland gibt es nicht genügend Pflegekräfte für Intensivstationen.
2 Auf Messen und durch Werbeaktionen konnte kein zusätzliches Pflegepersonal gewonnen werden.	5 Die neuen spanischen Pflegekräfte sind vor allem Frauen.
3 Pflegekräfte müssen einen Sprachkurs absolvieren.	6 Sie sind zunächst als Praktikant/innen angestellt.

b Note down any other information you consider useful to Abadía.

2 Explaining specific terms

When mediating information from German into English, you will have to paraphrase or explain words, either because you (or the person you are talking to) don't know their English equivalents or because your partner has a different cultural background.

a Imagine you knew the translations for the words below. Which of them would you explain to Melissa Abadía all the same? Say why.

▶ LP 16: Avoiding Germanisms

> **LANGUAGE HELP**
> • continue/conclude/ cancel/end a contract
> • a contract expires after …
> • dismiss sb.

1 *Intensivstation*	4 *Praktikantenvertrag*
2 *Arbeitspraktikum*	5 *unbefristeter Arbeitsvertrag*
3 *Sprachkurs*	6 *Probezeit*

b Paraphrase or explain the words from **a**. ▶ LANGUAGE HELP

▶ SF 9: Paraphrasing

3 Choosing the correct register

The place where a conversation takes place and your relationship to the addressee influence the way you speak to them. Read the two beginnings of the conversation with Melissa Abadía and decide which of them would be more appropriate in the given situation. Say why.

▶ LP 11: Using the right register

'Well, actually, I read an article just a few days ago and I think it might interest you. Basically it was all about how Germany really needs nurses and …'	'Bearing in mind the situation you have been telling me about I would like to inform you about the opportunities that have opened in Germany for qualified nurses.'

4 Speaking to the addressee

a Structure your ideas and prepare your side of the conversation, bearing in mind your results from tasks **1–3**.

▶ CC 4: Meeting and greeting

b Work with a partner to role-play the conversation. Answer their questions and pay attention to their facial expression or gestures to find out whether they have understood you. Rephrase your statements if necessary. Then swap roles.

▶ LP 12: Avoiding German-sounding sentence patterns

Find a recording tool here:
 Webcode context-55

Chances and risks of globalization

B1 How big is the impact?

Globalization is a complex process that affects various aspects of life. The video you are going to watch explains how it works.

▶ LP 7: The passive

1 Identifying the players in globalization

Describe the aspects of globalization that are presented in the picture below. Based on what you already know about globalization try to say how they are connected.

🎬 **DVD**

▶ SF 15: Marking up a text / Making and taking notes

COMPREHENSION ◀

2 Defining globalization

a Watch the video and note down the main topics mentioned in it. Compare notes with a partner.

b Watch the video for a second time and add information on the topics from **a**.

c Compare your notes in a group and add to them if necessary.

▶ SF 24: Giving a presentation

d As a group give a short presentation on globalization with each group member contributing 1–2 sentences on each topic.

ANALYSIS ◀

▶ SF 23: Analysing a film

3 Examining the video

Describe the devices that are employed in the video and explain their function. ▶ LANGUAGE HELP

LANGUAGE HELP

- explainer video / instructional video
- hand-crafted drawings showing … / scraps of paper
- put sth. on screen / remove sth.
- use audio effects to …

BEYOND THE TEXT ◀

4 YOU CHOOSE ▶ Illustrating globalization

a Comment on the quotation below and find examples that illustrate it further.

OR

b Find a picture that illustrates your personal view on the impact that globalization has on people. If necessary, collect background information about it. Present your findings in class.

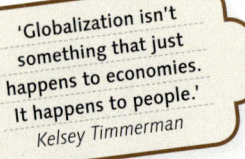

'Globalization isn't something that just happens to economies. It happens to people.'
Kelsey Timmerman

B2 The need for a new label   *Lucy Siegle*

- What information do the labels on the right give? What information might be missing?

Imagine a label, one that reads: 'An actual, living, breathing human used their own hands to help make this product.' This is just what the (western) world needs, a label affixed to consumer goods. We need this urgent reminder because in those seconds when we decide to purchase another piece of life's apparatus we are strikingly effect-
5 ive at suppressing any ethical doubt over its provenance.

The first thing we do (with varying levels of awareness) is convince ourselves that – from the hottest bits of sleek hi-tech gadgetry to highly embellished fashion garments – these were made by very clever robot arms that can apply toxic chemicals to a touch screen or expertly sew a sequin or bead. But as today's Observer report on
10 Apple products lays bare, our consumer goods still arrive courtesy of the blood, sweat and tears of many human beings. [...] The habitual use of unpaid, enforced overtime is common across many sectors. In the fashion industry, garment workers are effect-ively set up to fail. When a multinational places an order at the behest of a buyer the workers are set quotas to meet the order. Professor Doug Miller, an expert on the
15 garment supply chain and workers' rights, has identified a discrepancy between the estimated and real time taken for a garment worker to complete an order. So the multinational buyer's calculations are based on standard minute values (SMVs) – virtual minutes based on a factory that operates at near 100% efficiency. However, in countries such as Cambodia (the British high street is heavily reliant on Cambodian
20 production), the efficiency of factories rarely rises above 30%. Garment workers can therefore work flat out without any hope of meeting their targets within their paid working hours. At this point, they are forced to work overtime and sometimes gates may be shut or locked (including the fire escapes). [...] As consumers, we still tend to be most receptive to the voices of brand spokespeople. Time after time, we trust their
25 soothing words: 'We're working on these challenges', 'We've been let down badly by a supplier', 'These are not our values' etc. and placated by their corporate social responsibility reports. Robert Reich warns in his recent book, *Supercapitalism*, corporate social responsibility is 'as meaningful as cotton candy'. But Reich's ultimate position is that we should stop expecting corporations to do the right thing. And I can't
30 see any way of absolving the consumer of responsibility. I used to advocate going through a sort of consumerist catechism before making any consumer purchasing decision. Who made this product? Why did they make it? Why do I need it? I feel as if I urgently need to return to this way of buying. An understanding of the provenance of the product is key.

From: The Guardian, 1 May 2011

Glossary

5 **provenance** ['prɒvənəns] place that sth. has come from
7 **sleek** elegant, shiny
   gadgetry collection of modern devices/tools
9 **sequin** ['siːkwɪn] small shiny disc sewn onto clothes as decoration
   bead small piece of wood or glass that can be put on a string and worn as jewellery
10 **lay sth. bare** (*fml*) make sth. known that was a secret
   courtesy of sb./sth. ['kɜːtəsi] as the result of sb./sth.
11 **overtime** time that you spend at your job after the normal work hours
13 **at the behest of sb.** because sb. has ordered it
14 **quota** amount of sth. that sb. needs to achieve
21 **flat out** (*adv*) completely
26 **supplier** *Lieferant/in*
   placate sb. [plə'keɪt] make sb. worry less about something
28 **cotton candy** *Zuckerwatte*
30 **absolve sb.** [æb'sɒlv] state formally that sb. is not responsible for sth.
   advocate sth. ['ædvəkeɪt] advise/recommend sth.
31 **catechism** ['kætəkɪzəm] set of questions and answers used to instruct people about Christian beliefs

---

COMPREHENSION ◀

1 Collecting information
Collect information from the article about the situation in the garment industry, how we consumers deal with it and what we *should* do. Write down 5–9 keywords for each of these topics, then present your results.

ANALYSIS ◀

2 Examining the text
Analyse the tone of the text.

▶ SF 18: Analysing non-fiction

BEYOND THE TEXT ◀

3 Promoting transparent labelling   **SUPPORT** ▶ p. 214
a Design a clothing label that helps buyers make responsible choices.
b Write an article for a magazine in which you promote this new label.

▶ SF 37: Doing a creative writing task

B3 The Dutch footballer from Japan *Elko Born*

▶ SF 14: Reading strategies

• Skim the text. Within 1–2 minutes find out the gist of the text.

2 **maritime** ['mærɪtaɪm] (*fml*) near the sea
4 **trade route** route that people follow to buy and sell things
kickstart sth. make a process or project start more quickly
10 **recent** in the near past
decade ['dekeɪd] period of ten years
12 **gradual** step by step, slow
diminish sth. reduce sth.
13 **Kettle crisps** brand of crisps
15 **coincide with sth.** [ˌkəʊɪn'saɪd] happen at the same time as sth.
16 **negotiate sth.** [nɪ'gəʊʃieɪt] arrange something by formal discussion
supranational referring to more than one nation
17 **perimeter** [–'–––] outside edge of an area of land
dub sth. sth. else call sth. sth. else
19 **Pelé** (born 1940) former Brazilian footballer, often considered the best football player of all time
26 **Premier League** ['premɪə liːg] English professional football league
30 **Champions League** annual continental football competition organized by the UEFA, the Union of European Football Associations
31 **deem sth. to be sth. else** consider sth. to be sth. else
prestigious [pre'stɪdʒəs] having a lot of prestige

Some scholars argue that the process of 'globalization' (broadly defined as the global integration of various aspects of culture) started in the 16th century, when maritime empires such as Portugal and the Dutch Republic started colonizing parts of Asia and the Americas, setting up trade routes and kickstarting modern capitalism along the way.　　　　　　5

Others argue that it wasn't Columbus who 'discovered' the Americas, that the ancient Greeks and the Romans used the so-called 'Silk Route' to trade with China, and that the process of 'globalization' started when humans first started interacting with others of their kind.

Nonetheless, it's fair to state that in recent decades, the process of globalization –　10 whenever it may have started – reached a new phase: the phase of automatization and the gradual diminishing of the relevance of national borders. Just think of the Internet, the EU, and of eating Kettle crisps whilst crossing the border between France and Belgium without showing anyone your passport.

The birth of modern football, of course, largely coincided with this new phase in　15 globalization. During the 1960s, when politicians were negotiating the supranational perimeters of the European Union (dubbed by some as the modern day Habsburg Empire), football produced its first superstars.

The fame of footballers like Pelé reached far beyond Brazil, and across the world, people took time off to sit in front of their black and white television sets to watch the　20 South American legend play. Indeed, when Pelé jokingly put himself ahead of Jesus Christ by telling a reporter that 'there are parts of the world where Jesus Christ is not so well known', he wasn't even being absurd.

In modern day football, we see different manifestations of the ongoing process of globalization. National leagues filled with foreign players provide the obvious　25 example: so far in 2013/2014, only 32.26% of minutes in the Premier League – an 'English' league, but followed intensely by people from all over the world – were completed by English players, with a remarkable 8.1% completed by players from France.

Another obvious example of globalization in football is the Champions League: an　30 international competition, deemed as one of the most important and prestigious in

An early example of globalization: 13th century merchants on the silk route

the world. And it's not just international competitions that make football fans and stadium-goers travel outside the borders of their countries. To name just one example: this season Championship-side Leicester City was pleasantly surprised by a large

35 contingent of R.S.C. Anderlecht fans showing up at the King Power Stadium to sing songs in praise of their former player Marcin Wasilewski – a Polish player – on multiple occasions. Unconstrained international travel and the internet make it all possible. [...]

Back in the early-modern period, trading diasporas functioned as communities of

40 merchants living in foreign lands. They were semi-permanent residents. Not quite Dutch, English or Portuguese, but not quite native either. Often, these diasporas would be linked: with the mother-country, but with other diasporas as well.

Diasporas, and the people living in them, were 'stateless': they lived in the world's twilight-zone, more or less unconfined by regionalism or primitive nationalism. In

45 many ways, football clubs are today's world's trading diasporas, employing footballers as merchants. They travel around, performing their profession.

But while we might be able to typify some of Vitesse's players as 'merchants', we would do well to rid the term of some of its negative connotations. The Arnhemmers' flirt with globalization has manifested itself in wonderful things as well. Take

50 Mike Havenaar, a 6 foot 4 striker who looks Dutch, sounds Dutch, plays in the Dutch league ... but is Japanese.

Mike was born in 1987 in Hiroshima, where his father, the Dutch goalkeeper Dido Havenaar, played for Mazda FC (now called Sanfrecce Hiroshima). Dido had initially planned to only stay in Japan for a short while, but the months became years and the

55 years became a decade, until finally, the family decided to stay forever: 'When I was little, I spoke Dutch with my parents but Japanese with all of my friends. Initially I felt somewhat torn between the two countries but as I got older, my love for the country where I was born grew. When I had to make a decision about my nationality, there was never any doubt', Havenaar told Fifa.com in an interview in 2013.

60 Havenaar, who conducts his interviews in English rather than Dutch, has a Japanese passport, and as such, he plays for the Japanese national team, making his debut in 2011 and scoring 3 goals in 16 matches.

Besides his name and his appearance, there's little to reveal his Dutch roots. Indeed, when Havenaar first moved to The Netherlands, he felt like a foreigner. 'At first I had

65 trouble acclimatising,' he told Fifa.com, 'but since then the Dutch in me – which I had kind of forgotten – has really come to the fore. Today I feel great, just like at home actually.'

In this regard, the humility he displayed after injuring Stijn Schaars in Vitesse's 6–2 defeat of PSV in December 2013 spoke volumes. Havenaar visibly apologized

70 about ten times, and his whole demeanour contrasted starkly with the reaction of the Dutch on and off the pitch.

Indeed, while merchants travel around and perform their profession, they not only take things, they leave things behind as well. Wonderful things, in the case of Mike Havenaar. The ongoing process of globalization, driving people as well as culture to

75 travel from The Netherlands to Japan and back again, allows for the birth of the hybrid and unique.

Who knows, maybe one day Havenaar will move on to yet another league, and maybe he'll decide to stay there for a long time. Maybe he and his kids will stay there forever.

From: *The False Nine*, 9 January 2014

Mike Havenaar

35 **contingent** [–'– –] group of people who share sth., usually the place they come from
39 **trading diaspora** [daɪˈæspərə] community of merchants who live in a foreign country
40 **semi-permanent** [ˈpɜːmənənt] living in the same place for most of the time
resident person living in a certain place
41 **native** (here) born in the country you live in
44 **twilight** time between day and night
unconfined by sth. not held back by sth.
47 **Vitesse** football club based in the Dutch city of Arnhem
65 **acclimatize** [əˈklaɪmətaɪz] (here) start feeling at home
66 **come to the fore** start playing an important role
68 **humility** [hjuːˈmɪləti] quality of not thinking that you are superior to others
display sth. show sth.
69 **PSV** (= PSV Eindhoven) football club from Eindhoven in the Netherlands
speak volumes [ˈvɒljuːmz] tell a lot about sb./sth.
70 **demeanour** [dɪˈmiːnə] behaviour
stark obvious, easy to see
71 **pitch** football field
75 **hybrid** [ˈhaɪbrɪd] mix of two or more different things

▶ LP 5: Infinitive or gerund after certain verbs

▶ SF 14: Reading strategies

READING **FOCUS ON SKILLS**

Using reading strategies (non-fictional texts)

Reading strategies help you to read more effectively. They can help you to find information quickly, to see if a text is relevant for you or to come to an in-depth understanding of the content.

*Before actually reading the text **B3**, you were asked to skim it to find out what it's about. Now practise your scanning and close-reading techniques.*

1 Scanning
  a Scan the text on pp. 168–169 to find the answers to the following questions. For each question decide what keyword, name or number you are going to look out for in the text.
    1 What are the characteristics of people living in diasporas?
    2 What has Pelé got to do with a globalized world?
    3 How does Mike Havenaar feel about his nationality?
  b Locate the following ideas in the text and say in which order they appear. What keyword, name or number are you going to look for?
    1 Unconstrained international travel and the internet allow fans to visit football matches outside their country.
    2 Mike Havenaar felt like a foreigner when he first moved to the Netherlands.
    3 Mike Havenaar's father worked as a goalkeeper in Hiroshima.
    4 Globalization has reached the phase of automatization.
    5 In 2013/2014 less than half of the minutes in the Premier League were completed by English players.

A global sport: football

2 Close reading I: content and structure
  a Read the text carefully and make notes on the content of each paragraph.
  b Write a summary of the text.
▶ SF 31: Writing a summary
  c Read the text again and examine its structure. Add the words below to your notes from **a** where they fit. You can also add your own categories.

    background information · cause · conclusion · detail · example · opposite viewpoint · outlook · result quotation · thesis · …

▶ SF 16: Identifying text types (non-fiction)
3 Close reading II: identifying the text type
Explain what type of text this is and analyse its *tone.

English as a global language

C1 Keeping the accent   *Aoife Mannix*

- What do you expect after reading the title of the poem?

> The barman makes me repeat my order
> three times before he finally understands me.
> Heads turn and stare, I can feel my hands sweat
> and my throat close over the way it did years ago.
> Then he tells me my accent is so cute,   5
> he's going to give me one of the drinks for free.
> And all the people at the bar smile at me.
> And it doesn't make up for the way
> they laughed at me at school,
> repeating how I said the word potato   10
> over and over like a needle in my ear,
> or Alexis Fortgang dropping a worm in my hair
> and telling me to fuck off back to the little hole
> in the ground I crawled out of.
> But still, now that the way I speak is sweet,   15
> I swallow my bitterness
> and try not to think about how opening my mouth
> used to feel like a betrayal.
> The words sounding out of tune,
> a fork dropped on a china plate.   20
> Suddenly it's interesting and cool
> and everyone wants to go there.
> But I still hide behind my pride,
> the way I used to long to talk
> like everybody else.   25

From: *The Elephant in the Corner: New & Selected Poems*, 2005

COMPREHENSION ◀

1 Understanding the situation
Describe the speaker's experience in the bar and the memories it provokes.

LANGUAGE AWARENESS ◀

2 Examining the present participle
  a Identify the present participles in ll. 8–14, then reformulate these lines without using participles.
  b Compare with the original and explain why the participle constructions are especially helpful in the poem.

ANALYSIS ◀

3 Examining the poem
  a Subdivide the poem by introducing *stanzas, which may vary in length. Explain the structure you have chosen. Compare it to the original version.
  b Examine the *stylistic devices used in this poem to highlight the speaker's attitude towards her accent. Focus on the choice of words and the *imagery used.

FACT FILE

The term ***third culture kid*** (TCK) is applied to children who spend a considerable time of their childhood or adolescence outside their parents' home country, usually because their parents work abroad. Third culture kids experience the culture they are living in plus the culture from which their parents originated – without really belonging to either of them: they belong to a third culture, which is a mix of the other two cultures. In the era of modern globalization, the number of third culture kids has increased: global job mobility, proximity to neighbouring countries, international school attendance, multi-ethnic homes and worldwide adoption are on the increase and bring with them not only cultural, but also linguistic opportunities and challenges.

Compile possible advantages and challenges of early cross-cultural education.

Aoife ['iːfə]
1 **order** *(n)* request for food or drinks in a pub or restaurant
4 **throat** *Kehle*
  close over become very narrow
5 **cute** sweet, nice
8 **make up for sth.** do sth. that corrects a bad situation
19 **out of tune** containing wrong notes and therefore sounding unpleasant
20 **fork** *Gabel*
  china ['tʃaɪnə] *Porzellan*

▶ LP 18: Writing about texts

▶ LP 15: Connecting your thoughts (sentence structure)

▶ SF 21: Analysing poetry
▶ SF 17: Analysing stylistic devices

— BEYOND THE TEXT ◀

4 YOU CHOOSE▶ **Creative writing** SUPPORT▶ p. 214

a Write a *short story based on the poem.

OR

b Write a dramatic *scene based on the poem.

C2 English as a global language *David Crystal*

- Try to define the term *global language* and collect reasons why a language might become a global language.

— COMPREHENSION ◀

1 Understanding the main idea

Listen to David Crystal and decide which statement fits the text best:

1 English-speaking nations are powerful because they speak the global language English best.
2 Throughout the centuries people have had the power to decide which language is the global language.
3 The global language is the language of the people who have the most power globally.

2 Connecting language and power

Listen again and describe the connection between power and language as seen by Crystal.

— BEYOND THE TEXT ◀

3 Thinking about global languages of the future

Discuss when and how the four types of power mentioned by David Crystal might one day be dominated by other languages. Which languages might they be? Justify your answer by giving examples.

C3 Linguistic diplomacy: the Eurovision Song Contest *R. L. G.*

- Do you prefer listening to songs in English or in your mother tongue? Explain what difference it makes to you.

Last Saturday saw Denmark win the Eurovision Song Contest, the country's third win in the contest's history. A prototypically apple-cheeked blonde took the trophy for her country, but she did so with the rather un-Danish name of Emmelie de Forest and the equally un-Danish title, 'Only Teardrops'.

The contest has always been about more than music. Every year comes a slew of articles about the political nature of the voting. Countries that share ethnic or political friendships routinely give each other high marks: Greece and Cyprus typically give each other the maximum of 12 points while stiffing Turkey with nul points, for example. Estonia and Latvia this year gave Russia 12 points, no doubt because those countries' large Russian populations voted for their neighbour.

Language, of course, plays a role in this as well. 'Ethnicity' in Europe is often linguistic: an ethnic Russian is not apparent on the streets of Riga until he opens his mouth. Linguistic neighbours will tend to be generous to one another. Finland and Estonia are friendly not only because they are nearby but because their Finno-Ugric languages resemble each other, while being utterly unrelated to their neigbours'. (Hungarian is also Finno-Ugric.) Each country can give 12 points to only one other

Emmelie de Forest, winner of the 2013 Eurovision Song Contest

2 **apple-cheeked** having cheeks (= *Wangen*) the colour of apples
5 **slew** (*infml*) large number
8 **stiff sb. with sth.** (here) reject / mildly insult sb.
nul points [nyl pwɛ̃] (*French*) nil (= *no*) points
11 **ethnicity** [eθˈnɪsəti] fact of belonging to a particular race
12 **Riga** capital of Latvia

5

10

15

country, and this year Denmark and Sweden gave their 12's to Norway, Norway its 12 to Sweden, as befits the Scandinavian language continuum.

20 But the Scandinavians share something else besides apple-cheeked blondes and North Germanic languages: their tendency to sing in English. In that, they are like most countries nowadays. But some interesting variation clouds the picture.

The French, of course, overwhelmingly prefer French. (France has, however, sent two entries in Corsican and one, in 2008, mostly in English.) Spain nearly always opts for Spanish, and Italy for Italian. But it isn't true that big countries sing in their
25 own languages while small ones opt for English. Germany has sung just one German title ('Frauen regieren die Welt', or 'Women Run the World') in the past ten years. And a few small countries opted for linguistic pride over Anglophone Euro-cheer this year. Iceland's EyþórIngi offered up a dreary ballad in Icelandic, the perfect accompaniment to an official video in which he glumly fillets a fish in the rain. The highest-rank-
30 ing song not sung in English this year was technically Greece's 'Alcohol is Free', an upbeat ska tune in which the verses were in Greek and only the three-word chorus in English. It came in 6th place. The highest-ranking song entirely devoid of English was Italy's 'L'Essenziale' (7th).

Songs mostly in English have won 24 times, while songs in French have won 14.
35 That leaves just about a third of the contests won in any other language. This is despite two periods (1956–1965 and 1977–1999) in which contest rules required countries to sing in their own languages. [...]

It is clear that pop is just another area in which English is taking over Europe, alongside business and the politics of the European Union. French is holding a solid second
40 place, as it does elsewhere. The rest of Europe's many language communities divide up what remains. Whether you find this linguistic convergence cheerful as an Abba foot-stomper or depressing as an Icelandic fishing trip will say as much about your politics as it will about your views on language.

From: *The Economist*, 20 May 2013

18 befit sb. (*fml*) be suitable for sb.
21 cloud sth. make sth. unclear
23 entry (here) song that takes part in a competition
24 opt for sth. choose sth.
28 dreary sad and boring
accompaniment music that is played to support singing
29 glum quiet, sad, unhappy
31 upbeat (*infml*) cheerful/enthusiastic
ska fast and rhythmic music, related to Reggae
chorus part of a song that is sung after each verse
32 devoid of sth. without sth.
41 convergence [kən'vɜːdʒəns] process of moving towards each other and meeting at a point
ABBA Swedish pop band that won the ESC in 1973
42 foot-stomper lively music that makes you move your feet

COMPREHENSION ◀

1 Understanding the content
Structure the text (introduction, main body, conclusion), then make notes on the content of each part.

▶ SF 15: Marking up a text / Making and taking notes

2 Mediation (English ➔ German)
You are watching the song contest together with a friend who claims that language does not play any role in the ESC today since almost all songs are sung in English. In German, tell him why he is not quite right using information from the text.

▶ SF 41: Mediation of written and oral texts

ANALYSIS ◀

3 Examining the tone
a Analyse which elements contribute to the neutral *tone of the text.
b Identify the text type.

▶ SF 18: Analysing non-fiction
▶ SF 16: Identifying text types

BEYOND THE TEXT ◀

4 Reacting to a statement
Explain the last sentence and comment on it.

5 Discussion `SUPPORT` ▶ p. 215
In groups of five prepare and hold a panel discussion in which you discuss the question of whether each country should be obliged to enter songs in their national language only. One student is the moderator, the others argue either for or against the topic.

▶ SF 27: Having a discussion

Find a recording tool here:
 Webcode context-55

CULTURE SPOT

Keeping our language clean?

🎧 CD2 15

1. You're Skyping with an Irish friend of yours and talking about music. She has just come across a song by the a cappella group Wise Guys that she doesn't understand. Listen to the song, then tell her what it's about and what message you think it conveys.

2. Collect other examples of English (or pseudo-English) words often used in German. State for each example whether you accept it and use it or whether you avoid using it.

3. What does this use of English tell you about the role of English in German culture?

4. Radio stations, e.g. in France and Italy, are obliged to play a considerable number of songs in French or Italian, respectively. What do you think of this attempt to promote the native language?

'Slavery? Not today, not in Germany!' Preparing an exhibition

For the project week at your school, you are preparing an exhibition on the topic 'Slavery? Not today, not in Germany!' As a lot of visitors from your foreign partner schools will be attending, posters and presentations will be in English.

Work in groups of five.

1 Planning your work

   a Do some research to get a general idea of the topic and to identify suitable subtopics. **SUPPORT** ▶ p.215

   b Divide the work up among yourselves.

2 Preparing your poster

   a Research your part. Make sure to use German publications too. Notes, articles, books or worksheets you read at school, including in other subjects like History or Latin, may also be helpful. Make notes.

   b Organize your findings and prepare your poster. **SUPPORT** ▶ p.215

   c In your group, swap posters and check each other's.

3 Preparing and giving your presentation

   a In your group, organize and practise your presentation.

   b Give your presentation in class.

4 Assessing presentations

Using the assessment sheet your teacher will give you, assess the other groups' posters and presentations. In class, discuss how they might be improved.

Find some helpful links here:
 Webcode context-24

▶ SF6: Doing project work

▶ SF5: Doing research

▶ SF7: Making visual aids
▶ SF40: Proofreading

▶ SF24: Giving a presentation

Find a tool to help you create your poster here:
 Webcode context-50

9 Work and Business – Careers and Perspectives

WHEREVER YOU GO

GO WITH YOUR HEART

A

Download a list of chapter vocab here: **Webcode** context-25

B

▶ SF 11: Analysing pictures
▶ SF 13: Analysing cartoons

1 Talking about pictures

a Choose one of the pictures A–E. Think about the situation it shows and prepare to talk about your response to it. Find other students who have picked the same picture and exchange your thoughts. Select one spokesperson for your group to report back to your class.

b Work with a partner and choose another picture. Think of a question raised by this picture and write it on the board or on a strip of paper that you attach to the board. Take a class vote about the two most interesting questions and start discussing them.

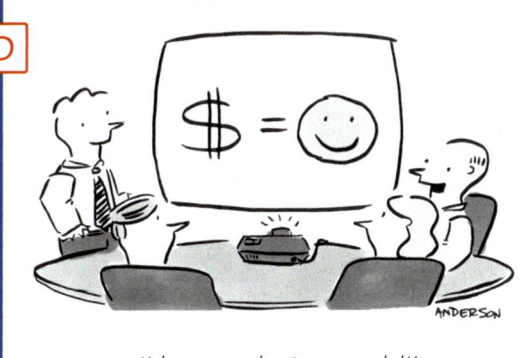

'I love your business model!'

'I really enjoyed my job. Management found out about it and fired me.'

Career decisions: priorities and consequences

You enjoy doing it.

Poor but happy

Just a dream

The perfect job

You're good at it.

Rich but unfulfilled

It's well-paid.

> ■ **FACT FILE**
>
> **Venn diagrams** – named after John Venn (1834–1923), a British logician, philosopher and mathematician – use over-lapping circles to illustrate all possible logical relations between a number of sets.

2 Talking about charts and diagrams

With a partner, explain the Venn diagram above with regard to business and entrepreneurs. Try and find an example of a person and a business idea that fits the field in the centre.

▶ SF 12: Analysing charts and graphs

PREVIEW

In this chapter you will learn about today's challenges and prospects of entering the world of work and business.

Main topics

Focus on Skills: SPEAKING and WRITING

Chapter Task:

The world of work and business

 CD3 02

Listen to an audio version of the text on the CD or download it here:
Webcode context-26

The right to a job – the right job

World economy has two faces. Many countries are recovering from a difficult period of recession. In many countries, average wages have risen so that many people have been lifted out of poverty. Despite minimum wage and unconditional basic income being under discussion, there is a global rise in income inequality – the rich are getting richer, and the poor are getting poorer. The fact that budget cuts have claimed many jobs makes the situation even more tense: people collecting unemployment benefits often have to face tough odds.

Stepping into the world of work

Building a career is not always easy nowadays. In some university courses competition among students is unusually high – for some the job hunt is already on. And once people get into their dream job, more often than not they are expected to move around the world and to adapt to new situations quickly. Furthermore, it is not unusual to change jobs often.

To get your career on track, it is therefore essential to access career advice and gain work experience. Career advisers can do you a huge service, e.g. by telling you which applicants are really needed out there because they are in short supply. Too often there is a massive mismatch between young people's career expectations and the realities of the market. In a paid or unpaid internship you can catch up on missing experience: schools do not, for example, tell you how to deal with difficult customers – this is what you learn best in an internship. Once you know that you have a head for, say, numbers, or that you have a passion for languages, you can narrow down your job sector or employment area.

Applying for a job

Research the companies that have caught your interest and start your application. For example, report on your ability to solve problems and showcase your skills in a professional letter of motivation.

Job interviews

Even though face-to-face interviews are still most popular, you might also be invited for a telephone interview or to an assessment centre. As applicants come from a wide range of backgrounds, it is important that you leave a positive impression on the interviewer. Successful candidates convince employers not only with their interview responses but with professional body language and demeanour too. Don't spoil your chances by asking about the salary package right away!

5

10

15

20

25

30

35

40

► SF 2: Learning new words

1 Words and phrases

Complete these phrases (1–6) with the help of the highlighted words from the text and match them with the correct German equivalent (a–f).

1	income …	a	Durchschnittsgehalt
2	… package	b	Etatkürzungen
3	job…	c	Berufsberatung
4	… advice	d	Arbeitserfahrung
5	… cuts	e	Gesamtgehalt
6	average …	f	Einkommensgefälle

2 Prepositions

Test yourself: do you know the right prepositions?

► LP 19: Collocations

- recover … recession
- be lifted … poverty
- a rise … inequality
- be … short supply
- deal … customers
- report … your skills
- a mismatch … expectations and reality

3 Opposites

Find the opposites of these words and expressions:

- have no particular talent for sth.
- employee
- do sb. a disservice
- hide sb./sth.

4 Collocations

Which words usually go together? From the three words offered, choose the correct one.

► LP 19: Collocations

- make/build/form a career
- gain/make/find work experience
- from a big/great/wide range of backgrounds
- the elected/successful/winning candidate

5 The situation in Germany

Using the text as background information, describe the situation for (young) job hunters in Germany. You may draw on the experiences of people you know.

6 Showcase your skills

Think about a talent that you have, or that you have always dreamed of possessing. Talk to your partner about how you can use this talent to start a unique career.

'I see under "special talents" that you always land on your feet. Tell me about that.'

▶ DVD

■ **FACT FILE**

The **State of the Union address** is an annual *speech by the US president delivered to the US Congress in January in which she or he describes the condition of the nation and outlines the administrative policies.

▶ Historical documents:
The Bill of Rights (1791), p. 345

2 **necessitous** *(fml)* [nəˈsesɪtəs] poor, needy

5 **self-evident** [ˈevɪdənt] obvious, needing no proof or further explanation

7 **prosperity** success, material or financial well-being
station *(fml)* social position

9 **remunerative** *(fml)* [rɪˈmjuːnərətɪv] well-paid

11 **recreation** [ˌrekriˈeɪʃn] *Freizeit, Erholung*

13 **decent** [ˈdiːsnt] of a sufficient standard or quality

■ **FACT FILE**

F. D. Roosevelt giving his State of the Union address on 11 January 1944

Franklin D. Roosevelt [ˈrəʊzəvelt] (1882–1945), commonly known by his initials FDR, was the 32nd President of the United States (1933–1945). Not to be confused with Theodore Roosevelt (1858–1919), US President of the United States 1901–1908, FDR led the US during times of worldwide economic depression and during World War II. He was a strong supporter of social welfare programmes and work projects, by which the US government created many jobs.

26 **implementation** realization of sth. that has been officially decided

28 **rightful** correct, appropriate, legal

The right to a job – the right job

A1 The second Bill of Rights   *Franklin D. Roosevelt*

In his State of the Union address of 11 January, 1944, US President Franklin D. Roosevelt suggested that an 'economic bill of rights' be adopted to complement the political rights guaranteed by the US Constitution and the Bill of Rights of 1791.

We have come to a clear realization of the fact that true individual freedom cannot exist without economic security and independence. 'Necessitous men are not free men.' People who are hungry and out of a job are the stuff of which dictatorships are made.

In our day these economic truths have become accepted as self-evident. We have 5 accepted, so to speak, a second Bill of Rights under which a new basis of security and prosperity can be established for all – regardless of station, race, or creed.
Among these are:

• The right to a useful and remunerative job in the industries or shops or farms or mines of the nation; 10
• The right to earn enough to provide adequate food and clothing and recreation;
• The right of every farmer to raise and sell his products at a return which will give him and his family a decent living;
• The right of every businessman, large and small, to trade in an atmosphere of freedom from unfair competition and domination by monopolies at home or 15 abroad;

• The right of every family to a decent home;
• The right to adequate medical care and the opportunity to achieve and enjoy good health;
• The right to adequate protection from the 20 economic fears of old age, sickness, accident, and unemployment;
• The right to a good education.

All of these rights spell security. And after this war is won we must be prepared to move forward, 25 in the implementation of these rights, to new goals of human happiness and well-being.

America's own rightful place in the world depends in large part upon how fully these and similar rights have been carried into practice for 30 all our citizens.

For unless there is security here at home there cannot be lasting peace in the world.

From: the website of the Franklin D. Roosevelt Presidential Library and Museum

─────────────────────────── **COMPREHENSION** ◀

1 Looking at the text
   a In your own words, give a brief description of each of the eight rights that Roosevelt wants guaranteed.
   b Outline what Roosevelt means by 'People who are hungry and out of a job are the stuff of which dictatorships are made' (ll. 3–4).

◀ LANGUAGE AWARENESS

2 Finding the 'right' constructions

a Collect all the expressions from the text which contain the word 'right' followed by a preposition. Write them down in a table like this:

the right of … to + *verb*	the right to + *noun (phrase)*
the right of every farmer to raise …	the right to a useful and remunerative job …

b Find a simple rule explaining how you can use the prepositions *of* and *to* in connection with the noun *right*.

ANALYSIS ◀

3 Examining the text

a Analyse how Roosevelt attempts to convince his audience of his idea of economic fairness. Take the language and the line of argument into account.

b Explain why the realization of the rights listed is essential for Roosevelt.

BEYOND THE TEXT ◀

4 Reacting to the text

Choose the three rights which you consider most important and explain your choice to your partner. After listening to your partner's reasons, work together to decide which in your opinion are the three most important rights.

5 YOU CHOOSE ▶ Commenting or giving a speech

'Necessitous men are not free men.' (ll. 2–3)

a Prepare a three-minute speech on the basis of this quote. **b** Write a *comment of 200–300 words.

▶ SF 4: Using a grammar book
▶ LP 19: Collocations

▶ SF 17: Analysing stylistic devices
▶ SF 25: Giving a speech

Find a tool to improve your speaking skills here:

 Webcode context-51

▶ SF 25: Giving a speech
▶ SF 34: Argumentative writing
▶ LP 14: Linking words and phrases

A2 Moving on after recession *Barack Obama*

This is an excerpt from President Barack Obama's State of the Union address, delivered on 28 January, 2014. Obama presents a country that is still struggling but gradually recovering from a difficult period of recession.

Over more than three decades, even before the Great Recession hit, massive shifts in technology and global competition had eliminated a lot of good, middle-class jobs, and weakened the economic foundations that families depend on.

5 Today, after four years of economic growth, corporate profits and stock prices have rarely been higher, and those at the top have never done better. But average wages have barely budged. Inequality has deepened. Upward mobility has stalled. The cold, hard fact is that even in the midst of recovery, too many Americans are working more than ever just to get by – let alone get ahead. And too many still aren't working at all. [...]

10 I'm also convinced we can help Americans return to the workforce faster by reforming unemployment insurance so that it's more effective in today's economy. But first, this Congress needs to restore the unemployment insurance you just let expire for 1.6 million people.

Let me tell you why.

15 Misty DeMars is a mother of two young boys. She'd been steadily employed since she was a teenager. She put herself through college. She'd never collected unemployment benefits, but she'd been paying taxes. In May, she and her husband used their

Job seekers wait to attend a job fair.

4 **corporate** ['kɔːpərət] of or belonging to a large business company
stock prices *Aktienpreise*
6 **budge** (v) move
stall (v) stop suddenly

18 **claim sth.** (here) cause the loss of sth.

29 **shake sth. up** change sth., e.g. an organization, to make it more efficient

30 **incentive** [ɪnˈsentɪv] *Anreiz*

31 **price sb. out of sth.** prevent sb. from having sth. by making it expensive

32 **cap sth.** *eine Obergrenze für etwas festlegen*

34 **reach out to sb.** show sb. that you are interested in them

35 **corporation** large company or group of companies

38 **Ronald Reagan** [ˈreɪɡən] (1911–2004) US President 1981–1989

39 **Tom Harkin** (born 1939) US Senator (Demokrat, Iowa) 1985–2015

George Miller (born 1945) US Representative (Democrat, California) 1975–2015

Graduation ceremony

► SF 10: Working with closed test formats

life savings to buy their first home. A week later, budget cuts claimed the job she loved. Last month, when their unemployment insurance was cut off, she sat down and wrote me a letter – the kind I get every day. 'We are the face of the unemployment crisis,' she wrote. 'I am not dependent on the government ... Our country depends on people like us who build careers, contribute to society ... care about our neighbors ... I am confident that in time I will find a job ... I will pay my taxes, and we will raise our children in their own home in the community we love. Please give us this chance.' [...] 20

Of course, it's not enough to train today's workforce. We also have to prepare tomorrow's workforce, by guaranteeing every child access to a world-class education. [...] We're working to redesign high schools and partner them with colleges and employers that offer the real-world education and hands-on training that can lead directly to a job and career. We're shaking up our system of higher education to give parents more information, and colleges more incentives to offer better value, so that no middle-class kid is priced out of a college education. We're offering millions the opportunity to cap their monthly student loan payments to ten percent of their income, and I want to work with Congress to see how we can help even more Americans who feel trapped by student loan debt. And I'm reaching out to some of America's leading foundations and corporations on a new initiative to help more young men of color facing tough odds stay on track and reach their full potential. [...] 25 30 35

Of course, to reach millions more, Congress needs to get on board. Today, the federal minimum wage is worth about twenty percent less than it was when Ronald Reagan first stood here. Tom Harkin and George Miller have a bill to fix that by lifting the minimum wage to $10.10. This will help families. It will give businesses customers with more money to spend. It does not involve any new bureaucratic program. So join the rest of the country. Say yes. Give America a raise. 40

From: the website of the White House, 28 January 2014

COMPREHENSION ◄

1 Close reading

Decide whether the following statements about this text are true, false or whether the information is not given. Give line numbers to support your answer and correct the statement where necessary.

1 The elimination of good jobs began with the Great Recession.

2 On average, wages have fallen despite economic growth.

3 If the current system of unemployment insurance is changed, it will speed up many Americans getting back to work.

4 There is not enough training for today's workforce.

5 School buildings will be redesigned.

6 Misty DeMars and her husband had to sell their home.

7 People who are out of work do not have to pay taxes.

8 Since Ronald Reagan's presidency, wages have fallen by 20%.

ANALYSIS ◄

2 Comparing two State of the Union addresses

Make a list of the issues that Obama wants to tackle. Compare it with the problems mentioned by Roosevelt (cf. **A1**). Explain similarities and differences in the promises made by the two presidents.

► SF 17: Analysing stylistic devices

3 Political speeches: convincing the audience

Look at Obama's style and language and show how he tries to convince his audience of the steps that to his mind need to be taken to come out of recession. **SUPPORT** ► p. 216

► SF26: Taking part in an interview

— BEYOND THE TEXT ◄

4 Reacting to the text

Imagine Misty DeMars is invited to the local TV station for an interview. Choose a partner. One of you is Misty, the other a reporter.

a Before getting together, work on your own:
Misty prepares herself for the kind of questions she might be asked.
The reporter thinks of questions the local audience might be interested in.

b With your partner, conduct a trial interview, then decide which questions should be kept.

c Together, practise your interview. Prepare to present it in class.

A3 Income inequality and guaranteed income
Felix Oberholzer-Gee

The idea of an unconditional basic income has many supporters in western Europe, but also among US Americans. Felix Oberholzer-Gee, professor at Harvard Business School, seeks an explanation for this.

In Western Europe, there is a lively debate about proposals to guarantee every citizen a basic income. The idea, which has a long history dating back to the 1920s (at least), is increasingly popular in policy circles and the broader population. The German and Spanish parliaments explored it. The Swiss will soon vote on an initiative that would
5 guarantee everyone $2,800 each month — no questions asked, irrespective of whether a person works. Early polls indicate that more than 45 percent of Swiss voters will support the initiative.

The supporters of a guaranteed income are a varied lot. They range from unreconstructed communists to humanists with a strong sense of dignity and the
10 wealthy. One concern that many of them share, however, is the global rise in income inequality. In the past few decades, economic growth lifted hundreds of millions out of poverty. But, at the same time, the distribution of income became increasingly skewed in favor of wealthy individuals.

The current situation is exceptional from a historical point of view. For example, the
15 top 10 percent of earners in the U.S. captured 35 percent of income through the 1950s and 1960s. Today, this share stands at 50 percent. Rising inequality reflects gains at the top in all sources of income: salaries and business income, as well as capital income and capital gains.

There are many reasons why income inequality has risen. One is technology, which
20 tends to benefit the well-educated. Machines increasingly take over routine tasks, leaving low-paid service jobs for unskilled workers. As a result, U.S. employment and wages tend to grow at the very bottom and at the very top of the distribution in skills. The middle is hollowed out.

Import competition from poorer countries is a second reason. Chinese imports, for
25 example, explain about one quarter of the decline in U.S. manufacturing from 1990 to 2007.

Third, globalization produces so-called superstar effects. In a flat world, top talent is handsomely rewarded for its broad appeal. The Brazilian soccer player Pelé, the best ever, earned $1.1 million in 1960 (adjusted for inflation). The Portuguese forward
30 Cristiano Ronaldo made $17 million this past year. Pelé played for 350,000 television sets in Brazil. At the [2010] World Cup, 700 million people watched Ronaldo, as Eduardo Porter writes in *The Price of Everything*.

From: *PBS Newshour*, 7 April 2014

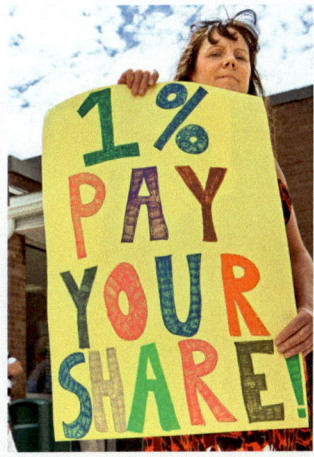

Protesting against income inequality

■ FACT FILE

In his bestselling book *The World Is Flat: A Brief History of the Twenty-First Century* (2005), Thomas L. Friedman analyses the globalization of markets and the resulting challenges and opportunities both for societies and for individuals. The term **flat world** has become a widely-used catchphrase.

---

5 **irrespective of sth.** regardless of sth.
9 **unreconstructed** *(adj) (derog)* hartnäckig, unverbesserlich
dignity ['dɪgnəti] sense of your own importance
13 **skewed** *(adj)* not accurate or correct, distorted
23 **hollow sth. out** *(fig)* diminish sth.
27 **flat world** cf. Fact File above

Part A

1 Looking at the text

   a Outline the concept of an unconditional basic income.

   b Point out what information is given in the text in connection with these countries: Brazil, China, Germany, Portugal, Spain, Switzerland, the USA.

   c Using keywords, sum up the three reasons given for the United States' current problem of income inequality.

▶ SF 18: Analysing non-fiction

2 Money and motivation

Analyse how the *article presents the idea of an unconditional basic income. Pay special attention to the writer's line of argumentation and *stylistic devices and use the information in the Venn diagram on p. 177 as a backdrop to your analysis.

▶ SF 24: Giving a presentation
▶ SF 41: Mediation of written and oral texts

3 Mediation (English → German)

The topic of income inequality comes up in your Social Studies class. You offer to give a talk in German about the situation in the USA and its causes as presented in this article. Sum it up for a presentation of about three minutes. Make notes and practise the talk.

4 An unconditional basic income for all?

Suppose Germany adopted the concept of an unconditional basic income for all citizens. Think of possible consequences …

   a … for employees.

   b **CHALLENGE** ▶ … for self-employed people and businesses.

Write an article for your school magazine.

■ FACT FILE

The concepts of **minimum wage** and an **unconditional basic income** (UBI) are essentially different from each other. While one stipulates a certain level of pay
5 to all employees, the other guarantees an income to all, whether they are currently holding a job or not, in addition to any other income they might receive. In Switzerland, there have been initiatives for
10 both concepts. In May 2014, a majority of voters rejected the proposal for a minimum wage of 22 Swiss francs per hour. Preparations for another, more far-reaching referendum began in
15 September 2013, when activists advocating the introduction of UBI collected around 130,000 signatures from supporters.
  As this is the first referendum of its kind
20 anywhere in the world, it requires thorough preparation and is not expected to be held before 2019.

Make appointments with two students and exchange your views about the idea of an unconditional basic income.

Basic-income activists dumped eight million Swiss coins – one for each citizen – in front of the parliament building in Bern in the autumn of 2013.

A4 Teenagers' career aspirations *Sean Coughlan*

In March 2013, a survey listed young Britons' job ambitions according to popularity. Before you read the summary of findings, look at the table below and do task 1 on page 186. Then read the text and continue with tasks 2–4.

Most popular jobs	Percentage 15–16	Least popular jobs	Percentage 15–16
Teacher/Lecturer	4.4%	Locksmith	0.2%
Lawyer (barrister/solicitor)	4.2%	Welder	0.2%
Accountant	4.0%	Surveyor	0.2%
Actor/Actress	3.7%	Speech therapist	0.2%
Police	3.6%	Personnel/HR	0.2%
IT consultant	3.4%	Miner	0.1%
Doctor	3.4%	Call centre	0.1%
Sportsman/woman	3.3%	Audiologist	0.1%
Army/Navy/Airforce/Firefighter	3.2%	Factory worker	0.1%
Psychologist	3.1%	Glazier	0.00%

From: Nothing in Common report, Education and Employers Taskforce, UK Commission for Employment and Skills, B-Live (March 2013)

> **TROUBLE SPOT**
>
> *Schauspieler* = **actor**
> *Schauspielerin* = **actor** (also: **actress**)
> *Gastgeber* = **host**
> *Gastgeberin* = **host** (also: **hostess**)
> *Kellner/in* = **waiter, waitress, server**
> *Flugbegleiter/in* = **flight attendant** (not: ~~stewardess~~)
> *Polizist/in* = **police officer**
> *Schriftsteller/in, Autor/in* = ***author**
> *Dichter/in* = ***poet**

accountant sb. who keeps or checks financial accounts
welder *Schweißer/in*
surveyor [sə'veɪə] *Landvermesser/in*
glazier ['gleɪzɪə] sb. who fits glass into the frames of windows, etc.

There is a 'massive mismatch' between young people's career expectations and the reality of the jobs available, a major survey of teenagers suggests. [...]

The study, based on a survey of 11,000 13- to 16-year-olds, is an attempt to map the job ambitions of teenagers against the employment market up to 2020. It shows teen-
5 agers have a weak grasp of the availability of jobs – and that large numbers will be aiming for jobs that are in short supply.

For instance, there are 10 times as many people aiming for jobs in the culture, media and sports sector than there are jobs likely to be available. And even though almost a quarter of jobs are in the distribution, hotels and restaurant category, only
10 about one in 40 youngsters are considering careers in these industries. Fewer than one in 30 young people are considering jobs in banking and finance, even though one in five jobs are expected to be in this sector.

This 'misalignment' could mean long-term problems for young people, the report says, because they are making decisions about qualifications and subjects with little
15 awareness of the jobs market ahead of them. And the report warns it can be difficult in later years to catch up with missing qualifications. This lack of informed choices fuels the problem of employers struggling to find suitably skilled staff, even though there are high levels of youth unemployment.

The report also looks at the perceptions of young people about types of employ-
20 ment. Among the 10 least preferred occupations are jobs such as surveyor and speech therapist, even though they are likely to earn above-average pay. The two least preferred jobs, as identified by teenagers, are factory work and glaziers. The most preferred employment areas, from the perspective of teenagers, include teaching, the law, the police, psychology and sport. These might be influenced either by role models
25 such as teachers at school – or else by media images. But the report says it suggests the narrowness of young people's view of the types of work available – and the failure of employers to present a broader picture of opportunities. [...] ·····▶

5 **grasp of sth.** understanding of sth.
6 **in short supply** not available in great numbers, scarce
13 **misalignment** [ˌmɪsə'laɪnmənt] state of not being in the correct position to sth. else
17 **fuel sth.** increase sth.
19 **perception** belief or opinion

Education and Employers Taskforce director Nick Chambers said: 'As a country we are doing our young people a huge disservice if we don't give them enough information to allow them to make proper informed decisions about their futures.' This 30 charity has campaigned to improve the quality of careers education, highlighting the link between social mobility and access to career advice and work experience.

From: the website of the BBC, 19 March 2013

1 Popular and unpopular job aspirations

a The table on p. 185 shows the ten most popular as well as the ten least popular jobs according to a UK survey among young Britons aged 15–16. Do you find anything surprising? Talk to your partner. ▶ LANGUAGE HELP

b Carry out a class survey: What kind of job(s) do you want to do later? Make a list, ranking jobs according to popularity. Then compare the results with the UK survey, pointing out similarities and differences.

— COMPREHENSION ◀

2 The central message

a Spot these percentages in the text and say what they stand for:
'ca. 2.5%'   'less than 3.3%'   '20%'   'nearly 25%'

b List the consequences of the 'massive mismatch' (l. 1) as mentioned in the text and say who is most affected by it.

c Sum up the main message of the text in one sentence.

— ANALYSIS ◀

3 Examining and reflecting

Find reasons why the jobs at the top of the list are so popular and why the ones further down are unpopular among teenagers. Work on your own and make notes, then compare with your partner.

— BEYOND THE TEXT ◀

4 Writing

Should you pursue the career of your choice or should you consider only those careers where job demand is fairly certain?
Write an argumentative text in which you consider both sides and state your own view. **SUPPORT** ▶ p. 216

LANGUAGE HELP
If you don't know the English term for a certain job or profession, describe in your words what duties and responsibilities this job involves in order to arrive at a more general job description for the class survey. You can also check in a dictionary.

Find a tool to conduct your own survey here:
 Webcode context-56

▶ SF 14: Reading strategies

▶ SF 15: Marking up a text / Making and taking notes

▶ SF 34: Argumentative writing
▶ LP 15: Connecting your thoughts (sentence structure)

SPEAKING FOCUS ON SKILLS

From informal to formal dialogues

In any form of successful conversation, you should stick to the topic and contribute to a pleasant atmosphere. Moreover, you should adapt your style, vocabulary and your reactions to the situation in general and to the other person's social and professional standing. Sometimes you can be informal and sometimes you have to be more formal, depending on the situation.

▶ CC 5: Making smalltalk

▶ SF 14: Reading strategies

1 An informal conversation

a Imagine you meet somebody your age at a party. You talk to each other about your career aspirations and your dreams about the future.
Before you start, scan **A4** (cf. pp. 185–186) again for phrases and words you might need for this conversation. Then talk to a partner for at least three minutes.

b You probably talked to your partner in a rather colloquial way.

THINK Assess your conversation and make notes on the following aspects:

- style of language
- phrases that you used repeatedly
- sentence structures
- the way you adapted to the given situation
- problems, mistakes, breaks

PAIR Exchange your findings with your partner and add to your notes and your list of phrases.

SHARE Share your most interesting findings with your class. Explain how you could have improved your conversation.

2 A formal conversation

a Imagine you have to have a similar conversation in a more formal context and with somebody older than you and in a different position, e.g. a guidance counsellor at school, an advisor at university or a board member of an organization that awards scholarships, internships or something else you are very interested in. What would you have to change in this form of discourse? Make notes.

b Match the following sentences and phrases with the stages of a formal conversation in the box below. Pick out the ones you consider too blunt or even impolite to be used in such a conversation.

▶ CC 1: Cultural awareness
▶ CC 2: Polite behaviour
▶ CC 3: The language of politeness
▶ CC 5: Making smalltalk
▶ LP 11: Using the right register

Bye. – It's very convenient for me to meet you here. – I absolutely hate that kind of job. – I actually think I am quite good at working in a team as … – Oh, really, you studied at ABC University! I have heard a lot about it. – I don't think I'm qualified for such a career. – Excuse me for taking up some of your time, but … – Hi, my name is Tom. – It was very nice talking to you. Thank you for devoting some of your time to me. – I actually always wanted to talk to you in person. – I don't care for other people's experience. – You can't be serious! – It was a pleasure meeting you. Thank you very much for your advice. – Would you mind me asking you a few questions?

> - Introducing yourself
> - Getting into the conversation
> - Showing interest in the other person
> - Talking about your qualities, likes and dreams
> - Expressing dislikes and rejections politely
> - Saying thank you and goodbye

In groups of 3–4, collect more ideas and phrases and add them to your list.

3 Role-play

Talk to a partner about your plans and career aspirations as described in task 2 for at least five minutes.

Partner A: You are a student. You have plans and career aspirations, but you are not sure how to go about them.

Partner B: You are an influential older person and you are willing to give Partner A some help or advice.

After five minutes swap partners and take over the other role.

*Satisfaction at work –
what does it take?*

A5 Do you love your job? *Uwe Jean Heuser*

*In a job interview you may be asked about your ideas of your future workplace
and how you can achieve satisfaction at work. The following excerpt from an
article in the German weekly DIE ZEIT *gives an insight into job satisfaction and
its implications.*

Lange gingen Ökonomen davon aus, dass Arbeit reine Last sei: Statt ihre Freizeit zu
genießen, litten die Menschen acht oder zehn Stunden am Tag – und für dieses Übel
würden sie bezahlt. Eine traurige Theorie war das und gottlob eine falsche. Heute
erforschen Wirtschaftswissenschaftler, in welchem Maße der Beruf ihr Lebensglück
beeinflusst und wie zufrieden Menschen sind. Und siehe da: Menschen, die sich als   5
hochzufrieden bezeichnen, werden von anderen auch so wahrgenommen. Sie sind
offener für positive Einflüsse, nehmen leichter Kontakt auf und blicken optimisti-
scher in die Zukunft. Sogar ihre Immunabwehr ist besser, sie sind selten krank. [...]

   Nach einer Umfrage der Beratungsfirma Gallup sind mehr als 90 Prozent der
Arbeitnehmer mit ihrem Job zufrieden, aber fast 25 Prozent spüren keine innere   10
Bindung an ihr Unternehmen. Manchmal liegt das an ihnen, oft aber an Firmenkul-
tur und Chefs. Wo Kollegen kooperationswillig sind, wo Führungskräfte schwelende
Konflikte rasch lösen und die Mitarbeiter beruflich unterstützen, entsteht Zufrieden-
heit. Umgekehrt geht es den meisten auf die Nerven, wenn Streitigkeiten ungelöst
bleiben, niemand Apathie oder Mobbing entgegentritt. Noch schlimmer ist es nur,   15
wenn Angestellte – zu Recht oder Unrecht – ihren Job permanent für gefährdet
halten und keine Möglichkeit für einen Wechsel sehen.

   Produktiv ist dieses Gefühl des Ausgeliefertseins nicht, auch wenn umgekehrt ein
Wohlgefühl bei den Angestellten noch keine gute Leistung garantiert. Die Wirtschaft
braucht eine Atmosphäre, in der sich zufriedene Mitarbeiter über den Dienst nach   20
Vorschrift hinaus engagieren. Und sie schafft umso mehr Wohlstand, je treffsicherer
sich die Menschen erst ihren Beruf und später ihre Jobs aussuchen.

   Die Bedingungen in der Wirtschaft ändern sich heute rasant, also müssen sich
Erwerbstätige öfter fragen, ob die Arbeit ihre Erwartungen erfüllt. Gerade diejenigen,
die sich im Job aufzehren, stellen sonst irgendwann fest, dass das übrige Leben leidet.   25
[...] Kein Wunder, dass auch flexible Tätigkeiten und Phasen von Teilzeit das Glück
des Einzelnen beflügeln. Und sei es nur, weil er merkt: Ich habe mein Leben selbst
in der Hand.

From: *DIE ZEIT*, 23 Oktober 2013

1 Translating or paraphrasing?
   Not every word or phrase can be directly rendered in another language;
   sometimes you have to find a paraphrase.
   a Find out whether *luck* or *happiness* are both good equivalents of *Glück*
      in the context of this article (cf. l. 26). Likewise, check whether *binding*
      for 'Bindung' (l. 11), and *wellness* for 'Wohlgefühl' (l. 19) are suitable
      equivalents.
   b Describe in German what is meant by the following expressions, then
      paraphrase them in English: 'dieses Gefühl des Ausgeliefertseins'
      (l. 18), 'Dienst nach Vorschrift' (ll. 20–21), 'sich im Job aufzehren' (l. 25).

2 Mediation (German → English)
   An English friend of yours thinks that the importance of job satisfaction
   is overrated. Sum up the main ideas of the article for her in English (ca.
   150 words).

▶ SF 3: Using a dictionary
▶ LP 16: Avoiding Germanisms

Find an online dictionary here:
🔊 **Webcode** context-52

▶ SF 9: Paraphrasing

▶ SF 41: Mediation of written
   and oral texts

3 A tricky question in your job interview

a Some of the aspects of job satisfaction mentioned by Heuser should not be brought up in a job interview. List them, then compare with your partner.
SUPPORT ▶ p.216

b Work with your partner again. One of you acts as the interviewer and asks 'How can you contribute to a healthy working atmosphere?', the other tries to answer this question. Then swap roles and ask or answer the question again.

◉ CULTURE SPOT

Corporate Head (1991)

The joint work of Terry Allen (sculpture) and Philip Levine (*poem on the plaque next to the sculpture), 'Corporate Head' is located outside the Los Angeles offices of the professional services firm EY (previously Ernst & Young).

They said
I had a head
for business.
They said
to get ahead
I had to lose
my head.
They said
be concrete
& I became
concrete.
They said,
go, my son,
multiply,
divide, conquer.
I did my best.

1 Describe 'Corporate Head'.

2 How do the sculpture and the poem relate to the topic of this chapter?

3 Discuss why the company EY may have commissioned 'Corporate Head'.

Stepping into the world of work

B1 Mitch's first glimpses of the world of work
Carl Deuker

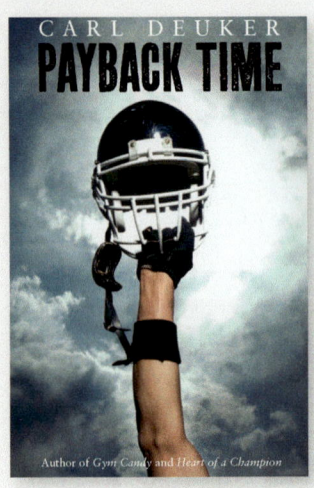

CARL DEUKER
PAYBACK TIME

Author of Gym Candy and Heart of a Champion

In the novel Payback Time *(2010), Mitch True, a not-too-popular high-school student, is a reporter for the school magazine. He has reluctantly accepted the responsibility for the sports section. In the following excerpt, Mitch is on his way to his first interview with the coach of the Lincoln Mustangs – his former PE-teacher McNulty.*

I parked my mom's Ford Focus by the gym, eased out of the front seat, and looked around. When I spotted McNulty loading tackling sleds into a school van, I tensed. To him, I'd always be a fat loser and nothing more. But a reporter has to have the courage to approach people, ask them questions, and get them to talk. 'I'm Mitch True,' I said as I neared him. 'I'm the school sports reporter. I'd like to ask you some questions.'   5

'I was hoping you'd come around,' he said. 'Step into my office.'

I gaped, dumbfounded. He was hoping I'd come around? When I recovered, I nearly had to run to catch up as he strode across the field and into the coaches' office in the gym. He took a seat behind a neatly organized desk while I squeezed into a wobbly blue plastic chair across from him.   10

'What's your name again?'

I told him again.

'You were in my gym class last year, right?'

'Two years ago.'

'Well, Mr. True, you are now an important member of the Lincoln Mustang football   15
family.'

I smiled.

'What's funny?' McNulty said, his blue-gray eyes glittering like shiny stones.

Like an idiot, I patted my jiggly belly. 'Me? An important member of the football family. How?'   20

He leaned forward, pointing his pencil at me. 'You are the person who sends in a game recap to the Seattle Times. You write exciting articles, and the Times will push them to the top of the high school page. That happens, and other newspapers will pick them up, which translates into publicity for the players and for me. It also means a byline for you, some cash, and a summer internship to boot. You remember last year's   25
sports writer, Boyd Harte. He interned at the Bellevue Journal.'

I hadn't thought about the connections I'd be making, but as a sports stringer, I'd be dealing with editors of real newspapers, something that would not have happened if I'd remained the news reporter for the Lincoln Light – unless the big dailies suddenly become interested in the accomplishments of Lincoln High's chess club.   30
'Sounds great,' I said. 'In fact, it sounds fantastic.'

McNulty leaned back. 'See. We're all part of one big family.'

I cleared my throat. 'How about we get started? I've got some questions. First –'

'No, no, no,' McNulty said, pointing the pencil at me again. 'No questions – not today, not ever. This job takes forever and pays peanuts. Here's how it works. You write   35
down or tape what I tell you. When I'm done, jazz it up whatever you want, but never make me, my coaches, or my players look bad. Understand?'

2 **tackling sled** *„Angriffsschlitten"
(schweres Trainingsgerät im
American Football)*
7 **gape** *(v)* stare with your mouth
open
dumbfounded [dʌmˈfaʊndɪd]
(adj) very surprised and unable
to speak
19 **pat sth.** touch sth. gently
22 **game recap** summary of a game
24 **translate into sth.** change into
sth.
25 **byline** line at the beginning or
end of a newspaper article that
gives the writer's name
to boot *(adv) (old-fashioned/
humorous)* obendrein
26 **intern** [ˈ– –] *(v)* be on an internship *(Praktikum)*
27 **stringer** [ˈstrɪŋə] freelance
journalist
36 **jazz sth. up** *(infml)* make sth.
more interesting or attractive

Mr. Dewey had warned us about people like McNulty, but this was my first time dealing with one. 'A reporter who lets himself be pushed around is a traitor to his
40   profession.' That's what Dewey had said.

I could feel myself trying to say: 'Coach, I will ask the questions I want to ask, and I will write what I want to write.'

In the classroom, practicing with bald, bowtied Mr. Dewey, I had spit out similar words like a machine gun spits out bullets. But McNulty's eyes were scary. I squirmed
45   as he stared at me, feeling like a snot-nosed preschooler who'd been caught marking a wall with crayons. 'Understood?' he said again, a threat in his voice, as though he might force me to do cartwheels in front of the football team if I argued.

'Yes, sir!'

From a drawer he took three sheets of paper covered with black type and showed
50   them at me. 'Here's the information for the football preview. Horst Diamond will be the focus, and you'll be leading every game story with his name, too. He's a lock for a D-I scholarship. UW is drooling over him, but he's got a shot at a bigger school – Notre Dame, or even USC. Your job is to get him publicity.'

I scanned the three sheets. 'But what if somebody else has a better game?'

55   'Nobody's going to have a better game. Run or pass – everything we do goes through Horst. I want a swarm of college coaches around here. They'll see him, and they'll see me and the program I run. I do not intend to spend my life coaching high school.'

McNulty stood. 'Read those pages, prepare a few questions, and before practice tomorrow you can interview Horst. He'll be at the field fifteen minutes early. Have
60   your photographer come along for that.' He paused. 'You've got a photographer, right?'

'A photographer?'

'Every sports story needs pictures. Either you've got to take them yourself, or you've got to get a photographer. Didn't you know that?

From: *Payback Time*, 2010

TROUBLE SPOT

intern ['– –] (n) = Praktikant/in
intern ['– –] (v) (l. 26) = *ein Praktikum machen*
internship ['– – –] (l. 25) = *Praktikum*
apprentice = *Auszubildende/r, Lehrling*
apprenticeship = *Ausbildung, Lehre*
trainee [– '– –] = *Auszubildende/r, Trainee*
hand = *Helfer/in (z.B. in einer Fabrik)*
employee [– –'– –] = *Mitarbeiter/in, Angestellte/r*
employer = *Arbeitgeber/in*
superior [suːˈpɪəriə] = *Vorgesetzte/r*
boss = *Chef/in, Vorgesetze/r*
chief = *Leiter/in, Chef/in*

43 **bowtied** [ˌbəʊˈtaɪd] (*adj*) wearing a bow tie (*Fliege*)
44 **squirm** *sich winden*
46 **crayon** ['kreɪən] *Buntstift*
51 **lock** (n) (*infml*) sure thing, certainty
52 **D-I = Division I** in the USA, highest level of college and university athletics
UW = University of Washington
drool over sb./sth. *für jdn./etwas schwärmen*
53 **USC** = University of Southern California

COMPREHENSION ◀

1   Who said it?
Using the text, point out who says the following and what is being talked about or what is happening at this particular moment: 'I'd like to ask you some questions.' / 'What's funny?' / 'Sounds great.' / 'How about we get started?' / 'Understood?' / 'Nobody's going to have a better game.'

▶ SF 14: Reading strategies

ANALYSIS ◀

2   Power relations
Work on your own first, then tell each other about your findings.
Partner A: Analyse the meeting between Mitch and McNulty and explain how one of them shows his power and superiority through non-linguistic means (e.g. facial expressions). `SUPPORT` ▶ p. 216
Partner B: Analyse the meeting between Mitch and McNulty and explain how one of them uses language to demonstrate his power and superiority.
`SUPPORT` ▶ p. 217

▶ SF 19: Analysing narrative prose
▶ SF 35: Writing a character profile

BEYOND THE TEXT ◀

3   Writing about Mitch's experiences
a   Outline what Mitch has learned about the world of work. Make notes.
b   In an email to a friend Mitch writes about the experience he has gained. Write his email using your notes from **a**.

▶ SF 15: Marking up a text / Making and taking notes
▶ SF 37: Doing a creative writing task
▶ LP 11: Using the right register

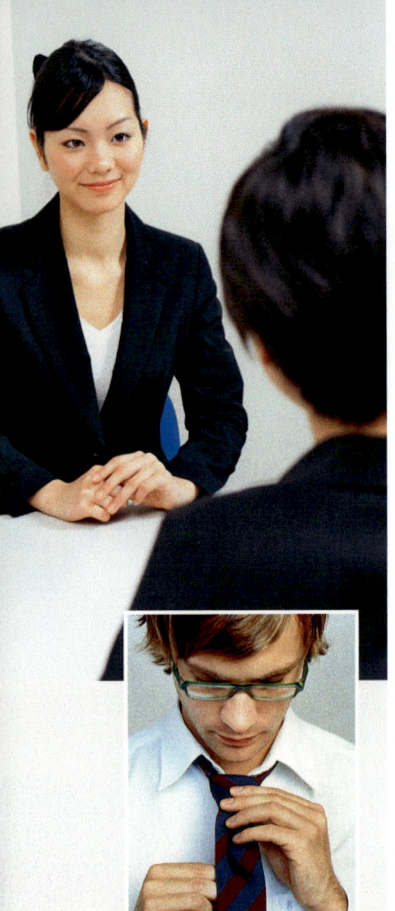

B2 Ten things not to say in a job interview *Mark King*

Getting invited to an interview is a big step on the way to getting a job. Now it's important not to spoil one's chances by saying something stupid. The Guardian's Mark King has some useful advice.

With the jobs market more competitive than ever it can be hard work just to get an interview, so once you're actually in front of potential employers you don't want to ruin your prospects with an ill-chosen comment.

Sadly, some job hunters still do speak before they think. Corinne Mills, managing director of Personal Career Management, says she can recall many instances of inter- 5 viewees saying the wrong thing. 'I remember when one man was asked why he wanted the job, he replied, "Because my mum thought it was a good idea",' she says.

She adds that some job hunters have also been known to say they've applied for a job 'because it will pay the rent while I look for a job I really want to do', and a common response to a question about what candidates like to do in their spare time 10 is 'go to the pub'.

Richard Nott, website director at CWJobs.co.uk, says candidates should avoid discussing religion and politics. 'Employers like people who can talk passionately about their own interests as it helps them to get to know you as a person. But we would always advise against sharing your views on these two topics without knowing if the 15 interviewer shares that point of view.'

We asked Nott, Mills and Nik Pratap of Hays Senior Finance for their list of the top things to avoid saying at a job interview:

1. 'Sorry I'm late.' It goes without saying that punctuality is key. Your interviewer doesn't want you to arrive for work 20 minutes late every morning. 20
2. 'What's your annual leave and sickness policy?' It doesn't look good if, before you've even been hired, you're planning your absence from the company.
3. 'I'll just take this call.' Mills says a large number of candidates think it is OK to take telephone calls, texts etc. during an interview. It isn't.
4. When asked, 'Where do you see yourself in five years?' never say, 'Doing your job.' 25 As much as this might be a genuine answer, Nott says candidates should 'try to build a response around the experience they would like to have gained and the level of responsibility they'd like to have, rather than threatening the interviewer's job.'
5. 'My previous employer sucked.' No matter how mind-numbingly boring those 30 roles might have been, 'speaking badly of a previous employer is not only unprofessional, but also reflects on your character,' Pratap says. Your new employer will contact your former employer for references following an interview, so it's never wise to burn your bridges.
6. 'You make widgets? I thought you made cricket bats.' Failing to research your 35 prospective employer fully is a big faux pas. 'Saying you've looked at their website is only marginally better – employers expect far more research,' Mills explains.
7. 'Bloody hell.' Never swear in your interview. It can happen, especially if your interviewer is themselves prolific with the profanities, but don't let them set the standard of the interview and remain professional at all times. 40
8. 'I was very good at sorting out PEBs by using ARCs.' Don't fall into the industry jargon of your previous employer or assume the interviewer knows anything about your experience, Pratap advises. Instead, speak clearly about your skills and experience to avoid any confusion or misunderstanding.

■ TROUBLE SPOT

apply to sb. for sth. (l. 18) = *sich bei jdm. um/für etwas bewerben*
applicant ['–––] = *Bewerber/in*
applicable [–'–––] = *anwendbar*
application = *Anwendung*

21 **leave** (n) time away from work, holiday
30 **suck** (v) (sl) be very bad
mind-numbingly ['nʌmɪŋli] **boring** very boring
34 **burn one's bridges** (idiom) do sth. that makes it impossible to return to the previous situation
35 **widget** ['wɪdʒɪt] simple software application
36 **faux pas** [ˌfəʊ 'pɑː] (French: 'wrong step') embarrassing action or remark *(Fehler)*
37 **marginally** ['mɑːdʒɪnəli] (adv) very slightly
39 **prolific** [prə'lɪfɪk] producing a lot
profanity [prə'fænəti] (usu. pl) swear word

45 9. 'Do I really have to wear that uniform?' Any criticism of staff uniform will go down like a lead balloon. Do you think your interviewer enjoyed wearing that fluorescent green ensemble when they performed your role?

10. When asked, 'What do you expect to enjoy most about this role?' never reply with any of the following: the perks, the pay, lunchtimes, my co-workers or the holidays,
50 Nott says.

From: *The Guardian*, 10 May 2012

47 **ensemble** [ɒn'sɒmbl] set of clothes that are worn together
49 **perk** *(usu. pl.)* Vergünstigung

COMPREHENSION ◀

1 Understanding the rules

In groups of three or four, quickly decide which of the mistakes in the list (cf. ll. 19–50) are ones that are easily made and which ones you are sure you would never make.

ANALYSIS ◀

2 The language of the text

a Explain how King tries to amuse the reader. **SUPPORT** ▶ p. 217

b Explain how King makes his advice easy to understand and to remember.

▶ SF 17: Analysing stylistic devices

BEYOND THE TEXT ◀

3 Your five golden rules

King gives tips for people being interviewed – but what about those asking the questions? In a group, think of five golden rules for interviewers.

▶ CC 3: The language of politeness
▶ CC 4: Meeting and greeting

B3 The best job in the world is back! *Emanuel Wetterqvist*

In order to promote the Great Barrier Reef as an international tourist attraction, Australia launched a competition for 'the best job in the world'. The winner of the contest would live on a Queensland island, explore and enjoy the area and write a blog about it.
In 2013, the second round of 'the best job in the world' was announced.

Yes, you read right. As our ex-island caretaker is regretfully handing over the keys to his island hacienda we're looking for someone to take his place.

As our Park Ranger you will be exploring the world's oldest rainforest, watching whales migrate on the Great Barrier Reef, and showcase our five World Heritage areas
5 to the world through blogs and social media.

This is the perfect opportunity for an outdoor lover with a sense of adventure to promote some of the world's most awe-inspiring natural wonders to an international audience. The position is a six-month contract attracting a generous salary package of AUD $100,000 and a free jar of vegemite.

10 **Your responsibilities**

- Patrol the beaches – you have 7,400 kilometres of palm and beach-fringed coastline within your jurisdiction, but you only need to show us your favourites.
- Swim, dive and snorkel the world's biggest aquarium. With 600 islands and 1,500 species of fish to hang out with, we're sure the 30°C water will keep you
15 occupied.
- Feed the fish, and meet and greet with local wildlife, including kangaroos, crocodiles and the short-tempered cassowary.
- Get up close and personal with hatching turtles and migrating whales and share your experience with the world.
20 - Showcase the best of our 300 national and marine parks and state forests. Like a well-paid Tarzan.

2 **hacienda** [ˌhæsɪ'endə] large farm
4 **showcase sth.** show the best aspects of sth.
7 **awe-inspriring** impressive
8 **attract sth.** (here) be worth sth.
9 **vegemite** ['vedʒɪmaɪt] type of food paste, very popular in Australia
17 **short-tempered** *(adj)* getting angry easily
cassowary ['kæsəwəri] *Kasuar (Laufvogel)*

- Report on your adventures through photo blogs, social media channels and media interviews.

Who we're looking for – We will consider applicants from a wide range of back-grounds, but believe you should possess these traits: 25

- Excellent oral and written English communication skills
- Be adventurous by nature and willing to try new things
- Have a passion for the outdoors and nature
- Good swimming skills and enthusiasm for snorkelling and/or diving

About the job package – The position of Park Ranger attracts a AUD $100,000 salary 30 package (AUD $50,000 salary and AUD $50,000 to cover living expenses) for the six-month contract.

The successful candidate will live amongst the stars with a range of rent-free accom-modation. You might spend one night camping on an island and the next in a bunk on a luxury yacht. 35

You'll receive return airfares from your nearest capital city (in your home country), travel insurance and the cameras and gadgets required to show the world a good time. The six-month contract commences on 1st August 2013.

About your new office – Queensland is regarded as having one of the world's richest natural environments and boasts a rich and diverse array of World Heritage areas 40 including the Great Barrier Reef, Daintree Rainforest and Fraser Island.

The state is home to hundreds of national parks, conservation areas, resource reserves and state forests.

How to apply – The position is open to adventure-hungry outdoor lovers from Australia and overseas. Apply online at http://bestjo.bs/Park_Ranger. 45

From: *Hello Sunshine*, the official travel blog of Queensland, 5 March 2013

▶ SF 14: Reading strategies

▶ SF 16: Identifying text types (non-fiction)

▶ LP 11: Using the right register

---

37 **gadget** ['gædʒɪt] small and useful device
38 **commence** [kə'mens] (v) start
40 **boast sth.** have sth. you can be proud of
array [–'–] large collection of things

COMPREHENSION ◀

1 Making sense of numbers
Pick three numbers from the text and ask your partner to point out what they refer to. Then swap roles. *Example: '6.' – 'The contract is valid for six months.'*

ANALYSIS ◀

2 Text type and target group
a Examine characteristic aspects of the text type 'job advertisement' and illustrate them with examples from the text. **SUPPORT** ▶ p. 217
b Identify the target group of this text and explain which aspects of the advertisement are likely to appeal to them most.

LANGUAGE AWARENESS ◀

3 Language and target group
Show how the *tone and language of the ad aim at its target group.
Pay special attention to humorous and colloquial elements.

BEYOND THE TEXT ◀

4 What's your opinion?
THINK Is the above text about proper work or a leisure activity? About a real application process or a casting show? Find evidence to support your argument.
PAIR Exchange your ideas and arguments with your partner. Try to agree on a position.
SHARE Tell your class about your view(s).

WRITING FOCUS ON SKILLS

Writing a letter of motivation

When applying for any type of position – an internship, a place at a university, a job – you are usually expected to write a letter of motivation, in which you explain why you are interested and what recommends you for the position. Such letters, which may also be called personal statements, cover letters, statements of purpose or letters of intent, are mostly formal letters.

Imagine you want to apply for the 'best job in the world' (cf. B3, pp. 193–194).

1 Thinking about your motivation
  a Reread the 'job ad' on pp. 193–194. ▶ LANGUAGE HELP
  b THINK List three reasons that motivate you to apply for this job. If you are not really interested in the job, list the reasons of an invented other person who is.
  c PAIR AND SHARE Work with one or two partners and exchange your ideas from **b**. Add convincing ideas to your list.

2 Presenting your assets
Of course, it is not enough to just write that you have all the requirements as listed in the job ad – you must prove it, either by presenting convincing arguments or by handing in relevant certificates.
  a List arguments and certificates proving that you answer the description given in the section 'Who we are looking for'.
  b Work with a partner you know well. Exchange your lists and give feedback to each other.

3 Writing your first draft
  a Turn your lists from **1** and **2** into a text. Stick to the conventions of formal letters.
  b Add typical application phrases to your text.

4 Typing your final version
  a Reread your first draft after one or two days.
  b Type it up on a computer and use your spellchecker to correct it.

5 The winner's application
Watch the application video of Elisa, the young woman who was eventually chosen for the 'best job in the world'. Discuss similarities and differences in content between her video and your letter of motivation.

▶ LP 11: Using the right register
▶ CC 2: Polite behaviour

■ LANGUAGE HELP

- I have a strong interest in …
- I was particularly impressed by …
- I understand that this position requires …
- I have demonstrated the desired qualities through …
- I would value the opportunity to gain experience in …
- I am very keen to …
- I see that this position offers … In respect to this, one of my key strengths is the ability to … I recently demonstrated this quality through …
- This experience taught me the importance of …
- I have developed skills in …
- My experience in …
- As you can see from the attached CV …
- In addition, my role as …
- My responsibilities included …

▶ SF 29: Writing a formal letter or email
▶ SF 30: Writing an application

▶ SF 40: Proofreading

 DVD

take a leap of faith *(idiom)* try one's luck
'roo *(infml)* kangaroo
fervent sincere, dedicated
anthropologist sb. who studies the human race

▶ SF 23: Analysing a film

▶ EE 4: Making phone calls

▶ SF 22: Listening

🎧 **CD3** 03

sophisticated *(here)* intelligent, complex
résumé *(AE)* = *(BE)* **CV / curriculum vitae**

▶ SF 26: Taking part in an interview

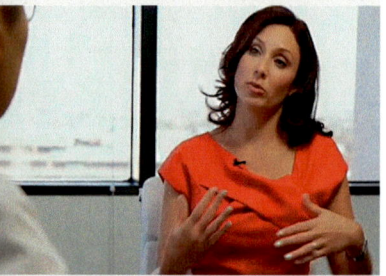

▶ SF 11: Analysing pictures

🎞 **DVD**

non-negotiable *(here)* obligatory
succinct short and precise
jack of all trades *Alleskönner/in*
unruly disorderly

▶ SF 26: Taking part in an interview

B4 Surviving a telephone interview

Telephone interviews have become increasingly popular in the business world. Easy as they might seem, there are practical dos and don'ts applicants should be aware of, as the audio explains.

———————————————————————————— **COMPREHENSION** ◀

1 Expectations
Before listening, arrange the following headings in the order of appearance you expect from the listening text:
Thank your interviewer / Research the company / Practise responses for your phone interview / Keep notes about your work experience / Be friendly during the phone interview
Then listen to the audio and check whether you were right.

———————————————————————————————————— **ANALYSIS** ◀

2 After listening
Explain the functions of the following in the context of a telephone interview: *paper, sticky tape, voice recorder, water, letter.*

———————————————————————————— **BEYOND THE TEXT** ◀

3 Act out an interview
   a Here are some typical questions asked by interviewers. With a partner, add three more questions:
      What is important to you in a job? How would you describe your present workplace? How do you handle stress and pressure? What motivates you? Where do you see yourself in three years' time? In what kind of company do you enjoy working? What does success mean to you?
   b Let your partner interview you.

B5 Look them in the eye – the job interview

Though the most frequent type of interview, a face-to-face meeting between an employer and a job seeker has its pitfalls. This video gives helpful advice.

———————————————————————————— **COMPREHENSION** ◀

1 First looks are (not) deceiving
Look at the still on the left and talk to your partner about how this person might come across in a job interview.

2 Do's and don'ts
Watch the video. With your partner, list and rank the given dos and don'ts of job interviews. **SUPPORT** ▶ p. 217

———————————————————————————— **BEYOND THE TEXT** ◀

3 Body language
   a Compare Lauren Ferrara's body language to that of the presenter.
   b Take your own pictures in which you show good and bad examples of body language in job interviews and/or the oral exams of the *Abitur*. Evaluate the body language and rank the pictures from good to bad.

4 Surprising advice
Which piece of advice given in the video did you find surprising?

Writing your personal statement

'Personal statement' is the term commonly used for a letter of motivation that you send to the university at which you want to study. In this letter you present yourself and explain why the university should offer you a place to study. A standard text type in the English-speaking world, personal statements are becoming increasingly popular with German universities too. They may also be required when applying for an internship, for volunteer work or for a year abroad.

1 Think about yourself

   a Imagine you want to apply to a university for a particular course or subject. Alternatively, think of what kind of internship or volunteer work you are interested in.
      Then study the table below and make notes on the points in the left column ('What?').

▶ SF 15: Marking up a text / Making and taking notes

Your personal statement	
What? • reasons why you are choosing higher education • reasons for your interest in the subject • things you already know about your subject • the subject and its connection to your education, work experience and to your hobbies	**How?** • catchy introduction • coherent main part • concise conclusion • max. 600 words • perfect grammar, spelling and punctuation • reader-friendly layout

   b Add some notes as to why you think you should be offered a place. Describe your skills, your knowledge and your experience.
   c Finally, add any other achievements and attributes that you might mention in your personal statement.

2 Ask for feedback
Work with a partner you know well. Let your partner read your notes and ask if there are any aspects of your personality that you forgot to mention. Then swap roles.

3 Get down to work
Now write out your personal statement for a course of your choice. Make use of your partner's advice, of the tips in the table above ('How?') and of the phrases given on p. 195 (Language help). Your teacher will give you an assessment sheet.

▶ SF 30: Writing an application

global warming

qualification

literature

nationalism

communication

knowledge

lingua franca

civil rights

ethnicity

language awareness

skills

future plans

literacy

analysis

power

multiculturalism

happiness visions

culture

application

stereotypes morals

rhetoric

going abroad

role models

talents

word power

responsibility

disappointments

research

environmental awareness

immigration

intercultural learning

dreams globalization

leadership identity

This context task gives you the opportunity to consider the topics you have dealt with in class again and to think about their relevance for your future life.

YOU CHOOSE ▶

1 Giving a presentation I

Work on your own or in a group. Choose 3–5 items from the word cloud on the left and prepare a presentation on the topic 'Skills and insights I got from my English course that might be helpful for my future life'. Your presentation should be 5–7 minutes long if you are working on your own or 10–12 if you're in a group. You may want to add examples from your course work to illustrate your statements.

▶ SF 6: Doing project work
▶ SF 24: Giving a presentation

OR

2 Giving a presentation II

Work on your own. Think of 3–5 items that are not in the word cloud and use them as the basis of a presentation as explained in **1**.

▶ SF 24: Giving a presentation

OR

3 Making an advertisement

Work on your own, in pairs or in a group. Make an advertisement for your English class that tells younger students what to expect and/or what to look forward to. Choose a suitable form (e.g. leaflet, poster, electronic presentation, blog ...) and present it in class (and, if possible, on the school website).

▶ SF 37: Doing a creative writing task

Find a tool to design your poster or flyer here:
 Webcode context-50

OR

4 Having a debate

Work in a group. Prepare and conduct a debate on the motion 'This house believes that English is the most important subject at school'.

▶ SF 28: Having a debate

OR

5 Writing a quiz

Work in a group.

a Choose five chapter topics or items from the word cloud and write a quiz consisting of three questions/tasks for each topic/item, e.g.
Example *lingua franca*:
  1 Name three situations in which English is used as a lingua franca.
  2 Why is a lingua franca so important in a country like India?
  3 Name two possible disadvantages of using a lingua franca.

b Ask fellow students to do your quiz.

▶ SF 6: Doing project work

Support Pages

A1 Lonely friends   p. 14

4 Poetic devices

Examine the means the poet uses to draw our attention to the influence of social media on our lives. Poetic devices are tools used by the poet to emphasize the meaning of a poem. These questions might help you to do the task:

- What effect does the title have on the reader?
- What is striking about the endings of the lines?
- What means does the poet use to make the content appear more vivid and appealing to the reader?
- How does the poet involve the reader in the poem?
- What is the tone of the poem, and what effect does this tone have on the reader?

Now go back to task **5** on p. 14.

A2 Online learning in 2044   p. 17

2 Telling names

Refer to the annotations on pp. 16–17 and analyse what the names reveal about the *character and the *setting.

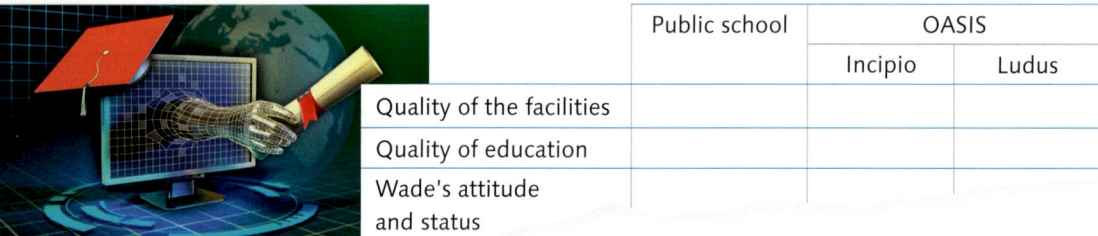

	Public school	OASIS	
		Incipio	Ludus
Quality of the facilities			
Quality of education			
Wade's attitude and status			

Step 1: Gather and structure the relevant information given in the text, using a grid like this one.
Step 2: Relate your findings to the names and explain their significance in the story.

Now go back to task **3** on p. 17.

B1 Should classrooms have video cameras?   p. 23

3 Discussing the pros and cons of surveillance at school

   c Present your concept to the school board (i.e. the class).
     Step 1: Make notes for each of the following steps.
       1 Address the members of the school board.
       2 State your group's attitude towards surveillance at school.
       3 Give reasons for your opinions and provide examples to illustrate your points. Present your concept in a clearly structured way with your most substantial argument at the end.
       4 Briefly sum up your main points.
       5 Invite the school board to ask questions or comment on your concept.
     Step 2: Plan how to present your reasons visually on the board / interactive whiteboard.
     Step 3: Use your notes to present your concept.

C1 Big Brother out of this world   p.27

2 What makes the text appealing?

Analyse the methods used to make the text engaging for the reader (e.g. heading, *register, *stylistic devices, quotes, objective/biased?).

Step 1: Copy the table below. Examine the aspects listed and find more examples from the text to illustrate each aspect. Look at all the examples again and try to identify what the author has done to make the text engaging. Add a few notes in the 'Methods' column.

Aspects you should examine	Example from the text	Methods used by the author
Ways of attracting the reader's attention from the very beginning	• Big Brother out of this world • Not only will they require mental and physical strength, but now, they will also need to have the makings of the next reality-TV star.	…
Style/Use of words	• The ticket is one-way. • 'the world's toughest job interview'	…
Structure	…	• The different stages of the project are described chronologically. • …
Way(s) of presenting the content	• The applicants have now been shortlisted to 705 candidates – 418 men and 287 women.	…
Author's attitude towards the topic	…	…

Step 2: Use your points to organize your analysis.

Now go back to task **3** on p.27.

C2 The ultimate reality TV show   p.28

2 Lally's mode of argumentation

a Explain Lally's line of argumentation to convince the reporter and the audience of his idea. Answer the following questions:

1 What historical reason does Lally mention to support his view of broadcasting prisoners' executions? What conclusion does he draw from this argument for society?

2 What political reason does he put forward? What would be a positive effect of his idea?

3 What economic reason does he state? Who might profit from the show?

4 What legal and ethical reasons does he present? In what way would the prisoners benefit from the reality TV show?

Now go back to task **2b** on p.28.

Chapter 2   Science – Enhancing Life?

A1 A saviour sibling   p. 35

3 Argumentative structure

Analyse the argumentative structure of the text.

1 Structure the text by finding headlines for each paragraph (see example on the right).

2 Examine the direct quotes: Who is quoted and what do they say? Are the quotes in favour or against the procedure?

ll. 1–2	Introduction: sibling was saved
ll. 3–6	Medical history of first sibling
ll. 7–12	Problems facing a second sibling
ll. 13–23	Medical treatment

3 Examine the indirect quotes: Who is quoted and what do they say? Are the indirect and direct quotes from the same person? If so, decide how the direct quotes relate to the indirect quotes.

Now go back to task **4** on p. 35.

A3 At the lab   p. 38

4 Practising speaking

a Prepare a monologue on whether designer babies are desirable or not. Think of a catchy introduction to your speech, e.g. start with a provocative statement like 'designer babies are the future' or 'a child has to be smart, intelligent, healthy and cute'.

- State your opinion on the topic clearly: In my opinion …, The point is that …, The way I see it …, My point is …, What I'm trying to say is …
- Make sure you have at least three good arguments in favour of or against the topic:
  Pro: reduced risk of genetic diseases, better opportunities in life, the child can have better genes than his or her parents
  Con: imperfect embryos are killed, no more individuality, only the rich can afford the perfect child, altering a human being is unethical
- Summarize your points at the end of your speech and clearly state your opinion:
  To sum up …, That's why I think …, All things considered …, All in all …

B2 Gene doping p. 44

4 Examining the tone

Identify how the writer's use of language reveals his attitude to the topic. It may be useful to look at these quotes when deciding on the writer's attitude:

- 'a battle like no other in sport' (l. 1)
- 'The authorities are so concerned, they have been preparing for it for more than 10 years.' (ll. 1–2)
- 'as anyone who had a vague brush with professional cycling in the 90s knows' (ll. 14–15)
- 'the illicit dope of choice for competitors' (ll. 17–18)
- 'the wonder drug' (l. 18)
- 'Could this be an undetectable way of improving oxygen delivery?' (ll. 23–24)
- 'even better for the would-be doper' (l. 29)
- 'So what is the World Anti-Doping Agency (Wada) doing about it?' (ll. 30–31)
- 'it could be lethal' (l. 33)
- 'your blood thickening into sludge' (ll. 34–35)

Now go back to task **3** on p. 44.

C4 Biofuels – the green alternative? p. 50

3 Conducting a debate

Find arguments in favour of and against biofuels. The motion could be as follows: 'Governments should subsidize biofuels.'

Discussion boxes for a debate:

Agreeing with and supporting an argument
Exactly!
Definitely!
I couldn't agree more!
That's right!
I agree with …
What … said is (absolutely) right.
I'm of the same opinion (as …)
I would like to support what … said.
You've got a good point there.

Interrupting – Asking for clarification
Sorry to interrupt, but …
I would like to add something here.
What do you think about …?
What is your opinion on …?
Could you explain that again, please?

Disagreeing
I can't agree with you …
I think you're (absolutely) wrong there!
I (completely) disagree with you!
Do you really mean that?
But you just said that now.
I'm sorry, but that can't be right!
But what you've just said is …
I must contradict you …

Chapter 3 Visions of the Future – Utopias and Dystopias

A2 Don't let me get bored   p. 57

3 Analysing genre and technique

b Evaluate Anderson's narrative technique.

The extract from *Feed* is told by a *first-person narrator. A first-person narrator is a character in the story who tells us what happened to him or her and how he or she felt about it. The following aspects are often relevant to texts with first-person narrators. Read the list, decide which aspects are most relevant to *Feed*, and use them to structure your analysis.

1 With a first-person narrator it is usually easier for the reader to identify with what is happening, the reader is somehow walking in the character's shoes and may find it easier to understand this character's actions and feelings.

2 In some stories, first-person narrators may refer to information they hear from the other characters, to try to give the reader a larger point of view.

3 If the narrator uses a conversational tone it can feel as if they are telling the reader a story about themselves. This could create more of an air of sympathy because as reader is more likely to relate to a person or feel sympathy for that person if you are in direct contact with them.

4 With direct insight into the narrator's thoughts and motivations, the reader can understand a character that would seem otherwise immoral, boring, stupid or otherwise not relatable.

Now go back to task **4** on p. 57.

B2 Living in the compound   p.67

3 Utopia or dystopia?

Analyse both utopian and dystopian elements in the text. You can use the following hints to help you consider particular points and structure your analysis.

1 Remember that utopias often depict paradise-like places in which people are safe and can lead happy lives. Try to find elements in the text that support this idea. Think of basic categories such as the need to eat, drink, breathe, to live in a clean and supportive environment. Think of a person's need for safety and security, for relationship and education etc.

2 Remember that this better society also needs to deal with individuals who do not conform to the rule. Is this aspect explored in the extract?

3 Remember that a dystopia is often a utopia gone wrong. Which elements in the text support the idea that the society is not perfect in every way?

4 Remember that utopias mirror the failures of society as it is today. Which present-day developments are shown as a future menace?

Now go back to task **4** on p. 67.

C2 Big Brother is watching you   p.70

3 Interpreting key aspects

b Analyse the atmosphere of the extract by looking at the content of the dialogue and Winston's thoughts on the one hand, and the fact that this is a dialogue between lovers on the other hand.

1 Use a table to collect examples of the dialogue's key content and examples of Winston and Julia as lovers. The following quotes should help you.

Dialogue's key content	Winston and Julia as lovers
• 'If I confess, they'll shoot you, and if I refuse to confess, they'll shoot you just the same.' (ll. 17–18) • 'If you can FEEL that staying human is worth while, even when it can't have any result whatever, you've beaten them.' (ll. 32–33) • …	• 'Yes, dear' (l. 4) • 'If they could make me stop loving you …' (ll. 26–27) • …

2 Think about the feelings that the quotes convey to the reader through the choice of words, Winston and Julia's emotions, the things they mention, etc. First consider the quotes in the left column, then the quotes in the right.

3 Now think about the effect that the quotes have when they are combined together to make one dialogue. Is the atmosphere tenser? Does this combination add new aspects to the atmosphere?

4 Think of a good structure for your analysis and make sure you use quotes from the text to illustrate your points.

Now go back to task **4** on p. 70.

Chapter 4   The Power of Words – from Shakespeare to Today

A2 Richard courts his enemy   p. 81

3 Working with imagery

Work with a partner. Identify the images each speaker uses. Explain them with the help of the annotations and from the context they are used in.

It is useful to become aware of your personal mental images when reading any text, and in particular a poetic passage like the one you are dealing with here. Consider
- names that Lady Anne calls Gloucester and whether these are straightforward or evoke certain images,
- personification of abstracts or of body parts,
- *similes,
- *metaphors.

5 Understanding character

On the basis of your analysis, describe the speakers' characters. Gloucester (= Richard) keeps twisting Anne's insults around to make them say something flattering
to her in response – which she does not seem to accept, at least verbally. In this context you have analysed her response to Richard's offering her his sword to kill him.

All these things are indicators of what kind of people these two dramatic characters are.
When describing them, consider
- what motivations they have for acting as they do,
- what emotions they display while they are speaking,
- what their actions reveal about them,
- whether their original emotions change and what that tells you about their characters.

B1 My future wife   p. 83

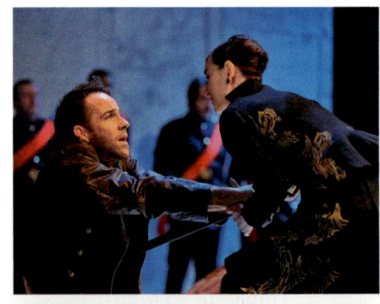

2 Comparing dialogues

Compare the way Petruchio woos Katharina to the way Gloucester woos Anne (**A2**, pp. 79–81). Evaluate what each man reveals about himself and how effectively they each use words to achieve their aims. First look at your answers to **A2**, tasks **4** and **6** on p. 81. Then use the following questions to help you examine Petruchio.
1 How does Petruchio respond to Kate telling him that her name is Katharina? (ll. 4–8)
2 What does he say he has heard about her from others? (ll. 4–14)
3 How does he respond to her attempts to make fun of him? (ll. 20–24)
4 How does Katharina come across?
5 How does Petruchio describe Katharina? (ll. 34–40 and ll. 49–50)
6 How does he propose to her? (ll. 41–52)

Now consider what sort of person Petruchio is, and whether you think he is successful at wooing Katharina. Then find similarities and differences between Richard and Petruchio, considering the context of each man's wooing and the emotions involved. Finally, decide which of the two men will be more successful.

5 Evaluation
Evaluate how successful the director has been in adapting the material. Name the elements that were changed and the effect the scene has on you. Use the following categories to create a table in which you contrast the play and the film:
setting *(What is the setting in each genre?)* • **characters** *(How did they come across in the play/film?)* • **relationship** *(What was the characters' relationship like in each genre?)* • **changes** *(What elements were added to/missing in the film?)* • **extras** *(How did the film maker use lighting, music, noise?)*

B2 Responding to a sonnet   p.86

2 GALLERY WALK **Comparing the sonnets**
Compare the two sonnets. Examine structure, development of the idea and style. Present your findings on posters and evaluate them in a gallery walk. These steps may be useful:
1 Look at the structures of the poems by examining the rhyme scheme.
2 State the main idea presented in each poem.
3 Divide each poem up according to the images in it.
4 Examine how the idea of alteration is addressed in each poem.
5 Examine how Simmons uses phrases and ideas from Shakespeare in his own poem.

Find a tool to make your poster here:
Webcode context-50

C1 Performance poetry   p.88

7 Reviewing a poetry performance
Watch the performance again. Pay special attention to the speaker's gestures. Then write a review for the English pages of your school magazine. In order to write a review, first consider what your opinion of the poetry performance is.
1 Describe the performance.
2 Decide what you think about how Zephaniah performs his poem.
3 Decide whether the performance helped you to appreciate the poem, or whether you would have preferred just reading it.
4 Write the review by following these steps:
   • Find a suitable introductory sentence.
   • When writing the body of the review, remember to combine elements of description and of comment, and consider both the poem itself and the performance by the poet.
   • Finish by giving either a recommendation or a short statement that summarizes why you are not recommending the poem or the performance.

C2 The psychological power of words   p.89

2 a + b Understanding the general idea
Draw a table like the one below. It will help you to examine the verbs and their connotations and to understand the images that the poem conveys.

Person	Verb/phrase	Connotation	Image
terrorist	lurk in the shadows	lie in wait, as if for an attack (negative)	dangerous person
freedom fighter …	take shelter …	wait somewhere safe until a danger has passed (neutral) …	person who needs safety and protection …

Chapter 5   The UK – a Kingdom United?

A1 Dangerous books   p.97

4 Creative writing

b Write the dialogue between the footman and his wife and include the events that probably took place while the Queen was opening the Parliament. The following questions might help you to collect ideas:

- How did the footman experience the incident?
- What is probably the most important aspect for him?
- Imagine the footman's feelings during his encounter with the Queen. Do you think he was embarrassed, frustrated, angry, unhappy, etc.? How could he express this in his conversation with his wife?

Don't forget: You are going to write a dialogue. So the footman and his wife should refer to each other and react to what the other person says.

A royal footman waits for the Queen to arrive in the royal carriage.

B2 Between two cultures   p.104

2 Analysing character relationships

Analyse the relationship between Kelly and her father Ibrahim. Reflect on what they talk about and how they speak to each other. Read the following quotes that Kelly and Ibrahim say to each other. How do you imagine the actors are meant to say them? What emotions are being portrayed?

IBRAHIM   Would you prefer it if I had been an American? (l. 9)
IBRAHIM   I wish we could've met earlier. (l. 23)
IBRAHIM   I imagined you might look like Kate Winslet. (l. 32)
IBRAHIM   Because you are English. And you don't know any better. (l. 81)

KELLY   But I told you I'm not going to go to Iraq, am I? (ll. 12–13)
KELLY   This isn't going very well, is it? (l. 34)
KELLY   Why are you here? Now, what do you want? (l. 42)
KELLY   Yeah, all right then, tell me what I think. (l. 69)

B3 The British and their tea   p.105

2 Analysing style

How does the speaker of the podcast try to hold the audience's attention and entertain his listeners? First make notes on the following aspects of the podcast. What further examples can you find? What effect do they have on you as a listener? Use your points to organize your analysis.

Aspect	Example	Effect
Statistics	By the end of the day, the counter will reach 165 million – that is three cups of tea per person per day.	…
Interesting facts	And it is well-known that the Queen likes a nice cup of tea, as well.	…
Personal facts	Yukk! I cannot stand tea with sugar!	…
Exaggeration	… in the interests of international harmony and understanding I shall now explain …	…

C1 A referendum on the EU   p. 108

3 Analysing style

Listen again. Analyse how Cameron tries to convince his listeners of his views. Focus on language and content. Is he successful?

a First fill in the 'Explanation' column of the table. What are the different stylistic devices?
b List examples of the different devices you can hear in the text.
c Describe the effect they have on you as a listener.
d Use your points to organize your analysis of the speaker's style.

Stylistic device	Explanation	Example from the speech	Effect
Alliteration	• …	• Rules and regulations • …	• …
Empathy	• …	• …	• …
Antithesis, contrast	• …	• Some people say … but the question mark is already there. • They say, but I don't believe	• …
Parallelism Repetition Anaphora	• The same word / structure is repeated	• It will be … • …	• …
Rule of three	• …	• Weeks, years and months • …	• …

C3 It's OK to like the Germans   p. 110

1 Summarizing

Summarize the writer's main points concerning Britons' relationship to Germany.
In the text, there are several main ideas you need to communicate in your summary.
Choose the seven most important facts from the list below:

- name of the text, author, date and source
- main idea: how British people feel about Germans
- background: the 2014 World Cup final
- quote: "I can't quite believe it … but I find myself supporting Germany."
- stereotypes about German people
- the state of Britain's economy
- what Britain cannot copy from Germany
- what Britain can learn from Germany
- German problems
- The chance of a British team winning the World Cup

Now summarize the text, then go back to task **2** on p. 110.

Chapter 6 India – a Kaleidoscope

A2 Colonizers and colonized p.117

Comparing a quote and photos

When studying the quote, you could consider the following:

- Who spoke the words?
- What is the speaker's view of colonialism?
- What is the speaker's view of the colonized people?
- What is the main message?

When studying the photographs, you should take the following aspects into account:

- When and where was the photo probably taken?
- Who can you see in the picture?
- What does body language reveal about the relationship of the people in the picture?
- What can you deduce from the picture about India under British rule?

A3 The British Empire from an Indian perspective p.119

5 The legacy of the Raj

Discuss whether the British Raj was a good thing for India. Consider the following points in **A2**:

- What does Curzon say that he hoped he gave the Indians? Consider whether some of these might have been given to the Indians, and whether the Indians needed what he hoped to give.
- How might the Indians in the photos feel? Has their lives changed much since the Empire?

Also, consider the following points in text **A3**:

- the positive elements listed in ll.1–2, 6–7, 16–21,
- the failures of the Empire in ll.2–9, 10–14, 18–19.

B1 Urbanization in India: the big picture p.123

1 Indian urbanization

When describing a graph, or diagram, start out by mentioning the topic, the type of presentation used (e.g. a bar chart, a line graph, etc.), the span of time it covers and its source and date of publication (if available). Then describe the diagram in detail by turning the graph into words. In the end summarize what you have learned.

Now go back to task **2** on p.123.

B3 Celebrating Indian culture p.125

6 Mediation (German → English)

Before writing your email, have a look at the following opening and closing formulas and decide which of them are best used in formal, which ones in informal emails (or letters). Decide on the best for your email.

Dear Dr. Smith, • Dear Madam, • Dear Ms. White, • Dear Prof. Smith, • Dear Sir or Madam, • Dear Mike, • Dear Sir(s), • Dearest • Hello, Mike! • Hey, babe! • Hi, • Tony,	*Best regards • Best wishes • Hugs and kisses • Lots of love • Love • Regards • Sincerely yours • With best wishes • With kind regards • Yours ever • Yours faithfully • Yours sincerely • Yours truly • Yours*

Now choose the most appropriate opening and closing formulas for your email.

C1 The Indian diaspora p. 127

2 Locating the Indian diaspora
  a When designing your poster, take the following points into consideration:
- Overall appearance: Does the poster attract your attention? Is it informative? How creative is the work that went into its making?
- Title: Does the poster have a title banner? Is the title clear? Is it eye-catching? Can it be read easily from 3 metres away?
- Layout: Is the text large enough to be read from 2 metres away? Is there sufficient 'resting space for the eye' (i.e. blank space)? Are colours and graphic highlighting used effectively? Are texts and illustrations/photographs integrated in a meaningful way?
- Writing: Is the writing concise? Is the information included in the texts relevant? Can the texts be read easily? Is language used correctly (e.g. vocabulary, grammar, spelling)?

C3 English lessons p. 130

3 The use of tenses
The following passages from 'English Lessons' illustrate the use of the narrative past, narrative present and narrative future tenses in the story:

narrative past:

The police came looking for him. Oh no, not for my protection – no. They were rounding up all Sikh boys between the ages of fifteen and twenty-five for 'questioning'. Tony's parents knew what was in store and they hid him in the servant's quarter, a concrete room on the flat roof of the house. (ll. 75–78)

narrative present:

The phone rings and my heart starts to pound – *dharak, dharak*. Our answering machine message has Valerie's voice, and I follow the words with her accent. (ll. 8–9)

narrative future:

I will tell Tony I will take English lessons, and that she will be my teacher. (ll. 98–99)

Find more examples like this in the story to illustrate each type of narration, then answer the following questions:
- Which type of narration lends the story a sense of immediacy?
- Which type of narration has a distancing effect?
- Which type of narration could be said to add a prophetic tone to the story?

Go back to 'English Lessons' and use your findings to interpret the story: Why are there so many tense switches in 'English Lessons'? What do they reveal about the first-person narrator? And what is their effect on the reader?

Now go back to task **4** on p. 130.

Chapter 7   The USA – Still the Promised Land?

A1 ¡Viva América!   p.137

3 Words that convey emotion

b The following text sounds bland because it lacks words that convey feelings. You can give it more emotional impact by adding the words from the box.

anxious • feared • hastily • hoping • nervously • overjoyed • tearfully • thrilled

My father … that his life would change for the worse if Castro came to power in Cuba. He … applied to the US Embassy in Havana, … for an immigration permit for himself and his family. After waiting three … months, he was … to receive a letter saying we could leave for the USA. My parents … packed their belongings and … said goodbye to their friends and relatives in Cuba. On March 11th, 1958, on board a small passenger ship bound for Miami, they were … to have their first glimpse of the US mainland.

When you have finished, compare texts with someone who did not use the Support option. Talk about different ways of modifying sentences to give them more emotional appeal.

B1 The new neighbours   p.143

6 The other side of the coin

Form groups of four. Two of you are Bev and Russ, the other two are the African American couple who have bought the house in Clybourne Street. Imagine that after Karl has left, the black couple come to look at the house. How would Russ and Bev behave? How might the black couple explain their wish to move to an all-white neighbourhood? Discuss the issues at hand, then prepare role cards for your parts.

Step 1: Give the black couple names (e.g. Francine and Albert). Each member of your group chooses one of the characters. Read the list below and decide whether the attitude would better fit the white couple or the black couple:

- a bit embarrassed by the situation
- looking forward to changing neighbourhoods
- want a better life for their children
- feel guilty about their behaviour

- worried about the reaction of the neighbours
- believe in equality and progress
- avoid talking about race and skin colour
- want their share of the American dream

Step 2: Now work together in 'couples' to prepare your role cards. Write down (in keywords) questions your person might ask and statements they might make.

Now practise the scene, then perform it for your class.

D1 Facts and figures   p.152

1 Understanding the figures

a Compare the figures in the table by completing the eight sentences on the opposite page with phrases from the box.

	USA	China	Germany	Brazil	Russia	India
1 GDP	16,244,600	8,277,103	3,428,131	2,252,664	2,014,775	1,841,710
2 Military spending	682,478	166,107	45,785	43,576	90,749	46,125
3 Balance of trade	−784,775	155,142	219,938	19,169	198,760	−154,401

1 The GDP of the USA is almost … as that of China, the country with the … largest economy.
2 The Russian GDP is only about … as China's.
3 China's GDP is … that of Germany, Russia and Brazil together.
4 Russia's GDP is … that of Brazil.
5 No country spends … money on the military as the USA.
6 Germany ranks only … in terms of GDP, but … in terms of balance of trade.
7 Russia has a healthy trade surplus, whereas India imports … it exports.
8 China's trade surplus is almost … India's trade deficit.

> *as many • as much • first • fourth • half as big • larger than • (slightly) less than • more than • one quarter as big • second • the same size as • third • twice as big*

■ FACT FILE

GDP (**Gross** [grəʊs] **Domestic Product**) is defined as the total value of goods and services produced in a country. The **balance of trade** is the difference between the total value of exports from a country and imports into the same country. A negative balance (**deficit** ['defɪsɪt]; opposite: **surplus** ['sɜːpləs]) means the country imports more than it exports.

D3 **Better than its reputation**   p. 154

3 The author's bias

a Point to examples from the text that illustrate the author's bias (selection of facts, word choice, use of *emphasis, *juxtaposition, sentence structure, etc.). Match the words and expressions that have been highlighted to one or more of the categories in the box and describe the effect they have on the reader. ▶ Glossary, p. 322

> *comparison • *juxtaposition / selection of facts • *contrast word choice (e.g. positive / negative *connotations) • *emphasis • *repetition / *anaphora*

> But the American response is already larger – by a factor of hundreds – than that of the largest economy in East Asia. The United States is sending an aircraft carrier to the worst-hit regions and has promised $20 million in emergency aid. Millions more will be raised by U.S. charities. The British are sending a warship and $16 million. Even the Vatican has promised $4 million. And the government of China, the new land of opportunity? $100,000.
> (Lines 18–27 of the text on p. 153)

Journalist Anne Applebaum

> Americans, like Europeans, have long believed that strength and wealth entail responsibility. That's why two American ex-presidents voluntarily coordinated the international response to the 2004 tsunami, even though Indonesia was not the site of a U.S. naval base. That's why massive amounts of U.S. aid went to victims of the 2005 earthquake in Kashmir, even though relations between the United States and Pakistan were deteriorating at the time.
> That's also why an American president who is actively uninterested in engaging with the Syrian conflict has pledged more than $1 billion in humanitarian aid to Syrian refugees, accounting for nearly 30 percent of all such aid; European contributions as a whole make up a good percentage of the rest. China's contribution, meanwhile, comes to $3 million, less than that of Luxembourg. China plays an enormous political role in Syria – the Chinese veto has helped keep the United Nations firmly sidelined there – but clearly does not feel obligated to help those affected by its decisions.
> The Chinese do give development aid, but differently: not in response to tragedies, not to counter disaster, but to facilitate the export of raw materials to China.
> (Lines 36–51 of the text on pp. 153–154)

Now go on to **3b** on p. 154; if possible, choose a partner who has not made use of the Support option.

Chapter 8 Beyond the Nation – Europe and a Globalized World

A2 Young, educated – and leaving the country p. 163

4 Creative writing

Form groups of four. Each select one important moment of Melissa Abadía's immigrant experience and write a diary entry. Read out your entries to your group and join your texts to form one coherent diary entry.
1 Look for the description of an important moment in the text.
2 Make notes on what happened and how Melissa Abadía felt at that moment.
3 If necessary add other events and feelings Melissa Abadía may have had.
4 Write your diary entry.

B2 The need for a new label p. 167

3 Promoting transparent labelling

a Design a clothing label that helps buyers make responsible choices.
  1 Make a list of aspects that are important for responsible clothing production.
  2 Choose the most important points and think of a system to evaluate them.
  3 Write the text for a clothing label that contains information about these aspects.

Now go back to task **3b** on p. 167.

C1 Keeping the accent p. 172

4 `YOU CHOOSE` **Creative writing**

a Write a *short story based on the poem.
  1 Outline the events and emotions you would like to include in your story.
  2 Decide from which character's *point of view to tell the story – the *speaker of the poem, the barman or other people in the bar.
  3 Decide what type of *narrator to use.
  4 Start writing. Do not write an introduction, but start in the middle of the scene, e.g. 'I can feel their looks piercing my back'.
  5 Do not write a clear, conclusive ending, but leave it open, even a bit vague.
  6 Hold writing conferences among four or five students to improve your texts.

 OR

b Write a dramatic *scene based on the poem.
  1 Decide on how you are going to convey the *speaker's feelings or memories. You might make her speak a *soliloquy or you might have a second actor who acts as the speaker's 'shadow', articulating her feelings and thoughts.
  2 Write your scene, starting the action right in the middle of the action, e.g. with the barman saying 'Sorry, what was that?'.
  3 Imagine the actors' gestures or movements and write stage directions.

C3 Linguistic diplomacy: the Eurovision Song Contest   p. 173

5 Discussion

In groups of five prepare and hold a panel discussion in which you discuss the question of whether each country should be obliged to enter songs in their national language only. One student is the moderator, the others argue either for or against the topic.

Moderator:
- Think of possible arguments and their counter-arguments.
- Collect questions or remarks that might make the participants put these arguments forward.

Discussion participants:
- Think of arguments for your position and collect examples to illustrate your point.
  Don't just talk about the very obvious topics, but search for arguments and examples the others might not have thought about.
- Collect arguments that your opponents might put forward and think about ways to refute them.

Chapter Task   p. 175

1 Planning your work

a Do some research to get a general idea of the topic and to identify suitable subtopics.

Find some helpful links here:
Webcode context-24

1. Don't forget to provide a definition of slavery.
2. Define the areas you want to focus on:
   a. You might want to give a short historical survey of slavery. Consider e.g. the situation in Ancient Greece or Rome, the Middle Ages and/or the Americas.
   b. You might also want to outline the grievances that have led to slave rebellions throughout history.
   c. When considering modern-day slavery, think of e.g. the catering trade or agriculture, the construction industry, private households, the entertainment industry (football) or sexual slavery.
3. Decide whether you want to present a case study or general aspects of slavery.

Now go back to task **1b** on p. 175.

2 Preparing your poster

Find a tool to make your poster here:
Webcode context-50

b Organize your findings and prepare your poster.
1. Structure your text and visual aids in a way that guides the reader of your poster through it: Use symbols, lines, arrows, colours, and fonts in a clear and meaningful way.
2. You may use pictures and/or quotations taken from films and/or literature dealing with slavery.

Now go back to task **2c** on p. 175.

Chapter 9   Work and Business – Careers and Perspectives

A2 Moving on after recession   p. 182

3 Political speeches: convincing the audience
Look at Obama's style and language and show how he tries to convince his audience. Pay attention, for instance, to how Obama appeals to the audience by
- varying sentence lengths,
- referring to historical events,
- …

Also, observe the effect the story of Misty DeMars has on the audience.

Now go back to task **4** on p. 183.

A4 Teenagers' career aspirations   p. 186

4 Writing
Should you pursue the career of your choice or should you consider only those careers where job demand is fairly certain? Write an argumentative text in which you consider both sides and state your own view. For ideas *for* wanting to pursue your preferred career / studies programme, i.e. *against* considering only those careers where job demand is projected, consider
- motivational aspects,
- your talents,
- achieving the goals you set yourself,
- potentially good results in examinations, etc., if you are diligent and hardworking.

For ideas *against* wanting to pursue your preferred career / studies programme, i.e. *for* considering only those careers where job demand is projected,
- look for arguments, facts and figures from the article for support,
- think of the possibility of combining talents and interests with promising career paths.

A5 Do you love your job?   p. 189

3 A tricky question in your job interview
  a Some of the aspects of job satisfaction mentioned by King should not be brought up in a job interview. List them, then compare with your partner. Remember, for instance: Your future employer is interested in your well-being and job satisfaction, but also wants employees who can work in a team.

Now go back to task **3** on p. 189.

B1 Mitch's first glimpse of the world of work   p. 191

2 Power relations
Partner A: Analyse the meeting between Mitch and McNulty and explain how one of them shows his power and superiority through non-linguistic means (e.g. facial expressions). Focus and take notes on
- Mitch and McNulty on their way to the coach's office,
- where and how they are sitting in the office,
- McNulty's eyes and voice,
- McNulty's pencil.

Partner B: Analyse the meeting between Mitch and McNulty and explain how one of them uses language to demonstrate his power and superiority. Focus and take notes on
- who is asking the important questions,
- who is using imperatives,
- who is trying to be funny,
- who controls the conversation.

Now go back to task **3** on p. 191.

B2 Ten things not to say in a job interview   p. 193

2 The language of the text
a Explain how King tries to amuse the reader. Consider the following *stylistic devices used by King: absurd example, exaggeration, metaphor. Find examples of these devices in lines 30, 35 and 46–47.

Now go back to task **2b** on p. 193.

B3 The best job in the world is back!   p. 194

2 Text type and target group
a Name characteristic aspects of the text type 'job advertisement' and illustrate them with examples from the text. The subheadings of the text give you a first idea about typical elements of job ads. Match the subheadings with their corresponding explanation:

Subheading	Explanation
Your responsibilities	financial information
Who we're looking for	contact information
About the job package	information about the employer
About your new office	description of the ideal candidate
How to apply	description of duties

Now go back to task **2b** on p. 194.

B5 Look them in the eye – the job interview   p. 196

2 Do's and don'ts
Watch the video. With your partner, list and rank the given dos and don'ts of job interviews. Five of the following aspects are dealt with in the video:

1   conversation openers
2   dress code
3   first impressions
4   hairstyle

5   no-go questions
6   professional documents
7   punctuality
8   selling yourself and your strengths

Now go back to task **3** on p. 196.

Language Practice

> *Download the suggested answers to the tasks here:*
> **Webcode** context-29

Focus on Grammar

▶ LP 1 Simple and progressive verb forms

1 **BASIC** Choose the right form of the verb for each of the sentences below (make sure you choose the correct tense).

1 A man came running out of the bank and (*jump*) into the waiting car.
2 Sorry, I can't talk now – I (*make*) dinner for the family.
3 Smoking (*cause*) over 600,000 deaths in the EU every year.
4 It was a cold evening, and a light drizzle (*fall*). When no one (*come*) to unlock the gates the crowd (*get*) restless.
5 The housing prices in London (*always be*) high, but at present they (*skyrocket*).
6 The last time I talked to her, she (*look*) for a new job.

Most English verbs can be used in all tenses in both the simple and the progressive form:
Jasmin *practises* *the piano three hours a day. She's* *practising* *now for her concert on Saturday.*

Simple form	Progressive form
• For states[1]: Our house *needs* repainting. • For actions that follow a plan or physical law: *Our plane* *leaves* *at 8:05 am. Water* *boils* *at 100 °C.* • Actions in a series (narration) • Verbs that describe what the author of a text does: *The author* *criticizes* *the government's lack of initiative.*	• For actions that are taking place at the present moment or were taking place at a certain point in time in the past: *I've* *been waiting* *here all morning! When the police arrived, two men* *were loading* *boxes into a van.* • For trends and developments: *It's* *becoming* *more and more difficult to find a permanent job. It's* *getting* *dark – let's go home.* • For descriptions of circumstances (weather, clothing, etc.): *A cold wind* *was blowing. She* *was wearing* *a red woollen sweater over a plaid skirt.*

---

[1]**state** *Zustand*

Verbs that describe a state (i.e. not an activity) are called **state verbs**. Normally, they can only be used in the simple form:
I heard a voice. Someone needed help. I wanted to help them, but I didn't know how.
A few state verbs can also be used in the progressive form, but with a different meaning. Compare the sentences in the table below and explain the difference in meaning:

Simple form	Progressive form
What do you think of his decision?	What are you thinking about?
You look upset – what's the matter?	Why are you looking at me like that?
For her, success is all that counts.	We're counting on you to help us.
How do you feel about same-sex marriage?	He stayed at home because he wasn't feeling well.
Everybody has a bad day now and then.	We were having lunch when my phone rang.

2 Choose the right form of the verb for each of the sentences below:
  1 I (*think*) you should go to her and tell her how you (*feel*) about what happened.
  2 Lydia (*love*) going to parties, but she never (*feel*) like organizing one herself.
  3 While I (*look*) at the photos on our website I (*have*) a great idea for our next campaign.
  4 Everyone (*need*) the feeling that their life (*count*) for something.
  5 The last time I (*see*) Bruce and Charlene they (*have*) a big argument about something .
  6 When I visited Bob in hospital, I (*think*) he (*look*) awful, but he said that he (*feel*) better.

> ▊ **TROUBLE SPOT**
> With **everybody/everyone**, the plural form of the possessive pronoun is commonly used.

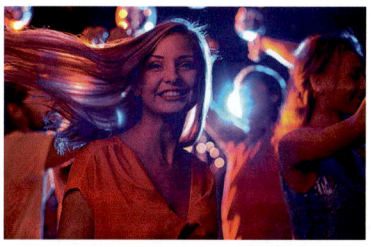

Special uses: the progressive form used for emphasis
- Some speakers use the progressive form of state verbs, especially in the present perfect, to underline their message: *'New York? I've been wanting to go there for ages!' / 'I've been meaning to write to you since Christmas!'*
- In some situations, the progressive form of the verb *be* is used to refer to behaviour that is temporary and (perhaps) not genuine: *Why are you being so stubborn? – Ignore him; he's just being a trouble-maker again.*
- The slogan of a US fast-food chain (*I'm loving it!*) belongs to the same category: using the progressive form of the state verb *love* has the effect of underlining the message and makes the slogan more memorable.

▶ LP2 Present tense or future?

1 **BASIC** Spot and correct the mistakes in the sentences below:
  1 I don't know how he reacts when we tell him the truth.
  6 'I need a can opener for this.' – 'No problem, I go look for one.'
  3 Is it true that Kai goes abroad next year?
  4 The weather forecast says there are scattered showers throughout the afternoon.
  5 I'm sure my parents don't let me go to the rock festival.
  6 The German students will wait at Stansted until their bus will come to collect them.

Generally speaking, English – like German – uses the **present tense to talk about the present** and the **future to talk about the future**. However, there are a few exceptions to keep in mind:

- In English, when offering to do something, the **will-future** is used (whereas the present tense would be used in German): *Hast du Durst? Ich hole uns etwas zu trinken. / Are you thirsty? I'll fetch us something to drink.*
- In German, it is possible to talk about the future in the present tense: *Wir fahren morgen an die See*. You can do this in English too, but only with the **present progressive** when you talk about plans for the future: *We're leaving* for the coast tomorrow. A sentence like *Morgen regnet es wieder* can only be expressed in the *will*-future: *It will rain again tomorrow*.
- **The future is not used** after *if, when, unless, until, as soon as*, etc., even when you are referring to the future: *Phone me as soon as you arrive. – You won't get tickets unless you book in advance.*

2 Use the keywords and phrases to make complete sentences. All verbs are in the present or the future:
1. There's someone at the door. You / please / go / see who it is?
2. The PM says / he / attend to the problem / as soon as / government report / published.
3. In the course of the week / temperatures / drop slightly.
4. By the time / we / arrive at the airport / it / be / too late.
5. The people next door / have / their house repainted / next month.
6. The assistant director says / he / talk to the staff / before / situation / escalate any further.

▶ LP3 Simple present and present perfect

1 BASIC Decide which of the following sentences are correct. Correct the faulty ones:
1. I have wanted to meet her for as long as I can remember.
2. For the past three years, John is saving his money for a trip to New Zealand.
3. The author and her family live in London since 2006.
4. Four hundred years after his death, Shakespeare has continued to fascinate audiences around the world.
5. We are waiting for this bus for the last half an hour – I don't think it's coming.
6. Leonie has been an avid reader ever since she taught herself to read at the age of five.

The **present perfect** is used in English for actions and states that began in the past, but are still going on or hold true. German uses the present tense in such cases.

German	English
Hunneman leitet die Organisation seit 2008.	*Hunneman has led the organization since 2008.*
Rowling arbeitet seit drei Jahren an einem neuen Roman.	*Rowling has been working on a new novel for three years.*

The **present perfect** is closely connected with the present time. For that reason, English speakers often choose verbs in the present perfect where a German might use a different verb in the present.

German	English
Kennst du den Roman Doktor Faustus?	*Have you ever read* Doktor Faustus?
Ich kenne Bratislava nicht.	*I've never been to Bratislava.*
Weißt du, ob Justin heute da ist?	*Have you seen Justin this morning?*
Wissen die Praktikanten schon Bescheid?	*Have the interns been informed yet?*

2 Translate the following sentences into idiomatic English. Use the verb in brackets in the present perfect.
1 Kennst du den Film *Casablanca*? (see)
2 Kennst du Paris? (be)
3 Kennt ihr schon das neue türkische Restaurant am Zimmerplatz? (check out)
4 Ich bin noch nie Ski gelaufen. (try)
5 Weißt du über das Treffen heute Nachmittag Bescheid? (hear)
6 Kennst du dich mit 3D-Druckern aus? (use)

▶ LP4 Present perfect and simple past

1 **BASIC** Complete the sentences with the correct form of the verb (present perfect or simple past).
1 When … you last … Thomas? (see)
2 The centre … opened in 2004. (be)
3 Until today, no one … a cure for cancer. (discover)
4 Sarah … me the revised version of the text just five minutes ago. (hand)
5 We're still friends, although I … her since we graduated. (not see)
6 I … the book when it first came out, but I … it. (read; not like)
7 Julia and Tobias … at a youth camp in Ireland in 2012. They … in contact ever since. (meet; keep)
8 My brother … to New Zealand yesterday, but we … from him yet. (fly; not hear)

Present perfect (This tense refers to a time that has not yet ended.)	Simple past (This tense refers to a time that is over.)
Use this tense • to present results: *Engineers at the Wyss Institute have developed a new kind of biodegradable plastic.* • to talk about states that have existed since some time in the past: *How long have you lived in Germany?* • to talk about actions in the past without saying when they happened: *She's been there before.* • to talk about actions that have happened more than once (or never): *I've seen that film at least five times. I've never been to Denmark.*	Use this tense when talking about events that happened in the past: *When I was a student, I lived in Exeter.*
Examples of signal words and phrases: • *already, ever, never, yet, often* • time phrases with *since* and *for (since 2013, for ten years)*	Examples of signal words and phrases: • *before, yesterday* • time phrases of the past (*ten minutes ago, last June, in 2010*) • *When …?*

> ■ **TROUBLE SPOT**
> Signal words of the past can **never** be used together with the **present perfect**. Sentences such as *When have you last talked to him?* and *I have seen her just a few minutes ago* are always wrong!

2   Choose the correct form of the verbs in brackets in the following text. You may use the present, the simple past or the present perfect:

Almost everyone (hear) of Stephen King, the best-selling author of dozens of horror stories. King (be) born in 1947 in Maine, USA, where many of his stories (be) also set. After graduating from the University of Maine in 1970, King (find) a teaching position at Hampden Academy. His first novel, Carrie, (be) published by Doubleday in 1973 and (bring) King national attention as well as financial independence. In the summer of 1999, King (be) walking down a road when he (be) hit by a car and badly injured. He (survive), but since his accident, he (write) much less. His son Joseph Hillstrom King, who (use) the pen name Joe Hill, (write) three novels and numerous stories, all of which (belong) to the genre fantasy/horror. Similar to his more famous father, Hill (win) numerous writing awards.

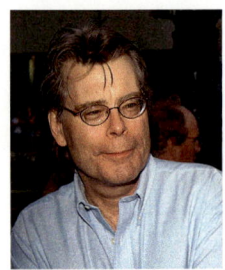

World-famous author, Stephen King

▶ LP 5   Infinitive or gerund after certain verbs

1   **BASIC**   Choose the correct form of the verb complement (infinitive or gerund) in the following sentences:
1   You can leave as soon as you have finished (clean up).
2   Many people dislike (be told) what to do.
3   How long have you wanted (go) there?
4   I don't mind (get) my hands dirty.
5   As she had never intended (take) the job, Sandy was surprised (receive) an offer.
6   She hoped (get) a better offer from a firm in Shanghai.

Infinitive or gerund?	Verbs	Example
verb + **infinitive**	most verbs that can take a complement	*I want to go to Hawaii.* *I wish to speak to your boss.* *I'm planning to study physics.*
verb + **gerund**	*admit, avoid, consider, deny, dislike, enjoy, finish, give up, imagine, include, involve, justify, keep, mention, mind, miss, practise, risk, suggest*	*I dislike waiting for the bus.* *I miss going to school.* ▬ **TIP** To avoid mistakes, try learning these verbs by heart and then use the infinitive with the rest.
verb + **gerund or infinitive** (same meaning)	*love, like, hate, prefer, begin, start, continue*	*I love to play badminton. / I love playing badminton.*

A small number of verbs have **different meanings** when they are used with an infinitive or a gerund. Compare the sentences in the table below. What does the verb mean in each case?

Verb	Used with a gerund	Used with an infinitive
stop	*Stop shouting like that!*	*Let's stop to have a break.*
remember	*I don't remember seeing him at the meeting.*	*Did you remember to lock the door?*
forget	*I'll never forget seeing London for the first time.*	*I forgot to buy a litre of milk – sorry!*
mean	*Sustainability means not using more than we produce.*	*I didn't mean to make her upset.*
try	*If you have the hiccups – try holding your breath.*	*We tried to make him change his mind, but he wouldn't listen.*

2 Decide between a gerund or an infinitive in the following sentences:
1 For Melissa, the job in Los Angeles was a dream come true, but it meant (leave) her family and friends behind.
2 If we don't stop (dump) waste into the world's oceans, it may soon be too late.
3 Suzie mentioned (go) on a date but avoided (tell) us with whom.
4 I tried (reach) you by mobile, but I only got your mailbox.
5 John stopped (read) the newspaper and missed the train.
6 Anthony considered (run) the red light but then imagined (cause) an accident.
7 Students often say that they forgot (do) their homework, but no one really believes them.

▶ LP6 Infinitive or gerund after certain nouns

1 **BASIC** Spot the mistakes in the following sentences and correct them. Careful: not all sentences are wrong.
1 I don't know why she entered the competition – she doesn't have a chance of winning.
2 I'm afraid we don't have time of discussing the matter any longer.
3 Mark Zuckerberg wasn't the first person who had the idea to create a social networking site.
4 Our plan of camping in the wild turned out to be completely unrealistic.
5 Rosa Parks was one of the first African Americans who had the courage of speaking out against racism.
6 After their traumatic experience, the victims had the need of talking to someone who could help them.
7 Students often face the problem to find affordable accommodations.
8 The stipend helped Jens of going to New York for a year.

In German, you can add information to any noun using an infinitive phrase: *der Wunsch, reich und berühmt zu sein.*
In English, generally an **infinitive** is used, a **gerund with *of***, or a ***that*-clause**:
the right to state your opinion
the dream of becoming a star
the fact that she could speak five languages.
However, these complements cannot be used interchangeably:

Infinitive or gerund?	Nouns	Example
noun + infinitive	*right, wish, desire, longing, will, courage, strength, decision, time, need, ability*	*the right to bear arms, time to say good-bye, the will to live*
noun + *of* + gerund	most other nouns	*the risk of getting lost, the fear of being left behind*
special cases	• *chance, opportunity, plan*: Either the infinitive or *of* + gerund can be used. • *a/any chance*: *of* + gerund is used more often. • *the chance*: The infinitive is used more often.	*This is my chance to earn lots of money. / This is my chance of earning lots of money. Any chance of seeing him again? The chance to win this game is pretty slim.*

There are a few **more special cases** worth remembering:
- The word *reason* can be used either with an infinitive or with *for* + gerund. When *reason* is followed by *for* + a person, an infinitive must be used: *There's no reason for us to give up without a fight.*
- The word *attempt* can be followed either by an infinitive or by *at* + gerund: *The government's attempt at covering up / to cover up the matter only made things worse.*
- The expression *(to) have trouble / difficulty* is used with a gerund without any preposition: *I had trouble starting the motor. Difficulty* can also be followed by *in* + gerund: *We had difficulty* (not: ~~difficulties~~) *in persuading her to come to the meeting. Careful:* In other contexts *difficulty* is treated like a normal noun (*of* + gerund): *the difficulty of living with a permanent disability*.

2   Put the verb in brackets into the correct form; in some cases there is more than one correct solution:
1. All our attempts (reach) an agreement have failed.
2. The dream (find) a better life was reason enough for millions of immigrants (leave) their homeland.
3. The producer had trouble (find) a child star who could both act and dance.
4. Steven spent his first weeks in Kerala learning (cope) with the difficulties (live and work) in India.
5. I would be interested in hearing your reasons (reject) the proposal.
6. You can't imagine the difficulty we had (locate) a garage in Sofia that could repair our car.

▶ LP 7 The passive

1   `BASIC`   Make complete sentences in the passive using the keywords:
1. Fitzgerald's classic novel, *The Great Gatsby* / first publish / 1925
2. To date[1] / it / adapt for the screen / six times
3. The most recent version / released / 2013
4. It / be / the first screen adaptation / that / film (v) / in 3D format
5. The title role / play / Leonardo DiCaprio
6. The film / criticize / some critics / as a costume spectacle
7. Most of the scenes / shoot / in Australia, / where huge sets / build / for the film

Rules for using the passive	Examples
The passive in English is formed using the verb **(to) be** and the **past participle**.	*Tchaikovsky's ballet* Swan Lake *was first performed in 1877.*
Generally, the passive is used when the person who does an action is unknown or unimportant.	*Three paintings were stolen from the museum last weekend.*
If the person or force that does something (the 'agent') is named in the sentence, it is introduced using the preposition **by**.	*The tower was damaged by lightning in 1988.*
Verbs that use a preposition keep the preposition in the passive.	*discriminate against sb.* → *African Americans have often been discriminated against, not only in the past.*
If the so-called **personal passive** can be formed, it is usually first choice.	*We were given our ID cards at the main desk.* (The 'normal' passive would sound awkward here: *Our ID cards were given to us at the main desk.*)
Passive forms of the **infinitive** and the **gerund** can also be formed.	*(to) love* → *(to) be loved* *loving* → *being loved*

[1] **to date** *(adv)* bisher, bis jetzt

2 Use an infinitive or a gerund in the passive to rewrite the <u>underlined</u> parts of the following sentences. You may have to change the word order. Avoid using a *by*-agent.

1 After the flood <u>they had to rebuild</u> most of the houses in the village. *(After the flood most of the houses in the village had to …)*
2 Teenagers hate <u>it when adults treat them</u> like children.
3 Even in his darkest moments, Colin never gave up the hope <u>that he would be rescued</u>.
4 It was her fear <u>that people would laugh at her</u> that held her back.
5 She told her doctor that she wanted <u>him to tell her the truth</u>.
6 No one likes the feeling <u>that someone is discriminating against them</u>.

Special uses: the *get*-passive

In colloquial English, many speakers form the passive using **_get_** instead of **_be_**. Common phrases are *get hurt, get killed, get lost, get caught.*
The *get*-passive is also used to emphasize the difference between an action and a state:
We soon got lost in a maze of tiny alleyways that all looked the same.
I couldn't spot a single familiar landmark and finally had to admit that I was lost.

▶ **LP8 Conditional sentences**

1 **BASIC** Complete the following sentences with the correct form of the verb in brackets:

1 If I discover a cancer cure, I (become) famous.
2 If I discovered a cancer cure, I (become) famous.
3 If I had discovered a cancer cure ten years ago, I (be) famous.
4 If someone (be) famous, everyone recognizes them on the street.
5 If Romeo (not crash) the Capulets' party, he might never have met Juliet.
6 If the sea level (rise) one meter, hundreds of coastal cities would be in danger.

A variety of conditional sentences are possible in English. Their use depends on the situation.

An imagined condition in the **past** with an imagined consequence in the **past**.	*If Sheila had taken part in the competition, she might have won a prize.*
An imagined condition in the **past** with an imagined consequence in the **present**.	*If you hadn't wasted all your money, you could afford to go with us to Greece.*
An imagined condition in the **present** with an imagined consequence.	*If Sarah worked harder, she would get better marks.*
A possible condition in the **present** with a possible consequence.	*If you have trouble with the new software, Kevin can / will help you.*
A condition that can happen at any time and its consequence.	*If the polar ice caps melt, the sea level rises / will rise.*

2 The text below presents some facts concerning the settlement of North America and its consequences. Draw conclusions from the facts using conditional sentences.
Example: *If European settlers had not come to America, herds of buffalo might still roam the Great Plains.*

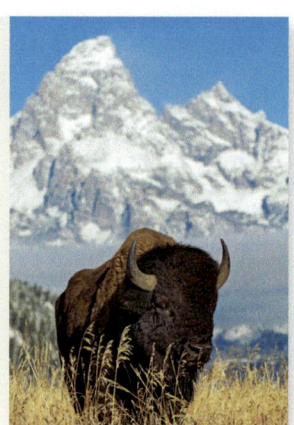

When the first European settlers arrived at the shores of the New World, there were about three million Native Americans living in North America. Having no natural immunity to European diseases, thousands of natives fell ill and died. As they moved farther west, the white settlers pushed the natives off their land, at the same time decimating[1] the large herds of buffalo that roamed[2] the Great Plains. The Native Americans, whose way of life depended on the buffalo, could no longer exist. Ancient grasslands disappeared as farms were followed by railroads, towns, highways and factories, further restricting the freedom of movement of the native tribes. An ecological balance between man and nature that had existed for thousands of years was destroyed within a few decades.

▶ LP 9 Articles, quantifiers and countability

1   **BASIC**   Translate the nouns and noun phrases in brackets, deciding whether you need a singular or a plural and whether or not the definite article is necessary.

1 *(Die menschliche Gesellschaft)* hasn't made *(viele Fortschritte)* in dealing with the forces of *(das Böse)*.
2 We found *(einige interessante Informationen)* on the internet concerning *(die Kunst)* of the Aborigines.
3 *(Die Wissenschaft)* can provide us with *(Erkenntnisse)*, but it can't give us any *(Ratschläge)* on how to use it.
4 Despite all the *(Forschungen)* on cancer, there has been relatively *(wenig Fortschritte)*.
5 Although she grew up in L.A., her *(Kenntnisse)* of *(die Natur)* and *(die Umwelt)* is really impressive.

> *Find more information on articles, quantifiers and countability here:*
> **Webcode** context-30

2 The table below shows which social networking site five young people regularly use:

	Sandy	Carol	Andrew	James	Marvin
Spacebook	X	X	X	X	X
Lightnigram	X		X	X	X
Chatter	X	X	X		
Mumblr			X		X
OurSpace					

1 Make four statements about the group. Example: *A few of them use Mumblr.*
2 Make two statements about Sandy and Carol: what have they got in common?

---

[1]**decimate sth.**   kill large numbers of sth.   [2]**roam**   walk around with no fixed goal

▶ LP 10 Using adjectives and adverbs

1 **BASIC** Put the words in brackets in the right form (adjective or adverb):
1 In science-fiction films, robots (traditional) appear in the role of (soulless) killing machines.
2 The engineers who develop robots for new applications (passionate) believe that they will make our lives (happy and safe).
3 For example, they will free us from (boring) tasks like cleaning the house or mowing the lawn.
4 Most of the (heavy) work in farming is already done (automatic) by machine.
5 (Remarkable) progress has been made in developing robots for a (large) number of everyday uses.
6 Ideas that sounded (impossible) only ten years ago are (rapid) becoming reality.
7 Perhaps someday we will be (complete) dependent on (intelligent) machines for almost everything.

Adjectives	
Adjectives are used to modify (i.e. describe) a noun. They can be used directly before the noun (*a short holiday, a famous tourist spot*) or they are used after certain verbs:	
Verbs of being, seeming, becoming, etc.	*Why are you sad? She seemed unhappy. Don't get nervous. Injustice always makes me angry.*
Verbs that describe sense impressions	*He looks nervous. That sounds wonderful. The soup smells great and it tastes great too. The stone felt cold to the touch.*

Adverbs	
Adverbs of manner are made from adjectives by adding *-ly*. (Exceptions: *fast, hard, early* and *late* are used as both adjectives and adverbs.) Adverbs modify verbs, adjectives, or other adverbs:	
Adverb modifies **verb**.	*She got up quickly and ran to the window.*
Adverb modifies **adjective**.	*The team has been incredibly successful this season.*
Adverb modifies **adverb**.	*The experts worked extremely cautiously to defuse the bomb.*
Certain adverbs can also be used to modify a whole sentence. Such adverbs are known as **sentence adverbs.** They always stand at the beginning of the sentence and are often separated by a comma from the rest of the sentence.	
Adverb modifies **sentence**.	*Fortunately, none of the passengers were seriously injured.*
Other common sentence adverbs: *actually, admittedly, apparently, consequently, eventually, evidently, hopefully, incidentally, luckily, obviously, presumably, surprisingly, ultimately, understandably*.	

2 Use a sentence adverb instead of the underlined words in each of the sentences below:
1 More and more cars hit the road every year. <u>As a result</u>, the number of traffic jams also increases.
2 <u>A surprising fact is that</u> the interest in car ownership is declining.
3 <u>It seems that</u> many young urbanites regard a car as an unnecessary expense.
4 <u>It is easy to understand that</u> the interest in car ownership is lowest where cheap, reliable public transportation is available.
5 <u>In the course of time</u> cars may disappear altogether from our city streets.
6 <u>I hope that</u> this development will mean cleaner air in cities that presently have a huge smog problem.

Focus on Style

▶ LP 11 Using the right register

1 **BASIC** In the following excerpt from a student's film summary, the teacher has underlined some expressions in red to indicate that they are inappropriate. Rewrite the text, correcting the stylistic problems.

The film Outsourced *is about this guy named Todd Anderson. He works for an American firm that has outsourced its call centre to India to save money. Todd gets sent there to bring the Indian workers up to US standards. When he gets there, he's totally lost, cause he doesn't know the first thing about India. He tries to get the Indians to act like Americans, but it doesn't work out. He only starts getting somewhere when he begins listening to the Indians and taking them seriously.*

Like other languages, English has different registers for different situations:

Register	Typical situations	Typical features
Informal	Everyday communication between friends, spoken English	Short or incomplete sentences, short forms (*they've, gotta*), phrasal verbs, colloquial expressions (*make it big, chill out,* etc.)
Neutral	Articles and essays on subjects of general interest	Mix of short and more complex sentences, no short forms, words of the general vocabulary
Formal	Official documents and speeches, business letters	Complex sentences, specialized or technical words

When writing essays for school, use the neutral register. Some teachers allow you to use short forms of negations in your writing (*don't, can't,* etc.); ask if you aren't sure.

2 After finishing school in Germany, you apply to a College of Arts in the United States. One day you receive the following letter:

> On behalf of the Admissions Committee I am pleased to inform you that you have been offered a place in the incoming freshman class. Your application convinced us that you have the talent and motivation required for academic success. Furthermore, after careful review of your family's financial situation, we have decided to award you a full scholarship, comprising all tuition fees as well as room and board for the duration of your studies.
> All our students are guaranteed on-campus accommodation in our newly-renovated dormitories (dual occupancy). Furthermore, the College provides a comprehensive 24/7 meal service. Should you decide to accept our offer, please reply by June 10th.

Look up the words and expressions you don't understand; most of them belong to the vocabulary of formal correspondence. Then write an email to your former host family in the US, telling them about the letter and its contents and asking about points that are unclear to you. Use a *neutral or moderately informal* style.

▶ LP 12 Avoiding German-sounding sentence patterns

1 **BASIC** Find the mistakes in the following sentences and correct them.
  1 If you ask me, Roland paid for his new smartphone far too much.
  2 In 2010 was the number of severe storms higher than ever before.
  3 Many teenagers use every day the internet to communicate with friends.

4 I download always the latest version of the program.
5 The author writes that the USA ignores all too often the rest of the world.
6 She points out in her latest book the decline of America's influence in the world.
7 This last point illustrates the author with an anecdote.
8 The summer months can be in some parts of Germany quite cool.

You already know that in some ways German and English sentences are formed differently. Here are some points to observe when you are writing English:

German	English
Dependent infinitives and participles are placed at the end of the sentence (*Satzklammer*): *Er kann* hervorragend *Klavier spielen.* *Er hat* neulich in der Aula *ein Konzert gegeben*.	A 'cluster' instead of a 'bracket' is used, i.e. closely connected words (subject, verb, object) stay together: *He can play the piano* marvellously. *Recently he gave a concert* in the school hall.
The subject moves to third position if there is an adverbial phrase at the beginning of the sentence: *Im November 1989 / wurden / die Übergänge zwischen Ost- und West-Berlin / überraschend freigegeben*.	The subject always comes before the verb; in other words, the word order (S–V) stays the same when an adverbial phrase is put at the beginning of the sentence: *In November 1989 / the checkpoints between East and West Berlin / were unexpectedly opened*.
Verb and object are often separated: *Thomas und Harald spielen jeden Mittwoch Tennis*.	Verb and object **must** stay together: *Thomas and Harald play tennis every Wednesday*.

Even if there is no two-part verb, Germans tend to form a 'bracket sentence': *Dies ist in einigen Fällen ein Problem*.
In English the sentence would sound strange: *This is in some cases a problem*.

> **■ TIP**
>
> Begin your sentences with an adverbial phrase. This helps you to avoid the monotony of sentences that all begin with the subject: *Friedman is an optimist in this respect.* → *In this respect, Friedman is an optimist.*

2 Rearrange sentences in the following text to make it more idiomatic:

Thomas L. Friedman and Michael Mandelbaum collaborated on the book *That Used to Be Us*, which in 2011 was published. The authors point out using numerous examples how the US in global competition has fallen behind. America has lost sight according to the authors of its traditional strengths and values. The authors make in the second half of the book a number of suggestions as to what should be done. Some of these suggestions sounded to a few of the book's critics quite unrealistic. The book was in spite of its gloomy message an instant bestseller.

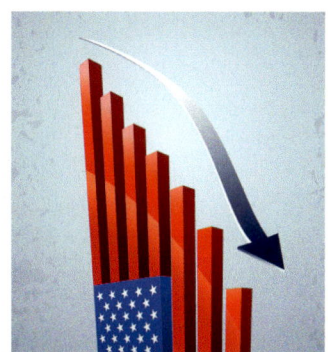

▶ LP 13 **Placing emphasis on key points** 🎧 **CD3** 07

1 **BASIC** Listen to three short conversations, then match them to the following techniques:
   1 The important words in the sentence are stressed, i.e. spoken louder than the others.
   2 The emphatic do-form of the verb is used.
   3 The important word is made the subject of the reply.

> *Listen to the audio file on the CD or download it here:*
> 🔘 **Webcode** context-31

Some of the techniques for emphasis that are used when speaking can also be used in written English; others sound rather formal in spoken English and are mainly used in writing:

Speaking/ Writing	Technique	Example
Speaking	Stressing the important words in the sentence, i.e. speaking them louder than the others	–
Speaking and writing	Using the emphatic *do*-form of the verb	I *do* think that's the wrong decision.
	Making the important word the subject of the reply	*Running* is the sport I love most.
Speaking (esp. in formal contexts) and writing	Special use of *very*	*Very* is used in English to modify words like *first* and *last*: In *the very first* scene of the film… • At *the very last* moment … It can also be used where in German you would use *gerade* or *genau* to emphasize something: *Gerade die Anonymität des Internets …* • *The very* anonymity of the internet …
	especially, in particular	Careful: Unlike *besonders*, you hardly ever find them at the beginning of a sentence: *Sitting still for 45 minutes can be a challenge, especially for young children.*
	Other expressions	German compound nouns like *Hauptgrund* or *Hauptfaktor* can be translated with *the main* reason, *the most important* factor, etc. To emphasize that you are naming the most important item in a list of facts or arguments, use *above all* or *most importantly* to introduce your sentence.

2 Now decide how you could reply emphatically to the following questions using one of the techniques in the table:

1 Do you like Indian cuisine? (You like some dishes, but not the really spicy ones.)
2 What would you like – apple juice or cola? (You choose.)
3 Didn't you read the novel over the weekend? (You didn't finish, but you read the first half.)
4 You're from Hamburg, right? (You went to school there, but you were born in Kiel.)

3 Translate these sentences into English:

1 Die Hauptursache von Hass ist Angst.
2 Besonders in den Entwicklungsländern haben viele Menschen keinen Zugang zu sauberem Wasser.
3 Wir erreichten unser Flugzeug in allerletzter Minute.
4 Vor allem gibt es eine wachsende Kluft *(a widening gap)* zwischen den armen und den reichen Ländern.
5 Schon im ersten Satz macht der Autor seine Meinung deutlich.
6 Die Hauptsache ist wohl die, dass es genug qualifizierte Arbeitskräfte *(workers)* gibt.

In written English, there are ways of structuring a sentence so as to emphasize a certain word or words:

Technique	Example	Comment
Using a subordinate clause that points to the most important idea in the sentence	*Ralph Nader first criticized the US automobile industry.* → *It was Ralph Nader who first criticized the US automobile industry.* *Society needs people who put the common good above personal gain.* → *What society needs is people who put the common good above personal gain.*	Pay attention to the forms of *be* used in the examples; why are they both in the singular?
Using a negation (*never, nowhere, not once*, etc.) or *only* + time phrase (e.g. *only later*) at the beginning of the sentence. The verb is put in the question form (inversion).	*Never before have young people had so many opportunities.* *Only then did she realize her mistake.*	This structure is common in political speeches.
Using contrast	*It was greed and arrogance, not simply bad timing, that led to the collapse of the bank.* *Unlike earlier SNS, Facebook appealed to users of all age groups.* *Compared with the US, China lacks a culture of creative entrepreneurship.*	

4 Rewrite the sentences to make them more emphatic, using the techniques from the table above.
  1 Shared values hold a society together.
  2 China's economy is growing rapidly; that of the EU isn't.
  3 It has never before been so easy to communicate with people around the globe.
  4 Western countries need a vision that includes the rest of the world.
  5 Not lack of ambition, but fear of failure holds most people back.

▶ LP 14 Linking words and phrases

1 **BASIC** Complete the following text with suitable linking words or phrases from the choices below.

at the same time · for example · for one thing · furthermore · moreover · on the other hand · for instance

Are Americans environmentally friendly? There is no simple answer to this question. In a recent survey, … (1), 65% of American adults agreed that 'preserving the environment is very important.' … (2), 22% of consumers who remodeled their homes in the last 12 months said they had used environmentally friendly products for their renovation. … (3), data from the last five years indicate that consumers are now less willing to pay more or give up convenience for green products. … (4), the percentage of U.S. adults who agreed with the statement 'I am willing to give up convenience in return for a product that is environmentally safe' has declined 16% in the past five years, from 56% in 2007 to 47% in 2011.

… (5), there is definitely a trend among younger Americans toward more environmental awareness. … (6), consumers aged 18–24 are the only adult age group whose willingness to give up convenience or pay more for green products has held steady over the past five years. … (7), 53% of consumers aged 18–24 recycle products and 4% participated in environmental groups or causes in the past 12 months.

Statistics from: Bart King, 'American Environmentally Friendly Buying Habits', 6 April 2012

Linking words and phrases are the signposts of written and spoken communication; they help readers and listeners find their way through texts. Choosing the right phrases also helps you as a writer to think critically about the relationship between your sentences. The table below shows you a selection of useful phrases and their functions.

Use	Linking word or phrase
Stating your opinion	*In my opinion … • To my mind … • I think/feel/believe that …*
Listing facts, arguments, etc.	*First of all … • Firstly … • For one thing, …* *Secondly … • Furthermore … • What is more, … • Besides … • In addition … • Moreover …* *Finally … • Above all … • Most importantly …*
Giving an example	*for example … • for instance … • such as …*
Emphasizing	*In fact, … • As a matter of fact, … • Actually, …*
Contrasting	*On the one hand … On the other hand … • However … • … though … •* *Nonetheless … • Whereas … • Although … • In spite of …*
Conceding a point	*Of course … • Naturally … • Admittedly …*
Referring to a point in time or a development	*At the/that time … • In those days … • Eventually … • In the course of … •* *In the long run … • Meanwhile … • At the same time … • As a result …*
Coming to a conclusion	*All in all … • In the final analysis … • In conclusion … • Ultimately … • For the reasons mentioned above … • To sum up … • To conclude … • I would like to conclude by saying …*

2 In the following text, linking words and phrases have been left out. Decide where such 'signposts' are missing and choose appropriate ones from the table above. Then write an improved version of the text.

Google wants to change the world – again

Google revolutionized the way we use the Web in the 1990s with a new kind of search engine. Now it wants to change the way we navigate physical space. The California firm has developed a small
5 car that drives itself. The car is equipped with GPS and a host of sensors that collect information about the surroundings as it moves. There is a steering wheel and a brake (for emergencies), but the car is programmed to work without a
10 human driver.

Google is not interested in going into the car business. The real purpose is to change how we think about mobility. Why should you buy a car if you can get one whenever you need or want it?
15 You want to go downtown, you flip open your smartphone and call for an autonomous taxi. The vehicle drops you off at your destination, then goes on to its next job. There would be less need for huge parking lots and parking garages. There would be fewer emissions as people waste less
20 time cruising around looking for a parking space. People who are unable to drive (because of age, disability, or because they are drunk) could still get from one place to another. Self-driving cars would be a new form of public transportation.
25 The way cities are designed would change.

There are still problems to be solved. Who is responsible when an autonomous vehicle is involved in an accident? Will people overcome their fear of losing control over their cars? What
30 about the transition period when human and non-human drivers share the same roads? It is only a question of time until these issues have been settled. The future is coming, and Google wants to get there first.
35

▶ LP 15 Connecting your thoughts (sentence structure)

1 **BASIC** Your partner has given you this text to proofread. Rewrite it to improve the style without leaving out any information.

Frank McCourt was born in Brooklyn, New York in 1930, which was the first year of the Great Depression. Both of his parents were immigrants from Ireland. They had come to America like millions of other Irish men and women who were looking for a better life. But they didn't find a better life, they only found poverty and misery. The McCourts, who were disappointed with life in America, decided to move back to Ireland. But their new life in Limerick, which was the hometown of Frank's mother, was no better than their life in Brooklyn. Young Frank had to leave school to support his family. He did odd jobs to earn a few pounds. After he had saved enough money for a ticket to New York, he left Ireland for good and didn't even tell his family.

Texts that contain unnecessary words or that connect ideas too loosely don't read well. A few simple techniques can help you make your sentences more compact and connected:

Loose connection		Stronger connection
Relative clause: *Frank McCourt was born in Brooklyn, New York in 1930, which was the first year of the Great Depression.*	→	**Apposition:** *Frank McCourt was born in Brooklyn, New York in 1930, the first year of the Great Depression.*
Relative clause: *They had come to America like millions of other Irish men and women who were looking for a better life.*	→	**Participle construction:** *They had come to America like millions of other Irish men and women looking for a better life.*
Compound sentence: *But they didn't find a better life, they only found poverty and misery.*	→	**Gerund construction:** *But instead of finding a better life, they only found poverty and misery.*
After he had saved enough money for a ticket to New York, he left Ireland for good and didn't even tell his family.		*After saving enough money for a ticket to New York, he left Ireland for good without even telling his family.*

Participle phrases can also be used instead of adverbial clauses with a variety of meanings:

Example	Function of participle construction
Arriving in New York, he looked for a cheap room.	Time (simultaneous action)
Having served in the Army during the Korean War, Frank was offered the chance to go to college.	Time (antecedent action)
Wanting to improve his status, he got a degree in English from NYU.	Reason
McCourt taught in New York schools for thirty years, never forgetting the bitter poverty he had experienced in Ireland.	Accompanying circumstance

2 Rewrite the final paragraph of the text on Frank McCourt, using participle phrases in suitable places to improve the style.

After he had retired from teaching, McCourt began writing his memoires. They appeared in fictionalized form in 1996 as Angela's Ashes. The novel was a worldwide success and also won its author a Pulitzer Prize. McCourt looks back on his childhood in Limerick with irony and wit, and he describes how hard life was for poor Irish families in the 1930s and 40s. McCourt was amused at the unexpected success of his book and said that it was the first time in history that a man had become rich by writing about being poor.

Focus on Vocabulary

▶ LP 16 Avoiding Germanisms

1 **BASIC** Each of the following sentences contains a 'typically German' mistake in red. Copy the sentences and correct the mistakes:

1 The plot of the film is typical for romantic comedies.
2 Jackie stepped into the corridor to phone with her lawyer.
3 Young people often use the internet to watch videos or hear music.
4 Music critics wondered when the single 'Thrift Shop' by a little-known rapper duo stormed the US charts in 2013.
5 We can meet us later in the city centre.
6 Some schools have introduced programmes to prevent cybermobbing.

German and English have much in common. This is often a help, but sometimes it is a source of confusion. The table below lists some common pitfalls:

	Source of confusion	Examples
a	similar word, different meaning	aktuell ≠ actual; eventuell ≠ eventual; Meinung ≠ meaning; spenden ≠ spend; sich wundern ≠ wonder
b	similar expression, different preposition	married **to** sb. = verheiratet **mit** jdm.; contact **with** sb. = Kontakt **zu** jdm.; example **of** sth. = Beispiel **für** etwas; typical of sb. = typisch **für** jdn.; do sth. **about** sth. = etwas **gegen** etwas tun
c	word-for-word translation of German phrase	~~hold~~/make a speech; ~~with 29 years~~/at the age of 29; on the one ~~side~~/hand; ~~make~~/take a photo; ~~hear~~/listen to music
d	verb used with/without a preposition	phone sb. = mit jdm. telefonieren; surf the internet = im Internet surfen; discuss sth. = über etwas diskutieren; comment on sth: = etwas kommentieren; discriminate against sb. = jdn. diskriminieren
e	Denglish used instead of English	~~beamer~~ (projector); ~~mobbing~~ (bullying); ~~handy~~ (mobile/cellphone); ~~boxes~~ (loudspeakers)
f	reflexive in German, non-reflexive in English	meet = sich treffen; identify with sb. = sich mit jdm. identifizieren; concentrate on sth. = sich auf etwas konzentrieren; feel = sich fühlen

2 For each of the following sentences, decide which word is missing (if any). If you aren't sure, the letter in brackets will tell you where to look in the table.

1 People write letters to the editor when they want to express their … (a)
2 The press secretary refused to comment … the minister's decision. (d)
3 In a speech that he … on March 4, Obama called for a new initiative on gun control. (c)
4 Jared is the only character in the novel that readers could possibly identify … with. (f)
5 Some teens spend far too much time surfing … the internet. (d)
6 The author names three examples … the abuse of power by the present government. (b)
7 It's high time for the town council to do something … this problem. (b)
8 To show the DVD in our classroom, we need a … and a pair of … as well as a laptop. (e)

▶ LP 17 Spelling

1 **BASIC** Copy the words below, adding the missing letters. Careful: sometimes no letters are missing!

1 int■rested	5 mis■understanding	9 standar■	13 wel■fare
2 nec■essary	6 d■scribe	10 politic■an	14 consc■ous
3 happ■ly	7 public■ly	11 av■rage	15 desp■rate■
4 chara■ter	8 refer■ing	12 assist■nt	16 non-viol■nce

> Unfortunately, there are very few rules for English spelling. The best strategy is to keep track of the words that you frequently misspell and practise writing them, for example before exams.

2 The following text is a student's essay on a British novel. There are ten spelling mistakes. Correct them:

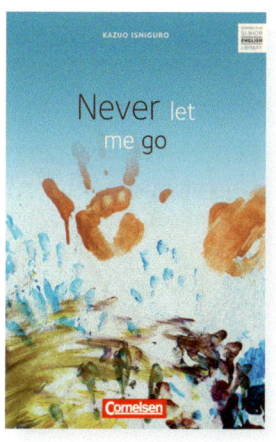

Never Let Me Go by Kazuo Ishiguro is one of the best novels I have ever read. The autor tells the story from the point of view of Cathy, a young women, who reflects on her live as a student at a boarding school called Hailsham, and later as a so-called 'carer'. At first the reader thinks this is
5 just an other story about adolesence, but as the novel progresses, we slowly realize that there is something special about the young people at Hailsham: as human as they appear to the reader, they are really clones who must donate their organs to others when they have reached maturity. Although they seem to know this, they don't really understand
10 their situation, and each of them clings to the hope that somehow they will be allowd to live a bit longer then the others. The novel has also been adapted for the screen, and although I usualy avoid films based on books I love, I have to admit that this one is outstanding and succedes brillantly in capturing the spirit of the novel.

▶ LP 18 Writing about texts

There are many special expressions that you need when you write essays in German. The same is true of English. Knowing these phrases makes it easier for you to express yourself clearly.

1 **BASIC** The table below contains German and English phrases for text analysis. Both lists are in alphabetical order. Copy the table, matching the German phrases and their English equivalents:

German	English	German	English
1 angesichts …	a according to …	8 im Großen und Ganzen	h in general
2 auf den ersten Blick	b as a rule	9 im Zusammenhang mit …	i in the process
3 bei näherer Betrachtung	c as for … / as far as … is concerned	10 in der Regel	j in view of …
4 in Bezug auf …	d at first sight	11 laut …	k on closer examination
5 dabei (d.h., während man etwas tut)	e focus on …	12 seitens …	l on the part of …
6 im Allgemeinen	f in connection with …	13 was … betrifft	m on the whole
		13 … auf den Punkt bringen	n put … in a nutshell
7 im Gegensatz zu …	g in contrast to …	15 … in den Mittelpunkt stellen	o with regard to …

2 Translate the following sentences into English with the help of your table:
1 Auf den ersten Blick hält man den Autor für einen Befürworter[1] der amerikanischen Umweltpolitik[2].
2 Bei näherer Betrachtung erkennt der Leser, dass er viele Dinge in den USA kritisch betrachtet.
3 Der Autor stellt die Auswirkungen der globalen Erwärmung in den Mittelpunkt.
4 Der Autor schildert die Folgen des Fracking in den USA. Dabei macht er deutlich, dass er diese Technik ablehnt.
5 Angesichts der Umweltbelastung[3] kann der Leser ihm nur zustimmen.
6 Im Gegensatz zu den Amerikanern, die Fracking im Großen und Ganzen akzeptieren, sind die Deutschen skeptisch eingestellt[4].
7 Im letzten Absatz bringt der Autor das ganze Dilemma auf den Punkt.

▶ LP 19 Collocations

Verbs and nouns

1 `BASIC` Choose the right verb for each of the sentences below:
1 Young people today sometimes find it hard to get/make a living in a tight job market.
2 Sam's teachers urged him to give/pay more attention to his school work.
3 The girls apologized to their victim, saying that they hadn't meant to do/make any harm.
4 The journalist calls/attracts attention to the problems in the region.
5 We think our school should make/set a good example by banning plastic tableware from the canteen.
6 The storm made/did considerable damage on its way northward.

> In English as well as in German, certain nouns are used together with certain verbs, e.g. you can only take (not ~~make~~) a photo in English. These 'natural pairs' are called collocations. Knowing the most common ones will help you avoid mistakes. The table below contains a selection of verb-noun collocations:

call attention (to sth.)	do damage	meet expectations	set an example
change your mind	exert influence (on sb.)	pay attention (to sb.)	take measures
commit a crime	make a living	put pressure on sb.	take offence (at sth.)
do justice to sth.	make history	put sth. to a vote	take a photo (of sb./ sth.)
do good/harm	make an impression	reach an agreement	tell the truth/a lie

2 Complete the following sentences with the missing verb. All collocations are from the table above:
1 Did the hotel … your expectations?
2 The only way we'll ever … an agreement is to … the matter to a vote.
3 Yesterday, history was … as government officials and rebel leaders met for direct talks.
4 As a member of the Board of Overseers she still … considerable influence on University policy.
5 It is important to … a good impression when you go for a job interview.
6 To my mind the film doesn't … justice to the novel.
7 The management … pressure on the workers to accept a pay cut.
8 The police agreed that further measures should be … to stop young people from … crimes.

[1] **Befürworter** supporter   [2] **Umweltpolitik** environment policy   [3] **Umweltbelastung** negative environmental impact
[4] **skeptisch eingestellt** sceptical

Adjectives and nouns

3 **BASIC** The grey boxes on the right contain adjectives and nouns that form collocations. Form matching pairs and use them to complete the sentences:

bright	*air*
equal	*damage*
fresh	*feelings*
heavy	*idea*
high	*opinion*
human	*parents*
negative	*publicity*
strict (2x)	*rights (2x)*
strong	*rules*

1 Let's step outside and get some … …
2 The firm finally agreed to the protesters' demands to avoid further … …
3 The Declaration of Independence names 'life, liberty and the pursuit of happiness' as basic … …
4 Listen, everybody! I just had a … …
5 The hurricane caused … … all along the coast.
6 African Americans have fought a long battle for … …
7 I can't believe how … Tamira's … are.
8 Don't make jokes about veggie burgers – Katrina has very … … about animal rights.
9 This boarding school has very … …, and all students are expected to obey them.
10 I wasn't surprised when Steve was chosen for the scholarship – I've always had a … … of his character.

> Some adjectives 'belong together' with certain nouns, forming a new 'compound noun': *a human being, fair play, real life*. Others are frequently used together and form a collocation (*hard work, poor health*). Knowing common adjective-noun collocations will help you avoid mistakes and express yourself more idiomatically.

4 What adjective(s) could you use to describe each of the following nouns? Write down your ideas first, then check them with the help of a monolingual dictionary (look at the usage examples):

1 burden	3 example	5 rise	7 topic	9 price
2 conscience	4 gesture	6 treatment	8 argument	10 working conditions

5 Use five of your collocations in sentences that illustrate their meaning, e.g. *In Germany, fracking is a very controversial topic*.

Prepositions

6 **BASIC** Choose the correct preposition for each of the numbered gaps in the following sentences:

I agree (1) the author that it is high time to do something (2) the problem of toxic waste. We can't just turn our backs (3) the problem or wait (4) industry to take the initiative. Everyone who is worried (5) the future of life (6) this planet should get involved (7) a campaign (8) toxic waste. Photos (9) young children playing on heaps of toxic rubbish in India or other countries can easily be found (10) the internet or (11) newspapers and magazines. No one can look (12) such photos without feeling their own responsibility (13) the present situation.

> Many common expressions in English include a preposition. You can't learn them all, but the more you know, the fewer mistakes you will make. If you aren't certain which preposition to use with a certain word, look at the example sentences under the corresponding headword in a monolingual dictionary.

7 Use a dictionary to find out which preposition(s) can be used with each of the following words:

1 a lack … something	6 appeal … something	11 remind someone … something
2 a novel written … someone	7 be critical … something	12 struggle … a goal
3 accuse someone … something	8 blame someone … something	13 sympathize … someone
4 allude … something	9 contribute … something	14 take a look … something
5 an attempt … something	10 good … sth.	15 thank someone … something

▶ LP 20 Word formation

Prefixes

1 **BASIC** In the table below, match the prefixes to the correct meanings.

Meaning		Prefix(es)	
1	against sth.	a	multi-
2	for sth., in favour of sth.	b	pseudo-
3	having two (sides, aspects, etc.)	c	re-
4	having only one	d	pre-
5	having or connected with several	e	anti- counter- neo-
6	not		
7	no longer	f	semi-
8	done badly or wrongly	g	ex-
9	one of two	h	pro-

Meaning		Prefix(es)	
10	new	i	non- dis-
11	happening before sth.	j	mono-
12	happening after sth.	k	co-
13	again, for the second time	l	bi-
14	not really	m	post-
15	referring to or done by yourself	n	ultra-
16	only half, not completely	o	mis-
17	extremely	p	self-

Adding a prefix to an existing word changes the meaning without influencing the grammatical class: *un + able → unable*. Knowing the meaning of prefixes can help you to understand words you have never seen before.

Some of the prefixes (especially anti-, non-, self-, neo- and pseudo-) are often separated from their root word with a hyphen: anti-aircraft, neo-Colonial, etc.). But as there are no fixed rules for English spelling, it is best to check your dictionary to be sure.

Find an online dictionary here:
🖐 **Webcode** context-52

---

2 Use a prefix from the list above to create an expression that matches each of the following definitions. Example: strong belief in your own abilities: *self-confidence*

1 a film that presents war in a negative light
2 a measure that produces the opposite of the intended effect
3 a former husband
4 one of the two captains of a team
5 a theory that pretends to be scientific but isn't
6 discover sth. for the second time, e.g. in later life
7 a person who is not a resident of the country they are staying in
8 interpret sth. the wrong way
9 an organization that operates in several countries
10 a worker who has some qualifications but fewer than a skilled worker
11 Germany after the war
12 having two poles

Suffixes

3 **BASIC** Copy the table below and sort the words on the right into groups. Underline the suffixes.

apparition • certify •
complicity • egalitarian •
enactment • furious •
hypothesize • identical •
laudable • marital •
notification • obligatory •
supportive

Nouns	Verbs	Adjectives

Like German, English can form a new word by adding a suffix to an existing root: *present + -able* → *presentable*. Since the suffix determines whether the word is a noun, verb or adjective, recognizing common suffixes can help you figure out the meanings of unfamiliar words. You probably haven't seen any of the words in the box above before, but the suffixes give you information about what they mean.

4 Drawing on your knowledge of English as well as other languages, make an intelligent guess as to the meaning of each word. When you have finished, check your answers using a dictionary.

Find an online dictionary here:

 Webcode context-52

Word families

5 **BASIC** The table below contains words related to each other. Copy the table and fill in the blanks, using a dictionary if necessary. Make sure you know the meanings of all the words:

Verb	Noun	Adjective	Noun
act	(1)	active	activity
create	creation	(2)	creativity
depend (on)	(3)	dependent/dependable	dependability
rely (on)	reliance	reliable	(4)
select	selection	(5)	selectivity
compare	comparison	(6)	comparability
tolerate	(7)	tolerable	tolerability
adapt (to)	adaptation	adaptable	(8)
criticize	(9)	critical	…
destroy	(10)	destructive	destructiveness

6 Use words from the table to rewrite the <u>underlined</u> parts of the following sentences. You may have to change the word order or add words in some cases:

Example: Meteorologists underestimated <u>how destructive Hurricane Ivor would be</u>.
   → *Meteorologists underestimated the destructiveness of Hurricane Ivor.*

1 We've had enough of speech-making; now is the time <u>to act</u>.
2 The author claims that classical music and popular music <u>can't be compared</u>.
3 All children <u>have a natural creativity</u>.
4 Gerald quit his job in India because <u>he could not tolerate</u> his working conditions.
5 Our firm expects all employees <u>to be reliable</u>.
6 <u>The fact that our country is dependent</u> on foreign oil and gas is a serious issue.
7 While doing her gap year in Uganda, Shirin demonstrated <u>how well she can adapt</u>.
8 The so-called Ivy League universities in the US are said to <u>select their students very carefully</u>.

Princeton, an Ivy League university

239

Everyday English

Download the suggested answers to the tasks here:
Webcode context-32

▶ EE 1 Eating in and out

Eating customs often vary from culture to culture and knowing a few basics can come in handy while abroad.

1 In what situation might someone use each of the following expressions?

1 Thanks, I'm fine.
2 Just help yourself.
3 It's delicious, but I'm full.
4 Could you pass the …, please?
5 This has been a wonderful meal!
6 Could I have some more, please?

2 ROLE-PLAY Use the phrases from part **1** and the role cards to act out a short dialogue.

You can find your role cards here:
Webcode context-33

■ **FACT FILE**

Eating out: American style

In sit-down restaurants in the United States where you are served at your table, there are a few customs that you should be aware of that are different from those in Europe:

- 'Please wait to be seated' is posted near the entrance in many restaurants. You are expected to wait to be taken to a table (even if the restaurant is completely empty!). Someone (a host or hostess) will probably ask how many are in your 'party' (e.g.: 'Just the two of you?' or 'How many are in your group?'), and either take you to a table or ask for your name so that they can call you when your table is ready.
- 'Designing your own meal' with your choice of meat and vegetable from the menu is not uncommon in the USA. A typical dish could be, for example, a sirloin steak with a choice of vegetable or side-salad and potatoes cooked in a specific way. Examine the menu and make your selection so that you are ready to order when the server arrives.
- 'Would you like a refill?' is a typical phrase in restaurants in the USA. Most restaurants offer free refills of at least coffee and soft drinks. The server exchanges your empty glass for a full one or refills your glass at your table. Tap water (usually with ice cubes) is provided for free.
- A 'service charge' is usually not included on the bill. Servers are not well paid in most regions of the USA and a tip of 15–20% is expected. You can either leave a cash tip on the table or, if paying with a credit card, there will be a place on the bill where you can add a tip to the total.

In groups of 4–5, write and act out a short theatrical scene that takes place in a US restaurant. Use the information above and the vocabulary below to help you.

■ **TIP**

Soft drinks are called different things in different parts of the USA. As a general rule:
On the East and West Coasts: **soda**
In the Midwest: **pop**
In the South: **coke**
(even for soft drinks that are not cola)

Some useful terms			
main dish entrée ['ɒntreɪ] (AE)	*Hauptgericht*	menu ['menjuː]	*Speisekarte*
starter (BE) appetizer (AE)	*Vorspeise*	four-course dinner / meal	*Vier-Gang-Menü*
side dish, side order	*Beilage*	tip	*Trinkgeld*
dessert [dɪˈzɜːt] sweet (BE), pudding ['pʊdɪŋ] (BE) afters (BE, *infml*)	*Nachspeise*	VAT (BE) sales tax (AE)	*Mehrwertsteuer*
bill; check (AE)	*Rechnung*	tap water	*Leitungswasser*

■ **TROUBLE SPOT**
Ger. *Menü* ≠ Eng. **menu**

■ **TROUBLE SPOT**
entrée (BE) ≠ **entrée** (AE)

► EE 2 Planning a trip using the internet

The internet is a handy tool for making travel plans. You can book travel arrangements and hotel accommodation, find out information about museums and other places of interest, order food and make restaurant reservations, as well as even reserve concert, theatre or movie tickets.
Imagine your class is planning a week-long trip to London. You will be in the city from Monday to Friday. Form three groups (A, B, C). Each group has its own planning task.

Group A: Getting around in London

Explore the options for public transport during your stay. London offers a variety of tickets with different prices and conditions. It might be helpful to know how many students there are in your class and their ages.

- Split your group into 3–4 smaller groups. Each of the mini-groups explores one option and presents it to the rest of the class.
- Consult relevant websites to find out what options are available, what conditions are attached to their use, and how much they would cost. Calculate the total cost for the group.

Find links to helpful websites here:
 Webcode context-34

Group B: A day trip to Greenwich

While in London, your class wants to take a day trip to Greenwich. How will you get there? The closest station to your hotel is Bayswater Tube Station.

- Divide your group into 3 mini-groups. Each mini-group researches a different way of getting to Greenwich.
  Mini-group 1: Docklands Light Railway
  Mini-group 2: Thames Riverboat
  Mini-group 3: Greenwich Foot Tunnel
  Take into account what interesting sights different travel options might offer along the way.
- What is the total price for the group (not including the cost of any Tube travel)?

Find links to websites of interest here:
 Webcode context-35

Group C: The Royal Museums Greenwich

The Royal Museums Greenwich (RMG) is a complex of buildings and sites of historical, architectural and scientific interest.

- What does the RMG consist of? Use the internet to explore the various possibilities.
- Divide your group into 3 mini-groups. Each mini-group puts together a different suggestion for a visit to the RMG.
- What can you see and do? When and where? How much does it cost for your group?
- Are there adequate food options available there for a group of your size?

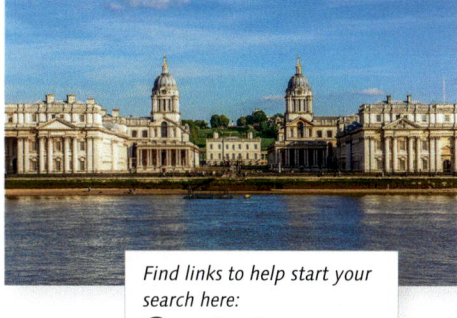

Find links to help start your search here:
 Webcode context-36

Some useful terms			
peak (hours, etc.)	*Spitzenzeiten*	fare	*Fahrpreis*
entry (to a building, etc.)	*Zutritt*	swipe card	*Magnetstreifenkarte*
opening hours	*Öffnungszeiten*	vending machine	*(Verkaufs-)Automat*
admission (fee)	*Eintritt(spreis)*	destination	*(Reise-)Ziel*
exhibition	*Ausstellung*	venue	*(Veranstaltungs-)Ort*
surcharge	*Aufschlag*	closing time	*Schließzeit*
concession/discount	*Ermäßigung*	pay-as-you-go credit	*Prepaid-Guthaben*

▪ FACT FILE

Greenwich ['grenɪtʃ], a district of South East London, is on 0° Longitude *(Prime or Greenwich Meridian)* and sets the global time standard *(Greenwich Mean Time)*.

▶ EE 3 Dealing with medical emergencies   CD3 08

A medical emergency can happen anywhere. The cause can be an accident or a sudden illness. Before you go abroad, make sure you have health insurance coverage[1] for your country of destination. Travel medical insurance[2] is inexpensive and covers all medical expenses during a brief foreign stay.

> **MY GOODNESS, MR. GRTPTZSK – HOW LONG HAS IT BEEN SINCE YOU HAD A VOWEL MOVEMENT?**

> ### ■ FACT FILE
>
> **Getting medical assistance**
> In the event of an emergency, call 999 (UK), 911 (USA) or 000 (Australia). From mobile phones, the number 112 will also connect you with the emergency services in many countries.
> 5   **Hospital:** If you or someone else needs medical help, consult a physician/doctor or go to the outpatient clinic[3] of the nearest hospital, where you can be treated without being admitted to the hospital[4].
> **Pharmacy:** In the UK and the US, shops that sell medicine are called pharmacies, drugstores (US) or chemist's (UK). They offer a wider range of products than a German *Apotheke*, including cosmetics,
> 10   health and beauty products, and sometimes travel essentials.
> **Prescriptions:** Medicine that has been prescribed by a doctor is dispensed at the pharmacy counter within the shop. In the US, you are given the exact dosage prescribed by the doctor. If, for example, your prescription says three capsules daily for five days, you will be given 15 capsules in a
> 15   small bottle, not the original package.

> ### ■ TROUBLE SPOT
> *ärztliches Rezept* = **prescription**
> *Kochrezept* = **recipe** ['resəpi]

A group of students in the eighth class at your school are about to go on their first exchange to the UK. Prepare an informative and funny two-minute talk for them in English on medical assistance abroad.

1   In the event that you need medical help, it is important that you understand the doctor's questions and can give precise answers. Test your knowledge by matching the English words to their German equivalents.

1 abdomen	11 have a temperature	a allergisch	k Schnittwunde
2 allergic	12 headache	b Bauch, Unterleib	l Schürfwunde
3 bowel movement	13 nausea ['nɔːziə]	c Durchfall	m Schwindel
4 bruise [bruːz]	14 numb	d Fieber haben	n sich übergeben
5 congested	15 scrape	e Halsschmerzen	o Stuhlgang
6 constipated	16 shiver	f Husten	p taub
7 cough [kɒf]	17 sore throat	g Impfung	q Übelkeit
8 cut	18 stomach ache [eɪk]	h Kopfschmerzen	r verschnupft
9 diarrhoea [daɪərɪə]	19 vaccination	i Magenschmerzen	s verstopft
10 dizziness	20 vomit	j Prellung	t zittern

2   Sabine is staying with her host family in the USA. She isn't feeling well and her host parents take her to the doctor. Listen to the dialogue and answer the questions.
   1   How does Sabine describe her symptoms?
   2   What information does Dr Felter want from her?
   3   What does Dr Felter give her?

> *Listen to the audio file on the CD or download it here:*
> **Webcode** context-37

3   ROLE-PLAY **Partner A** is cycling near Bristol with his or her British host-brother, Toby. All of a sudden, Toby hits a hole in the road and falls off his bike. He is badly hurt. Phone for help! **Partner B** will be the person taking calls for emergency services in the Bristol area. Use the role cards.

> *You can find your role cards here:*
> **Webcode** context-38

---

[1]**health insurance coverage** *Krankenversicherungsschutz*   [2]**travel medical insurance** *Auslandskrankenversicherung*
[3]**outpatient clinic** *Ambulanz*   [4]**admit sb. to the hospital** *jdn. stationär aufnehmen*

▶ EE 4 Making phone calls

Talking on the telephone has become less common in the age of text messages, but there are still situations in which it is unavoidable. The box below lists example phrases that can be used when talking on the phone.

1 Match the phrases from the box below to the following typical situations:

1 You phone a number and say who you are.
2 You explain why you are calling.
3 You answer the phone.
4 You are not the intended recipient of the call.
5 You ask for clarification.
6 You want to end the conversation and hang up.

a Hello. My name is Lisa Weber. I'm calling from Cologne in Germany.	k I think you've dialed the wrong number.
b The reason I'm calling is …	l I'm calling about the advert you posted …
c I'm sorry, I didn't catch that. Could you repeat your name please?	m Thank you for returning my call / Thanks for getting back to me. *(infml)*
d May I ask why you are calling?	n Good afternoon. Caroline Schlegel speaking.
e Can I take a message?	o Could you spell that, please?
f It was nice talking with you.	p I have a problem, could you connect me with Customer Services, please?
g Good morning. This is Max Kunze in Dresden, Germany.	q Robert Peters here. What can I do for you?
h I'm afraid she isn't here. Would you like her to call you back?	r Sorry, the line is busy. Would you like to speak to someone else?
i I'd like to speak to …	s Mr Adams tried to reach me while I was out. I'm returning his call.
j May I ask who's calling, please?	t Thank you for your call.

2 ROLE-PLAY Working together with a partner, use the information on the role cards to carry out a conversation on the phone.

You can find your role cards here:
Webcode context-39

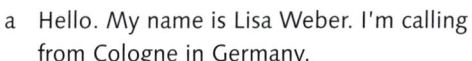

Some useful terms	
line	*Leitung*
engaged (BE), busy (AE)	*besetzt*
dial a number	*eine Nummer wählen*
answer the phone	*einen Anruf entgegennehmen*
return sb.'s call, get back to sb.	*jdn. zurückrufen*
hold	*in der Leitung bleiben*
put sb. through (to sb.)	*jdn. (zu jdm.) durchstellen*
hang up	*auflegen*

HELLO!
THIS IS LIBERTY SPEAKING——

▶ EE 5 Watch your valuables!

When staying abroad, whether on holiday or as part of an exchange programme, you will need money. There are different ways of taking money abroad.

1 Match the lettered boxes to their corresponding method of taking or accessing money abroad.

Money Management Methods:
1 a bank card/debit card (AE)
2 a credit card
3 traveller's cheques
4 cash

A
- must be exchanged for local currency
- no way of preventing a thief from using it

B
- equivalent to the German 'ec-Karte' or Girocard
- can be used to withdraw cash at an ATM[5] (more commonly called a cash machine or 'hole in the wall' in the UK) or to pay for goods and services in many countries

C
- can be used to pay bills in many hotels and restaurants without a PIN
- can sometimes be used with the PIN to withdraw cash from an ATM
- can be cancelled if lost or stolen

D
- must be bought before you leave home
- can be cashed in any bank during opening hours

Plastic money is very practical, but use caution:
- Before you travel, check whether your bank at home has a partnership with a bank where you're staying abroad. It might be cheaper for you to use that bank to withdraw cash.
- In many countries, ATMs are not inside banks, but on the walls outside. For safety reasons, try to use an ATM in a well-lit area or inside the bank building.
- Make sure nobody can see the number keys while you are entering your PIN.
- Be aware that there will probably be a fee every time you withdraw cash from a foreign ATM.

If your card is lost or stolen, take immediate action:
- Make sure you know how to reach your bank and/or credit card company in case you need to block or cancel your card. (The phone number can change depending on where you are travelling.)
- Phone and have the card blocked as soon as you realize your card is lost or stolen.
- Report the theft to the local police.

2 ROLE-PLAY Oh, no! You have been robbed! Report the theft to the local police. Use role cards and the vocabulary in the box below for your dialogue.

You can find your role cards here:
🔍 **Webcode** context-40

Some useful terms			
valuables	*Wertsachen*	bank card, debit card	*ec-Karte; Girocard*
purse/wallet	*Geldbörse, Portemonnaie*	have your card blocked/cancelled	*deine Karte sperren lassen*
cash	*Bargeld*	suspicious [səˈspɪʃəs] behaviour	*auffälliges Verhalten*
pickpocket	*Taschendieb/in*	report a crime, etc. (to the police)	*eine Straftat usw. anzeigen*

TROUBLE SPOT
rob sb. = steal sth. from sb.

[1]**ATM** *Geldautomat*

Communicating across Cultures

Download the suggested answers to the tasks here:
Webcode context-41

▶ CC1 Cultural awareness

Like a fish out of water: A fish doesn't know what water is – until the water suddenly isn't there anymore. Likewise, we often take the culture we grow up with for granted – customs, body language, how people interact in everyday situations – and don't really notice it while it surrounds us. As a result, experiencing different cultures can open our eyes to aspects of our own culture and also give us insight into ways other people behave.

1 Put yourself in each of the following situations and choose the reaction that comes the closest to your own.

  1 A crowded cafeteria at lunchtime. You have been waiting patiently for the last ten minutes. Someone comes into the room, spots a gap near the front of the queue and jumps in.

    a You look away and say nothing.

    b You grumble to your neighbour, 'So selfish!'

    c You shout out loud, 'Hey you! Go to the back of the queue!'

  2 While waiting at the bus stop, you see an exchange student who is in one of your courses. He comes over to chat and stops about thirty centimetres in front of you (try it out with a partner, using a ruler to measure the distance between the tips of your noses).

    a You take a step backward.

    b You turn a bit to the side to avoid facing the other student directly.

    c You stand your ground and look the other person directly in the eye.

  3 You get a note from a guidance counselor asking you to come to her office after school. When you arrive, the door is half open; the counselor is working at her desk.

    a You walk in, say hello and sit down opposite her.

    b You stand in the doorway and say, 'You wanted to see me.'

    c You knock lightly on the door and say, 'Excuse me, may I interrupt you?'

2 In groups of not more than three, compare your reactions to the situations in exercise **1** and your reasons for choosing them. Discuss the following points:

  ▪ How do you feel about (not) playing by the rules?

  ▪ How close is too close – when do you feel that someone is invading your personal space?

  ▪ What does eye contact signify?

  ▪ What does an open (or closed) door mean?

Compare your views and decide which forms of behaviour you think are typical in your society.

▶ CC 2 The language of politeness

1 People don't always say what they really mean; sometimes they even say the opposite:

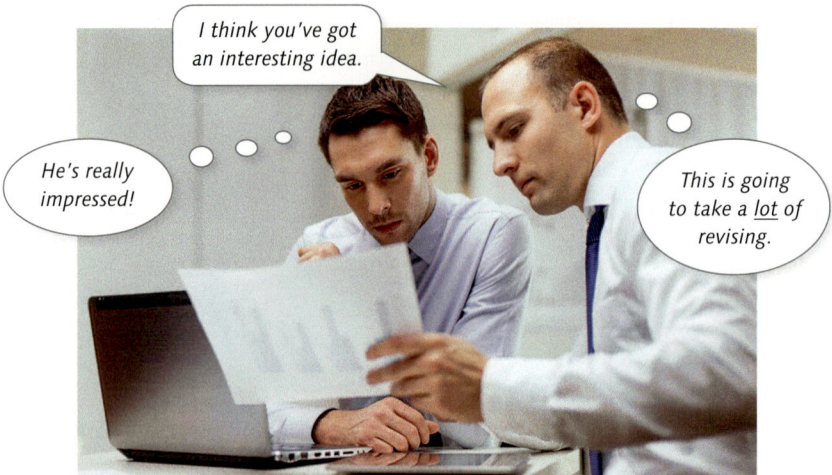

To a certain degree, understatement and exaggeration are part of national culture. Americans tend to be highly enthusiastic ('Fantastic!' – 'I'd love to!' – 'I'm dying to meet him!'), whereas the British are more reserved in their way of expressing themselves ('I'm afraid we've got a bit of a problem.'). These are, of course, just generalizations, as each person has their own style.

In conversations, always try to be friendly and polite, but remember that polite phrases cannot always be taken literally. The list on the left in the table below shows some polite phrases you might hear, especially in the UK. First, decide what you think they mean, then choose the 'translation' from the list on the right.

1 There's room for improvement.	a	I'm just being polite.
2 I wouldn't mind.	b	I'm very annoyed.
3 Very original work.	c	I expect you to read it.
4 You must come over for dinner.	d	I'd love to.
5 I was a bit disappointed that …	e	That's really good.
6 You might want to have a look at it.	f	I expect you to apologize.
7 I'm sure it was my mistake.	g	Hopeless stuff.

2 The table below contains polite phrases that can be used in everyday situations. Match them, then use one or two of the matching pairs to write a short dialogue (with a partner, if you prefer):

1 Would you mind if I borrowed one of these? I can't find mine.	a	Great idea! I'd love to!
2 Sorry, I didn't know …	b	Sure, come in and have a seat.
3 Thanks a lot!	c	Certainly. Here you are.
4 Is it all right with you if I …?	d	I'll have to think about that.
5 Could I bother you for a minute?	e	Sure, help yourself.
6 Would it be possible for me to …?	f	That's all right. Don't worry about it.
7 We were wondering if you would be interested in …	g	You're very welcome.
8 Could I get a …, please?	h	Of course. Feel free.

▶ CC3 Polite behaviour

Leon is an exchange student in the USA. Read the following descriptions of everyday situations and decide whether he breaks any rules of polite behaviour. Then discuss your reactions in a group. Have you experienced similar situations? Why do you feel that certain behaviour is polite or impolite?

> *Compare your views with additional comments here:*
> **Webcode** context-42

1 Leon meets his host parents and host brother, Matt, for the first time. He offers them his hand in greeting.
2 Leon calls his host parents 'Frank' and 'Brenda'.
3 At his American home, Leon always keeps his bedroom door shut.
4 Leon and Matt are watching TV when Matt's grandparents enter the room. Leon stays seated.
5 It's dinner time and Leon is very hungry. He starts eating as soon as he has something on his plate.
6 Leon can't follow the conversation at the dinner table, so he starts playing games on his smartphone.

▶ CC4 Meeting and greeting

1 The phrases below can be used in different social situations: when you meet someone for the first time, when you meet a friend on the street, or when you want to end a conversation. Copy the table below and put the phrases from the list in the correct column (some can be used more than once).

1 Fine thanks. And you?
2 Hi, how's it going? (infml)
3 Hi, nice to meet you. (infml)
4 How are things going? (infml)
5 How do you do? (fml)
6 Sorry, I've got to run. (infml)
7 I'd like you to meet XY.

8 It's been wonderful talking to you.
9 Not too bad. What about you? (infml)
10 (I'm very) Pleased to meet you.
11 Thanks, and the same to you!
12 See you later. (infml)
13 Bye now. Take care! (infml)
14 Have a good time!

Meeting someone for the first time	Meeting someone you know	Saying goodbye

2 Select an appropriate response from your table for each of the following situations:
1 You work for an organization that employs mostly young people. Your supervisor brings a new colleague over to meet you and says: 'Hi Rebecca, this is James, our new trainee.' You say:
2 You see a co-worker in the hallway. She says: 'Hi, how are things going?' You say:
3 Going back to your office, you see your supervisor talking to an older woman. He calls you over and says: 'Rebecca, I'd like you to meet our regional coordinator, Deirdre O'Connor.' You say:
4 After Ms O'Connor has asked you a couple of questions about your job, you want to end the conversation and go back to work. You say:
5 You drive a friend to the train station. As he gets out of the car, he says: 'See you later!' You say:
6 You're a bit late for work when you run into an old friend. When she starts telling you all about her new boyfriend, you make it clear that you're in a hurry and say:
7 On the last day of work before the holidays, a co-worker waves to you as you are leaving and calls out: 'Have a good break!' You say:

> **■ TIP**
> • 'How do you do?' isn't really a question; it is just a very formal way of saying 'Nice to meet you'.
> • When someone asks 'How are you?', they usually don't want a medical update. Just say 'Fine, thanks' or 'Not too bad, thanks'.

▶ CC 5 Making small talk CD3 09

Small talk is an art. That means that some people are, by nature, better at it than others. However, everybody can work on their skills and practise developing them.

1 Listen to two short conversations and describe the differences between them. Why is one more successful than the other?

Listen to the audio file on the CD or download it here:
Webcode context-43

2 The list below contains tips for making small talk. In each tip, one or more phrases is missing. Complete the tips with phrases from the box below right.

1 Stand roughly at arm's length from your partner and … while you are talking.
2 Choose a topic that involves something you and your partner … (e.g. social or regional background, personal experiences, present situation, the weather, etc.).
3 Don't ask any questions that you wouldn't …
4 Avoid … ('Do you like sport?'); use … instead ('What's your favourite sport?').
5 Give your partner the opportunity to talk about him- or herself before you make a comment or …
6 Encourage your partner to … by interjecting remarks such as 'That's really interesting!' or 'Wow! That must have been awesome!'.

a	change the subject
b	keep talking
c	have in common
d	end the conversation
e	coming to a natural end
f	open questions
g	look them in the eye
h	want to answer
i	'yes-or-no' questions

7 Pay attention to the silences; they may be a sign that your conversation is …
8 Phrases like 'It's been great talking to you' or 'We'll have to continue this conversation some other time' can help you to … elegantly.

3 **ROLE-PLAY** You meet someone new at a youth hostel in Germany. Use the role cards to guide your conversation with a partner.

You can find your role cards here:
Webcode context-44

4 Choose a new partner and practise making small talk without the help of role cards. Try to keep your conversation going for at least two minutes.

▶ CC 6 Talking about sensitive issues CD3 10

Which topics are considered sensitive and which are absolutely taboo varies from culture to culture. A good indicator is humour: which topics do people make jokes about? Which do they seem to avoid? (Watching comedy shows on TV can tell you a lot about social norms.)

1 Imagine you are going to the USA for a year. Rank the ten topics below on a scale from 1 (harmless) to 10 (taboo) as discussion topics. Compare lists with your partner or in a group and discuss your reasons.

food preferences • sports • patriotism • gun control • religion and church-going • parents' jobs • politics • race relations • career goals • the United States' role in the world

2 Emma, a German exchange student in Ohio, is asked by her American social studies teacher about her impressions of life in the USA. Listen to two different versions of the story and make notes on the differences. How is the tone of the conversation affected by the way Emma responds?

Listen to the audio file on the CD or download it here:
Webcode context-45

■ FACT FILE

Political correctness

In the mid-20th century in the USA, political correctness became an important topic when minority groups criticized how people spoke about them as
5 a form of discrimination. Other groups soon followed suit.

Racial minorities: During the Civil Rights Movement, African Americans rejected names such as 'negro' or 'colored' that identified them on the basis of skin
10 colour. They preferred the term 'African American', which was similar to traditional terms such as 'Irish American' or 'Italian American'. (Note: Today, it is also acceptable to use the adjective 'black'.) American Indians often want to be called 'Native
15 Americans' or 'First Nations Peoples', and the indigenous peoples of Canada and Alaska prefer to be called 'Inuit' or 'Alaska Natives' instead of 'Eskimos'.

Gender: There are various job titles in English that
20 refer only to the male (or, less often, to the female) gender: postman (*AE:* mailman), salesman, actress, stewardess, etc. Such terms have generally been replaced by gender-neutral ones: 'the chair' (instead of 'chairman/chairwoman'), postal carrier (*AE:* mail carrier), salesperson, flight attendant, etc. 25

Health: Certain terms used to refer to health issues are sometimes regarded as discriminatory, as they can suggest that there is something inherently wrong with people. People who are physically handicapped should be referred to as 'physically disabled' 30 and mentally challenged people have 'special needs', 'learning disabilities' or are 'intellectually impaired'.

Other politically correct terms would be, for example, 'vision impaired' for the blind or 'hearing 35 impaired' for the deaf.

Think of other politically correct terms that are used in German. Can you find the English equivalents?

▶ CC7 Making polite complaints 🎧 CD3 11, 12 and 13

Travelling abroad is always complicated, and mix-ups and misunderstandings can easily happen. The important thing is to stay calm and, if necessary, get competent help as quickly as possible.

1 Michaela Börner from Düsseldorf is spending a year abroad in North Carolina. When she arrives at the airport in Charlotte, her host family is waiting for her. Listen to the dialogue. What phrases do they use to greet each other? What questions have to be resolved before they can communicate easily?

2 At the baggage claim, Michaela and her host family wait for Michaela's suitcase. Listen to the sound file and identify the English words for the following terms:

1 Förderband 2 Gepäckstück 3 Haupthalle 4 Schalter 5 zurückbekommen

> *Listen to the audio files on the CD or download the audio files that correspond to exercises 1, 2 and 3 here:*
> **Webcode** context-46

3 Michaela and her host family go to the baggage services office. Listen to the sound file. Write down the English equivalents of the following expressions:

1 Kann ich Ihnen behilflich sein?   5 Sie dürfen sich jederzeit an uns wenden.
2 Darf ich bitte …?   6 Wäre es vielleicht möglich, dass unser Gast …
3 Ist das so richtig?   7 Sie waren sehr hilfreich.
4 Ihr Ärger ist verständlich.   8 Gern geschehen.

4 When you encounter a situation for the first time, you may be confronted with vocabulary you haven't heard before. Here is a short list of words that Michaela had trouble understanding. Just as Amanda would have tried to help Michaela, try explaining in English what the following terms mean.

1 baggage receipt   2 written confirmation   3 toll-free number   4 reimbursement

5 ROLE-PLAY Waiting at the airport baggage claim, you see your suitcase coming down the belt. Read the role card and act out the scene with your partner.

> *You can find your role cards here:*
> **Webcode** context-47

Skills File

P A task allows you to practise the skill.

Download the suggested answers to the *Skills File* PRACTICE tasks here:
 Webcode context-48

Language and study skills

▶ SF 1 Dealing with unknown words

READING, LISTENING AND MEDIATING ENGLISH INTO GERMAN

When you read or listen to texts, you usually won't understand every single word. Luckily, in many cases, you won't need to because you can understand texts without knowing each individual word. However, if the meaning of a word is essential to a sentence, there are some techniques that can help you work it out.

Look at the highlighted words in the text on the left and, on the right, read what strategies to use to work out their meaning.

> In order to remain competitive, the industrial nations have to raise their productivity, encourage innovation and lower their production costs.
>
> To reduce costs and to maximize profits, multinational companies often relocate facilities to other countries (= outsourcing) to profit from lower wages they pay their workers and from less restrictive laws. The problem is that it diminishes work prospects for workers here.

- *competitive:* think of words from the same word family *(competition / (to) compete / competitor)*
- *encourage:* identify parts of the word that you know *(courage → give someone courage)*
- *maximize:* think of similar words in other languages (German *maximieren*) but watch out for false friends *(prospects = Aussichten,* not: *Prospekte)*
- *multinational:* identify suffixes or prefixes *(multi = many → multinational = belonging to many nations)*
- *wages:* use the context of the word ('pay their workers')

PRACTICE

Using different strategies, try to infer the meaning of the <u>underlined</u> words:

> One of the Queen's <u>recurrent</u> royal responsibilities was to open Parliament, an <u>obligation</u> she had never <u>previously</u> found particularly <u>burdensome</u> and actually rather enjoyed: to be driven down the Mall on a bright autumn morning even after fifty years was something of a treat. But not any more.

From: Alan Bennet, *The Uncommon Reader*, 2008 (cf. *Context* p. 96)

SPEAKING, WRITING AND MEDIATING GERMAN INTO ENGLISH

When you want to express a certain concept in English when talking, writing or mediating and you don't know the word, you can paraphrase it. (▸ SF9: Paraphrasing)

▸ SF2 Learning new words

Learning vocabulary is a lifelong activity – even in your own language you never stop learning new words. There are different methods for expanding your vocabulary. Try out a variety of methods until you find the one that works best for you.

Step 1: Identify words that could be useful to you. These might be:
- words that are related to the topic you are dealing with (e.g. Shakespeare's dramas)
- words that help you talk or write about texts or topics in class
- words that go together with other words (collocations) or that belong to a word family that you already know
- words that belong to a neutral *register (words that are either very formal or very informal can only be used in limited situations).

Step 2: Arrange your words in a suitable form. This could be a mind map or a list – or you might want to use index cards. Indicate the meaning of your words by:
- giving synonyms (e.g. *dogma* = *belief / principle*)
- giving antonyms (e.g. *upheaval* ≠ *stability*)
- making sketches/drawings
- giving examples (e.g. the arts = *art, music, literature, etc.*)
- giving the German equivalent (e.g. *achievement* = *Errungenschaft*).

If possible, write down words in contexts or collocations; this will help you to use them in a sentence (e.g. *be torn between, remember sb. for sth.*).

The Elizabethan Age is often remembered as a Golden Age for its many achievements in the arts. However, England was struggling for peace and stability at home – religious, social, political and economic developments challenged society.
People were torn between a traditional world view and a more modern one; they generally accepted the Earth as the centre of the cosmos and the Church as the centre of life on Earth, but were keen to discover new truths beyond the old dogmas. Shakespeare's drama reflects this upheaval.

Find a mindmapping tool here:
Webcode context-53

Find an online thesaurus here:
Webcode context-52

Step 3: Use your new vocabulary as soon and as often as possible, e.g. include it in a short text, prepare a one-minute speech, study your index cards, etc.

Step 4: Revise your vocabulary regularly; first in short intervals, then in longer ones.

> **TIP**
>
> Be active when learning new words: do not just write them down, say them out loud as well. Sometimes movements, e.g. walking around while learning or giving them a rhythm or tune, can also be helpful.

▶ SF 3 Using a dictionary

There are both mono- and bilingual dictionaries. Both serve different purposes and they complement each other. They can be digital or print.

USING A BILINGUAL DICTIONARY

Here you can look up translations of words. For example if you do not know the English word for *Ruf* you can look it up in the German-English section or type it into your digital dictionary.

- The running heads at the top of each page help you find the right page quickly (top left-hand corner: first entry on page, top right-hand corner: last entry at bottom of page).
- In the example on the right, *Ruf* is the headword: the different translations are listed, numbers or letters in boxes indicate the different meanings.
- The notes in *italics* help you to find the particular meaning you are looking for.
- Examples and collocations are found below the headword.

> **Ruf**
> **1** *auch übertragen* call /kɔːl/; *lauter* shout /ʃaʊt/: **der Ruf nach schärferen Gesetzen** the **call for** tougher laws
> **2** ≈ *Ansehen* reputation /ˌrepjuˈteɪʃn/

From: *Schulwörterbuch English G 21*

> **TIP**
>
> - To find the pronunciation of an English word, check the English-German section of your dictionary or listen to the soundfile in a digital dictionary.
> - In the English-German section you will also find references to irregular verb forms, irregular plural forms, etc.
> - Always read the additional information next to your headword (above: in *italics*). This will prevent you from using the wrong translation.

USING A MONOLINGUAL DICTIONARY

Sometimes a monolingual dictionary can prove more helpful than a bilingual dictionary because it doesn't only give equivalents of words in another language, but definitions and example sentences. In this way, an English-English dictionary will help you to find the words that fit best to express exactly what you want to say. If you don't understand an English word of Latin or Greek origin, a monolingual dictionary will usually be more helpful than a bilingual one because the bilingual one will often give you a translation that is similar to the English word, e.g. *cosmopolitan* = *Kosmopolit*.

- In order to choose the right meaning from those given, always read the whole entry.
- The information on usage and style helps you to avoid using the wrong *register.
- Looking at the examples of common collocations and idioms can help you avoid false friends.
- Many dictionaries provide more specific information on typical error areas.

> **grim** /grɪm/ *adj.* (**grim·mer**, **grim·mest**) **1** looking or sounding very serious: a *grim face/look/smile* ◊ *She looked grim.* ◊ *with a look of* **grim determination** *on his face* ◊ **grim-faced** *policemen* **2** unpleasant and depressing: *grim news* ◊ *We face the grim prospect of still higher unemployment.* ◊ *The outlook is pretty grim.* ◊ *Things are* **looking grim** *for workers in the building industry.* **3** (of a place or building) not attractive; depressing: *The house looked grim and dreary in the rain.* ◊ *the grim walls of the prison* **4** [not before noun] (*BrE*, *informal*) ill/sick: *I feel grim this morning.* **5** [not usually before noun] (*BrE*, *informal*) of very low quality: *Their performance was fairly grim, I'm afraid!* ▶ **grim·ly** *adv.*: *'It won't be easy,' he said grimly.* ◊ *grimly determined* **grim·ness** *noun* [U]

From: *Oxford Advanced Learner's Dictionary*

> **PRACTICE**
>
> Translate the following sentences:
> 1 *Genetisch veränderte Lebensmittel haben in vielen europäischen Ländern einen eher schlechten Ruf.*
> 2 *Es gibt auch noch den Ruf nach mehr Beschränkungen für den freien Markt.*
> 3 *Sein Rufen schien niemand zu bemerken.*

Find an online dictionary here:
 Webcode context-52

▶ SF4 Using a grammar book

A grammar book is useful for correcting mistakes and improving your grammar. You should consult it when you come across a grammar problem while writing a text (e.g. if you are not sure whether or not to use a gerund) or when you realize that you keep making mistakes in certain fields of grammar. To identify these areas, analyse the feedback you receive from your teacher on your tests or homework.

Step 1: Find your grammatical problem area (e.g. word order or tenses) in the contents page or in the index pages at the back of the book. Read the relevant entry (both rules and examples).

Step 2: In order to avoid mistakes in the future, use your grammar book in different ways, e.g.:
- Copy problematic grammar rules onto index cards and use them to revise your grammar points. (Use the same colours for similar aspects or leave space on the cards for examples you add later, etc.)
- Create a poster with your own typical grammar traps.
- Look for the grammar point in question in texts you are working with or in your own texts.
- Do some exercises on the topic.
- Say the rule and some example sentences out loud, perhaps using your grammar card.

> *Find a tool to make your poster here:*
> **Webcode** context-50

PRACTICE

In your latest test the sentences below have been marked as wrong. Say what grammar topic you will look up in your grammar book, then correct the mistakes.
1 *They never went to England before.*
2 *They have known each other since six years.*
3 *If they would be older, they would do it.*
4 *Alicia feels not comfortable.*
5 *She asked me if I am happy.*
6 *They were all the time there.*

▶ SF5 Doing research

For projects, presentations or other school work you usually have to research individual aspects and find specific information. For this you can use the internet, but also other sources of information. Here are some ways to make your research more effective.

THE PREPARATION STAGE
Step 1: Clarify what your topic is, then brainstorm it. Decide what information you need so that you can structure your research accordingly.

Step 2: Plan your research:
- Decide which sources are helpful for your research: the internet, textbooks, encyclopaedias, newspapers or magazines, experts or contemporary witnesses?
- Concentrate on English language sources. Using German information and translating it into English will take a long time and often leads to unidiomatic English.
- Make a list of keywords that you want to check.

THE RESEARCH STAGE
Step 1: Check your sources: Older publications may contain outdated information; information published by individuals, interest groups or companies may be biased (i.e. have a tendency to be in favour of this group or company). Check for cross-references and do not just rely on one source.

Step 2: Make notes on the information you find. (▶ SF15: Marking up a text / Making and taking notes)
- Using index cards might make it easier to organize the information later.
- Copy the exact wording and note down the source (▶ SF39: Quoting a text), as it normally needs to be given in a bibliography (an alphabetical list of sources used) at the end of your presentation or project work.

·····▶

> ■ TIP
>
> **When doing research on the internet, the following tips may help you to find useful information:**
>
> | How can you determine whether a website provides reliable information? | Domain names ending with *.gov* or *.edu* indicate that the information is likely to be accurate, as it is usually an official website. Sites of scientific institutions are also usually reliable. |
> |---|---|
> | | Personal blogs or homepages often just give statements by individuals – they tend to be biased. |
> | How can you limit the number of hits so that you will find useful information more quickly? | Brainstorm which keywords would most likely appear in the perfect article to answer your search question. Combine them to get the most exact results. Typing in 5–7 keywords is better than just two or three. The more specific the word(s), the better. |
> | How can you find the original source of a quote? | Enter the full quote or parts of it, using quotation marks. This way you will only find websites with that exact quote. From these, you will normally be able to find the original source of a quote. |

PRACTICE

'German vs. British political system – similarities and differences'. Use the internet and/or printed works to find out about the German political system and compare it to your findings from Chapter 5, p. 98.

► SF 6 Doing project work

A project is a complex task usually done in a group, involving several hours of work and often resulting in a written or oral product, e.g. a wall display or a presentation. Project work typically proceeds along the following stages:

Step 1: Plan your work:
- Agree on a topic or look closely at the topic assigned to you.
- Decide what has to be done and how to present your results (e.g. a display, a presentation, a web page, a class magazine).
- Discuss how everybody can contribute best to the project and assign the tasks accordingly.
- Agree on a schedule, including regular group meetings at which all group members give status reports, present their results so far and discuss problems.

Step 2: Research your topic. (► SF 5: Doing research)

Step 3: Organize your findings (► SF 8: Structuring ideas) and start preparing your final result, i.e. your presentation (► SF 24: Giving a presentation) and/or any kind of written material (e.g. a wall display, a written text to be handed in, your web page, etc. (► SF 7: Making visual aids). Bear in mind any specifications you were given by your teacher (e.g. length of presentation or text, etc.).

Step 4: Check your written and visual material. Is it well organized and clear? Is the English correct? (► SF 40: Proofreading) Give your product to someone else in your group to check it again.

Step 5: Present your results. (► SF 24: Giving a presentation)

Step 6: After your presentation, assess your work. With your group, discuss what went well and what you could do better next time or ask your audience or teacher for feedback.

▶ SF 7 Making visual aids

Visual aids can have three purposes:
- *to help you get a clearer picture of the content of a text*
- *to structure information before writing a text*
  (▶ SF 8: Structuring ideas)
- *to present information to accompany a presentation*
  (▶ SF 24: Giving a presentation).

Some typical examples of visual aids are
- *timelines: order of events, dates*
- *flow charts: cause and effect*
- *pie charts: percentages, amounts*
  (▶ SF 12: Analysing charts and graphs)
- *clusters/mind maps: structured ideas.*

The following instructions explain how to make a flow chart after reading a text:

Step 1: Read the text and highlight the most important information. (▶ SF 15: Marking up a text / Making and taking notes)

> The reduction of oxygen-giving forests, especially the tropical rainforests, is one component of the climate change that scientists have been observing over the past few decades. This global warming appears to be causing the polar ice caps to melt, which could lead to the flooding of many coastal regions. At the same time as we rob the earth of its natural resources, we pollute the air and water with the waste products of those resources. Some of the emissions our technology produces are to blame for the greenhouse effect, which further contributes to the global warming phenomenon.
>
> 5
>
> 10

Step 2: Work out how the different aspects are connected.
- *reduction of forests: leads to climate change / global warming*
- *climate change / global warming: leads to melting of the polar ice caps*
- *melting of the polar ice caps: can cause floods*
- *pollution of air and water through waste: emissions cause greenhouse effect*

Step 3: Show the connection with arrows or other symbols.

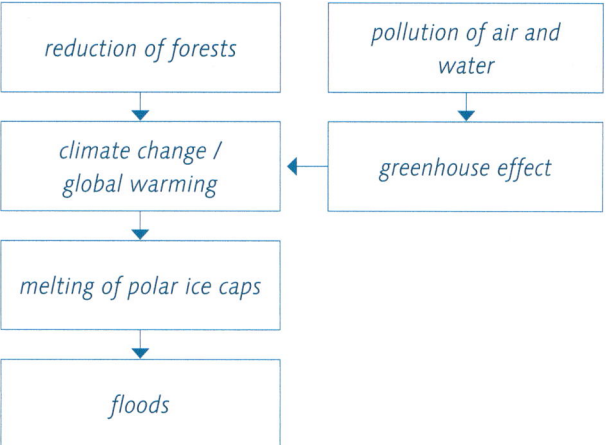

■ TIP

Use single terms or short phrases if possible; otherwise your chart will look too full and be visually confusing.

PRACTICE

Read ll. 22–34 of the Fact File on p. 101. Make a visual aid that presents the information on the Commonwealth in a suitable way.

▶ SF8 Structuring ideas

Structuring ideas is an important step after collecting information and before preparing a text (which may be written or spoken). Arranging your arguments in a logical order is a prerequisite to an effective text. (▶SF38: Writing a well-structured text)

Step 1: When you have collected your ideas, decide on an order in which to present them:
Most texts you produce will follow the general structure **1. Introduction → 2. Main part / Body → 3. Conclusion**. Decide on the order in which to present your ideas in the main part. Often the text-type you are being asked to produce will demand a specific structure (▶SF16: Identifying text types). For example, if you are asked to discuss a statement you will probably divide up your ideas into pro- and con-arguments (▶SF34: Argumentative writing). Other possibilities are a chronological order or *problem → cause → solution*. It may be helpful to use a flow-chart (▶SF7: Making visual aids) at this stage.

Step 2: Make an **outline** of your text (cf. the box on the right).
All 'main ideas' are of equal importance, as are the 'important facts', etc.

Step 3: Add the ideas you have collected to your outline. Use keywords.

Step 4: Before you start producing the final text or notes, review your outline. Make sure you have found the most appropriate place for each piece of information. (▶SF38: Writing a well-structured text)

> **OUTLINE**
> **1. Introduction**
> **2. Main part / Body**
>   I. Main idea 1
>   A. Important fact
>   1. Supporting fact
>   2. Supporting fact
>   a. Example or detail
>   b. Example or detail
>   B. Important fact
>   …
>   II. Main idea 2
>   …
> **3. Conclusion**

▶ SF9 Paraphrasing

Paraphrasing is useful when you don't know the exact word or phrase in a conversation, when writing a text or mediating into English. There are different techniques for paraphrasing:

Paraphrasing technique	Example
Antonym Antonyms denote the opposite of the original word.	*Reichtum:* 'the opposite of poverty'
Comparison Comparisons help you illustrate what you mean by creating images.	*Handschuh:* 'It's like a hat for your hand.'
Definition or explanation (often using relative clauses) With definitions or explanations, relative clauses help you add detail to general terms (e.g. 'a person', 'a machine').	*Freiwillige/r:* 'a person who offers to do something but doesn't ask for money in return' *Navigationsgerät:* 'a machine that tells you how to get to your destination; often in a car'

PRACTICE

Paraphrase the German words and phrases using the strategies in brackets:

Krankenschwester (definition/explanation)	*Dach* (comparison)
unangenehm (antonym)	*langweilig* (antonym)
Herbergsvater (definition/explanation)	*Garage* (comparison)

▶ SF 10 Working with closed test formats

In both lessons and written examinations you will come across test formats that don't ask you to write complete texts or answers to questions:

- *In **half-open formats** you write keywords only, e.g. when taking notes, completing tables or finishing sentences.*
- *In **closed test formats**, you don't write at all, but just indicate which of the given solutions is correct or which items go together. The most common forms are multiple-choice tasks, true/false statements, matching tasks and gapped texts (see below).*

Before an exam, ask your teacher which closed test formats you might expect.

The following strategies will help you deal with closed test formats.

Step 1: Preparing for the test
- Read the **instructions** carefully and work out what information you have to look for. It might help to underline keywords in the task.
- Try to **imagine** the situation of the text and anticipate what you might read or hear.

Step 2: Doing the test
- Focus on the **information that is necessary** to complete your task. Take notes. (▶ SF 15: Marking up a text / Making and taking notes)
- In **listening tasks**, complete as much as possible during the first listening. Use the second listening to add the missing information or to correct what you have done before. (▶ SF 22: Listening)
- Keep an eye on the time while working on **reading tasks**. Tasks that require you to read for gist only allow you a short time to skim the texts (▶ SF 14: Reading strategies). First work on the questions you are sure about, then go back to those you're struggling with.
- Never leave an **item unanswered**. If you do not know the answer, make a sensible guess – your chances of getting the credit for it are 25% in a multiple-choice task with four options!

Here are some specific tips for the different types of closed test formats:

Multiple-choice task (i.e. choosing the correct answer from multiple given options; cf. p. 50 above, task 1)
- Read the given options carefully – they may contain traps: They may use keywords from the text, but e.g. say the exact opposite of what is said in the text!
- If you are unsure which of the options is correct, go through them one by one and ask yourself why they might be incorrect.

True/false statements (i.e. classifying each given statement as 'true' or 'false'; cf. p. 143, task 2)
- In the case of false statements, you will typically find the opposite information in the text.
- In a half-open version of this format, you may be asked to give evidence for why you think an answer is right or wrong or to correct it.

Matching task (i.e. matching items from two lists, e.g. paragraphs with headings; cf. p. 46, task 1d)
- Don't match items just because they contain words or phrases that are similar. Instead, paraphrase the items and match those with a similar meaning.

Gapped text (i.e. identifying passages that have been left out of a text; cf. p. 118, task 1)
- Watch out for words that link sentences/ideas such as connectors (e.g. *therefore, moreover*), pronouns (e.g. *she, there, this*) or connected vocabulary (e.g. *bird – eagle, sparrow*) and pay attention to the sequence of time in the text. They may provide useful hints.
- After completing the text make sure that the grammar fits and the line of thought works (e.g. *cause and effect*).

Text skills

▶ SF 11 Analysing pictures

There are different types of pictures: photos, posters, paintings, drawings, or sketches. Often they are combined with written text, either as a title or a caption.

John Gast, *American Progress*, 1872

in the top right-hand corner

in the background

in the foreground

in the bottom left-hand corner

Step 1: Basic information
- State your first impression of the picture.
- Read the title or caption and identify the general topic.
- Check when (and where) the picture was created or published.

- *title: 'American Progress'*
- *general topic: American settlers moving west / conquering the continent*
- *artist, date: John Gast, 1872*

> ▪ LANGUAGE HELP
>
> - This picture/painting/photo/poster/drawing/sketch … shows / provides proof of / gives information on / introduces the topic of / conveys the impression that / depicts / portrays / illustrates / is about/ …
> - In the picture, … can be seen.

Step 2: Description
Choose one of these approaches:
- Start with the main subject, i.e. a dominant object, describe it in detail, then describe the background (useful for a picture with one dominant image).
  OR
- Start at the left of the picture and work across to the right or vice versa (useful for pictures with a lot of activity).
  OR
- Start at the top of the picture and work down to the bottom or vice versa (useful for pictures where the interest tails off towards the top or bottom).

- *dominant figure in the middle of the painting: woman, made to appear like a goddess or angel, holding a book in her left hand, moving towards the left of the picture, …*
- *painting shows landscape with a lot of detail*
- *right-hand side: bright, especially at the top; background: ships and railway lines*
- *in the bottom right-hand corner: farmers and a horse-drawn coach*
- *left-hand side: considerably darker / more threatening: clouds, ragged mountains, wild landscape*
- *bottom-left corner: Native Americans*
- *…*

Step 3: Analysis and interpretation

Draw conclusions about what the picture is meant to convey, whether it does this effectively and how it achieves its effect. You can look at …

- the technique, colours
- the effect on the viewer
- who is addressed and why
- the artist's/photographer's intention/ message.

- *right half of the painting (i.e. east) represents the American east (where the first settlers landed and lived); left half of the painting represents the 'wild west'*
- *colours and light: the east appears warm/bright; the west seems to be threatening and dark ('wild' west)*
- *all objects/people (trains, coaches, people, dominant figure) move from right to left → westward movement of American settlers → picture illustrates the idea of 'Manifest Destiny', which was …*
- *dominant figure: could represent culture, learning and progress (cf. the title); her angelic impression underlines the importance and positive connotation the artist places on those aspects*

■ LANGUAGE HELP

- The artist's/photographer's use of … creates … / conveys the impression of …
- By … the picture effectively illustrates …
- The dominance of … / The way the light/shadow … directs the viewer's attention to …

- As the foreground/ background is …, the impression given is that …
- … is a symbol of … / … helps to create an atmosphere of/ which …
- This has the effect that …

Step 4: Evaluation

Evaluate the picture by analysing how or how well it achieves an effect and by describing its effect on you.

- *painting clearly/effectively illustrates the idea that American people were chosen by God to conquer the American continent*

PRACTICE

Analyse one of the pictures on p. 114.

▶ SF 12 Analysing charts and graphs

Charts and graphs present complex information visually. There are different types, e.g. pie charts, bar charts, line graphs or tables.

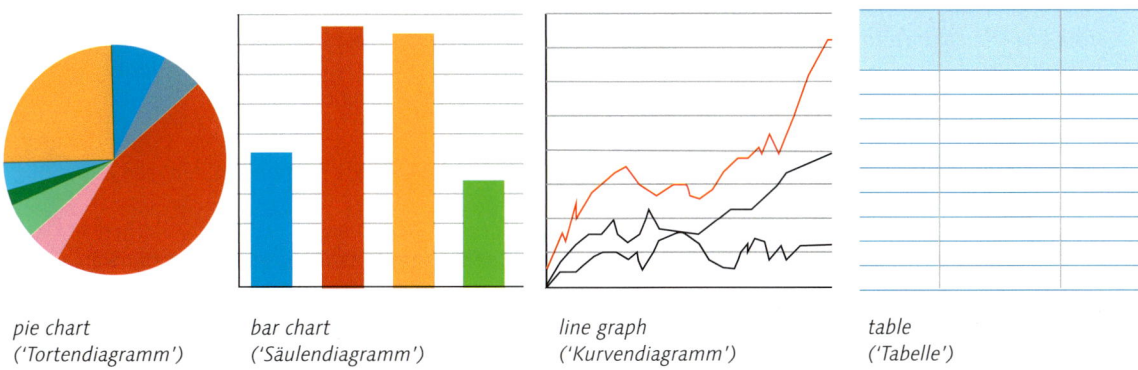

pie chart
('Tortendiagramm')

bar chart
('Säulendiagramm')

line graph
('Kurvendiagramm')

table
('Tabelle')

·····▶

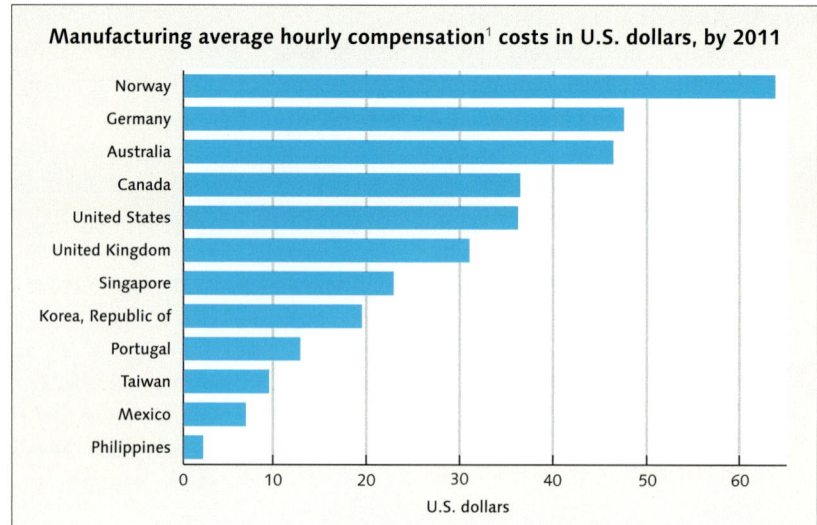

Manufacturing average hourly compensation[1] costs in U.S. dollars, by 2011

When analysing charts and graphs like the one on the right, follow these three steps:

From: the website of the U.S. Department of Labor

Step 1: Identify the type of chart or graph you are dealing with. Analyse the source:
- Is the source reliable?
- Is the data up to date?

- *bar chart*

- *source: U.S. Dept. of Labor: reliable*
- *data from 2011: not exactly up to date*

Step 2: Describe the graph/chart:
- What is it about and what information does it give?

- Does it show a development or does it compare different items at one point in time?
- Does it use absolute figures or percentages?

- *shows the differences in the hourly wage of workers in manufacturing in different countries in 2011*
- *gives the hourly compensation in $ (absolute numbers)*
- *compares data from 2011*
- *at the top of the ranking: countries with the highest hourly compensation (Norway: first, Philippines: last)*
- *countries at the bottom: hourly compensation is less than a sixth of the countries at the top*

LANGUAGE HELP

- The bar chart/pie chart/line graph/table ... shows the different/compares the size/number of .../ deals with/is about .../contrasts ... with ...
- It shows ... in contrast to...
- It is taken from/It contains data from .../It was published in ...

Bar chart:
- The bars are arranged horizontally/vertically.
- There are big/vast/surprising differences between ...
- At the top/bottom of the ranking comes...
- ... is first/last in rank
- ... has the largest/second largest ...

Pie chart:
- The chart is divided into ... segments, which show/represent ...
- The smallest/biggest segment/The segments representing ... and ... constitute the majority .../ A huge majority/minority is ...

Line graph:
- The graph shows the relationship between ... and ...
- ... is twice/three times as high as .../... There are more than/nearly twice as many ... as there are ...
- increase/decrease/reach a high point/rise/fall/ drop/grow steadily

---

[1]**compensation** *wage*

Step 3: Draw conclusions from the chart/graph.

- vast differences in the hourly wage → huge differences in the production costs of the goods → outsourcing of time-consuming jobs to countries with a lower hourly wage

Look at the table on the right and decide whether the figures would best be shown in a pie chart, a bar chart or a line graph and why. Use a computer to design the chart.

The world's most livable cities		
Rank	City	Score (out of 100)
1	Melbourne/Australia	97,5
2	Vienna/Austria	97,4
3	Vancouver/Canada	97,3
4	Toronto/Canada	97,2
5/6	Calgary/Canada Adelaide/Australia	96,6
7	Sydney/Australia	96,1
8	Helsinki/Finland	96,0
9	Perth/Australia	95,9
10	Auckland/New Zealand	95,7

From: *The Telegraph*, 6 August 2014

Find a tool to create info-graphics here:
Webcode context-57

▶ SF 13 Analysing cartoons

The following steps will help you to describe and analyse a cartoon systematically.

Step 1: Basic information

- What is your first impression of the cartoon?
  first impression: humorous, eye-catching, cartoon exaggerates a common school situation to illustrate a serious topic
- What is the cartoon about?
- What is its topic?
  topic: genetic engineering and its uncontrollable consequences
- (Where/when was it published?)

'Okay – is there anybody ELSE whose homework ate their dog?'

Step 2: Description

- Describe the cartoon systematically.
  – *classroom with students who all have brought colourful fantasy animals/monsters with them*
  – *in the background: blackboard with writing 'Genetic Engineering 101' (= name of the class); in front of the class: teacher looking angry*
  – *one student: putting up his hand, looking at his dinosaur-like animal*
  – *caption: the teacher's words*
- What people, events or trends does the cartoon refer to? Mention any labels, speech bubbles or captions. (▶ SF 11: Analysing pictures)

Step 3: Analysis

The following questions may help you when analysing a cartoon:

- Are the figures or issues presented in a positive or negative light? How is this impression achieved?
- Does the cartoon make use of *symbols or *irony? Explain their use.
- Does the cartoon depict well-known persons? Who are they and what is their role in connection with the topic of the cartoon?
- What point is the cartoonist trying to make? What means are used to get the message across?
  - *cartoonist reverses a common classroom cliché: a common excuse for students who don't have their homework is that their dog ate their homework; here, the homework (i.e. the genetically engineered animal) has eaten the dog*
  - *illustrations of the fantasy animals: exaggerated, eye-catching, funny shapes and colours*
  - *cartoon = criticism of uncontrollability of genetic engineering; even experts (here: the teacher) are unable to control the risks*

Step 4: Evaluation

Is think the cartoon effective or not? Give reasons, using your background knowledge about the topic.

*The cartoon criticizes the dangers of scientific research and genetic engineering effectively. To get its message across, it uses a funny twist by turning a well-known *cliché upside-down. By choosing a seemingly harmless setting to illustrate the devastating consequences of genetic engineering, the cartoonist criticizes it in a forceful way.*

PRACTICE

Describe and analyse the cartoon on the left.

DEAN OF STUDENTS

'I'd like to change my major from electrical engineering to English or something.'

▶ SF 14 Reading strategies

When working with longer texts, there are different ways of reading. Which strategy you need to apply depends on what you want to do with your text: look for the main ideas or specific information, read for pleasure or analyse it. You also need to have a strategy to deal with unknown words (▶ SF 1: Dealing with unknown words).

SKIMMING

Skimming (or reading for gist) means going through a text quickly to identify its main ideas. This technique is helpful when there is lots of material to be taken in and only a limited amount of time, e.g. when you are doing research on a certain subject and you have to find out which texts could be relevant for your topic.

Step 1: Look at illustrations, pictures, keywords, headings or subheadings to get an idea of the content of the given text.

Step 2: Don't read every sentence. Let your eyes run over the whole text and look for words or phrases that contain useful information.

Step 3: Read the first and the last sentence of each paragraph – one of them usually states the main idea of that paragraph and the very last sentence of the text often contains a summary.

Step 4: Summarize the text. If you are able to do this without a problem, your skimming was probably successful.

SCANNING

Scanning means looking out for for specific information. You can use this technique when you want to find answers to a particular question or to compare particular aspects in different texts.

Step 1: Think of keywords or phrases that might be useful to search for when looking for the information you need.

Step 2: Move your eyes quickly down the page. Stop when you find a keyword or phrase and read the part where you found it. Then continue scanning the text.

EXTENSIVE READING

Extensive reading means reading for pleasure, e.g. when reading a novel. You read at your own speed and concentrate on what's happening (the events of the plot) without looking up unknown words.

CLOSE READING

Close reading is necessary when analysing a text (▶ SF 17–21). You will need to understand not only what is being said in the text, but also how it is being said. To do that, you will have to read the text more than once and make sure you understand every word.

PRACTICE

1 Skim the text 'Young, educated – and leaving the country' (p. 162) and note down what the text is about in a few words.

2 Scan the third paragraph of 'India then and now' (p. 114) for facts and figures showing which challenges India has to face.

▶ SF 15 Marking up a text / Making and taking notes

When working with photocopied texts or printouts, you can mark up important information so that you can find it more easily when you are working with the text again, e.g. when you are writing about it or preparing for a test.

> **■ TIP**
>
> When working with a borrowed book, put a transparency on the page and mark important information on it.

MARKING UP A TEXT

Step 1: As you read the text, bear in mind what information you are looking for. You may want to read the task/question again.

Step 2: When you find the relevant information in your text, mark it by underlining, highlighting or circling the relevant words or passages. Only mark keywords.

> **■ TIP**
>
> 1. Use different colours for different tasks.
> 2. Also mark words which show that a different opinion or a contrast is being introduced to help you understand the logical structure of the text.

Step 3: Finally, add headings or keywords in the margin or summarize passages with short phrases or sentences.

Tasks: a Point out what recruiters do and how they work.

b Collect tips on how to write a CV to arouse a recruiter's interest.

How to please recruiters
Clare Whitmell

A recruiter can be your short cut into a new job. With a good understanding of industry trends – and insider knowledge of that particular employer's preferences and needs – a recruiter will be briefed to find exactly the right candidate with a specific set of skills, experience and qualities. To even be considered for the role, you need to make sure that your CV hits the right notes with them.

Recruiters can be generalists working in a number of sectors or headhunters specialising in one, but there are a few pet hates they all share. Avoid these and you'll be giving yourself a better chance of getting into the yes pile each time. [...]

Zena Everett, director and career coach at Second Careers and career guru at Mumsnet, has researched how headhunters, recruiters, employers and HR professionals screen CVs. She found that they all – without exception – looked first at the most recent work experience and job title. These must be relevant for the CV to get a second look in a competitive job market.

For recruiters to put you forward to an employer, they need to see that your background matches the role. A simple way to ensure that you're giving your CV the best possible chance is to search the job description for key criteria, then make sure you include relevant details on your CV that show you're a good match.

From: *The Guardian*, 8 April 2014

recruiters' knowledge

recruiters' tasks

recruiters' areas of work

Show that your most recent work experience is relevant for the job.

Show that you fulfil the most important criteria for the new job.

MAKING AND TAKING NOTES

In cases where you cannot mark up a text (either because you are not working with your own book or because you are listening to an audio file), you can first *take notes* (i.e. extract important information from the text), then *make notes* (i.e. organize your ideas). Making notes will also help you structure your own ideas, e.g. after brainstorming or when preparing for a speaking task (▶ SF 8: Structuring ideas; ▶ SF 24–28).

▶ SF 16 Identifying text types (non-fiction)

In class you often have to analyse texts. The first step of the analysis is to identify the text type you are dealing with.

Texts can be classified into two main categories:

Fictional texts (i.e. literary texts, *Dichtung*, ▶ SF 19–21)	Non-fictional texts (i.e. *Sachtexte*, ▶ SF 18)
• The text describes a world that was created in the mind of its *author. • Its *setting, *characters and events may or may not seem realistic.	• The text talks about the real world. • It was written to convey information, convince the reader or criticize something.

Knowing what type of non-fictional text you're dealing with and what characteristic features this text type has will help you to anticipate what kind of information might be given and how it might be presented. Follow these steps:

Step 1: Skim the text (▶ SF 14: Reading strategies) and try to get a general idea of its content:
- Sum up in one or two sentences what the text is about.
- If possible, find out when and where it was published (newspaper, book, journal, internet).

Step 2: Examine the text more closely. Look at:
- its content and purpose: Is the text meant to inform, persuade, entertain, …?
- its *style and *tone: Is the language formal or informal, simple or complex?

Step 3: Identify the text type. The following table will help you.

Non-fictional texts	
Text type and examples	**Contents and purpose**
Expository texts: *feature story, *news story, summary, etc.	• contain comprehensive and detailed information • are intended to be objective and factual • give no personal opinion • describe a situation, scientific findings, historic occurrences
Descriptive texts: travel book, biography, etc.	• describe actual places, objects, events or people based on the writer's observations and impressions • are intended to create a vivid picture in the reader's mind • tend to give a lot of detail
Argumentative texts: *editorial, *column, *letter to the editor, *review, *speech, *comment, etc.	• discuss problems and controversial ideas • evaluate a topic by giving reasons and stating the pros and cons of an issue • show a clear line of argument • tend to use expert opinions, statistics, quotations and technical/scientific language • aim to convince the reader
Persuasive texts: *speech, advertisement, etc.	• use stylistic devices • often use imperatives as an appeal to do something specific • try to persuade or convince the reader/listener
Instructive texts: manual, brochure, etc.	• are intended to instruct the readers, tell them what to do or how to do it • use imperatives and passive constructions (▶ LP 7: The passive)

▶ SF 17 Analysing stylistic devices

When you listen to or read texts, you will normally notice that they have some kind of effect on you – you might strongly agree or disagree or you might feel amused, entertained, informed or perhaps irritated. This effect is created through the way the text is written, and especially by the *stylistic devices used. So when analysing texts, you should try to find out how certain effects are created. Stylistic devices may relate to sound (e.g. *alliteration), structure (e.g. *repetition, *parallelism) or meaning (e.g. *imagery).

Step 1: When reading the text pay attention to the effects that certain passages have on you.

Step 2: Study the passages in question to find the stylistic devices that create these effects. In the table below there are some examples.

Step 3: Consider why these effects may have been intended in this context. (▶ SF 36: Writing a text analysis)

> ■ TIP
>
> If you cannot pinpoint any specific effects while listening or reading, you can try it the other way round: Study the text for the most common stylistic devices (cf. the table below) and see if you can find a reason why the author may have used them.

Example	Effect	Stylistic device
'The most restless, the most adventurous, the most innovative, the most industrious of people [...].' From: William J. Clinton, 'The changing face of America', 13 June 1998; cf. *Context* p. 144, ll. 14ff.	• reader/listener may feel overwhelmed, impressed by positive qualities	• *enumeration of superlatives
'What do the changes mean? They can either strengthen and unite us, or they can weaken and divide us.' From: William J. Clinton, 'The changing face of America', 13 June 1998; cf. *Context* p. 144, ll. 27ff.	• reader/listener may feel drawn into the argumentation by being asked a direct question • reader/listener feels a little under pressure, even manipulated to answer the question in a specific way	• *rhetorical question • *contrast of two possible answers: one with strongly positive, the other with strongly negative *connotations
'With a growing UK Muslim population currently standing at 2.7 million (Census 2011) with a £20.5 billion a year spending power and expected to rise to 5.5 million people by 2030 (Pew Report, *The Future of the Global Muslim Population* 2011) access to delicious halal food in the UK is becoming increasingly important.' From: the website of HalalFocus; cf. *Context* p. 106, ll. 15ff.	• reader may feel convinced by factual information/objective numbers	• statistical data • reliable sources (Pew Report)
'Many Indians despair over the divisiveness[1] of caste and would prefer to wish it away. However, the hold of the Indian way of life is also a bulwark[2] against the onslaught[3] of the global culture.' From: Gurcharan Das, *India Unbound*, 2001; cf. *Context* p. 117, ll. 14ff.	• reader may have difficulty understanding individual words, may find this irritating	• *register, sophisticated/academic choice of words ('divisiveness', 'hold', 'bulwark', 'onslaught')

[1] **divisiveness** force that splits people into different groups [2] **bulwark** *(fml)* thing that protects sth. [3] **onslaught** strong attack

From the beginning of a job advert for a park ranger: 'Yes, you read right. As our ex-island caretaker is regretfully handing over the keys to his island hacienda[4] we're looking for someone to take his place.' From: the website of the Queensland tourism board, 5 March 2013; cf. *Context* p. 193, ll. 1ff.	• reader may feel directly addressed and involved, connected to the writer	• direct address of reader without introduction • imitation of spoken language, of personal interaction • use of personal pronouns ('we', 'you')
'For me, school had been a Darwinian exercise. A daily gauntlet[5] of ridicule, abuse, and isolation.' From: Ernest Cline, *Ready Player One*, 2012; cf. *Context* p. 16, ll. 21ff.	• reader will be able to picture the situation very clearly	• *images/*metaphors ('Darwinian exercise', 'gauntlet of ridicule') • incomplete sentence
'War is as old as Europe. Our continent bears the scars of spears and swords, canons and guns, trenches[6] and tanks[7], and more.' From: Herman Van Rompuy, 'From war to peace', 10 December 2012; cf. *Context* p. 160	• reader gets a lively idea of the wounds inflicted on Europe through war • list of nouns draws reader's attention to the numerous weapons which caused the injuries	• *personification of an object ('continent bears the scars') • alliterations ('spears and swords', 'trenches and tanks')
'I fear the day technology will surpass our human interaction. The world will have a generation of idiots.' (Albert Einstein)	• reader may be taken aback by this provocative statement • the reader's interest will be aroused	• *exaggeration (to stress a point)
'... we're talking the ultimate reality TV, where the public can monitor [...] prisoners' whole lives on death row[8]. They can [...] make up their own minds about a convict's worthiness for punishment. Then each week, viewers across the globe can cast a vote to decide which prisoner is executed next. It's humanity in action – the next logical step toward true democracy.' From: DBC Pierre, *Vernon God Little*, 2003; cf. *Context* p. 27, ll. 9ff.	• reader will be irritated/shocked by the description of the game show as 'humanity in action' • text evokes indignation	• *irony: author uses the term 'humanity in action' to denote the exact opposite: a truly inhumane TV show

When analysing the effects created by a text, make sure you also pay attention to its *tone (i.e. the way a writer treats his/her topic). The tone may be formal, intimate, playful, ironic, humorous, etc.)	■ LANGUAGE HELP			
	The author	uses employs makes use of	a metaphor a simile enumeration irony personification	to illustrate … to show … to emphasize … to underline … to draw the reader's attention to …

[4] **hacienda** large farm   [5] **gauntlet** fight with a lot of people attacking you   [6] **trench** *Schützengraben*
[7] **tank** *Panzer*   [8] **death row** cells for prisoners who are waiting to be executed

▶ SF 18 Analysing non-fiction

When analysing a non-fictional text you have to say more than just what it is about. You have to find out what type of text it is, for example a *feature story, an *editorial or a *comment (▶ SF 16: Identifying text types). By looking at how its content, its structure and its language interact you can find out what its function and its message might be.

Here is an excerpt from a newspaper article written by a young British woman. Analyse the way she presents her own experiences as a non-white woman in Great Britain.

Step 1: Read the text and decide what type of text it is. Collect extracts that help you analyse the text, e.g. its line of argument, *stylistic devices, choice of words, etc. (cf. the highlighted passages). (▶ SF 17: Analysing stylistic devices)

> ... It's not that I'm embarrassed about my ethnic background. I don't think about it much, though it's good for jokes ('I'm half Iranian, half American – so basically, I hate myself'). But some people seem to want me to think about it. 'Why don't you visit Bombay?' they enthuse. 'You'd love it.' They may be right, but have yet to explain to me why I'd love it more than Tokyo, or Guatemala, or any of the other places I haven't yet been. It's an odd misconception that you should somehow feel connected to a far-flung country because your ancestors lived there centuries ago, even if your entire life has been spent morris dancing[1] in Loughborough.

5
10

From: Ariane Sherine, 'It may not be racist, but …', *The Guardian*, 3 March 2010

Step 2: Organize your findings. Make sure all examples e.g. for stylistic devices go together.

- *line of argument: does not think much about her background (l. 1), people seem to think she ought to care about it (ll. 3–4), she thinks her parents' country of origin is just as relevant for her as any other country (ll. 5–7)*
- **humour: joke (ll. 2–3), compares her parents' country of origin with other countries she does not know (ll. 5–7)*
- *choice of words: 'odd misconception' (l. 7), 'far-flung country' (l. 8), 'ancestors' (l. 9), 'morris dancing' (l. 10): humorous*
- **stylistic devices: *exaggeration 'centuries ago' (l. 9), quotations (ll. 4–5)*

Step 3: Analyse the effect that is created by the stylistic devices that you have identified.

- **humour, choice of words: give the text a light-hearted tone*
- *quotations: help the reader imagine the specific situation, make the text more lively*
- **exaggeration: shows how absurd she finds other people's ideas*
- *light-hearted tone: she's not seriously offended*

Step 4: Examine the connection between the effect identified in **Step 3** and the author's line of argument.

- *readers ought to realize how ridiculous it is to keep identifying the descendants of immigrants with their parents' country of origin, to not accept them as fellow-citizens*
- *no acid criticism, no fierce accusation of racism, but a fairly lighthearted account of people's everyday misconceptions*

---

[1] **morris dance** *(v)* do a traditional English dance

TIP
When working on **Step 1** do not only follow the chronology of the text and wait until something catches your eye. Make sure you examine the text systematically by checking its use of stylistic devices, its choice of words, etc.

LANGUAGE HELP
• The author uses vivid/collo-quial/objective/emotive … language. • The sentences are long-winded/paratactical/simple/complex/ … • The author's tone is friendly/humorous/critical/optimistic/sarcastic … • His/her choice of words under-lines … • The stylistic devices used support/emphasize/underline … • The reader can easily picture the situation / follow her/his train of thought / line of argument …

▶ SF 19 Analysing narrative prose

When you have to analyse a *short story, a *novel or any other *narrative text you are usually asked to pay attention to one or two specific aspects. The most common aspects for a text analysis are:

Aspect	Example
Character constellations or relationships (▶ SF 35: Writing a character profile) • Who is in the story? • What relationships do the *characters have to each other? Are they dependent on each other/equals, etc.? • Do they belong to similar/different groups (social/ethnic, etc.)? • Do they serve as foils for each other, i.e. do they contrast with another character to highlight particular qualities of the other character? • How does the author characterize them, *directly or *indirectly? • Are the characters *round or *flat?	High-school student Mitch is a reporter for the school magazine and on his way to his first interview with his former PE-teacher McNulty: I parked my mom's Ford Focus by the gym, eased out of the front seat, and looked around. When I spotted McNulty loading tackling sleds[1] into a school van, I tensed. To him, I'd always be a fat loser and nothing more. But a reporter has to have the courage to approach people, ask them questions […]. From: Carl Deuker, *Payback Time*, 2010; cf. *Context* p. 190, ll. 1ff. • *reporter and coach share a history* • *reporter feels inferior; tries to overcome his fear* • *…*
The *narrator or the narrative perspective • Who is telling the story and to whom? Is it a *first-person narrator, a *third-person narrator or an *omniscient narrator? • How much does the narrator know or not know? What are the limiting factors? Does the narrator have a *limited or an *unlimited point of view?	Some nights I lie next to Tony, here in America where I live like a worm avoiding the sunlight, and I wonder if he knows. And is it only because it was his brother that he does not sense that another man's body has come between us. From: Shauna Singh Baldwin, *English Lessons*, 1996; cf. *Context* p. 128, ll. 46ff. • *first person narrator (*protagonist), probably female, might be an immigrant* • *tells the reader a secret that apparently the husband does not know; but since the narrator cannot know the husband's thoughts, neither he/she nor the reader know for sure* • *…*

---

[1] **tackling sled** *Angriffsschlitten (schweres Trainingsgerät im American Football)* ⋯⋯▶

The *plot

- How are the events connected by cause and effect to form a plot?
- How does the author attract or keep the reader's attention by creating *tension or *suspense?
- Is there a *climax and/or a *turning point?
- Does the story have an ending or a conclusion? Or is there an *open ending / a *denouement?

Dan, a high-school student whose parents have recently lost their jobs, is approached by another student, who tries to recruit him for a protest march:

> I felt myself tense. All my friends, plus a couple of kids at the sign-up table, were watching and listening. 'Why do you ask?' 'Seems like a good time,' he said. Had he heard that we'd lost our home? Did he think that would make me more sympathetic to his cause? 'Why's that?' I gave him a hard look.

From: Todd Strasser, *No Place*, 2014; cf. *Context* p. 150, ll. 4ff.

- *tension between characters is building up*
- *suspense: reader does not know if the secret is going to be discovered*
- …

The *setting and the *atmosphere

- Where and when does the action take place?
- Are there any people? How do they react to the setting?
- How does the setting influence the atmosphere? (E.g. sunny spring days usually create an optimistic atmosphere, a crowded place may create a tense or exciting atmosphere, etc.)
- Are you told directly or do you have to draw your own conclusions?

Her Majesty the Queen is on her way to open Parliament:

> One of the Queen's recurrent royal responsibilities was to open Parliament, an obligation she had never previously found particularly burdensome[1] and actually rather enjoyed: to be driven down the Mall[2] on a bright autumn morning even after fifty years was something of a treat.

From: Alan Bennett, *The Uncommon Reader*, 2008; cf. *Context* p. 96, ll. 1ff.

- *autumn, sunny*
- *the Queen: about to do a job she enjoys*
- *positive atmosphere (to be concluded from the setting)*
- …

LANGUAGE HELP

- The relationship between the characters is strongly influenced by … Their power struggle reveals itself when … Their lack of communication shows …
- X's behaviour when … reveals that …
- The description underlines/emphasizes … / conveys the impression that …
- The image suggests …
- By using words like … the author stresses …

- The overall effect is … It can be portrayed as …
- The perspective is biased/one-sided …
- As the first-person narrator has a limited perspective, the reader must … The author chose an omniscient narrator because …
- The story has an open ending, so …
- In the end the conflict is solved when …

---

[1] **burdensome** implying hard work   [2] **the Mall** road leading to Buckingham Palace

▶ SF 20 Analysing drama

*A *drama or *play is a script in which a *playwright presents what *characters say and what they do. A drama is written to be performed on stage, so when you read a play, you will enjoy it more if you imagine what it would look and sound like on stage.*

When analysing drama, typical aspects to look at are:

Aspect	Examples and explanations
Structure • Is the play divided up into *acts and *scenes or is there a different structure? • What function do these divisions have in the play? • Do they correspond to action, time, place or a combination of these?	• Shakespeare's plays used to be performed without intermissions – *rhyming couplets would indicate the end of one scene. Nowadays his plays are conventionally edited to have four or five acts and scene divisions, which usually mark a change in the set of characters on stage. • Most modern plays have two or three acts. Some (e.g. *Artefacts*, cf. pp. 102f.) have no act division at all and are meant to be performed without a break. Still, *Artefacts* is divided into three parts, which are set in the two different countries. *Clybourne Park* (cf. pp. 141f.) has two acts, separated by a time gap of 50 years.
The construction of action • Does the script contain *stage directions? If so, what information do they provide? • How does the **action** unfold through the **dialogue**? • Are there *monologues? What function do they have? • What kind of **language** is used?	• In *Clybourne Park* (cf. pp. 141f.) there are some stage directions. They describe how actors should speak certain lines or move (e.g. 'chuckles with amazement, shakes his head', p. 142, ll. 109f.), but there are very few descriptions of settings or actions except at the beginnings of each of the two acts. • Dramatic dialogue has to be very carefully constructed (and yet sound realistic) so that it never gets boring and gives enough clues about what is actually happening. • Monologues usually serve to show a character's thoughts to the audience, but not to the other characters, i.e. they are not part of the interaction. Shakespeare often made use of them to give the audience more insight into a character's mind. • In the extract from *Macbeth* (cf. pp. 76f.) Lady Macbeth uses aggressive language, calling her husband a coward when he hesitates to commit the murder as planned. His question 'If we should fail?' shows his hesitation, whereas her answer 'We fail!' shows her determination to succeed (cf. p. 76, ll. 36f.). This interchange actually drives the action forward because it serves to persuade Macbeth to act as planned. • In *Artefacts*, Kelly's informal language (cf. pp. 102f.) serves to characterize her as a modern British teenager and makes the dialogue more realistic, e.g. 'Yeah, all right then, tell me what I think.' (ll. 69)

Characters
(▶ SF 35: Writing a character profile)

- Who are the *characters?
- What information do we get about them and what issues do they have to deal with in the play?
- Do they develop over the course of the play?

- Do they stand for a particular idea or are they part of the play's message?

- Normally it's not the playwright who tells us directly about the characters, but as in real life we get an idea of them through the way they act or talk about themselves, their lives or about others. *Monologues in particular can give the audience an insight into a character's motivations, feelings or problems.
- Macbeth (cf. pp. 76f.) develops from a man reluctant to kill into a ruthless murderer. In *Artefacts* (cf. pp. 102f.) Kelly first refuses to go to Iraq, but later we see that she has actually gone there.
- In *Clybourne Park* (cf. pp. 141f.), the members of the white community who oppose black neighbours represent racist ideas. Lady Macbeth (cf. pp. 76f.) represents ruthless ambition as she is even willing to commit murder to achieve the ultimate success she wants.

Audience

- What does the audience know or see that the characters don't know or see?
- What is left to the audience's imagination?

- In Shakespeare's *Romeo and Juliet*, Romeo has heard that Juliet is dead and kills himself. The audience however knows that she only looks dead – an example of *dramatic irony.
- Sometimes characters speak of actions that do not actually happen on stage, even though they are important for the plot.

■ LANGUAGE HELP

- The play is divided into … acts and … scenes / The development of the action corresponds with the play's division into acts / scenes …
- The overall theme of the play is …
- In the play the conflicts develop between …
- The audience is drawn into the plot by … / The action is supposed to please / shock / enrage / fascinate the audience …
- The … act ends in a cliffhanger / In the end the conflict is solved …

- The stage directions draw a concise picture of the scenery / There are almost no stage directions, so … / The play works with almost no props / a bare stage …
- Even though X appears as a friendly character at first, he later shows … / … stands for / represents …
- The social differences between the characters can be seen in the language they use … / The characters speak in *blank verse …

The Globe Theatre, London

■ TIP

play = Theaterstück
drama = Drama (i.e. text form), e.g. *modern drama* or *Elizabethan drama* (i.e. the plays produced during the time when Queen Elizabeth I reigned)
playwright, dramatist = Stückeschreiber/in, Dramatiker/in
character = Figur
actor, actress = Schauspieler/in

▶ SF 21 Analysing poetry

When you are asked to analyse a poem, you should not only look at its poetic features such as its form, its *rhythm or its language, you must also look at its content and link this to the poem's form. Only then will you be able to fully understand what the poem conveys.

Here is a poem by Gavin Ewart, followed by a step-by-step guide.

Ending   *Gavin Ewart*

The love we thought would never stop
  now cools like a congealing[1] chop[2].
The kisses that were hot as curry
  are bird-pecks[3] taken in a hurry.
The hands that held electric charges   5
  now lie inert[4] as four moored barges[5].
The feet that ran to meet a date
  are running slow and running late.
The eyes that shone and seldom shut
    are victims of a power cut.   10
The parts that then transmitted joy
  are now reserved and cold and coy[6].
Romance, expected once to stay,
  has left a note saying gone away.

From: Poetry Archive

Step 1: Read the poem two or three times, then summarize it in one or two sentences. Consider
- the poem's title, *setting and *theme
- the *speaker and the addressee
- the link between the title and the poem's content.

- *two people in a relationship that has lasted for some time*

- *title: ending of a relationship*
- *couple: one person is speaker, one is addressee*
- *contrast: what the relationship was like before and what it is like now*

Step 2: Look at the poem's structure (*stanzas, *rhythm, *rhyme scheme, *metre). (It may help to read the poem out loud to get a feeling for the way it sounds.)
- Is it built regularly or are there interruptions in the rhythm or rhyme scheme?
- Is there a *refrain?
- Is it a *sonnet?

- *seven couplets*
- *each couplet rhymes (aa,bb, cc, etc.) → regular pattern, conventional*
- *regular metre, regular rhyme scheme*

·····▶

---

[1]**congeal** (here) become unpleasantly dry   [2]**chop** thick slice of meat with a bone attached to it   [3]**peck** quick kiss / bird's bite   [4]**inert** unable to move   [5]**moored barge** *(here)* small boat that has been fixed to land   [6]**coy** not willing to give away much about yourself

Step 3: Examine the poem's language more closely. Look for
- *imagery, e.g. *simile, *metaphor, *analogy, *personification
- sound effects, e.g. *alliteration, *assonance, *onomatopoeia
- *contrasts, *repetitions and specific sentence structures (simple/complex sentence, *enjambement)
- mythological/literary/social/historical references
- *symbols.

- contrast between past and present, e.g. 'love that never ends' (l. 1) ↔ 'congealing chop' (l. 2)
- changes are conveyed through descriptions of body parts: hand (l. 5), feet (l. 7), eyes (l. 9), parts (l. 11)
- vivid images for love in the past, e.g. 'hot curry' (l. 3), 'electric charges' (l. 5)
- images of disconnectedness/cold/passiveness of love today, e.g. 'lie inert as four moored barges' (l. 6), 'power cut' (l. 10)
- personification: 'romance' (l. 13)
- short and simple sentences
- down-to-earth metaphors

Step 4: Describe the poem's effect and analyse how it is achieved by connecting your findings on its form to its content.

- clear and regular structure → monotony, conventionality
- clear and precise images → easy to understand, common problem
- → lack of drama
- …

■ LANGUAGE HELP

- The poem by … deals with/is about … In the poem … describes/reflects on … The poet addresses the topic of …
- The title reminds the reader of …/refers to …
- The poem is made up of …/consists of … verses/ stanzas.
- The rhyme scheme is …/There is no consistent rhyme scheme. The word … rhymes with … The use of … creates a certain rhythm.
- Line … runs into line …, which emphasizes …

- The poet employs specific images, such as metaphors or similes, in order to …
- The diction/register is simple/colloquial/formal, which intensifies the feeling of …
- The most prominent stylistic device used in the poem is …, which serves to …
- All in all, … The overall effect is … The poem aims to show/illustrate/convey/express the idea that … The overall message of the poem is …

Listening and viewing skills

▶ SF 22 Listening

When you have to deal with a listening task at school, you are normally first given time to read the questions you will have to answer. These questions may be closed such as multiple choice (▶ SF 10: Working with closed test formats) but they can also be more open. After reading the tasks you are usually allowed to listen to the audio file twice.

■ TIP

In contrast to listening at school, you will not normally have the opportunity to listen to something twice in real life situations, e.g. to a train announcement. You then need to be able to identify relevant information right away – or you may ask people for clarification who have listened to the same thing. In a conversation, you may ask the speaker to repeat what they have said.

LISTENING FOR GIST

Listening for gist is what you do to find out what the main topic of a spoken text is, e.g. when you want to see if an audio file is relevant for you.

Step 1: Before listening for gist, collect information on the following if possible:
- the text type (e.g. newscast, lecture, panel discussion, interview) and its addressee
- the situation and *setting
- the number of speakers and their role in the audio file. For example, will there be conflicting points of view?
- the topic dealt with in the audio file and what points of view or concepts you are likely to encounter.

Step 2: When listening for gist,
- do not try to understand every detail that is said
- watch out for 'signpost expressions' that show somebody's train of thought, e.g. *the biggest issue is …, the most important argument is, on the one hand …*
- listen carefully to a speaker's intonation; it may help you identify their attitudes or intentions.

Step 3: Summarize the text so as to prove that you can identify its topic.

LISTENING FOR DETAIL

You listen for detail if you need specific information, e.g. tips given for a specific problem.

Step 1: Before listening for detail,
- remember what you know about the text (its speaker, addressee, situation, setting and/or topic) and try to anticipate what might be said in the text
- collect keywords that are relevant to your question, e.g. names, dates or numbers
- prepare your notepad so that you can take notes quickly. (▶ SF 15: Marking up a text / Making and taking notes)

Step 2: When listening for detail,
- watch out for the keywords you collected
- take notes, using abbreviations and symbols.

▶ SF 23 Analysing a film

Watching a film can make you laugh or cry, feel angry or scared. Those reactions are not only caused by the story the film tells but also by the way it tells its story. Just like written texts can provoke a reaction in their readers through the choice of words and *stylistic devices, films can achieve a certain response in the viewer through, for example, their camera work, editing and sound.

BEFORE VIEWING

Step 1: Find out what kind of film you are going to watch and try to get an idea of what to expect by looking at available information on the film (e.g. film posters, reviews, DVD covers, magazine information). What genre does it belong to (feature film, documentary, video clip, commercial, etc.)?

WHILE VIEWING

Step 1: Watch one or more scenes and make notes on how the characters act, what the *setting is like or what information is presented. You may also add some observations on cinematic devices such as camera angle, sound and light. A **viewing log** can help you structure your notes. Here is one example for the first scene of *Never Let Me Go* (you may choose other categories to serve your own purposes):

Scene	What?	Where?	Who?	Camera	Sound	Light	Effect
1	a patient (Tommy) is being prepared for a surgery	hospital: operating room	carer (Kathy) and patient	close-up of Kathy, over-the-shoulder shot towards Tommy → Kathy's point of view	only voice-over of Kathy, no other sound	operating room is illuminated, no additional light	very emotional
…	…	…	…	…	…	…	…

Step 2: Watch the specific scenes once more and have a closer look at the cinematic devices used and the effect they achieve. Add your observations to your viewing log. The table below may help you.

Camera angle/movement or sound	Example	Possible effect
The camera seems to be looking through the eyes of the character or is looking directly over his or her shoulder (**over-the-shoulder shot**). One character's face is shown in **close-up** (cf. the picture on the right), while the other characters are presented through **long** or **medium shots**.		The character's emotions are revealed and you identify with that character.
A character is shown through a **low-angle shot**.		The character appears bigger. He or she seems to be dominant, i.e. to have power over the other characters in this scene.

A character is shown through a **high-angle shot**.		The character appears smaller. He or she seems to be inferior, i.e. to have less power than the other characters in this scene.
Two or more characters are shown through **eye-level shots**.		The characters appear to be on the same level.
The scene is rather dark. People and objects cannot be clearly distinguished. The **soundtrack** is eery or moves towards a *climax.		The viewer may feel tense or scared.
There are short **shots** and lots of **cuts**. *Flashbacks (showing past events) or **flash-forwards** (showing future events) are used.		The *action is fast-paced and exciting.
The camera takes a steady position.		The action appears slower.
The music is uplifting, pleasant or catchy.		The viewer feels relaxed and in a good mood.

LANGUAGE HELP

- The film is about …/shows …/tells the story of …
- The music intensifies/fades as …/creates/builds tension/suspense/joy/…
- The actor's body language and facial expressions add to the feeling of …
- In this scene the music and lyrics/the props support the plot/underline the feeling of …

- The soundtrack/lighting/editing establishes/re-inforces the mood of the scene.
- The camera movement creates a feeling of …
- The camerawork/soundtrack helps to …/under-lines/emphasizes …
- The close-ups reveal his/her emotional state.
- The props in her room characterize her as a … person.

▶ **DVD**   **PRACTICE**

You are going to watch an extract from *The Hunger Games*, a 2012 science fiction film. It depicts a dystopian state in which every year a group of teenagers, the 'tributes', are forced to take part in a televised event and fight each other to the death until only the victor remains alive. In the extract you are going to watch the protagonist Katniss is being chased by other tributes.

1 Watch the extract and use a viewing log to structure your observations. Work with a partner to complete your notes.

2 The extract is full of contrasts: the wild forest vs. the television headquarters, Katniss on her own vs. the group of other tributes, the wild chase vs. a moment of rest when the other tributes let Katniss be for some time. Choose one of the contrasts, watch the extract again and examine the cinematic devices used to create this contrast.

Speaking skills (monologues and dialogues)

▶ SF 24 Giving a presentation

Informing an audience about a topic is an important skill to master and one that will be useful not only in school (classroom presentations, etc.) but also in later life (university, work, etc.). To give a successful presentation the following steps may be a helpful guide.

PLANNING A PRESENTATION

Step 1: Find out about the general framework for your talk, e.g.
- its topic
- the time limit for your presentation
- your audience and their background knowledge of the topic
- the kind of equipment available (smartboard, blackboard, flip chart, digital/video projector, laptop).

Step 2: Research your subject and make notes in English. (▶ SF 15: Marking up a text / Making and taking notes; ▶ SF 5: Doing research)
- If you are working in a team, decide who is going to work on which aspect.
- Use different sources so that you cover all relevant aspects and your information is reliable.

PREPARING A PRESENTATION

Step 1: Decide what information you need and work out a structure for it. (▶ SF 8: Structuring ideas)

Step 2: Think of ways to make your talk interesting and easy to understand for your audience:
- Plan the beginning of your presentation carefully: refer to interesting facts or give anecdotes which lead to the topic of your presentation.
- Remember the KISS-rule: **K**eep **i**t **s**hort and **s**imple!
- Keep your audience's attention by naming interesting or funny details or examples.
- Check whether there are words or phrases that need to be explained to the audience so that they can follow your presentation.
- If suitable, prepare charts, visuals, diagrams, etc. to present facts and figures visually. (▶ SF 7: Making visual aids)

Step 3: Prepare a handout or poster or use a presentation programme to accompany your presentation:
- Design them in a way that helps your audience to follow your presentation (cf. the tips on the right).

  Find a tool to make your poster here:
   Webcode context-50

- Proofread your material. (▶ SF 40: Proofreading)
- Before the actual presentation, make sure that any electronic media you want to use are working and that you can handle them.

> ■ **TIP**
>
> When preparing a **poster** or **wall display**:
> - Give it a clear structure or line of thought that guides the reader through the various sections of the poster.
> - Make it visually attractive and informative.
> - Present complex information visually, e.g. through diagrams.
> - Keep a good balance between visuals and written information.
> - Make sure that the writing can be read from the back of the room.
> - Use bullet-points, short sentences or key-words and try to avoid any redundancies.
> - Indicate the sources you used.
>
> When preparing a **handout**:
> - Decide if you want to distribute it before the presentation so that it helps your audience to follow your talk (in that case it might make sense to leave room for notes) or if you want to hand it out after the presentation to remind your audience of the main points (in that case tell them that a handout will be distributed at the end).
> - Give it a clear structure.
> - Present the most important information, key quotations, diagrams and/or charts on it.
> - Use bullet-points, short sentences or key-words and try to avoid any redundancies.
> - Indicate the sources you used.

Step 4: If you are giving your presentation in a team
- decide who is going to present which parts
- check that the different parts add up to a coherent presentation
- make sure that everybody takes part in the presentation.

Step 5: Prepare notes that will guide you through your presentation and help you to speak freely without reading from the page. (▶ SF 15: Marking up a text / Making and taking notes)

> ■ **TIP**
>
> Write keywords or notes on index cards, number the cards and use only them during your presentation.

Step 6: Practise your presentation:
- Look up the pronunciation of difficult words in a dictionary.
- Practise your presentation in front of friends or a mirror or record it, e.g. using a smartphone. If you are doing a team presentation, practise as a team.
- Make sure you don't exceed your time limit.

Find an online dictionary here:
Webcode context-52

Find a recording tool here:
Webcode context-55

DOING A PRESENTATION

Step 1: Give your presentation:
- Wait until the audience are quiet, then greet them and give an overview of your presentation.

> ■ **LANGUAGE HELP**
>
> 'Hello everybody. My talk today is going to be on … First I will give you a general idea of … After that I will tell you more about … At the end of the talk I will explain why … and give you some examples.'

- Speak clearly, loudly and not too fast. Make suitable pauses.
- Speak freely and don't read out complete sentences.
- Avoid extremely long sentences and too many figures or new words. Remember that your audience can only listen to your presentation once.
- Refer to your poster, wall display or handout if appropriate, but don't read it out word for word.
- Try to maintain eye-contact with your classmates.
- If you use new or difficult words, help your audience by writing them on the board and explaining them.

> ■ **TROUBLE SPOT**
>
> **word by word** = one word at a time, one word after the other
> **word for word** = in exactly the same words

Step 2: Round off your presentation by
- summarizing the most important aspects
- thanking your audience for their attention
- asking them if they have any questions.

> ■ **LANGUAGE HELP**
>
> 'So, as I have pointed out, … It is important to keep in mind that … That was my presentation on … Thank you for listening. I hope you enjoyed my/our presentation. Do you have any questions?'

·····▶

▶ SF 25 Giving a speech

When you give a speech you want to reach your audience and persuade them of your point of view on a topic. In order to achieve this goal, you need two things: firstly, a well-structured text with carefully chosen words and *stylistic means and secondly, an effective way of delivering it.

PLANNING A SPEECH

Step 1: Find out about the general framework for your speech, e.g.
- its topic
- the time available

- task: convince your student body council that your school should become more environmentally friendly

- the purpose of your speech: do you want it to inspire people/lead to a specific action/…?
- your audience and their background knowledge/attitudes.

- purpose: lead to action

- audience: some students have talked about it in class; some might be tackling the issue already

Step 2: Brainstorm and/or research your topic: collect any ideas, stories or arguments that fit your topic and form your own opinion on it. Make notes (▶ SF 15: Marking up a text/Making and taking notes).

- things you can do every day, e.g. separate rubbish, turn off lights, don't use paper cups for your coffee, …
- may be inconvenient at first, but will become normal

PREPARING A SPEECH

Step 1: From your ideas choose essential points that are relevant to your topic and the message you wish to get across to your audience. Make notes and organize them
- by structuring them into introduction/body/conclusion (▶ SF 8: Structuring ideas)
- by choosing the best two to five ideas for the body of your speech and putting them in a suitable order (▶ SF 8: Structuring ideas).

- introduction: watching The Day after Tomorrow made me depressed – how can I make a change?
- body: little things done by normal people can make a change; it's no use blaming politicians for not acting; …
- conclusion: be the change!

Step 2: Unless you are a highly experienced speaker, write out your complete speech:
- Choose the correct *register for your specific audience, e.g. scientific, colloquial, … (▶ LP 11: Using the right register)

- register: colloquial, e.g. 'Look at this school. We are a huge number of people. Think about the mountain of rubbish we produce every day. Is it really necessary?'

- Use your own experience.

- personal experience: 'We throw away a lot of different things at school: paper, Kleenex, sweet wrappers, broken pens.'

- Use clear and short sentences. Make logical connections clear by using linking words (▶ SF 38: Writing a well-structured text).

- short sentences: 'So, take a stand. Ask the school for separate bins for paper, plastic and other rubbish.'

- Be persuasive: use *stylistic devices to convince your audience, e.g. *contrasts, *rhetorical questions, *enumerations, *alliterations, direct address of audience …

- *contrast: 'A small act – like closing the window before you leave – can have a big effect.'*

Step 3: Write introduction and conclusion:
- Write a conclusion: sum up the main points, give a final effective example supporting your message, further food for thought or an appeal for action.
- When you have prepared most of your speech, think of a good introduction, e.g. a true story, a quotation, a rhetorical question, an interesting statistic, a joke.

- *conclusion: 'You could argue that some students might not be interested in environmentally friendly behaviour and I have to agree. That is why I need your support. Set an example. Do the right thing. Help our school become active in our fight for a healthier planet.'*
- *introduction: 'Last Saturday I watched the film The Day after Tomorrow and felt really depressed. I don't want my world to be flooded or frozen over. I want to be able to live in a beautiful, clean world. So if I want that, what can I do to make a change?'*

Step 4: Prepare the presentation of your speech:
- Print out your speech in a format that is easy to read out from (fonts and margins not too small). If you know your speech by heart write keywords or notes on index cards.
- Mark passages and words that you want to emphasize.

Step 5: Practise your speech by reading or saying it out loud (check the pronunciation of difficult words if necessary). Even if you read it, try to make it sound as if you were delivering it freely. Practise it in front of friends or a mirror or record it, e.g. using a smartphone. Make sure you don't exceed your time limit.

> **TIP**
> Write keywords or notes on index cards, number the cards and use only them during your presentation.

Find a recording tool here:
 Webcode context-55

GIVING A SPEECH

Giving a speech is not like reading something out (even if you have written it down). Try to speak as freely as possible and maintain the attention of your audience.

- Wait until the audience are quiet, then greet them and state your topic.
- Speak clearly, loudly and not too fast. Pause in suitable places.
- Use facial expressions and gestures to emphasize important points.
- Try to maintain eye-contact with your listeners.
- Thank your audience for their attention.

Find a tool for improving your speaking skills here:
Webcode context-51

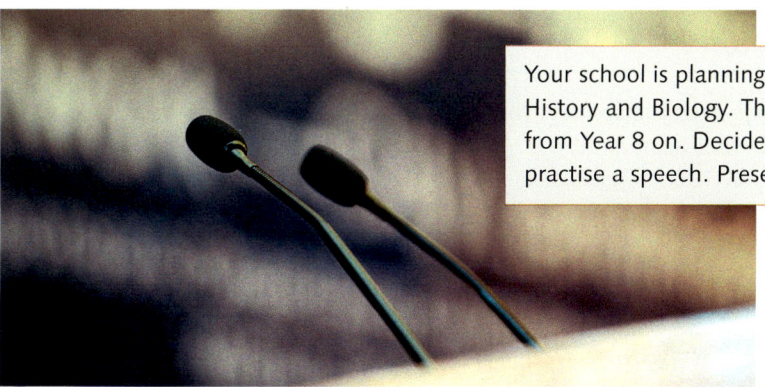

> **PRACTICE**
> Your school is planning to introduce bilingual classes for History and Biology. The lessons are to be held in English from Year 8 on. Decide on your position, then write and practise a speech. Present it to your classmates.

▶ SF 26 Taking part in an interview

In lesson situations but also when applying for a job you may be asked to take part in interviews, either asking or answering questions. It is essential to prepare for an interview and to follow some general guidelines.

PREPARING FOR AN INTERVIEW

- On the basis of your role card or the task given prepare questions you are going to ask (as interviewer) or think of possible answers to questions you might be asked (as interviewee).
- For **job interviews,** you need to be prepared to say why you might be suitable for the offered position. Do research on the company you are applying for and prepare some questions you might want to ask. It might be useful to rehearse a job interview with a friend or parent.

MASTERING THE INTERVIEW

- Speak loud enough and clearly. Be aware of your non-verbal communication: Try to maintain eye-contact with the interviewer/interviewee and smile when saying hello at the beginning or thanking your interviewer/interviewee at the end. (▶ CC 4: Meeting and greeting)
- As an **interviewer**: Start off by using your prepared questions, but be flexible – phrase new questions if some interesting aspect is touched on or rephrase a question if you feel that it was not answered fully.
- As an **interviewee**: Take your time to think about your answers rather than blurting out a reply that does not show you in a good light. Do not simply answer questions with *yes* or *no*, but use your answers to show your qualifications or to express your thoughts. If you have not understood a question fully, ask the interviewer to clarify it.

■ LANGUAGE HELP

Interviewer
- Nice to meet you./Thank you for coming.
- To start off, would you like to say something about …?/First, let me ask you …/My next question would be …/If you think so, then why didn't you …/Let's get back to my original question …
- You just said …, how does that relate to …?
- Thank you very much for taking part in this interview.

Interviewee
- Nice to meet you too./Thank you for inviting me today./I am fine, thank you.
- I am not sure I have understood your question correctly./Sorry, could you rephrase that?/I'm glad you asked that question because …/… is very important to me, as …/A good example of the aspect you mention is …/Let me explain that in some more detail.
- Thank you for the chance to speak to you.

PRACTICE

You want to find out your fellow students' priorities for their future lives – earning a lot of money or following their dreams? Choose someone from your class and prepare and conduct an interview with them.

▶ SF 27 Having a discussion

In a (classroom) discussion you exchange ideas and opinions with others. Discussions may be spontaneous or they may be more formal, e.g. in panel discussions or debates (▶ SF 28: Having a debate). If possible, you should prepare for the discussion so that you have your arguments and useful words and phrases ready.

THE PREPARATION STAGE

Step 1: Research the topic and make notes (▶ SF 5: Doing research, ▶ SF 15: Marking up a text/Making and taking notes). Form an opinion on it and note down arguments. In a role-play you may have to take a position which is not really your own, so make sure that your arguments are in line with *your role*. Think of counter-arguments and of ways to reject them.

Step 2: Structure your notes (▶ SF 8: Structuring ideas) and arrange them in a way that helps you to have the relevant facts ready during the discussion.

Step 3: Prepare an initial statement on the topic; this will ease your way into the discussion. If you are assigned a specific role, be prepared to introduce yourself.

THE DISCUSSION STAGE

Step 1: State your point of view on the topic, e.g. give your prepared statement.

Step 2: Listen to what others say and refer back to their statements, e.g. by saying which of their arguments do not convince you and why. You might also counter an argument by asking a provocative question. Remember to bring in the facts you collected to support your view.

■ LANGUAGE HELP

Stating your opinion	Agreeing	Disagreeing
• In my opinion/view … • As far as I'm concerned … • Well, I'd say … • It's a fact that … • The way I see it, … • Personally, I think … • If you ask me … • It seems to me that … • I think/feel/reckon/believe … • First of all …/To start with I'd like to point out that … • There can be no doubt that … • Nobody will deny that … • I'm absolutely convinced that …	• I quite agree. • I couldn't agree with you more. • Quite!/Exactly!/Precisely! • Certainly!/Definitely! • You're quite right. • I agree entirely/completely. • That's just how I see it/feel about it. • You've got a good point there. • That's exactly how I see it. • Yes, indeed.	**Polite disagreement:** • I'm afraid I don't quite agree there. • I'm not so sure, really. • Do you really think so? • Well, that's one way of looking at it, but … • I'm not convinced that … • Well, I have my doubts about that.
Asking for clarification	**Signalling that you would like to say something**	**Strong disagreement:** • I doubt that very much. • That doesn't convince me at all. • I don't agree with you at all. • I disagree entirely. • It's not as simple as that.
• I'm sorry, but I don't understand/know what you mean by … • Could you give an example/explain that, please? • Can you prove that?/I would be very interested in some data/examples that prove your statement.	• May I interrupt?/Excuse me, I would like to add to that. • An important aspect is missing here, namely … • That illustrates perfectly what … • Can I just say/explain that …? • I would just like to jump in here, to clarify that … • I hope you don't mind me interrupting, but it is important to stress …	**Adding a point** • Another thing is … • What's more, … • On top of that, … • We must also consider … • I would like to add to that … • Have you ever considered/thought about …
Buying time		
• Well, that is an interesting point./I see what you mean. • I think the question we were discussing was …	• You have given your opinion, however … • Why don't we see what X has to say about that?	

Step 3: At the end of the discussion, summarize your point of view or your main arguments.

■ LANGUAGE HELP

• I have shown that …/It has become clear that …
• Let me just state again that it is vital to …/The most important argument is …/At the end of the day you can't deny that …

• If we don't … then…/In spite of everything we have heard from the other side …

•••••▶

Step 4 *(optional):* If a chairperson has moderated the discussion, he/she may summarize the main line of the discussion and round it off.

LANGUAGE HELP

- We have seen/heard that …/The majority on the panel/in the audience thinks that …/Some are in favour of …, others against it, but in general you can say that …

- The general trend seems to be …/On the one hand, … On the other hand, …
- All in all this discussion has shown …

▶ SF 28 Having a debate

A debate is a formal discussion of a 'motion' (proposal) that ends in a vote. Similar to a discussion, the aim of a debate is to present arguments as convincingly as possible, so participants need well-prepared arguments as well as rhetorical skills. There is often a particular set of rules for the debate, which participants have to agree on before holding the debate. The following steps outline how you could go about holding a formal debate.

Step 1: Organizing a debate

The 'motion' (i.e. a controversial topic) is the starting point for a debate. Often it is provided by the teacher, but in other cases, your class may be asked to suggest a number of motions and then agree on one of them. The motion is then phrased in a formalized way:

- 'This house proposes that *(… students should be allowed to use smart phones during lessons).*'
- 'This house would *(… abolish the death penalty world-wide).*'
- 'This house believes that *(… minimum wages are a threat to the German economy).*'

The class is then divided into two groups, one for and one against the motion.
Usually a chairperson and a timekeeper are chosen and a time-limit for each speaker is specified (often 3–6 minutes per speaker).

Step 2: Preparing the debate

- In your group (either for or against the motion) research the topic, collect and note down arguments for your side. Your personal opinion on the motion is not relevant here – you must argue for your team. List and rank the arguments that you have for your team in order of importance.
- Write your arguments on index-cards so that you have them ready during the debate.
- Think of arguments for the opposing view and ways to reject them.
- Choose speakers for your side. The other students are the audience, called the 'floor'.

Step 3: Holding the debate

A debate follows a clear structure. The 'chair' will make sure that the rules are followed and that time-limits are respected.

A debate in the House of Commons

Team in favour of the motion

FIRST PROPOSAL: The first speaker proposes the motion (= argues in favour of the motion) and gives some main arguments.

> **LANGUAGE HELP**
> - This house firmly believes that …
> - Not only is … but also …

SECOND PROPOSAL: The second speaker of the affirmative team presents further arguments in favour of the motion. He/she also responds to the aspects mentioned by the first speaker of the opposing team, outlining where the positions conflict.

> **LANGUAGE HELP**
> - The opposing team has tried to create the impression that …
> - However, we can prove that …
> - It is therefore evident that …

Team opposing the motion

FIRST OPPOSITION: The first speaker of this team opposes the motion (= argues against the motion).

> **LANGUAGE HELP**
> - We strongly advise against following the proposed motion because …
> - The most obvious reason for this is that …

SECOND OPPOSITION: The second speaker of the opposing team presents further arguments against the motion and/or restates the position of his/her team. The main task here is to defeat the arguments presented by the team in favour of the motion.

> **LANGUAGE HELP**
> - Again it needs to be stated that by following the arguments, …
> - … would lead to/cause …

A short recess may be taken here to prepare for the following 'rebuttals'.

FIRST REBUTTAL: The team against the motion defends their arguments and tries to rebut the arguments of the affirmative team.

SECOND REBUTTAL: The affirmative team supports their point of view and tries to rebut the arguments of the opposing team.

THIRD REBUTTAL: The opposing team give their closing statements.

FOURTH REBUTTAL: The affirmative team give their closing statements.

Rules for the debate:
- Speakers may not interrupt each other at any point.
- Speakers must wait their turn.
- The time-limits as given by the chair must be respected.
- Speakers must remain polite and respectful of the other team.
- Statements must be backed up by giving examples or proof, by referring to research, experience, etc.

Step 4: Concluding the debate
- The 'floor' (i.e. the audience) may ask questions and/or present their ideas on the topic.
- The 'house' (i.e. everyone present) may take a vote on the motion by a show of hands, not based on what they personally agree or disagree with, but on who made the better case by presenting the best arguments and speaking most convincingly.
- Members of the two debating teams may get some feedback from their classmates.

Writing skills

▶ SF 29 Writing a formal letter or email

When applying for a place at university, asking for information from a company or organization, etc., your email or letter should follow certain formal rules.

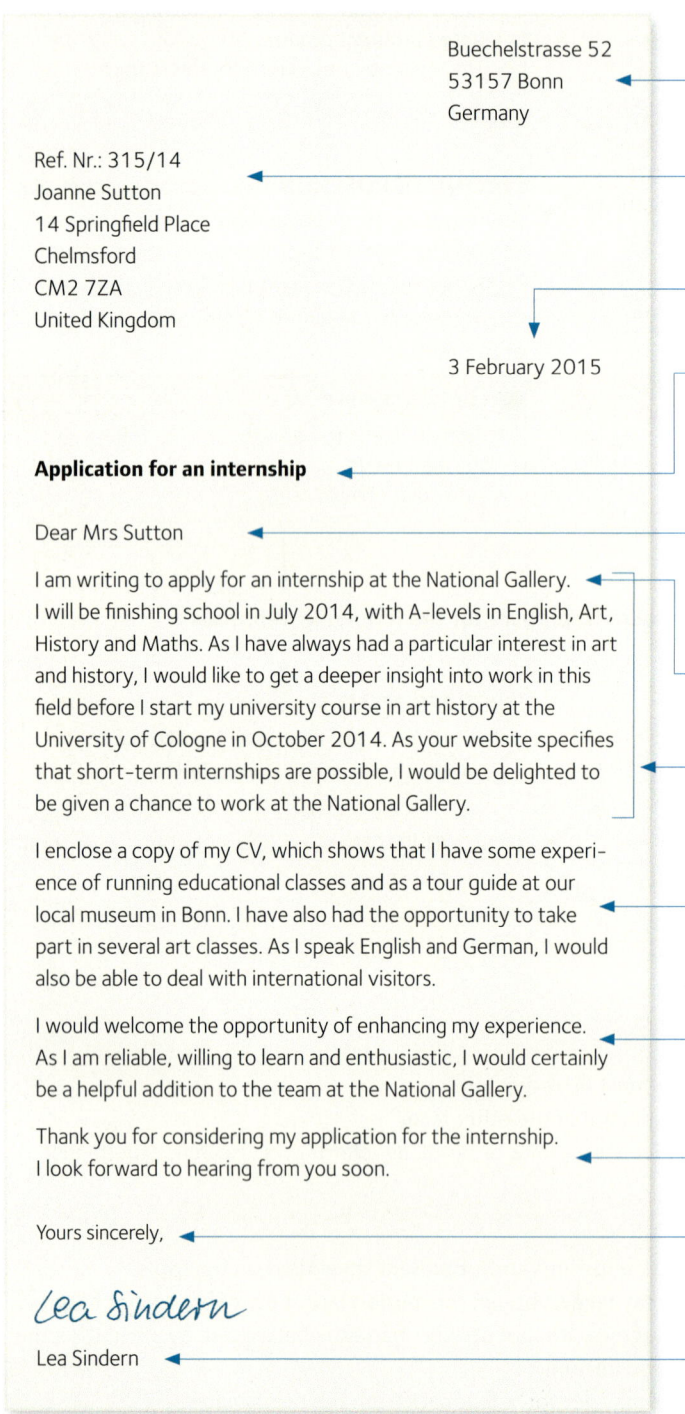

Buechelstrasse 52
53157 Bonn
Germany

Write your address (without your name) in the top right corner of your **letter**. Don't use typical German letters like *ä, ö, ü* or *ß*.

Ref. Nr.: 315/14
Joanne Sutton
14 Springfield Place
Chelmsford
CM2 7ZA
United Kingdom

Write the address of the person or company you are writing to on the left. If you have a reference number, write it above the recipient's address.

3 February 2015

Write the date on the right.

Show what the letter is about in a heading.

Application for an internship

Start your letter with *Dear Madam or Sir* if you don't know the recipient's name, otherwise write *Dear Mr/Mrs/Ms …* In BE, there is usually no comma after the greeting; in AE a colon after the greeting is used in formal letters.

Dear Mrs Sutton

I am writing to apply for an internship at the National Gallery. I will be finishing school in July 2014, with A-levels in English, Art, History and Maths. As I have always had a particular interest in art and history, I would like to get a deeper insight into work in this field before I start my university course in art history at the University of Cologne in October 2014. As your website specifies that short-term internships are possible, I would be delighted to be given a chance to work at the National Gallery.

Always start with a capital letter (e.g. *With great interest, I read …*).

State the reason you are writing in the opening paragraph.

I enclose a copy of my CV, which shows that I have some experience of running educational classes and as a tour guide at our local museum in Bonn. I have also had the opportunity to take part in several art classes. As I speak English and German, I would also be able to deal with international visitors.

Add more detailed information in the following paragraphs (reasons for applying, qualifications, why you are the right person for the position etc.).

I would welcome the opportunity of enhancing my experience. As I am reliable, willing to learn and enthusiastic, I would certainly be a helpful addition to the team at the National Gallery.

Use long forms (*I am/We are/I would*) rather than short forms (*I'm/We're/I'd*) and abbreviations.

Thank you for considering my application for the internship. I look forward to hearing from you soon.

If you are asking for information or a favour, thank the recipient in advance.

Yours sincerely,

Finish your letter with *Yours faithfully* if you don't know the recipient's name, otherwise write *Yours sincerely* (AE: *Sincerely, Sincerely yours* or *Yours truly*).

Lea Sindern

Lea Sindern

Type your name at the end of the letter, leaving space for a handwritten signature.

When writing a **formal email**
- you don't need to include the recipient's address or the date in the body of your email, as they appear automatically in the header
- open and close your mail the same way you would when writing a formal letter
- do not use emoticons, smileys, etc.
- type your name and contact details at the bottom.

A **letter to the editor** follows most of the conventions of a formal letter or email. Note the following, however:
- Nowadays, letters to the editor are very often sent by email. Watch out for contact information on the magazine's or paper's website.
- Your letter should be brief.
- Start like this: *Sir or Madam* (i.e. leave out *Dear*).
- Omit the closing remarks (*Yours faithfully/sincerely*).
- Don't forget to give your name, address and phone number.

▶ SF 30 Writing an application

If you want to apply for a holiday job or a position in a company (e.g. an internship), you should send them a cover letter and a CV (curriculum vitae).

THE COVER LETTER
The cover letter for an application (cf. p. 286) follows the rules of a formal letter (▶ SF 29). Since you are presenting yourself, it is important to avoid mistakes and to use formal language (▶ LP 11: Using the right register). State in what ways you are suited for the position you are applying for. Show that you have collected information about the company you are writing to and that you have a real interest in the position advertised. Mention what documents you are enclosing. At the end of the letter, express hope for a reply or an invitation to an interview.

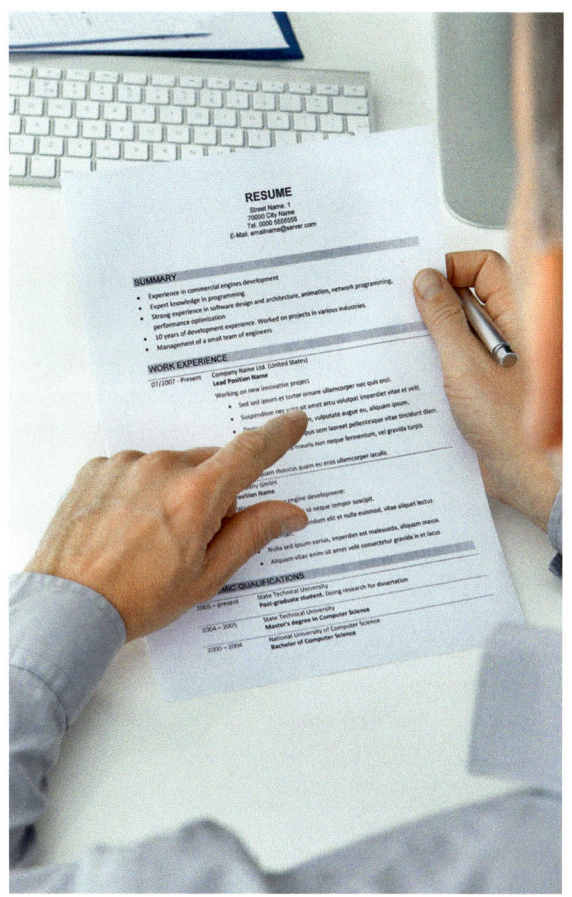

THE CV (*AE*: résumé ['rezəmeɪ])
Your CV (cf. p. 288) gives information about you, about your education, qualifications, etc. to the person you are applying to. A CV should be clear and effective – remember the KISS rule ('Keep it short and simple'). Use a clear and easy-to-read font, highlight particularly relevant information, and don't forget to check your CV for spelling mistakes.

•••••▶

CURRICULUM VITAE
Lukas Meister

Rheinuferstrasse 2, 53158 Bonn, Germany
Telephone: +49(0)201 000 8177 Mobile: +49 178 000 4235
Email: Lukasmeister@mail.de

Give your personal details: name, contact details, nationality, etc.

Personal statement

I have always enjoyed working with visual media, i. e. films, photographs, etc. and with computers. Being creative, I enjoy developing ideas to solve problems.
English is my favourite subject at school and I expect to improve my language skills further and to become a more independent person by spending time in the UK.

Add a personal statement explaining why you are suitable for the specific place or job.

Education

| 2008–date | Secondary School: Alfred-Krupp-Schule, Essen |
| 2004–2008 | Primary/Elementary School Gartenstrasse, Essen |

Show the stages of your education so far (schools, exams, etc.).

Qualifications/skills

IT skills	Excellent knowledge of MS Word, PowerPoint, Excel, web design, photoshop
Language skills	German native speaker; good written and spoken English, basic French
Technology	Winner of the gold medal 2014 for 'school inventors' in the 'Junior Ingenieur Akademie' (school engineering course)

List your qualifications and present your key skills, especially those the employer is looking for.

Work experience

| May 2014 | Placement: two weeks at local IT company, organized by my school |

Give information on any work experience.

Hobbies and interests

Member of school drama club, member of school computer club, member of after-school basketball club. I enjoy listening to and playing music and making films.

Write something about your hobbies or interests.

References
Available on request

Note down that references are available on request.

Read the job advert on the right. Then write an application, consisting of a cover letter and your curriculum vitae, for the position of management assistant. (You may also make up a person applying for the job.)

SELLIT

International advertising company based in Nottingham, UK, is looking for a Management Assistant (entry level) for office-based work.
Requirements:
• degree in International Management
• good IT-skills
• fluent English (spoken and written)
• long-term availability.

CONTACT:
Sellit
Peter Miller
pmiller@sellit.co.uk
12 Springfield Road
Nottingham
NG1 5ZA
Great Britain

▶ SF31 Writing a summary

When you work with written or spoken texts, you are often asked to summarize the text or certain aspects of it. To do this, you need a proper overview of the text, its content and its message. Then you have to decide what to include in your summary and what to leave out. The following steps and rules can guide you.

PLANNING YOUR SUMMARY

Step 1: Listen to or read the text carefully. Either make notes or mark the most important words and phrases (▶ SF15: Marking up a text / Making and taking notes). Find out which text type you are dealing with (▶ SF16: Identifying text types).

Step 2: Listen to or read the text again and try to answer the '5 Ws' (*Who? What? Where? When? Why?* Perhaps also *What is the consequence?*). To get a better understanding of the text, you may also want to use the reading strategies explained in ▶ SF14: Reading strategies.

Step 3: Decide which passages of the text (marked green in the example below, cf. *Context* pp. 172ff.) contain essential information that needs to be part of your summary and which passages can be left out. Take your time to check which parts of the text contain examples, numbers, comparisons, quotes, *imagery, direct speech, etc. – these parts do not belong in a summary.

Linguistic diplomacy: the Eurovision Song Contest R.L.G.

Where?/What? Last Saturday saw Denmark win the Eurovision Song Contest, the country's third win in the contest's history. A prototypically apple-cheeked[1] blonde took the trophy for her *Who?* country, but she did so with the rather un-Danish name of Emmelie de Forest and the *What?* equally un-Danish title, 'Only Teardrops'.

The contest has always been about more than music. Every year comes a slew[2] of artic- 5
What/Why? les about the political nature of the voting. Countries that share ethnic or political friend-
(Examples) ships routinely give each other high marks: Greece and Cyprus typically give each other the maximum of 12 points while stiffing[3] Turkey with *nul points*[4], for example. Estonia and Latvia this year gave Russia 12 points, no doubt because those countries' large Russian populations voted for their neighbour. 10

What? Language, of course, plays a role in this as well. 'Ethnicity'[5] in Europe is often linguis- tic: an ethnic Russian is not apparent on the streets of Riga until he opens his mouth. *Why?* Linguistic neighbours will tend to be generous to one another. Finland and Estonia are *(Examples/* friendly not only because they are nearby but because their Finno-Ugric languages resem- *numbers)* ble each other, while being utterly unrelated to their neigbours'. (Hungarian is also 15 Finno-Ugric.) Each country can give 12 points to only one other country, and this year Denmark and Sweden gave their 12's to Norway, Norway its 12 to Sweden, as befits[6] the Scandinavian language continuum.

But the Scandinavians share something else besides apple-cheeked blondes and North *What?* Germanic languages: their tendency to sing in English. In that, they are like most coun- 20 tries nowadays. But some interesting variation clouds the picture.

From: *The Economist*, 20 May 2013

·····▶

---

[1] **apple-cheeked** having cheeks (= *Wangen*) the colour of apples [2] **slew** (*ifml*) large number
[3] **stiff sb. with sth.** (*here*) reject / mildly insult sb. [4] **nul points** [nyl pwɛ] (*French*) nil (= no) points
[5] **ethnicity** fact of belonging to a particular race [6] **befit sb.** (*fml*) be suitable for sb.

WRITING YOUR SUMMARY

Step 1: Write your summary in your own words.

1 Write an introductory phrase, mentioning the essential aspects, such as the title, *author, topic, main message and source of the text. (▶ LP 18: Writing about texts)

> ### ■ LANGUAGE HELP
>
> - The story/text is about …
> - The text deals with …
> - In the text the reader gets to know …
> - The topic of the text is …
> - The article shows …

The article 'Linguistic diplomacy: the Eurovision Song Contest', written by an author abbreviated as R.L.G. and published in The Economist *on 20 May 2013, investigates the languages of songs entered for the Eurovision Song Contest and points out that English has had a leading role over the years.*

2 Use the present tense (▶ LP 3: Simple present and present perfect). Don't copy the original text – use your own words. Use linking words to connect your ideas (▶ SF 38: Writing a well-structured text).

In the article, the author takes Denmark's win of the last ESC as a starting point to look into different influencing factors of the voting.
After mentioning political reasons, i.e. neighbouring or politically close countries, the writer moves on to the main topic: the chosen languages of the songs being entered. Countries seem to give more points to songs from countries sharing the same language. Using the starting point of Denmark's win again, the writer focuses on the dominance of English …

3 Round off your text by restating the main message or *action.

All in all, the text focuses on … and invites the reader to make up their mind whether …

Step 2: Check your summary. Does it contain the most important facts and ideas from the original text? Have you left out examples, unnecessary details, etc.? Have you checked the spelling, punctuation, tenses, etc.? (▶ SF 40: Proofreading, ▶ LP 12: Spelling)

> ### PRACTICE
>
> Summarize the extract from Alan Bennet's *The Uncommon Reader* (pp. 96f.) in no more than 200 words.

▶ SF 32 Writing a review

When writing a review, you provide information on a book, play or film you have read or watched, as well as expressing your opinion about it. Reviews are meant to either recommend the work in question or to discourage people from reading or seeing it.

PREPARING YOUR REVIEW

Step 1: Read the book or watch the film/play you want to write about, making notes of interesting, very good or very bad aspects. It may be useful to consider typical elements of the text-type in question (▶ SF 16: Identifying text types).

Step 2: Add to your notes, writing down important information about the book or the film. Structure your ideas (▶ SF 8). The grid on the next page will help you to identify the relevant aspects, but you could also use a mind map to structure your ideas.

> *Find a mindmapping tool here:*
> 🖐 **Webcode** context-53

Header	
Title	*2012*
Running time	*157 minutes*
Your rating	*** (out of five) (= okay)*
Year	*2009*
Director's name	*Roland Emmerich*

Introduction	
Basic information: type of movie/book, characters	• *disaster film / science fiction action film* • *science fiction writer Jackson Curtis tries to rescue his two children and his ex-wife from a geological and meteorological super-disaster*

Main part	
Short summary of the plot (Be careful: perhaps your readers don't want to be told the ending before they have read the book or watched the film themselves.) Cast/characters	• *2009: scientist discovers that the temperature of the Earth is rising unexpectedly; international leaders plan to save a certain number of people on Arks* • *2012: Jackson Curtis (John Cusack), a divorced writer of science fiction, takes children Noah (Liam James) and Lily (Morgan Lily) camping in Yellowstone National Park, hears fears about the end of the world by Charlie Frost (Woody Harrelson)* • *they return home; earthquakes are everywhere; Jackson rents plane for his children and ex-wife; they leave LA before California is destroyed* • *family tries to get to the Arks; the President of the US dies in a tsunami* • *Jackson and his family reach the Arks and manage to get on board*

Scenes from the film 2012

Comments	
Your opinion, e.g. on *plot, *actors, *characters, *dialogues, special effects, the 'message', etc.	• *great special effects in the depiction of the catastrophe, impressive when famous buildings collapse* • *dramatic music/great sound* • *the film is fun to watch if you like action films* • *John Cusack convincing as Jackson Curtis: not the typical action hero, but likeable and a bit quirky – good contrast to the action scenes* *BUT:* • *parts of the film are not logical, i.e. characters use mobile phones while the earth is exploding around them* • *film has some quite scary parts* • *film is far too long* • *all in all, film seems to be a bit far-fetched*

Conclusion	
Summary of your opinion, recommendation/target group	• *quite good science fiction disaster film with great action scenes* • *too long and partly exaggerated* • *only suitable for lovers of action/disaster movies – don't expect too much!*

WRITING YOUR REVIEW

• Start with a catchy title and a **header** which contains basic facts. • Use the present tense. • Avoid imprecise words like *good*, *really bad*, etc. • Start with an **introductory paragraph** with basic information.	*A film review:* **2012:** *not quite the perfect disaster* *2009 running time: 157 minutes rating:* *** *(okay)* *The science fiction disaster film 2012, directed by Roland Emmerich, is an action-packed and generally enjoyable film, which has some riveting images and lots of gripping scenes, but which is also rather far-fetched in many places …*
• In the **main part** first give a short summary of the plot without giving away the end of the film/book.	*After a scientist …* *After having obtained a map from Charlie, who dies while reporting about the events, the family tries to get to the Arks, …*
• Then **comment** on the positive or negative aspects of the book/film/play.	*The special effects in 2012 are definitely worth seeing: images of the earth being destroyed are powerful and often scary. The special effects are sometimes truly breath-taking …* *… all this is underlined by a dramatic score. So for all lovers of action films, 2012 definitely is fun to watch. It even has some good acting: John Cusack shines in his role as …*
• Finish your review by **summarizing** the main aspects and by giving a **recommendation** whether the book/film is worth watching/reading. • Use linking words to connect your ideas. (▶ SF 38: Writing a well-structured text; ▶ LP 12: Linking words and phrases; ▶ LP 15: Connecting your thoughts)	*But is the film a real masterpiece? Unfortunately not. It is irritating for the viewers that …* *… And last but not least, the film might be considered just a bit too scary for the faint-hearted!* *All in all, it might have been a good idea to tone the film down a little.* *So here is my final verdict. Is 2012 a perfect film or is it a disaster? It is neither one nor the other but it is a perfect disaster film, and lovers of action films and disaster are going to get their money's worth – and perhaps even more than they bargained for. However, if you are looking for a scientifically correct, logical plot and deeper insights into life, I recommend finding a different film for your Saturday night.*
• Proofread your text. (▶ SF 40: Proofreading; ▶ LP 17: Spelling)	

PRACTICE

Choose a film that you enjoyed watching in the past six months. Write a short review, focusing on the film's strengths and – if you found any – weaknesses and recommending it to your classmates.

▶ SF 33 Writing a report

Reports offer factual information about a recent event. The information is given in a chronological order and the language used is objective and formal.

The following instructions will guide you through the steps of writing a report. Your task is to write a report on a family dispute that caused extreme reactions on the parents' side.

Steps	Example
Step 1: Gather as much information about the event as possible. Try to answer the '5 Ws' (who? where? what? when? why? and if possible: what are the consequences?). If your report is based on a fictitious event (e.g. from a novel or play) you might need to add missing details such as last names, place names or dates.	(The story deals with the experiences of second-generation Indian immigrants in London. The narrator, Karim, is visiting his cousin, Jamila. Jamila and her father, Anwar, are fighting.) 'What's going on here?' I asked her. 'Look at him, Karim, he hasn't eaten or drunk anything for eight days! He'll die, Karim, if he doesn't eat anything won't he!' 'Yes, you'll cop it[1], boss, if you don't eat your grub[2] like everyone else.' 'I won't eat. I will die. If Gandhi could shove out the English from India by not eating, I can get my family to obey me by exactly the same.' 5 'What do you want her to do?' 'To marry the boy I have selected with my brother.' 'But it's old-fashioned, Uncle, out of date,' I explained. 'No one does that kind of thing now. They just marry the person they're 10 into, if they bother to get married at all.' This homily[3] on contemporary morals didn't exactly blow his mind[4]. 'That is not our way, boy. Our way is firm. She must do what I say or I will die. She will kill me.' From: Hanif Kureishi, *The Buddha of Suburbia*, 1990
Step 2: Put the information in chronological order. If necessary, add further details.	• *London* • *family of Indian origin* • *domestic dispute* • *daughter's refusal to agree to arranged marriage* • *day eight of father's hunger strike* • *...*

Step 3: Write your report:
- Use the simple past. (▶ LP 4: Present perfect and simple past)
- Start off with a summarizing sentence.
- If you write a longer report, divide it into paragraphs. (▶ SF 38: Writing a well-structured text)
- Use linking words to connect your ideas. (▶ SF 38: Writing a well-structured text)
- Make your report sound formal and matter-of-fact by using objective language and the passive voice where possible. (▶ LP 7: The passive; ▶ LP 11: Using the right register)
- Don't state personal thoughts, feelings or opinions. Try to focus on the facts, even if you use quotes from witnesses.

Step 4: Proofread yout text. (▶ SF 40; ▶ LP 17: Spelling)

---

[1] **cop it** *(BE, infml)* die   [2] **grub** *(infml)* food   [3] **homily** *(fml)* talk that gives advice on how to live
[4] **blow sb.'s mind** *(infml)* produce a strong feeling in sb.   ·····▶

LANGUAGE HELP

- On … an incident/occurrence of … was reported to …
- … domestic disputes such as …/another case of …
- It is believed/assumed that …
- … confirmed/claimed/revealed that …
- People are concerned about …/that …
- … took it to extremes when …/The intervention by … has not been successful …
- neighbours / a relative

PRACTICE

Look at the examples given for **Step 2**. Add further details from the text or invent them. Then put them in a suitable order and write your report. You may start like this: *Last night a middle-aged man of Indian origin was brought to St George's Hospital after having nearly starved himself in a hunger strike.*

▶ SF 34 Argumentative writing

When writing an argumentative text, you have to structure your text clearly and argue in a logical manner.

THE PLANNING STAGE

The starting point for an argumentative text can be a statement, a text you have read or a thesis you have been given, for example:

- 'For learners of English at German schools, Shakespeare's plays are incomprehensible, outdated and simply irrelevant. Therefore, his plays ought to be deleted from the curriculum of English classes.' Discuss.

In a written **discussion** (*Operator: discuss*) you give arguments for and against something and come to a justified conclusion. In a **comment** (*Operator: comment on/write a comment*) you want to convince the reader of your own opinion on an issue. You have to give arguments to support it and may even introduce counter-arguments which you refute to make your own arguments even stronger.

Step 1: Brainstorm your topic and make notes.

Step 2: Collect pro and con arguments.

Pro: *Shakespeare's plays ought to be deleted from the curriculum of English classes.*	**Con:** *Shakespeare's plays should not be deleted from the curriculum of English classes.*

- *Students struggle with the language and ideas of the Elizabethan Age and therefore don't enjoy studying Shakespeare's works.*
- *Students would benefit more from reading about events, characters and stories that are relevant to their own daily lives.*
- *…*

- *Shakespeare's works are a vital part of English culture – learning about him and his works is part of general knowledge.*
- *The topics and conflicts dealt with in Shakespeare's works are universal and can easily be transferred to a modern world (cf. the numerous modern versions of his plays).*
- *…*

Step 3: Arrange your arguments in a logical way, following either of these two patterns:

Pattern A Present the arguments for and against in separate paragraphs: 1. Introduction 2. Arguments pro 3. Arguments con 4. Conclusion	**Pattern B** Answer each argument immediately with its counter-argument: 1. Introduction 2. Argument 1 ▸ counter-argument 1 3. Argument 2 ▸ counter-argument 2 4. Argument 3 ▸ counter-argument 3 5. Conclusion

It is usually a good idea to finish with the argument that supports your position most strongly because this is the one the reader will remember most. Sometimes, however, it may be helpful not to postpone your strongest argument until the very end, because you want to catch the reader's attention.

- *my position: con*, *i.e. Shakespeare's works should not be deleted from the curriculum*
- *line of argument*: *pattern B (argument → counter-argument)*
- *argument 1*: *Most students find Shakespeare's texts difficult to read.*
  → *counter-argument 1*: *Shakespeare's texts are a vital part of English culture and are often referred to in everyday speech, so understanding them will eventually help students in everyday situations.*
- *argument 2*: *Shakespeare's texts are set in a remote past, so students can't profit from them in their everyday lives.* → *counter-argument 2*: *Once students have understood a text from Shakespeare's plays, they will realize that the themes dealt with depict universal conflicts which can easily be transferred to modern life.*
- *…*

THE WRITING STAGE

Step 1: Write your introduction. Refer to the topic. In a comment, you can give your point of view here.

Young people today are confronted with a world that is becoming more and more complex and which offers new technology, new information and new forms of literature. Classic literature, notably the plays by William Shakespeare, no longer seem to be relevant to some people today. So they claim that Shakespeare's plays ought to be taken off the curriculum for English classes.

Step 2: Present your line of argument, following either pattern A or B (see above). Use linking words (▸ SF 38: Writing a well-structured text; ▸ LP 14: Using linking words and phrases; ▸ LP 15: Connecting your thoughts)

Many students claim that reading Shakespeare's plays is a challenge and not worth the effort: they argue that not only his language but also the ideas from his times are incomprehensible to young people in the 21st century.
However, Shakespeare's plays are a vital part of English culture – quotations from his plays have found their way into everyday English, into sayings and proverbs. Knowing about Shakespeare's works provides an important background for understanding the heritage of modern language and modern texts.
When I was first made to read Romeo and Juliet *in school, I also struggled with Shakespeare's language and ideas and initially only saw the story in its historic context. But once I had fully understood …*

> ■ TIP
> Your arguments will appear more convincing if you
> 1. quote authorities, experts or statistics; present facts
> 2. refer to your personal experience whenever possible

·····▸

Step 3: Write a conclusion. Round off your text by stating your thesis once again, but do not give new information and do not use the same phrases that you used in the introduction.

In conclusion, it seems clear that taking Shakespeare's plays off the curriculum for English classes would mean that students would be denied the chance of getting to know …

Those precious works of English literature should therefore remain a compulsory part of the curriculum for English classes.

Step 4: Proofread yout text. (▶ SF 40)

▶ SF 35 Writing a character profile

Characters in fictional texts are presented through descriptions by the *narrator or other characters (*direct characterization) and through their appearance, language, attitude, behaviour, relationships to other characters and their thoughts and actions (*indirect characterization).

> ■ **TIP**
>
> When writing a character profile, do not describe *what* the character does, but explain *why* he/she says or does what he/she does.

Read the excerpt from the *novel *Payback Time* on pp. 190f. and describe Coach McNulty's character.

Step 1: Collect relevant passages in the text and make notes on

- general information we get about the character (outward appearance, social background, etc.)

  - 'He took a seat behind a neatly organized desk.' (l. 9)

- what the narrator or other characters say about the character you are dealing with

  - (Mitch:) 'To him I'd always be a big fat loser and nothing more.' (l. 3)
  - 'But McNulty's eyes were scary. I squirmed[1] as he stared at me, feeling like a snot-nosed preschooler who'd been caught marking a wall with crayons[2].' (l. 44)

- what the character says about him-/herself

  - 'I do not intend to spend my life coaching high school.' (l. 57)

- what the character says and does.

  - ' "What's funny?" McNulty said, his blue-gray eyes glittering like shiny stones.' (l. 18)
  - ' "No, no, no," McNulty said, pointing the pencil at me again. 'No questions – not today, not ever.' (l. 34)
  - 'You write down or tape what I tell you. When I'm done, jazz it up[3] whatever you want, but never make me, my coaches, or my players look bad. Understand?' (l. 35)
  - ' "Understood?" he said again, a threat in his voice.' (l. 46)
  - 'Every sports story needs pictures. Either you've got to take them yourself, or you've got to get a photographer. Didn't you know that?' (l. 63)

---

[1] **squirm** *sich winden*   [2] **crayon** *Buntstift*   [3] **jazz sth. up** *(infml)* make sth. more interesting or attractive

Step 2: From your notes draw conclusions about the character.
Always note down examples from the text to give evidence on what you have concluded.

- *according to Mitch: judges people by their outward appearance and athletic ability, not their character → superficial, biased*
- *neatly organized desk → disciplined, conscientious*
- *controls what is being done and said → hungry for power superior, patronizing*
- *uses intimidation to achieve his aims → ruthless, cold*
- *makes others feel stupid → patronizing, condescending*

> **■ LANGUAGE HELP**
> - X appears to be … is portrayed as … This behaviour shows/indicates … Evidence for this can be found in lines … The way she/he talks implies that …
> - Her/his dress sense shows … This proves that … X is a person who can be considered courageous/optimistic/trustworthy/unreliable/disloyal/…

Step 3: Write up your text.
- Structure your text (▶ SF 8) into
  - introduction (should include names, general information, the role the character plays in the story, etc.)

    - *Coach McNulty is a PE teacher and high school football coach who considers himself destined for greater things and therefore openly displays his superiority and power.*
    - *…*

  - main part (should include details about the character, e.g. character traits, ambitions, aims, problems, inner conflicts, etc.)

    - *McNulty is very ambitious and does not 'intend to spend [his] life coaching high school football' (l. 57).*
    - *To make sure he can achieve that goal he is willing to use threats ('Understood?', l. 46)*
    - *He is very condescending towards the reporter.*
    - *…*

  - conclusion (should summarize why the character acts/reacts she way he/she does).

    - *In summary, one can say that Coach McNulty's ruthless ambition, his condescension and his patronizing manner reveal him to be an unfeeling, cold-hearted character and not a stereotypical friendly high school coach and teacher.*

- Use the present tense. (▶ LP 3: Simple present and present perfect)

- Use linking words to connect your ideas. (▶ SF 38: Writing a well-structured text; ▶ LP 14: Linking words and phrases)

- Support your findings using quotes from the text. (▶ SF 39: Quoting a text)

Step 4: Proofread yout text. (▶ SF 40; ▶ LP 17: Spelling)

▶ SF 36 Writing a text analysis

Text analyses can be done with different types of texts, *fictional or *non-fictional texts. The aspects you analyse may differ from text type to text type (see the entries in the Skills File to find out which information is relevant for each text type, ▶ SF 18–21), but the process of analysing texts is usually the same for all of them.

PREPARING YOUR TEXT ANALYSIS

Step 1: Read the task carefully to make sure you know exactly what you are asked to do (cf. 'Verbs for tasks', pp. 340f.). Sometimes you will be given a specific aspect to analyse, sometimes you will be free to select aspects yourself. The following are some suggestions for questions you might ask yourself:
- Which *stylistic devices are used? To what effect? (▶ SF 17: Analysing stylistic devices)
- Which noteworthy words and phrases are used? To what effect?
- How does the structure of the text add to its general meaning / *line of argument?
- How is the reader influenced by the text? To what effect?
- What information is being withheld? Why / To what effect?
- In what way does this text differ from other texts of the same type? (▶ SF 16: Identifying text types)
- …

Step 2: Read the text carefully and make sure you understand it properly. Use a dictionary where necessary (▶ SF 3). Make notes on features or aspects of the text that strike you as relevant to your analysis (▶ SF 15: Marking up a text / Making and taking notes). Remember to note down references from the text that support your analysis (▶ SF 39: Quoting a text).

> *Find an online dictionary here:*
> 🔊 **Webcode** context-52

Step 3: Structure your ideas (▶ SF 8). Do not follow the text chronologically, but structure your ideas according to the different aspects you are analysing.

WRITING YOUR TEXT ANALYSIS

Step 1: Write an introductory sentence in which you give the source and author of the text, the topic and a first general idea to answer your question. Write only one short paragraph, e.g.
In his speech given at Portland State University on 13 June 1998, President Bill Clinton focuses his speech around the topic of ethnic diversity in the US and stresses its positive aspects and the opportunities it offers, using various stylistic devices to bring his message home. (Cf. pp. 144f.)
Use the present tense. (▶ LP 18: Writing about texts)

Step 2: Write the main part of your text:
- Present your findings to support the central idea you stated in the introduction.
- Use different paragraphs for different ideas and introduce these paragraphs with topic sentences to guide the reader. Use linking words. (▶ SF 38: Writing a well-structured text)
- Remember to provide evidence from the text, i.e. to use quotations. (▶ SF 38: Quoting a text)

Step 3: Write a short conclusion:
- Refer to your introduction and write a concluding sentence in which you restate your first general idea or your main findings.
- Do NOT add new aspects at this point!
- Do NOT give your personal opinion or an evaluation!

Step 4: Proofread yout text. (▶ SF 40; ▶ LP 17: Spelling)

> **PRACTICE**
>
> Read the text 'Linguistic diplomacy: the Eurovision Song Contest' (pp. 172f.). Write an outline (▶ SF 8) for the following task: 'Analyse the different means the author of this article uses to get the reader's attention.'

▶ SF 37 Doing a creative writing task

Most creative writing tasks ask you to create a text using an existing piece of writing as a starting point.

NON-FICTIONAL TEXTS

Your creative task may take a *non-fictional text (such as a *speech or newspaper *article) as a starting point. In this case you usually have to assume a certain perspective and evaluate a situation through the eyes of a fictitious *character. You might, for example, be asked to read an article on a climate conference and then write an article from the perspective of a reporter who attended the conference. (▶ SF 18: Analysing non-fiction, ▶ SF 34: Argumentative writing).

FICTIONAL TEXTS

When dealing with *fictional texts a common creative task might be to write an ending to a story or to rewrite the story from a *character's point of view, i.e. to change perspective.

Continuation of a story

Step 1: Brainstorm ideas. Look at the *setting, events, dates, characters and their relationships in the original text and watch out for hints as to how the story might continue.

Step 2: Compare your ideas to the original text to make sure they don't contradict the reality depicted in the story.

Step 3: Identify the *narrative perspective of the original text (e.g. *first-person or *third-person narrator) and consider what limitations that specific perspective might have or not have.

Step 4: Write your continuation. Try to imitate the style and language used in the original.

Change of perspective

A change of perspective means that you take over the role of one of the characters in the story from whose perspective the story is *not* told. You retell its events from your point of view e.g. in a diary entry, a letter or an interior monologue.

Step 1: Brainstorm ideas. Pay attention to the relationships your character is involved in and to specific features such as his/her social status, age or special character traits.

Step 2: Ask yourself what your character might think and feel in a specific situation and also what your character knows and doesn't know.

Step 3: Write your text in a way that is appropriate to your character. Age, social status and other features usually determine how you speak or write.

Step 4: Pay attention to the *text type you're using. For example if you write a letter, you must address the addressee and sign it; if you write a dialogue, you should use typical elements of spoken language; if you write a diary entry you should focus on thoughts and feelings.

> ■ TIP
> - Do not stray too far from the original text because your text may become illogical or far-fetched.
> - Do not invent things that contradict the events of the original story.

·····▶

▶ SF 38 Writing a well-structured text

A well-structured text makes it easy for your reader to follow your line of thought and to understand your text. The structure you use will depend on the kind of text you are writing. For instance, if you are telling a story or writing a report (▶ SF 33: Writing a report), you might want to relate the events in a chronological order. However, there are some rules which apply to all kinds of texts.

Step 1: Collect ideas. Make an outline for your text and structure your ideas accordingly. (▶ SF 8: Structuring ideas)

Step 2: Write your text:
- Begin a new paragraph for each new event, point, argument or idea.
- Structure your text visually, for example by leaving spaces between your paragraphs.
- Make the first sentence in each paragraph a **topic sentence**, i.e. a sentence that states what the paragraph will be about.
- Use **linking words** to make the connections between individual ideas clear (▶ LP 14: Linking words and phrases; ▶ LP 15: Connecting your thoughts).

Step 3: Proofread your text. (▶ SF 40: Proofreading; ▶ LP 17: Spelling)

■ LANGUAGE HELP

Linking words

Enumeration/ Structure	first, second, third; firstly, secondly, …; to begin/start with …, in the first place …; next, then; finally, last (but not least), lastly, to conclude
Addition	furthermore, moreover, in addition (to that), above all, what is more …
Comparison	equally, likewise, similarly, in the same way …
Summary/Conclusion	then, all in all, to conclude, to sum up, in summary/conclusion …
Exemplification	namely, for instance/for example (e.g.), that is to say …
Reasoning	that is why … because …, one reason for this is that …
Result	consequently, as a consequence, therefore, thus, after all, as a result, this leads to/ results in …
Reformulation	or rather, to put it another way, in other words …
Alternatively	on the one hand … on the other hand …, either … or, neither … nor …
Contrast	on the contrary, in contrast to, opposite to, unlike …
Concession	however, nevertheless, still, though, in spite of that, despite that, …

▶ SF 39 Quoting a text

*Quoting is used when you want to support your own statements (e.g. in an analysis) by giving evidence from other texts or the text you are working on. You can either paraphrase / **quote indirectly** (i.e. use your own words to express ideas from a text, ▶ SF 9) or you can use a **direct quote** (i.e. use the exact words of the text).*

Here are some rules for quoting properly:

- With a direct quote, repeat exactly what the author wrote – this also refers to spelling, punctuation, etc.
- Use quotation marks to show where the direct quote begins and ends: A direct quote must be clearly indicated as someone else's thoughts to avoid giving the impression of plagiarism. Remember that in English, quotation marks start and end above the line ('…').
- Always give the exact **source** of your quotation: line or verse numbers and – when dealing with longer texts – page numbers). If you are quoting from more than one text, indicate the author and year of publication. Remember these **abbreviations**: *p./l.* is used for one page/line (e.g. 'p. 4'); *pp./ll.* for more than one page/line (e.g. 'pp. 11–14'); *f./ff.* after the number of a page/line means 'and the following page(s)/line(s)'.
- Especially when working on projects, you may have to quote from more than one text. In this case you need to indicate in a **bibliography** which texts you have used. For each text, provide the author, title, place and date of publication, publisher or URL.

Strategy	Example
Indirect quotes If you use an indirect quote (i.e. you paraphrase or summarize ideas from a text in your own words) you do not use quotation marks, but indicate that you are referring to somebody else's ideas by using *cf.* (= German *vgl.*) and the page number and/or line.	*Franklin D. Roosevelt suggests in his speech that people who are threatened by poverty are easy prey for dictators (cf. p. 180, ll. 2f.).*
Direct quotes: complete sentences When quoting complete sentences make sure that you explain them, refer to or comment on them, so as to avoid disconnected quotations. Using quotes without further comment may give the impression that you have no ideas of your own! Use a colon (:) to separate the quotation from your introductory phrase or sentence.	*Americans and Europeans feel that their wealth and power oblige them to get involved: 'Americans, like Europeans, have long believed that strength and wealth entail responsibility' (p. 153, ll. 35–36).*
Direct quotes: words or phrases If you want to refer to individual words from the text (e.g. in an analysis), you can incorporate words/phrases into your own sentence. Be careful: Work the quotations into your sentences as smoothly as possible so that they fit syntactically.	• *In the prologue to* Romeo and Juliet, *the unhappy ending of the play is already foreshadowed by the phrase 'starcrossed lovers' (Prologue, v. 6).* • *In her text 'Better than its reputation' Applebaum claims 'that the American dream is looking rather tarnished' (p. 153, l. 8), especially when compared to East Asia, which she describes as 'the new land of opportunity' (p. 153, l. 11).*
Direct quotes: poems or plays in verse With texts written in verse, indicate the end of lines with a slash (/). When quoting from plays, provide the act, scene and verse, i.e. II/2/6 = act II, scene 2, verse 6.	*In Aoife Mannix's poem 'Keeping the accent' the speaker experiences that her accent is seen as something positive: 'Then he tells me my accent is so cute, / he is going to give me one of the drinks for free' (p. 171, ll. 5f.).*

······▶

Deleting from or adding to a direct quote If you want to leave out part of a quote indicate this by using square brackets [...]. If you need to add to a quote, for example to make it fit into your sentence syntactically or logically, indicate this by adding words in square brackets, too. Make sure that you don't change the meaning of the quote and that it is still syntactically correct.	• *'But these differing responses [...] also signify a different set of attitudes to power [...]: Americans, like Europeans, have long believed that strength and wealth entail responsibility'. (p. 153, ll. 34f.)* • *At some point Imtiaz Dharker realizes that 'No words can help [her] now'. (p. 89, l. 20)*
Direct quotes: texts containing quotation mark When quoting a passage that includes quotation marks (e.g. in direct speech), use two different kinds of quotation marks, i.e. '...' and "...".	*In Genesis, the first book of the Bible, it says: 'And God said, "Let there be light" and there was light' (Genesis 1.6).*

■ TIP

Check your assignment before using quotes – when answering comprehension questions, you are often asked to express ideas from the text in your own words and are therefore not supposed to quote.

PRACTICE

In the following extract from an essay on why people emigrated to the US, certain passages have been underlined. Quote them to complete the sentences given below the text. Add line references.

Political and Economic Freedom   *Milton and Rose Friedman*

Ever since the first settlement of Europeans in the New World – at Jamestown in 1607 and at Plymouth in 1620 – America has been a magnet for people <u>seeking adventure, fleeing from a tyranny, or simply trying to make a better life for themselves and their children</u>.

An <u>initial trickle</u>[1] swelled after the American Revolution and the establishment of the United States of America and became <u>a flood</u> in the nineteenth century, when millions of people streamed across   5
the Atlantic, and a smaller number across the Pacific, driven by misery and tyranny, and attracted by the promise of freedom and affluence[2].

When they arrived, they did not find streets paved with gold; they did not find an easy life. <u>They did find freedom and an opportunity to make the most of their talents</u>. Through hard work, ingenuity[3], thrift[4], and luck, most of them succeeded in realizing enough of their hopes and dreams to encour-   10
age friends and relatives to join them.

From: *Free to Choose*, New York 1980

1. The text states that the people who came to the US did this for a variety of reasons, as there were people …
2. The text describes the rising number of immigrants as … after the American Revolution and as … during the nineteenth century.
3. Even though the immigrants couldn't expect to become rich without effort, they did get the chance to fulfil their dreams if they were willing and able to work hard: …

---

[1] **trickle** *Rinnsal*   [2] **affluence** wealth   [3] **ingenuity** ability to find solutions to problems   [4] **thrift** careful spending of money

▶ SF 40 Proofreading

Whenever you write a text, it is important to check the correctness and the style of the English you have used. Ideally ask someone else to read it through. Others will often see more because they are not as involved with the text as you are. If possible, read your text out loud. This will help you spot if you have accidently left out any words.

Step 1: Checking structure

- Check that you have included an introduction and a conclusion. (▶ SF 8: Structuring ideas)
- Check that you have followed all the rules for a sensible text structure, e.g. topic sentences, paragraphs, etc. (▶ SF 38: Writing a well-structured text)
- Make sure that your paragraphs include more than one sentence but still focus on one basic thought, argument or idea.

Step 2: Checking style

- Look at your sentences. If your text consists of lots of unconnected main clauses only, then add linking words to express logical connections between your ideas and thus make your text more readable. (▶ SF 38: Writing a well-structured text)
- Make sure you used the right collocations. (▶ LP 19: Collocations) If in doubt, look them up in a dictionary. (▶ SF 3: Using a dictionary)
- Check for repetitions. Substitute words you have used repeatedly with synonyms.

> *Find an online dictionary and a thesaurus here:*
> **Webcode** context-52

- *He is a very conscientious* ==person. He== *goes to work even when he feels* ==sick. People== *know that when he is not at work, something serious must have happened.* →
  He is a very conscientious ==person who== *goes to work even when he feels sick.* ==That is why== *people know that when he is not at work, something serious must have happened.*
- *Social networks can* ==hurt people's privacy.== →
  Social networks can ==violate people's privacy.==

- *Not everybody can* ==achieve== *the American Dream but there are some people who work hard and* ==achieve== *it in the end.* →
  Not everybody can ==achieve== *the American Dream but there are some people who work hard and* ==reach== *it in the end.*

Step 3: Checking correctness

- Keep a checklist of mistakes you have regularly made in the past, e.g. correct tenses in the *if*-clause, the use of adverbs, etc. Look specifically for these mistakes when reading your text.
- Check spelling and punctuation. (▶ LP 17: Spelling) If possible take advantage of your computer's spell-checker, but always double-check its suggestions rather than accepting them blindly.

- **She is* ==terrible== *upset about her husband's death.* →
  She is ==terribly== *upset about her husband's death.*

> **TIP**
>
> Try to think in English when you write because otherwise phrases or sentence patterns sometimes sound more German than English.

······▶

PRACTICE

The following is the beginning of a student's text analysis. It includes nine mistakes (both grammatical and stylistic errors). Find all the mistakes and correct them.

In the short story 'No speak English' from Sandra Cisnero the main character which is called Mamacita, is a beautiful woman. Actually she never leave her apartment, instead the narrator basically speculates about why she behaves in this way. He only knows that she is married and has one kid and he only knows that she speaks only eight words of English. The narrator thinks that she doesn't like English. She always listens to the Spanish radio shows. The husband wants that she integrates into US-American society but she misses her real home, Mexico, too much.

Mediation skills

▶ SF 41 Mediation of written and oral texts

Not everybody speaks and understands both German and English. So you may sometimes find yourself in a situation where you have to help people understand each other – where you have to mediate between speakers of German and English or where you have to explain what is written in texts in the other language. A mediation is not *a translation, i.e. you do* not *translate a text word for word.*

Your English-speaking e-pal is leaving school next year but is finding it difficult to decide on his career plans. You have just read the article below and want to send him an email giving some advice on how to proceed.

Hilfen bei der Berufswahl

Wenn die Berufswahl für Jugendliche ansteht, dann tun sich viele häufig schwer. Sie wissen nicht so recht, ob sie lieber studieren sollen oder erst einmal einen Beruf erlernen möchten. Weiter lernen oder gleich Geld verdienen? Ein Studium nach der Ausbildung beginnen und damit weiter auf Unterstützung angewiesen sein? Oder in einem handwerklichen Beruf Karriere machen? Alles scheint offen und alles möglich. […] 5

Was soll man nun aber tun, wenn man als Jugendlicher eine Ausbildung finden möchte? Erst einmal sollte für die Berufswahl des Jugendlichen klar sein, welche Interessen er hat. Dafür gibt es im Internet oder auch bei der Bundesagentur für Arbeit verschiedene Tests. Soll lieber mit Menschen oder Tieren, mit Maschinen und Geräten gearbeitet werden? Sind die eigenen Fähigkeiten eher theoretischer Natur oder besteht eine Veranlagung zum 10 praktischen Basteln? Gibt es aus der Schule Neigungen, die sich beruflich nutzen lassen? […] Wichtig ist, dass mit der Suche nach einem Ausbildungsplatz für den Jugendlichen zeitig begonnen wird, denn häufig endet die Einstellung der neuen Azubis schon im Jahr vor dem Abschluss in der Schule. Auch für einen Studienplatz sollte sich der Schüler rechtzeitig bewerben, vor allem wenn es sich um einen Studienplatz handelt, der an einen Numerus 15 Clausus gebunden ist, oder um einen, für den es nur eine begrenzte Zahl an freien Plätzen gibt.

From: *Deine Stärken*

How to proceed	Example
Step 1: Select the relevant information from the text, bearing in mind what specific information your partner needs. Remember: the mediated text will usually be much shorter than the original because you select only the information you need.	• *first find out what you enjoy doing* • *get some help from online-tests or the 'Bundesagentur für Arbeit'* • *start early*
Step 2: Analyse the communicative situation: • Who are you talking or writing to? What is the appropriate *style and *register? (▶ LP 11: Using the right register) • What text type are you expected to produce (an informal letter or email, an article for a school magazine? (▶ SF 29: Writing a formal letter or email; ▶ SF 33: Writing a report) • Will you be speaking or writing? (Speaking allows you to use gestures and other non-verbal means of communication.)	• *Your friend needs to know the basic steps he can take to decide on his career.* • *a friend → informal language* (If you were e.g. giving a speech at a symposium on young people's career choices you would use a formal style.) • *an email* • *written text*
Step 3: Structure the relevant information, then phrase it in the target language. (▶ LP 12: Avoiding German-sounding sentence-patterns) Watch out for aspects that are specific to one culture and explain them in more detail. (▶ LP 12: Avoiding Germanisms) If you don't know words in the other language, paraphrase them. (▶ SF 9: Paraphrasing)	*The article I have read gives you some advice:* • *The first step is to find out what you enjoy and what you are good at. You can use online-tests or you can get help at the Job Centre.* • *It's important to start early – here in Germany you have to apply well before for trainee programmes or places at university.* • *'Bundesagentur für Arbeit': Job Centre / a state institution that helps people find jobs*

Find a tool to improve your speaking skills here:
 Webcode context-51

PRACTICE

A 'career's night' is being held at your school for your entire year group. You are asked to give a short talk in German about what careers young people tend to choose and why. Using the text 'Teenagers' career aspirations' (p. 185), prepare a script for your speech (▶ S25 Giving a speech).

P A task allows you to practise this skill.

> Download the suggested answers to
> the PRACTICE tasks here:
> **Webcode** context-49

▶ EP 1 How to do exams in general

You are likely to come across many different tests and exams for English at school, for your *Abitur* or after school. Before sitting an exam, you should therefore familiarize yourself with its specific format. However, there are certain general tips that might help you to be successful. In this *Exam Practice* you will find guidance for both written and oral test formats.

BEFORE THE EXAM
Start early and organize your work.

Collecting information
- Make sure you know how to use aids that are allowed in the exam, e.g. dictionaries. (▶ SF 3: Using a dictionary; ▶ SF 4: Using a grammar book)
- Find out details of the exam situation. Who will be present? Where will it take place? How long will you have? (Especially for oral exams:) Will you be given preparation time? (▶ EP 5)
- Try to get hold of old test papers to see what they require.
- Make sure you understand what the different tasks require from you (cf. 'Verbs for tasks', pp. 340–341).
- Learn about the evaluation criteria of the exam – this will help you to focus on the relevant aspects.

Practising
- Go over old tests or homework tasks to identify your problem areas and learn from your mistakes.
- Don't practise what you already know but focus on your weak areas. (▶ LP 1–20)
- Practise the specific type of exam you will be sitting. If you have to pass an oral exam, practise with a partner. If you have to write a comment, write comments or different parts of a comment.

IN THE EXAM
- Be on time for the exam.
- Read the instructions of the test carefully, they provide crucial information. Make sure you understand what you are supposed to do – it may help to highlight the instructions.
- If you are allowed to choose between different tasks, read all alternatives before deciding which one you want to do.
- If you notice that you are becoming nervous, take a quick break before continuing.
- Use your time efficiently, e.g. leave enough time for checking your work.

A teacher has added this comment to a student's text:

The argumentation of your comment is convincing. You might put forward some more arguments though and back up all your findings with passages from the text. The overall structure of your text is well-chosen, but try to connect the paragraphs more effectively. Linking words and special phrases may help you to do so. Your style of writing is your strength: you write fluently and right to the point. You have expanded your vocabulary successfully and most passages are idiomatic. There are hardly any mistakes, but you should revise conditional sentences.

1 Look at the following list of criteria and say whether the student's text fulfilled them very well or just satisfactorily or whether it needs improvement in that area.

Criteria		
▪ Content: quality	▪ Content: quantity	▪ Structure
▪ Use of quotes	▪ Linking words	▪ Useful phrases for interpretation
▪ Vocabulary: general flexibility	▪ Ability of expression	▪ Grammar

2 Look at the sections Skills File (pp. 250–305) and Language Practice (pp. 218–239) and identify relevant sections that could help the student to improve his/her weak areas.

3 Now collect your own 3–5 weak areas and identify the relevant sections in Skills File and/or Language Practice. Develop an action plan to work on your weak areas.

▶ EP 2 Working with texts

In most of your exams you will be faced with one or more texts, which you have to respond to (▶ SF 11–13, ▶ SF 16–21). These may include:
- *fictional texts (e.g. *short stories, *poems; extracts from *novels, *dramas or *film scripts)
- *non-fictional texts (e.g. articles, *speeches)
- visuals (e.g. *cartoons, pictures, films, advertisements, leaflets).

You may be given a single written text or a written text combined with another text or a visual. You will be expected to work on different tasks. For instance, you may be asked to analyse a short story or to mediate a newspaper article. In order to be successful you will need to apply different skills, e.g.:
- skimming, scanning (▶ SF 14: Reading strategies)
- underlining or highlighting important sections (▶ SF 15: Marking up a text / Making and taking notes)
- making notes in the margin (▶ SF 15: Marking up a text / Making and taking notes)
- making notes on a separate piece of paper, e.g. mind maps, outlines, drawings (▶ SF 7: Making visual aids; ▶ SF 8: Structuring ideas)
- writing a well-structured text (▶ SF 38).

Find a mindmapping tool here:
Webcode context-53

In general, when dealing with a text you will be asked to consider the following three aspects:

Anforderungsbereich I	*Anforderungsbereich II*	*Anforderungsbereich III*
comprehension (focus on content) ▶ EP 2.1	analysis/interpretation (focus on form and function) ▶ EP 2.2	composition (focus on evaluation and re-creation) ▶ EP 2.3

In an exam, you may be given tasks that clearly relate to one of these three aspects, or there might be complex tasks that combine two or all three of them.

► EP 2.1 *Anforderungsbereich I*: comprehension

This type of task focuses on the content of a text and is intended to check whether you have understood the information. Comprehension tasks can be quite open, i.e. they require you to write a free text, as in summary writing (► SF 31) or answering comprehension questions. They can also occur in the form of closed test formats, e.g. multiple choice or true/false exercises (► SF 10: Working with closed test formats; ► EP 6).

TYPICAL INSTRUCTIONS FOR *ANFORDERUNGSBEREICH I* (OPEN TASKS)
Here are some instructions that are frequently used for *Anforderungsbereich I*. To see the complete list of instructions, have a look at pp. 340–341 ('Verbs for tasks').

Instruction	Example	What you are expected to do	Tips
outline ['– –] *umreißen, skizzieren*	**Outline** the writer's views on …	*Give the main features, structure or general principles of a topic, omitting minor details.*	Structure your answer using main and subordinate points.
state *darlegen*	**State** the author's opinion on the main character's decision.	*Specify something clearly.*	Be precise and brief.
summarize (*also:* **give/write a summary of; sum up**) *zusammenfassen*	**Summarize** the incident in the church in no more than four sentences.	*Give a concise account of the main points of something.*	Be concise; leave out details and examples.

To practise *Anforderungsbereich I*, have a look at **Practice I** (p. 312) or **Practice II** (p. 313).

► EP 2.2 *Anforderungsbereich II*: analysis/interpretation

In this part of the exam, you 'read between the lines' of a text. You might examine why an author gives the text a certain form, why he/she characterizes the figures in a drama in a certain way, etc. To do exactly what you are asked to do, make sure you understand the instructions (cf. 'Verbs for tasks', p. 340). Also, provide a suitable structure for your findings (► SF 8: Structuring ideas).

TYPICAL INSTRUCTIONS FOR *ANFORDERUNGSBEREICH II*
Here are some instructions that are frequently used for *Anforderungsbereich II*. To see the complete list of instructions, have a look at pp. 340–341 ('Verbs for tasks').

Instruction	Example	What you are expected to do	Tips
analyse (BE), **analyze** (AE) ['ænəlaɪz]/ **examine** [ɪgˈzæmɪn] *analysieren, untersuchen*	**Analyse** the main elements of the poster. **Examine** the writer's attitude towards the protagonist.	*Describe and explain certain aspects and/or features of the text in detail.*	Do not just list e.g. stylistic devices the author uses, but always connect them to the effect they are used to create.
explain *erklären*	**Explain** the main character's reaction to her mother in the first scene.	*Describe and define in detail.*	Do not just describe something, but give reasons why it is the way it is.

Authors always write their texts to achieve an effect – they may want to persuade or inform the readers, they may try to arouse compassion or contempt for a character in their story, etc. When analysing a text, you need to examine which means the author has used to create a specific effect (▶ SF 17: Analysing stylistic devices; ▶ SF 18: Analysing non-fiction; ▶ SF 19–21: Analysing fiction). The table below gives some examples.

Category	Some typical means	Possible effects
techniques of persuasion	quote from or use of statistics from reliable sources and experts	creates credibility
	example from everyday life	makes an argument more comprehensible and concrete
	direct address of reader	makes the reader sympathize with a concept or adopt the writer's view
use of language	use of *images (e.g. *metaphor, *symbol, *simile, *personification)	helps to evoke a graphic, vivid picture in the reader's mind
	use of *stylistic devices such as *anaphora, *alliteration or *repetition	stresses a certain aspect
	use of *irony, *sarcasm	creates humour, emphazises a point or message
	use of technical jargon	creates credibility, makes the writer appear more expert
narrative techniques	use of a *first-person narrator	helps the reader to identify with the narrator, to understand his or her attitude

To practise *Anforderungsbereich II*, have a look at **Practice I** (p. 312) or **Practice II** (p. 313).

▶ EP 2.3 *Anforderungsbereich III*: beyond the text

Part III of the exam requires you to produce a text. It may be based on a text or on visuals (e.g. cartoons or photos) or it may take just a topic as a starting point. It may be called *comment, composition, creative writing* or *writing*.

In some exams you will be asked to write a certain type of text. The task may also give you aspects that need to be (or may be) taken into consideration. The following table gives you an idea about the most common text types, their purpose, content/structure and specific language.

Text type	Purpose	Content/Structure	Language
*feature story/ article	• inform sb. • entertain sb. • provide background information	• catchy headline • first paragraph must arouse reader's interest (example, anecdote) • use of anecdotes, examples, quotes • personal angle	• less formal language, some slang may be used
report (▶ SF 33: Writing a report)	• inform sb. • provide background information • influence sb.	• catchy headline • clear paragraphs • from general aspects to detail	• less formal language, some slang may be used

*comment (▶ SF 34: Argumentative writing)	• pass judgment on an issue • express and support your opinion	• introduction: outline of topic and attitude • body: arguments for personal position, refutation of counter-arguments • conclusion: summary of personal position • use of examples to illustrate arguments	• formal/neutral language
argumentative essay/ discussion (▶ SF 34: Argumentative writing)	• weigh up both sides of an issue remaining fairly neutral	• introduction: outline of topic • body: pros and cons of the issue • conclusion: summary of arguments, statement of personal opinion • use of examples to illustrate arguments	• formal/neutral language
(written) **interview** (▶ SF 37: Doing a creative writing task; ▶ SF 26: Taking part in an interview)	• present a topic/a person's views • portray a celebrity	• introduction: basic facts on interviewee • official welcome of interviewee • body: interviewee's answers to questions (which should be polite, may be provocative) • concluding statement or question; words of goodbye and expression of gratitude	• imitation of spoken language • polite language
*letter (e.g. letter to the editor, cover letter for an application, personal letter) **email** (▶ SF 34: Writing a formal letter or email)	• various, e.g. apply for a job, tell reader about a topic, express your opinion	• content varies according to addressee and purpose • structural elements: letterhead, greeting, body, signature	• varies according to addressee and purpose
review (▶ SF 32: Writing a review)	• describe something you have read or experienced (book, film, etc.) and express your opinion on it • make recommendations	• introduction – body (brief summary, evaluation) – conclusion	• varies according to type of magazine or newspaper • use of words that describe the film, book, etc. and your opinion in a differentiated way (adjectives, adverbs; words with positive or negative connotations)

*speech script (▶ SF 25: Giving a speech)	• various, e.g. move/ convince/inform/ entertain sb.	• introduction: welcome audience; outline topic and intention of speech • body: well-structured arguments backed up with evidence/examples • conclusion: summary, appeal to listeners, expression of gratitude	• varies according to context, i.e. audience, speaker, occasion • stylistic devices

Your task may also be creative writing (▶ SF 37: Doing a creative writing task), i.e. you may be asked to add something to an already existing text (mostly fictional) or to change it. You might change the *point of view of a text, add an ending to a story (or write a different one), add a part to the text or fill a gap in it (e.g. an *interior monologue). Remember that your writing must match the language style of the original.

You may also come across 'free' creative writing tasks. They are not based on or linked to a certain text but require you to apply your knowledge and skills – as for example when writing a poem on a given topic.

TYPICAL INSTRUCTIONS FOR *ANFORDERUNGSBEREICH III*

If you are not given a certain text type to write, you may find one of the tasks listed in the table below. See pp. 340–341 for a complete list of instructions ('Verbs for tasks').

Instruction	Example	What you are expected to do	Tips
comment on ['kɒment] *kommentieren, Stellung nehmen zu*	**Comment on** the speaker's belief that …	*State clearly your opinions on the topic in question and support your views with evidence.*	Say exactly what you think and why.
discuss *diskutieren, erörtern*	**Discuss** how education influences attitudes towards immigration.	*Investigate or examine by argument; give reasons for and against.*	Structure your ideas clearly. Weigh up both sides of an issue and support your final position with arguments.
justify *begründen, rechtfertigen*	**Justify** your answer.	*Show adequate grounds for decisions or conclusions.*	If possible and suitable, use statistics or research results as support.

In all your writing tasks make sure to apply general writing skills such as structuring a text or linking ideas (▶ SF 8: Structuring ideas; ▶ SF 38: Writing a well-structured text).
To practise *Anforderungsbereich III*, have a look at **Practice I** (p. 312) or **Practice II** (p. 313).

Working with a non-fictional text: *Anforderungsbereich I, II* and *III*

A great honour   *Ewen MacAskill*

NSA whistleblower Edward Snowden said he was humbled and honoured after Glasgow University students voted overwhelmingly for him to serve as their rector for the next three years. In a statement to the Guardian, Snowden described it as bold and historic decision in support of academic freedom. 'In a world where so many of our developing thoughts and queries and plans must be entrusted to the open internet, mass surveillance is not simply a matter of privacy, but of academic freedom and human liberty,' Snowden said. The vote is purely symbolic as Snowden is unlikely to be in a position to become a working rector, able to represent students at meetings of the university's administrators. He is wanted by the US for leaking tens of thousands of documents to journalists and has been granted temporary asylum in Russia. The result of the online election was announced to candidates and their supporters shortly after polls closed at 5pm on Tuesday. Snowden was nominated by a group of students at the university who said they had received his approval through his lawyer. He defeated the former champion cyclist Graeme Obree, the author Alan Bissett and the Rev Kelvin Holdsworth, who also stood for the post. Chris Cassells, Snowden's spokesman for the rectorial election campaign, said: 'We are delighted to see Edward Snowden elected as the new rector of the University of Glasgow. We have a proud and virtuous tradition of making significant statements through our rectors and today we have once more championed this idea by proving to the world that we are not apathetic to important issues such as democratic rights.' [...] Charles Kennedy, the outgoing rector and former Lib Dem leader, said: 'It has been a pleasure and a privilege to serve the students of the University of Glasgow for the past six years. The post of rector is an important one, and I would like to wish my successor all the very best for his term of office.'

Snowden, in his statement, said: 'I am humbled by and grateful to the students of Glasgow University for this historic statement in defence of our shared values. We are reminded by this bold decision that the foundation of all learning is daring: the courage to investigate, to experiment, to inquire.' He added: 'If we do not contest the violation of the fundamental right of free people to be left unmolested in their thoughts, associations, and communications – to be free from suspicion without cause – we will have lost the foundation of our thinking society. The defence of this fundamental freedom is the challenge of our generation, a work that requires constructing new controls and protections to limit the extraordinary powers of states over the domain of human communication. This election shows that the students of Glasgow University intend to lead the way, and it is my great honour to serve as their rector.'

From: The Guardian, 18 February 2014

---

1 **whistleblower** *Enthüller*
2 **rector** *(BE)* head of a university or college
3 **bold** (here) brave
8 **leak sth.** (here) reveal sth.

13 **Rev Kelvin Holdsworth** clergyman of the Scottish Episcopal Church in Glasgow
17 **Lib Dem** (= The Liberal Democrats) a socially liberal political party in the United Kingdom

21 **humble sb.** *jdn. mit Demut erfüllen*
23 **daring** ready to do dangerous or unusual things, brave
24 **unmolested** not disturbed by anybody

1 Possible task for *Anforderungsbereich I*
Summarize what the article tells you about Snowden's election and his personal reaction to it.
(▶ SF 31: Writing a summary)

2 Possible task for *Anforderungsbereich II*
Examine how MacAskill expresses his indirect support for Snowden's actions. Consider his line of argument, his techniques of persuasion and his use of language.
(▶ SF 18: Analysing non-fiction)

> ■ TIP
>
> Reread EE 2.2, then collect ideas and structure them before starting to write.
> (▶ SF 8: Structuring ideas)

3 Possible tasks for *Anforderungsbereich III*

Before working on the tasks you might want to do some research on the controversy around Edward Snowden.

a Some people have called Snowden a traitor because he leaked confidential information from the NSA. Discuss this view. ▶ LANGUAGE HELP (▶ SF 34: Argumentative writing)

b Write an interview with an American politician who considers Snowden a hero who opened the world's eyes to mass surveillance. ▶ LANGUAGE HELP (▶ SF 37: Doing a creative writing task)

c Imagine you are a student at Glasgow University before Snowden's election as rector. You have been asked to give a speech in front of undecided fellow students convincing them (not) to vote for him. Write a speech.
▶ LANGUAGE HELP (▶ SF 25: Giving a speech)

▮ LANGUAGE HELP

- endanger national security
- destabilize international relationships
- commit a crime
- cause unpredictable political turmoil
- be on an ego-trip
- brave hero
- support freedom of speech
- fundamental democratic right
- trigger a much needed debate
- defense of democratic values
- principles of the American Dream
- international peacekeeping

Working with a fictional text: *Anforderungsbereich I, II* and *III*

PRACTICE II

In the novel *The Uncommon Reader* Queen Elizabeth II discovers a travelling library outside of Buckingham Palace. She starts to borrow books regularly and slowly, her character begins to change. In this excerpt she is talking to her equerry after performing a ceremony.

The monarch's truly human side *Alan Bennett*

'Less spontaneous this morning, ma'am,' one of the bolder equerries ventured to say.

'Was I?' said the Queen, who would once have been most put out at even this mildest of criticisms, though these days it scarcely impinged. 'I think I know why it is. You see, Gerald, as they kneel one looks down on
5 the tops of people's heads a good deal and from that perspective even the most unsympathetic personality seems touching: the beginnings of a bald patch, the hair growing over the collar. One's feelings are almost maternal.'

The equerry, with whom she'd never shared such confidences before and who ought to have been flattered, simply felt awkward and embarrassed. This was a truly human side to the monarch of which he'd never been
10 previously aware and which (unlike its counterfeit versions) he did not altogether welcome. And whereas the Queen herself thought that such feelings probably arose out of her reading books, the young man felt it might be that she was beginning to show her age. Thus it was that the dawn of sensibility was mistaken for the onset of senility.

Immune to embarrassment herself, as she was to any that she might cause, the Queen would once not have
15 noticed the young man's confusion. But observing it now she resolved in the future to share her thoughts less promiscuously, which was a pity in a way as it was what many in the nation longed for. Instead she determined to restrict her confidences to her notebooks, where they could do no harm.

The Queen had never been demonstrative; it was not in her upbringing; but more and more these days, particularly in the period following Princess Diana's death, she was being required to go public about feel-
20 ings she would have preferred to keep to herself. At that time, though, she had not yet begun to read, and it was only now that she understood that her predicament was not unique and that she shared it, among others, with Cordelia. She wrote in her notebook: 'Though I do not always understand Shakespeare, Cordelia's "I cannot heave my heart into my mouth" is a sentiment I can readily endorse. Her predicament is mine.'

From: *The Uncommon Reader*, 2007

·····▶

2 **equerry** [–'––] male officer who acts as an assistant to the royal family
venture to do sth. *etwas zu tun wagen*
4 **scarcely** almost not
impinge have a noticeable effect
6 **bald patch** area on top of the head without hair
collar *Kragen*
7 **maternal** *mütterlich*

8 **be flattered** *sich geschmeichelt fühlen*
9 **awkward** uncomfortable
10 **counterfeit** fake
11 **arise out of sth.** happen as a result of sth.
12 **dawn of sensibility** *Anflug von Empfindsamkeit*
onset beginning
16 **promiscuously** *(here)* with lots of people
17 **harm** damage, injury

18 **be demonstrative** show your feelings in public
upbringing education
19 **Princess Diana** (1961–1997) first wife of the Queen's son Charles
21 **predicament** situation where it is hard to know what to do
22 **Cordelia** character from William Shakespeare's drama *King Lear*
23 **endorse sth.** say publicly that you support sth.

1 Possible task for *Anforderungsbereich I*

Briefly describe the situation as well as the monarch's and Gerald's attitudes and feelings.

2 Possible task for *Anforderungsbereich II*

Examine how the author employs narrative perspective to show the differences between the behaviour and views of the Queen and the equerry. (▶ SF 19: Analysing narrative prose)

Step 1: Put a transparency over the text and mark relevant passages revealing information on
    1 the Queen's behaviour and how she explains it
    2 the equerry's observations and how he explains them.

Step 2: Determine the narrative perspective and examine how it influences the reader's perception of both characters. What effect does it have on the presentation of both characters' behaviour and views?

Step 3: Add your observations to the structure below to create an outline. (▶ SF 8: Structuring ideas) Don't forget to use quotes and to indicate the lines. (▶ SF 39: Quoting a text)

Paragraph 1: *narrative perspective*
    ...

Paragraph 2: the Queen's behaviour and her self-image
    2.1. Her behaviour   *2.2. How she explains it*
    ...   *...*

Paragraph 3: the equerry's view
    3.1. The equerry's observations   *3.2. How he explains them*
    ...   *...*

Step 4: Add suitable notes for introduction and conclusion, then write a coherent text. (▶ SF 38: Writing a well-structured text)

Introduction
- *an 'uncommon' picture of the British monarch*
- *Queen's new hobby → effect on her behaviour → effect on her subjects / the equerry*

Conclusion
- *omniscient third-person-narrator → two perspectives (Queen, equerry)*
    ...

3 Possible tasks for *Anforderungsbereich III*

a Discuss whether the British monarch is supposed to 'go public about feelings' (l. 19) considering his/her duties and function. (▶ SF 34: Argumentative writing)

b The Queen takes Cordelia's utterance as a starting point for her notebook entry (l. 22f.). Finish her entry reflecting on her latest experience and self-image. (▶ SF 37: Doing a creative writing task)

▶ EP3 Mediation

Mediating basically means to summarize information (from a written or oral text) in another language. (▶ SF41: Mediation of written and oral texts). Note that a mediation is *not* a translation; i.e. you do *not* translate a text word for word.

Your task is normally embedded in some kind of context, so you have to consider the situation and your relationship to the addressee to find out what information to select from the original text and in what form to put it. *Form* here can refer to a specific *text type but also to a suitable *register.

To get the maximum number of points in your exam, it is helpful to know which criteria your teacher will apply when assessing your exam:

- **content:** selection of relevant aspects for the situation given (answers given to all the addressee's questions, but no superfluous information)
- **form:** choice of suitable text type and ability to apply its rules
- **appropriateness** of *style and *register for the given situation
- **powers of expression:** ability to deal with unknown words/technical terms or culture-specific concepts; lexical and syntactical flexibility, etc.
- **grammar:** amount and types of mistakes.

> ■ TIP
>
> Be aware of (cultural) misunderstandings, German idioms and false friends.
> (▶ CC 1–7) Do not translate word for word because cultural peculiarities often do not have a translation. Paraphrase.
> (▶ SF9: Paraphrasing)

PRACTICE

Your British friend is coming to visit you. She has heard that a new Primark shop has just opened in your town and cannot wait to go there during her stay with you. You come across the article below.

Erschütternder Hilferuf in Kleid von Primark eingenäht

In westlichen Kleiderläden verführen bunte, billige Klamotten zum Kauf. Die Arbeitsbedingungen der Näherinnen in den indischen Textilfabriken sind dabei meist ganz weit weg. Nicht so für eine britische Primark-Kundin: Denn jemand hatte eine Botschaft in ihr Kleid genäht. Die britische Primark-
5　Kundin Rebecca Gallagher hat überraschend erfahren, unter welchen Bedingungen ihr Kleid offenbar hergestellt wurde, berichtet die „South Wales Evening Post online". Sie habe in ihrem zwölf Euro teuren Sommerkleid von Primark ein Etikett mit einer Nachricht gefunden. „Forced to work for exhausting hours", zu Deutsch etwa „gezwungen, stundenlang bis zur Erschöpfung zu arbeiten", sei handschriftlich auf dem Etikett gestanden, das jemand mit der Hand zwischen die anderen genäht hatte. Es sei ihr
10　aufgefallen, als sie nach der Waschanleitung geschaut habe, erzählte die 25-Jährige der Zeitung. Daraufhin habe sie gelobt, das Kleid nie wieder anzuziehen. Sie fühle sich schuldig und habe Angst, dass eine übermüdete Arbeiterin sich dafür in einem Sweatshop irgendwo in einem fernen Land quälen musste. „Um ehrlich zu sein, habe ich noch nie darüber nachgedacht, wie die Kleider hergestellt werden", sagte sie. „Aber das hat mich jetzt zum Nachdenken darüber gebracht, woher wir unsere
15　billigen Klamotten bekommen." Ein Primark-Sprecher sagte der Zeitung, ihm seien keine weiteren Vorfälle dieser Art bekannt. Trotzdem bat er um Rückgabe: „Wir wären der Kundin dankbar, wenn sie das Kleid an uns übergeben würde, damit wir untersuchen können, wie das Schildchen an das Kleid gelangte und ob dieser Sache weiter nachgegangen werden muss."

Vor mehr als einem Jahr stürzte das Rana Plaza in Bangladesch ein. Beim schwersten Unglück in
20　der Textilindustrie starben mehr als 1130 Menschen, mehr als 2500 wurden teils schwer verletzt.

•••••▶

Die Arbeitsbedingungen der Näherinnen, die dort zu Dumpinglöhnen Hosen, T-Shirts und Kleider für westliche Kunden herstellen, gerieten in die Kritik. Zu den Unternehmen, die in einer der Fabriken in dem Gebäude produzieren ließen, gehörte auch das irische Unternehmen Primark.

From: *Focus*, 25 June 2014

Possible mediation task

After reading the article, you are concerned about buying new clothes. Write an email to your friend (in English) in which you tell her what you have found out about working conditions in Asian textile factories.

Step 1: Look at the following pieces of information from the text and say whether you would include them in your email or not.

1 A British customer found a message sewn into her Primark dress saying 'forced to work for exhausting hours'.
2 The customer is 25-year-old Rebecca Gallagher.
3 She found the message when looking for the washing instructions.
4 The shopper feels guilty because of the exploitation of workers in clothes factories.
5 Primark asked the young woman to return the dress to find out how the label got there.
6 In 2013, more than 1130 people were killed when a factory which produced clothes for western companies collapsed in Bangladesh.

Step 2: Collect more information from the text that you consider relevant for your email, then structure your ideas. (▶ SF 8: Structuring ideas)

Step 3: Read the following model answer, which is not at all perfect. Say what might be improved.

> Hi there,
>
> I have a serious problem. Primark forces children to produce cheap clothes. I read that in an article in some newspaper. A woman discovered a label sewn in her Primark dress saying 'forced to work for exhausting hours'. She only paid €12 for the dress. There was also an accident in one of those sweatshops abroad. It´s horrible, isn´t it? I suggest we don´t go there.
>
> Hope to hear from you soon!

Step 4: Write your email, bearing in mind the following points:
- form: email (fairly informal)
- addressee: a friend from the UK you do not know that well (→ don't be too informal!)
- situation: your friend wants to go to the new Primark shop, but you have found out about sweatshops and want to dissuade her.
  - Don't get right to the point: make polite small talk first, maybe tell her how happy you are about the visit.
  - Try to voice your doubts about the idea without offending your friend. You might suggest some kind of compromise.

► EP4 Listening and viewing

Your exam task may be based on a short audio (e.g. an interview, a speech) or video (e.g. an interview, a documentary, an extract from a film) of about four minutes.

To prepare for this exam, use every opportunity you get to listen to spoken English. For instance, listen to BBC radio or watch your favourite British or American TV show on DVD or online in English. Start with English subtitles and switch them off when you feel ready. If possible, listen to a wide variety of speakers (different accents, different speeds, various topics).

In listening tasks, you will often only be asked to answer questions on *Anforderungsbereich I*, i.e. text comprehension (► EE 2.1), and they are often closed test formats such as multiple choice (► SF 10: Working with closed test formats; ► SF 22: Listening). Viewing tasks, but also some listening tasks, go beyond simple understanding and require you to analyse the film clip or audio, so make sure you are familiar with aspects to examine. (► SF 23: Analysing a film)

There is usually a standard exam procedure when it comes to listening or viewing:

Step 1: You get some time to read the instructions and further information and vocabulary, if provided. The questions will normally come in the same order as the information in the recording.

Step 2: First listening/viewing: you are allowed to write while listening/viewing, so start working on your tasks right away. Try to complete as much as possible.

Step 3: Time to work on the tasks: fill in missing information and/or read through the tasks again. Mark things you are not sure about and any gaps that are still there.

Step 4: Second listening/viewing: try to fill any gaps that might be left and check the answers you've already noted down.

Step 5: Time to complete your tasks and check your answers.

In a viewing activity your teacher might show you the video a third time.

 TIP

Before listening/viewing:
- Read the instructions carefully and make sure you know what you have to focus on.
- Try to make predictions about the audio/video and the answers to the questions.

While listening/viewing:
- Read all answers, even if you are sure that you have found the correct one. The differences between the right and the wrong answers are often subtle or tricky.
- If you need to take notes, only jot down keywords or short phrases.
- If your task requires you to write a text, try to note down particular phrases from the audio/video and use them as quotes in your text.

After viewing/listening:
- Don't leave an item unanswered. If you don't know the answer, make an educated guess – you still stand a good chance of getting the credit for it (e.g. 25% in a multiple choice item with four options!)
- If you are asked to write a text, …
  - don't forget to use all the background information from the instructions.
  - back up your findings with concrete evidence, i.e. refer to relevant phrases or expressions used by a speaker/actor or describe special (cinematic) moments.

Listening (▶ SF 22: Listening)

Former First Lady Hillary Rodham Clinton was US Secretary of State from 2008 to 2012. You are going to listen to an extract from an interview with her broadcast in 2014, in which she speaks about the challenges as a female Secretary of State and women's issues in general.

🎧 **CD3** 14

perseverance *Beharrlichkeit*
hostility *Feindseligkeit*
private capacity private life
inconsequential unimportant
**break through the highest glass
 ceiling** *die letzte Hürde nehmen*
renowned famous
assertive *durchsetzungsfähig*

1 Choose the correct answers. Sometimes more than one answer is correct.

  a On women as US Secretary of State:
  1 When Clinton came to office, three women had done the job of US Secretary of State before.
  2 Having a female Secretary of State has changed the way people perceive women considerably.
  3 In countries like the UK, a female US Secretary of State is nothing special.
  4 Hillary Clinton never got used to being the only woman in the room on meetings in some foreign countries.

  b To Clinton, making women and girls an important element of US foreign states policy is …
  1 a necessity   3 both a luxury and a necessity
  2 a luxury   4 neither a luxury nor a necessity.

  c During her fight for women's rights she was often faced with …
  1 hostility
  2 interest
  3 people rolling their eyes at her
  4 people who considered this topic an unimportant hobby horse of hers.

2 List three brutal actions that girls are confronted with in a lot of countries according to Clinton.

3 List two fields of life in which women still face challenges in Western civilization.

4 List two ways in which women break the law in Saudi Arabia.

5 How does Clinton decide if and how to speak out in cases where women are treated badly?

Viewing (▶ SF 23: Analysing a film)

Margaret Thatcher was the first and only female British Prime Minister (1979–1990). Her nickname 'the Iron Lady' was coined because of her tough opposition towards the Soviet Union and socialism as such in the Cold War era. The scene from the film *The Iron Lady* (2011) that you are going to watch shows her with the members of her Cabinet discussing a new tax.

▶️ **DVD**

council estate (here)
(oft sehr armer) Wohnort
resent sth. (strongly) dislike sth.
slacker *(infml) Faulenzer/in*
sovereignty *Souveränität*
concession *Zugeständnis*
beret type of French hat

1 Possible task for *Anforderungsbereich I*
Briefly sum up the content of the scene.

2 Possible tasks for *Anforderungsbereich II*
  a Examine Margaret Thatcher's character as presented in this scene. Focus on her attitudes and her behaviour towards the members of the Cabinet present. (▶ SF 35: Writing a character profile)
  b Analyse the cinematic devices employed to create this picture of Thatcher. (▶ SF 23: Analysing a film)

3 Possible tasks for *Anforderungsbereich III*
  a Assess Margaret Thatcher's leadership qualities as shown in this scene.
  b After the meeting, two Cabinet members talk about the incident, commenting on Thatcher's leadership qualities. Write their dialogue. (▶ SF 23: Doing a creative writing task)

▶ EP5 Speaking

Many exams nowadays are exclusively communication exams or they may include a part in which you have to prove your communicative capacity. Preparing for and successfully passing a speaking exam is different from a written exam because you need to use different skills and strategies. (▶ SF24–SF28)

Usually, oral exams consist of two parts which are thematically linked, a monologue and a dialogue:

Monologue	Dialogue
In this part, you are asked to give a presentation based on e.g. a diagram, statistics, picture, cartoon, quote or short text.	In the second part, you are asked to interact with a partner or a group of students in a role-play or a discussion. It may be based on the material you have worked on for the monologue. Your fellow students have probably dealt with similar material.

To prepare for your exam, ask your teacher about the specific conditions of your exam, e.g.
- What kind of prompts can you expect (i.e. cartoons, pictures, quotes, etc.)?
- Will you be given time to prepare only the monologue or both parts?
- If there is preparation time for the dialogue, will it be at the very beginning or shortly before the dialogue?
- How long will the preparation time be?
- How long will both parts of the exam be?
- How many people will take part in the dialogue?
- Will the participants in the dialogue be other students or teachers?

To get the maximum number of points in your exam, it is helpful to know which criteria you teacher will apply when assessing your exam:
- **communicative strategies** (structure, eye contact, interaction with partners, etc.)
- **pronunciation** (clarity, fluency, intonation, accuracy)
- **powers of expression** (choice of words, ability to deal with unknown words/technical terms, flexibility, etc.)
- **grammar:** amount and types of mistakes
- **content:** quality and meaningfulness of statements/arguments, etc.

■ TIP

Before the exam:
- Practise monologues by describing a picture to a fellow student. (▶ SF24: Giving a presentation)
- Learn phrases which you can use during presentations, speeches or discussions (cf. the table on p.320).
- Study your classroom material and look for controversial issues which could be discussed, then collect arguments for and against them.
- Watch (current) political debates online to get an idea of the culture of reflection and debate.

In the exam:
- If there is a preparation time, use it to arrange your material so that you can use it effectively. Structure your ideas clearly. Use clear handwriting. Use abbreviations, keywords, etc. (▶ SF7: Making visual aids)
- You may have to adopt a role or defend a position which you don't like. Try to disregard your personal opinion, stick to the facts and give evidence if possible.
- In the dialogue part, take your time to react but do not hesitate too long. (▶ SF27: Having a discussion)
- Ask for clarification of crucial points. Be provocative and polite at the same time; avoid attacks or insults.
- Don't be too emotional.
- Use appropriate body language and facial expressions.
- Choose the right moment to sum up your points and introduce a new aspect.

Stages of conversation

Every communicative situation consists of different stages. If you know about these stages and useful expressions to use, you can keep a conversation going and make it successful:

Stage of conversation	Explanation	Phrases
starting a conversation	You either introduce the situation or explain the topic.	Well, our topic seems to be very controversial … Why don't we … first? Recently, I heard that somebody …
expressing one's opinion	You elaborate the arguments concerning the topic.	I'm convinced that … It seems to me that … To me …
involving a partner	You invite a partner who so far hasn't contributed much to the conversation.	What do you think about …? Is there anything you'd like to add? How about you? Would you agree with that?
contradicting	You politely express that you have an opposing opinion.	That's not the way I see it. That is true to a certain extent but …
interrupting	You try to find your way into the conversation without cutting the other person short.	Sorry to interrupt you but … May I interrupt you for a moment, please?
asking for clarification	You are not sure that you have understood your partner correctly.	Excuse me, I didn't quite catch your point about … Do you mean …? Sorry, could you say that again, please?
gaining time to think	You need time to think or work on your own argumentation.	Well, that's a good point, but I think … Well, now, let me see … It's difficult to say exactly, but … If I understood the question correctly, … I don't know whether this is what you meant, but …
summing up	You bring the conversation to an end, e.g. by mentioning the most important aspects or giving a view into the future or establishing a compromise.	So, to sum up … In brief … To cut a long story short …

·····▶

1 Monologue: preparing and giving a presentation (▶ SF 24: Giving a presentation)

  a Work with a partner. Each of you choose one of the cartoons below, then prepare a presentation in which you comment on it.

  b First partner A presents his/her cartoon, then Partner B.

'Congratulations, it's a Versace!'

2 Dialogue: discussing a topic (▶ SF 27: Having a discussion)

You are going to have a discussion on the benefits and dangers of scientific progress.

  a Work with a partner. Read the role cards below, then decide who is going to take which role.

Partner A	Partner B
Your little brother had leukemia and the doctors were able to treat it with a bone marrow transplant[1]. You are glad about scientific progress and the possibility that it might one day help to prevent leukemia.	You suffer from strong allergic reactions to certain foods and you suspect it's because you might have eaten genetically modified soy[2]. You are afraid of fast progress in science because you fear that its side effects cause more harm than good.

  b Collect arguments for your position. Also collect counter-arguments and think of possible ways to refute them. You might tackle the following issues: pre-implantation genetic diagnosis, designer babies, genetically modified food, genetic engineering in health care, stem cell research, etc.

  c Discuss the topic for about 10–15 minutes. Begin by introducing yourself and your general standpoint. You can take your cartoon as a starting point for the debate.

---

[1] **bone marrow transplant** *Rückenmarksspende*   [2] **soy** *Soja*

▶ EP6 Closed test formats

In many exams in and after school there are special forms of tests that are called 'closed test formats' (▶ SF10: Working with closed test formats). In closed test formats, you don't write at all, but just indicate which of the given solutions is correct or which items go together.

Closed test **formats** include:
- multiple choice tests with one or more correct answer/s
- true/false statements
- matching: matching questions, statements or headings to different texts or sections of a text
- gapped text: locating and replacing missing segments of a text

Before an exam, ask your teacher which closed test formats you might expect.

Closed test formats tend to occur mostly in listening and reading comprehension tasks (▶ EP2.1, EP4). In language tests such as TOEFL, Cambridge Certificate and TELC they may also be used for grammar or vocabulary.

To be successful in a closed test format, the following **skills** may be helpful:
- strategies of dealing with unknown words (▶ SF1: Dealing with unknown words)
- the ability to identify different *text types and to know what to expect from them. For example, if you follow a discussion, you can expect the speakers to have different opinions on a topic.
- knowledge about typical text structures and the use of linking words, which may indicate e.g. a contrast, an addition, a conclusion (▶ SF8: Structuring ideas; ▶ SF38: Writing a well-structured text).

If you are taking part in a test for a language certificate such as TOEFL, you should try to get information from this organization. Look for sample questions to get a better idea of what to expect in the exam. Since some of these tests are computer-based, you should get some computer practice in how to handle them.

■ TIP

- Read the instructions carefully and make sure you know what you have to focus on.
- Try to make predictions about the listening/reading text and about the answers to the questions.
- Read all answers, even if you are sure that you have found the correct one. The differences between the right and the wrong answers are often subtle or tricky.
- Fill in answers to questions that you are sure about straight away. If you are unsure, leave the item aside and come back to it later.
- Don't skip questions you cannot answer. Make educated guesses – you still stand a good chance of getting the credit for a question (e.g. 25% in a multiple choice item with four options!).

Glossary

When looking for a term in the Glossary, go to the alphabetical list of terms on p. 339 to find its exact page. An asterisk (*) before a term indicates that it is explained in the Glossary.

Literary texts

► Fiction

A fictional text is an imaginative work in which an author ['ɔːθə] creates his or her own world and/or presents an invented story. The reader is expected to accept this world or story as existing or true (this is called suspension of disbelief). Fiction can take different forms. The main types are *narrative prose (e.g. *novels, *short stories) and *drama.

Fiction usually comprises a variety of elements, such as *characters, *action and plot, *setting and *atmosphere. The *mode [məʊd] of presentation (scenic or panoramic) and the *point of view adopted (first-person or third-person, limited or unlimited, *reliable or *unreliable *narrator) play a central role in how the reader reacts to the story.

A literary text is often structured and held together by a specific theme [θiːm] or a so-called motif [məʊ'tiːf], which may be a recurring image or a specific phrase or sentence.

► Narrative prose

A narrative ['nærətɪv] prose text is a *fictional text which is told by a *narrator and is written in prose [prəʊz], i.e. writing that is formed by sentences in a continuous flow and is broken up only by paragraphs (cf. verse [vɜːs], which is used in poetry and refers to a single line of a poem, or a *stanza). Typical examples of narrative prose are *novels and *short stories. Fiction can further be subdivided by aspects of content (e.g. *coming-of-age stories or *fables).

novel ['nɒvl] *Roman* ▪ TROUBLE SPOT **novel** = Roman Not: ~~Novelle~~	A novel is a long and complex fictional narrative text often divided into chapters. The storyline and structure of a novel are normally more complicated than those of shorter fictional works and, accordingly, there may be greater variety and a more detailed development of *characters and *setting (i.e. the time and the place). In every novel the author must decide from which *point of view the story will be told. In some cases there is more than one *narrator. No other art form can recreate life on the same scale as the novel with its almost unlimited possibilities.
short story [,ʃɔːt'stɔːri] *Kurzgeschichte*	There is no generally accepted definition of the short story that clearly separates it from other narrative texts like the *novel. However, there are some elements that can be regarded as characteristic. Most short stories can be read at one sitting and concentrate on one *character, situation, dilemma or problem. In a short story the characters, the situation, etc. are not fully developed (unlike in a novel); the focus is on one single aspect which undergoes a change in the course of the story. There are different types of short stories, e.g. the *coming-of-age story or the slice of life story (which shows just one particular aspect of everyday life).
microfiction, **flash fiction** *Kürzestgeschichte*	Microfiction (or flash fiction) is an extremely short fictional text. It refers to a new literary genre [ʒɑ̃rə, 'ʒɒnrə] that originates from the *short story. Although there is no general agreement regarding its length, microfiction is much shorter than a short story and usually does not exceed one thousand words.

fable *Fabel*	A fable is a short narrative text in which animals represent human types or act like human beings. Fables are usually didactic since they intend to teach a moral lesson, make a satirical comment or illustrate some general truth. A moral may be understood from the text or there may be a moral (epilogue ['epɪlɒg]) at the end, which in modern fables is often *ironic.
coming-of-age story *Entwicklungsroman,* *Initiationsgeschichte*	A coming-of-age story is a *short story or *novel in which the process of growing up is portrayed. Usually the *protagonist is a child / an adolescent undergoing an experience which changes his/her outlook on life and marks an important stage in his/her development towards adulthood. It is also called story of initiation.
frame story *Rahmenhandlung*	A frame story is a *novel or *short story which contains one or more quite independent stories within it. The main story provides the frame for the other stories. Often the main story consists of a *character in one *setting recounting another story in another setting.

▶ Poetry

A poem is a piece of creative writing structured by lines and rhythm ['rɪðəm] (i.e. the arrangement of stressed and unstressed syllables in a line). The lines of a poem are often arranged into groups called stanzas ['stænzəs]. Phrases or lines repeated at intervals throughout a poem form the refrain [rɪ'freɪn]. To emphasize the structure and to create certain effects, traditional poets frequently make use of *rhyme. Modern poetry often uses free verse [ˌfriː 'vɜːs], which makes little use of rhyme. The poetry comes from *repetition, *imagery and the arrangement of words and stresses in the poem. Poems are often lyrical ['lɪrɪkl] (i.e. they express personal thoughts and feelings), but they can also be narrative (i.e. they tell a story). The speaker is the voice in which a poem is spoken, especially when the personal pronoun *I* is used. This speaker is not always identical with the voice of the poet.

sonnet ['sɒnɪt] *Sonett*	A sonnet is a special form of a poem that consists of 14 lines. Sonnets became popular in England in the 17th century and were mostly used for love poetry, but later they came to embrace a wide number of themes. There are various types of sonnets with different structures and forms. Shakespeare's sonnets comprised three quatrains ['kwɒtreɪns] (i.e. four lines with a shared rhyme scheme) and a couplet ['kʌplət] (i.e. two successive lines which rhyme). The couplet has a rhyme scheme that differs from the rest of the sonnet and it is used to sum up the theme or thought. The couplet is usually accompanied by the volta ['vɒltə], i.e. the turning point in a sonnet, which can be identified by words like *but*, *yet* or *and yet*. *Example:* William Shakespeare, 'Sonnet 116'; cf. *Context* p. 85
shape poem, **concrete poem** ['kɒŋkriːt] *konkrete Poesie*	A shape poem (also called a concrete poem) is a poem in which the printed words form a shape or picture. The shape usually reflects the theme or contents of the poem.
rhyme [raɪm] *Reim*	Rhyme is the similarity of sounds between certain words (especially stressed syllables), usually at the end of lines. When identifying the rhyme scheme ['raɪm skiːm] (i.e. which words at the end of the lines rhyme), it is usual to use small letters to indicate that words share a rhyme. If e.g. the words *abide*, *thee*, *wide* and *see* occur respectively at the end of four successive lines, the rhyme scheme is written as **a b a b** (this pattern is called alternate rhyme [ɔːl'tɜːnət]). If *abide*, *wide*, *thee*, and *see* occur respectively at the end of four successive lines, the rhyme scheme is written **a a b b** (this pattern is called rhyming couplets). Other letters are then used for other rhymes.

metre ['miːtə] *Metrum, Versmaß*	Metre is the regular rhythm of the words in a poem. Traditionally, this is achieved by the arrangement of stressed and unstressed syllables in the line of a poem. The most common metre in English is the iambic pentameter [aɪˈæmbɪk penˈtæmɪtə], which consists of a line of five feet (each foot consists of an unstressed syllable followed by a stressed syllable).	*Example:* O **no**! It **is** an **ev**-er *fix*-ed **mark** From: William Shakespeare, 'Sonnet 116'; cf. *Context* p. 85 The syllables **in bold** are stressed.

▶ Drama

A drama or play is written to be performed by actors or actresses in a theatre, in a film, on TV or on the radio. The author of a play is called a playwright ['pleɪraɪt] or dramatist ['dræmətɪst] while a scriptwriter creates scripts for films and television. Plays are usually divided into several acts (in classical drama, there were usually five acts, but modern plays normally consist of three and sometimes of only one act). An act may be subdivided into scenes.

A scene [siːn] is a smaller unit of action in which there is no change of place or break in time. The actors take on roles of *characters, perform the *action and express themselves in the form of dialogues, monologues or soliloquies. While a dialogue ['daɪəlɒg] involves at least two actors engaged in a conversation, the monologue ['mɒnəlɒg] is a lengthy speech by just one character in the company of others. The soliloquy [səˈlɪləkwi] differs from the monologue as it is spoken by one person who is alone on stage. It can give the audience more knowledge of events or individuals than the other characters and actions can take on different meanings for the audience than for the other characters of the play (this literary device is called dramatic irony). The actors' way of speaking, their appearance and their movements, as well as the *setting, the arrangement of props (i.e. all kinds of objects used by actors on stage or in a film), the sound and lighting, etc. are often given in the stage directions – this helps an acting company perform a play.

tragedy ['trædʒədi] *Tragödie, Trauerspiel*	A tragedy is a type of *drama in which the *protagonist passes through a series of misfortunes towards his or her downfall. Usually the downfall is brought about partly by the protagonist's own fault, e.g. through too much pride, weakness, uncertainty, etc. *Example:* William Shakespeare, *Macbeth*; cf. *Context* pp. 76f.
comedy ['kɒmədi] *Komödie, Lustspiel*	A comedy is a type of *drama which deals with a light topic or a more serious one in an amusing way. A comedy always has a happy ending. *Example:* William Shakespeare, *The Taming of the Shrew*; cf. *Context* pp. 82f.
feature film ['fiːtʃə] *Spielfilm*	A feature film is a full-length film that has a story and *characters, who are played by actors. A feature film is based on a film script, which the director then turns into a film. Important elements in a film are the dialogue, the use of camera techniques and the acting.
TV/radio series ['sɪəriːz] *Fernseh-/Radioserie*	A series is a regular programme on TV or radio about the lives and problems of a *character or, more usually, a group of characters. A series may centre on a couple or family life or a leading character's career, and some involve magic and/or fantasy. Each programme is self-contained, i.e. it deals with a particular issue or storyline which is concluded at the end of the programme. The lives of the characters evolve slowly over the course of a series. *Example:* Downton Abbey; cf. *Context* p. 111

sitcom *Sitcom*	A sitcom (= *situation comedy*) is a comic TV/radio *series which usually centres around a *character or group of characters. They are often stereotypes as they do not evolve over the series. It may be filmed in front of a live audience or have canned laughter added to make the audience aware of or to reinforce the funny lines.
soap (opera) 'Seifenoper'	A soap (= *soap opera*) is a regular TV or radio programme about the everyday lives of a group of people. The storyline of a soap, unlike that of a normal TV/radio *series, develops from programme to programme and may often end with a cliff-hanger ['klɪfhæŋə] (i.e. an exciting situation that makes you want to know what will happen next) to encourage the audience to tune in to the next episode.

▶ Narrator

The narrator [nə'reɪtə] is the voice or *character who tells the story and is part of the fictional world created by the author. There are three types of narrator:

first-person narrator *Ich-Erzähler*	The narrator is a *character in the story and refers to him- or herself as *I*. The reader must take care when reading the text, as only one person's point of view is given. *Example:* I'd attended school in the real world up until the sixth grade. It hadn't been a very pleasant experience. From: Ernest Cline, *Ready Player One*, 2012; cf. *Context* p. 16, ll. 1–2
third-person narrator *personaler Erzähler*	The narrator is not a *character in the story and refers to the characters as *he*, *she* or *they* or by their names. *Example:* It was with some relief that she got back into the coach and reached behind the cushion for her book. It was not there. Steadfastly waving as they rumbled along, she surreptitiously felt behind the other cushions. From: Alan Bennett, *The Uncommon Reader*, 2008; cf. *Context* p. 96, ll. 34–36 In this example, the narrator is a third-person narrator as he or she is not part of the fictional world and refers to the *protagonist by using the personal pronoun *she* (= the Queen). This excerpt is, however, told from the Queen's point of view (i.e. there is a *limited point of view) as the readers experience the story from her perspective. They are informed about her feelings and are also puzzled about the disappearance of her book.
omniscient narrator [ɒm'nɪsɪənt] *allwissender Erzähler*	The narrator has an *unlimited point of view, i.e. he or she can move freely in place and time and enter the minds of the *characters at will.

▶ Point of view

The point of view is the perspective from which *characters, events, etc. are presented in a *fictional story. This has an important effect on the reader: for example, we tend to respond more sympathetically to a character whose mind we enter, as we experience for ourselves what he or she goes through. A fictional work can have several points of view (depending on the *narrator):

limited point of view	A *first-person narrator can have a limited point of view: a *character in fictional work does not know everything that occurs, therefore he or she imposes his or her understanding and interpretation on the action.
	A *third-person narrator can have a limited point of view: the *narrator looks at the events and characters from the perspective of one of the *characters or from the outside (as an observer narrator) and so does not have access to the thoughts and feelings of all the characters.
unlimited point of view	A third-person narrator can have an unlimited point of view: the narrator can move freely in place and time and enter the minds of the *characters at will (here we speak of an omniscient narrator [ɒmˈnɪsɪənt]).

Often, the point of view changes to make for more interesting reading. A reader must ask him- or herself how reliable a narrator is. Often one cannot take everything in a fictional work at face value:

reliable narrator [rɪˈlaɪəbl]	The reader may take everything the *narrator tells at face value.
unreliable narrator [ˌʌnrɪˈlaɪəbl]	The reader must find out just how much of what the *narrator says can be accepted. *First-person narrators are usually unreliable as they give only one perspective on the action and the *characters.

▶ Mode of presentation

The way a writer narrates events is known as mode of presentation. There are two modes of presentation, and usually a combination of both is used in a narrative text:

scenic presentation	If the author shows an event in detail as it occurs, using dialogue, depicting thoughts and emotions, describing a scene, etc., he or she uses scenic presentation (also known as showing). *Example:*

When they arrived at the palace she had a word with Grant, the young footman in charge, who said that while ma'am had been in the Lords the sniffer dogs had been round and security had confiscated[1] the book. He thought it had probably been exploded.

'Exploded?' said the Queen. 'But it was Anita Brookner.'[2]

The young man, who seemed remarkably undeferential[3], said security may have thought it was a device. 5

The Queen said: 'Yes. That is exactly what it is. A book is a device to ignite[4] the imagination.'

[1]**confiscate sth.** take sth. away [2]**Anita Brookner** (born 1928) British novelist and art historian [3]**undeferential** showing no respect [4]**ignite sth.** *etwas entzünden*

From: Alan Bennett, *The Uncommon Reader*, 2008; cf. Context p. 97, ll. 42–50

interior monologue [ɪnˈtɪərɪə ˈmɒnəlɒg] *innerer Monolog*	This is a particular kind of *scenic presentation in which the author depicts the thoughts and feelings passing through a *character's mind. Often an interior monologue does not follow a chronological [ˌkrɒnəˈlɒdʒɪkl] order, since when people think, their thoughts jump from one subject to another. Interior monologues are normally narrated in the present tense. However, it is more common to find reported thought, in which the thoughts are presented as reported speech (i.e. in the past tense).

panoramic presentation	If the author tells the story as a condensed series of events, summarizing in a few sentences what happens over a longer period of time (e.g. an hour, a week, months), he or she uses panoramic presentation (also known as 'telling'). *Example:* For me, school had been a Darwinian exercise. A daily gauntlet[1] of ridicule, abuse, and isolation. By the time I entered sixth grade, I was beginning to wonder if I'd be able to maintain my sanity[2] until graduation, still six long years away. [1] **(run a) gauntlet** ['gɔːntlət] deal with a lot of people criticizing or attacking you [2] **sanity** ['sænəti] mental health From: Ernest Cline, *Ready Player One*, 2012; cf. *Context* p. 16, ll. 21–23

▶ Characters

Characters ['kærəktəz] are the people in a fictional text. They are usually presented through their actions, speech and thoughts as well as by description. The main character in a story is called the protagonist [prə'tægənist]. There are generally speaking two types of characters in *fictional works:

round character	A round character may be similar to real individuals and have several traits and behave in a way that is life-like. A round character usually changes in the course of a story. The main character in a story, the protagonist, is almost always a round character.
flat character	A flat character has only a limited number of traits or represents only a single quality. A crude representation of a character which is meant to be laughed at is called a caricature.

> ■ **TROUBLE SPOT**
>
> When talking about the characters in a fictional text, do not use the words *people* or *person*.

▶ Characterization

Characterization [ˌkærəktəraɪ'zeɪʃn] is the way in which the author presents his or her characters. We usually distinguish between two kinds of characterization, which are often combined by authors in their presentation of the characters.

direct [də'rekt, dɪ'-, daɪ'-] or **explicit characterization**	The reader is told about a character's personality directly by a) the *narrator, b) another character or c) the character him- or herself.	*Example:* 'But McNulty's eyes were scary.' From: Carl Deuker, *Payback Time*, 2010; cf. p. 191, l. 44
indirect [ˌɪndə'rekt, ˌɪndaɪ'rekt] or **implicit characterization**	The reader is expected to draw conclusions about a character by studying his or her behaviour, opinions, choice of words and/or way of talking. *Example:* I cleared my throat. 'How about we get started? I've got some questions. First –' 'No, no, no,' McNulty said, pointing the pencil at me again. 'No questions – not today, not ever. This job	

·····▶

takes forever and pays peanuts. Here's how it works. You write down or tape what I tell you. When I'm done, jazz[1] it up whatever you want, but never make me, my coaches, or my players look bad. Understand?'

[1]**Jazz sth. up** (*infml*) make sth. more interesting or attractive

From: Carl Deuker, *Payback Time*, 2010; cf. p. 190, ll. 33–37

TROUBLE SPOT

An author *characterizes* somebody, i.e. invents the traits of a character. A reader *describes the character* of somebody when talking about his or her traits.

LANGUAGE HELP

- main/central/major character/figure
- minor/secondary character/figure
- hero/heroine

▶ Action

Action ['ækʃn] is everything that happens in a *fictional story. Action may be on two levels:

external action [ɪk'stɜːnl]	The author describes what the *characters do and the events that take place. *Example:*
	[...] she got back into the coach and reached behind the cushion for her book. It was not there. Steadfastly waving as they rumbled along, she surreptitiously[1] felt behind the other cushions. [1]**surreptitious** subtle From: Alan Bennett, *The Uncommon Reader*, 2008; cf. Context p. 96, ll. 34–36.
internal action	The author describes what is going on in the minds of the *characters, i.e. the reader is shown the thoughts of the characters. *Example:*
	She was dreading the two hours the whole thing was due to take, though fortunately they were in the coach, not the open carriage, so she could take along her book. From: Alan Bennett, *The Uncommon Reader*, 2008; cf. Context p. 97, ll. 6–7.

▶ Plot

Plot [plɒt] refers to the structure of events in a *fictional story. The story is usually told through cause and effect. The English novelist E.M. Forster described plot in these terms: '"The king died and then the queen died" is a story. "The king died and then the queen died of grief", is a plot.' (*Aspects of the Novel*, 1927). The plot usually develops in a number of stages:

1. **exposition** [ˌekspə'zɪʃn]	The *characters, theme, *setting, etc. are introduced.
2. **rising action**	A conflict ['kɒnflɪkt] is developed (i.e. the struggle or opposition between different forces, characters, etc.).
3. **climax** ['klaɪmæks]	The conflict reaches its highest point.
4. **turning point**	There is a change in the conflict or *suspense.
5. **falling action**	The *suspense is reduced.

6. **denouement** [deɪˈnuːmõ] (also known as the **solution** [səˈluːʃn])	Some resolution of the conflict is achieved.
which may also be: **surprise ending**	The reader's expectations concerning the course of the story are not fulfilled but instead an unexpected solution of the conflict is presented.
or instead: **open ending**	The conflict is not fully resolved and the reader is left wondering what might happen next.

A plot will have some element of *suspense and *tension. In order to create suspense or to make a story more exciting, authors also make use of flashbacks and foreshadowing:

suspense [səˈspens] *Spannung*	Suspense is created when the reader does not know the outcome of a conflict or of the action.
tension [ˈtenʃn] *(An)spannung*	Tension is the feeling evoked in the reader when a story/drama is full of *suspense, i.e. the reader is curious about what will happen.
flashback [ˈflæʃbæk] *Rückblende*	Authors do not always tell their stories strictly chronologically [ˌkrɒnəˈlɒdʒɪkli]. In some stories the authors make use of flashbacks, i.e. the *narrator goes back into the past to describe a scene that has relevance to the plot.
foreshadowing [fɔːˈʃædəʊɪŋ] *Vorwegnahme*	Foreshadowing (also called anticipation) is the technique of hinting at later events in a *fictional text so that the reader is prepared for them or can anticipate them. *Example:* In William Shakespeare's *Macbeth*, the three witches allow the audience to believe that Macbeth will become king.

■ TROUBLE SPOT	■ LANGUAGE HELP
happy ending Not = ~~happy end~~	• open/surprise/unexpected/happy/sad/tragic ending • centre around sth. • a conflict between … and …

▶ Atmosphere

Atmosphere [ˈætməsfɪə] is the feeling or mood created by an author in his or her work. The *setting, use of language and *characterization all contribute to the atmosphere of a work.	*Example:*
	One of the Queen's recurrent royal responsibilities was to open Parliament, an obligation she had never previously found particularly burdensome[1] and actually rather enjoyed: to be driven down the Mall[2] on a bright autumn morning even after fifty years was something of a treat.
	[1]**burdensome** implying hard work [2]**the Mall** road leading to Buckingham Palace
	From: Alan Bennett, *The Uncommon Reader*, 2008; cf. Context p. 96, ll. 1–4
	Here the description of the Queen's drive down the Mall together with the bright autumn morning creates a positive atmosphere.

▶ Setting

Setting is the time and place in which a literary work takes place. The setting can have symbolic overtones; it may serve to reveal something about the characters and also contribute to the *atmosphere of the story. *Example:* The extract quoted above from the novel *The Uncommon Reader* by Alan Bennett (cf. Context p. 96, ll. 1–4) is set in contemporary Britain on a sunny autumn morning. The season contributes to the positive and light-hearted atmosphere of the story.

Non-fictional texts

▶ Non-fiction

A non-fictional [ˌnɒn ˈfɪkʃənl] text (e.g. *news story, *advertisement, *speech, *letter, etc.) normally refers to the real world whereas a *literary text creates its own fictional world. Non-fictional texts may serve a variety of practical purposes, e.g. to inform, persuade, express personal opinions, criticize, etc. There is a variety of non-fictional text types:

news story *Zeitungs-bericht*	The terms *news story*, *news item* and *news report* can be used interchangeably to refer to reports of recent events of general interest that appear in newspapers, on television or on the radio. News items can be of any length. In theory, they are meant to be objective and unbiased presentations of the facts, providing answers to the five w's, i.e. the questions *who?, what?, when?, where?* and *why?.* In practice, totally impartial reporting is impossible. The choice of words, the *style and *tone, the choice of detail and examples, the emphasis [ˈemfəsɪs] given to certain aspects of the story, the position of the article in the paper and on the page, the headline and layout all contribute to influence the reader. There are two common formulas used in news stories: a) The pyramid, in which the most important item or element in the story is reported first and then the rest of the information is offered in descending order of importance. b) The Wall Street Journal formula, in which the news story starts with a particular (usually personal) example to attract the reader's attention before the topic is discussed. It differs from a *feature story in that the latter puts more emphasis on the personal account in order to illustrate a topic, while the former uses the personal account merely to attract the attention of the reader.
biography [baɪˈɒɡrəfi] *Biografie*	A biography is a book or text written by one person about the life of another person. If the person writes his or her own life story, this is referred to as an autobiography [ˌɔːtəbaɪˈɒɡrəfi]. Usually the biography belongs to the genre of *non-fiction as it portrays the life of a person that really exists/existed. However, there are also *fictional biographies, where the author invents a *character and his life story (e.g. *Robinson Crusoe*).
feature story [ˈfiːtʃə] *Zeitungsre-portage*	A feature story deals with a topic by concentrating on a particular person or on particular people. It often takes an individual case as its starting point to discuss the different aspects of the topic on a personal level and leaves the reader to draw more general conclusions from this individual case. The writer of a feature story makes use of direct quotes from the people involved in the story and relies on first-hand reporting, i.e. the journalist writes mostly about things and people he or she has actually encountered. A feature story often opens with the description of an event or a person in order to attract the reader's attention. *Example:* 'Eastern Europeans in the UK'; cf. Context p. 107

editorial [ˌedɪˈtɔːriəl] *Leitartikel*	An editorial (in British English also known as a *leading article* or *leader*) is an article that expresses the opinion of the newspaper's editor or editorial team about an item of news or a political or social issue, etc. In American usage an editorial can also be a comment ['kɒment] on radio or television that expresses the opinion of the station or network. Unlike *columns, editorials are not supposed to be personal and do not appear with a byline, i.e. with a line that gives the writer's name.
column ['kɒləm] *Kolumne*	a) *Column* is the term used for any of the vertical sections into which the printed page of a newspaper is divided. b) *Column* is the term used for a regular item in a newspaper or magazine which either deals with a particular subject (e.g. gardening, gossip, financial, agony column) or is written by a particular writer (called a columnist). Columnists often write highly personal essays on topics of their choosing. Unlike *editorials, columns appear with a byline, i.e. with a line that gives the writer's name.
speech *Rede,* *Ansprache*	A speech is an address delivered to an audience. A speaker may try to establish contact with his or her listeners in various ways: by flattering them, addressing them directly (direct address) or using the first person plural (e.g. *we, our*) to involve them in what he or she is saying. A speaker may appeal to shared experiences and values, e.g. by quoting from or alluding to sources such as the Bible or history. A speaker often uses *stylistic devices to heighten the impact of what he or she is saying. Contrast ['kɒntrɑːst] may be used to highlight differences between the speaker and his or her opponents. *Repetition and *alliteration often help the audience follow the speech and remember key ideas and phrases. *Example:* '9/11 – A game changer'; cf. *Context* pp. 24f.
essay *Essay*	An essay is a text form in which the writer expresses his or her personal views on some topic. Essays can vary widely in length, subject matter and *tone, some being serious and others light-hearted and entertaining.
letter *Brief*	There are many types of letters. They can be personal or business-oriented, depending on the relationship between the sender and receiver, the occasion and the purpose of the letter. Letters are a very flexible text form and comprise thank-you notes, emails, covering letters (in American English, *cover letters*), letters of complaint, *letters to the editor, etc. The beginnings and endings of letters follow certain conventions. Usually, letters consist of the following parts: **1** the address of the sender (and in the case of a business letter, the address of the recipient), **2** the date, **3** the salutation (e.g. *Dear Mark*), **4** the body of the letter, i.e. the information the sender wants to convey, **5** a conventional phrase to close the letter (e.g. *Yours faithfully*, *Yours sincerely*, *Love*) and **6** the signature. *Example:* the letter from Chetan Bhagat to Gandhi; cf. *Context* pp. 119f.
letter to the editor *Leserbrief*	A letter to the editor is a letter in which a reader expresses his or her opinion concerning an article in a newspaper/magazine or a problem which is of public interest. The letter may criticize or support an article, or state a personal opinion concerning a topic which is being discussed in public or attract the attention of other readers to a topic that has been ignored or is worthy of attention.
blurb [blɜːb] *Umschlagtext,* *Klappentext*	A blurb is the short promotional text on the back cover of a book or a DVD case.
advertisement [ədˈvɜːtɪsmənt] *Werbung, An-* *zeige, Annonce*	An advertisement (informally also called an *advert* or *ad*) is a text which attempts to persuade people to do something (e.g. buy a particular product or contribute money to a cause). It normally consists of pictures and text (called *copy*) and is designed to catch the attention of the reader through its layout. ·····▶

Common elements of advertisements are *wordplay in the title or headings and *humour to win the sympathy of the reader. Advertisers often use the AIDA formula (**A**ttention, **I**nterest, **D**esire, **A**ction) in their advertisements. Newspaper or magazine advertisements dealing with job offers, buying, selling or renting something, etc. are called *small* or *classified ads.* Advertisements on the radio or on television are known as *commercials*.
Example: 'The best job in the world is back!', cf. *Context* p. 193

blog [blɒg] *Blog*	A blog is a regularly updated website created by an individual or a small group. Usually, the chosen language is colloquial and informal.
cartoon *Karikatur,* *Cartoon*	A cartoon is an amusing drawing in a newspaper or magazine that deals with human nature or a current political or social issue. Complex issues are reduced to memorable pictures. Cartoons often include captions or speech bubbles. Techniques employed by cartoonists include caricature ['kærɪkətʃʊə], *exaggeration, *wordplay and the use of *symbols. Cartoons usually presuppose that the reader has background knowledge of the political, social and cultural issues being dealt with, which often makes them difficult for the non-native reader to understand. *Example:* 'Being five. A boy and his blog'; cf. *Context* p. 10

Style and Language

▶ Style

Style [staɪl] is the way in which a text is written. In order to examine the style of a text it is necessary to examine aspects such as the *register, the *diction and the *tone of the text, as well as the grammar and the sentence structures used in the text.

tone [təʊn] *Ton(fall)*	Tone is the way in which a writer treats his or her topic, thereby reflecting his or her emotional attitude towards that topic and also towards the reader. The tone can be formal, intimate, solemn, playful, serious, ironic (cf. *irony), humorous (cf. *humour), angry, etc.
humour ['hjuːmə] *Humor*	Humour is based on the human ability to see and laugh at the strangeness of a *character, an action or comment, etc. because it is unexpected or unsuitable in a particular situation. At one end of the spectrum, humour is gentle, understanding and tolerant and makes the reader smile at human weaknesses; at the other end, it is divisive, bitter or sarcastic, evoking contempt and moral indignation at human vices and corruption. Not all forms of humour will be appreciated by every segment of society since humour relies on shared cultural values. *Example:* > [The Queen] got quite good at reading and waving, the trick being to keep the book below the level of the window and to keep focused on it and not on the crowds. From: Alan Bennett, *The Uncommon Reader*, 2008; cf. *Context* p. 96, ll. 7–9 Here the Queen's well-known behaviour of waving at the crowd is ridiculed by the fact that she is reading a book at the same time.

diction *Diktion,* *Ausdruck,* *Wortwahl*	Diction is the words a writer chooses for his or her text. Diction is very important as words influence the reader or listener. In many argumentative texts, for example, the writer will use words that have a positive connotation [ˌkɒnəˈteɪʃn] (i.e. the associations a word has beyond its literal or dictionary meaning) to support his or her arguments, or words with negative connotations to attack those he or she opposes. The choice of words often reveals the writer's attitudes. A writer can also use emotive language (i.e. words and expressions with particular connotations that appeal to the reader's or listener's emotions) and so influence him or her to react in a particular way. When the writer makes use of the literal and limited meaning of a word, regardless of the ideas and emotions it might connote, this is called denotation [ˌdiːnəʊˈteɪʃn].
register [ˈredʒɪstə] *Sprachebene,* *Stilebene*	Register is the level of language (the choice of words, grammar, etc.) used in a particular situation. The register in a text may be formal, neutral or informal.
	Formal style consists of difficult vocabulary, often of Latin origin, and complex sentence structure; it is usually only used for serious purposes, e.g. essays or academic publications, or in official situations, and would not be appropriate in normal everyday conversation. *Example:* A new widely-debated approach is gene pharming. Pharma crops are genetically modified plants like maize that produce much-needed medicines. From: 'Science – motor of progress?', cf. *Context*, p. 32, ll. 22–24 The writer uses difficult words and grammar so that the reader must examine the sentence closely to understand what the writer is saying.
	Neutral style falls between *formal and *informal style and is the style generally used by educated people; it is used in *feature stories, *news stories, etc. *Example:* [P]eople's 'likes' and 'dislikes' are carefully stored, along with a great number of other details gathered about the users, to be exploited by businesses or political organizations. From: 'Living interactive lives', cf. *Context*, p. 12, ll. 6–9 The writer uses straightforward sentences and words that are neither formal nor informal.
	Informal style is characterized by fairly simple, often incomplete sentences, short forms (e.g. *can't, you'll*), phrasal verbs and colloquial words, often of Germanic origin; it is used between friends or in a relaxed or informal situation. *Example:* That waitress sized us up in two seconds. We're black, and 'black people don't tip' so she wasn't gonna waste her time; someone like that, nothing you can do to change their mind. From: Paul Haggis, *Crash*, 2004 The short forms like 'we're', 'wasn't' or gonna, the use of simple words like 'do', 'go' and phrases like *to* 'size sb'. *up* indicate that the characters are using informal style. Informal style may include the use of slang and/or taboo words: Slang is very informal language, mainly used in dialogue between people of the same age or from a similar background, etc. Taboo words [təˈbuː] are generally considered obscene, vulgar or shocking and are used only if the writer is trying to make a particular point or shock his or her reader.

layout *Layout,* *Aufbau*	The way elements are arranged on a printed page is known as the layout. The layout includes elements such as the type and size of letters, the use of **bold** or *italic* typeface, <u>underlining</u>, headings and sub-headings, bullets (i.e. dots or other symbols used at the beginning of a text passage), the size and number of *columns, the length of paragraphs, the colour and the placement of illustrations. The layout determines whether a text attracts the attention of the reader and is pleasant to read, and it helps writers to structure their texts and to emphasize certain words, phrases or passages. The layout is particularly important when considering newspaper articles, *advertisements and brochures.
thesis ['θiːsɪs] *These*	An idea or a view that an author of an argumentative text presents and discusses in a formal way.
antithesis [æn'tɪθəsɪs] *Antithese*	An antithesis is an idea that is the opposite of an idea (thesis) already put forward by a writer. Often the writer will put forward the antithesis in order to stress his own thesis.

▶ Stylistic devices

Stylistic devices [staɪ'lɪstɪk dɪ'vaɪsɪs] (also called *rhetorical devices* [rɪ'tɒrɪkl dɪ'vaɪsɪs]) are methods and techniques used to produce a particular effect. Stylistic devices may e.g. relate to sound (e.g. *alliteration), structure (e.g. *repetition, *parallelism) or *imagery.

> ■ LANGUAGE HELP
>
> *The author uses alliteration/contrast/exaggeration/ repetition … (uncountable nouns)*
> *In line 5 there is a metaphor/allusion/symbol/rhetorical question/pun (countable nouns)*

Imagery

metaphor ['metəfə, 'metəfɔː] *Metapher*	A metaphor is a comparison between two things which are basically quite unlike one another without using the words *as* or *like* (cf. *simile).	*Example:* There's daggers in men's smiles. <div align="right">From: William Shakespeare, *Macbeth*</div>
personification [pə,sɒnɪfɪ'keɪʃn] *Personifikation*	Personification is the technique of representing animals or objects as if they were human beings or possessed human qualities. *Example:* Love's not Time's fool, though rosy lips and cheeks / Within his bending[1] sickle's[2] compass[3] come: / Love alters not with his brief hours and weeks, / But bears[4] it out even to the edge[5] of doom. [1] **bending** curved [2] **sickle** *Sichel* [3] **compass** *Reichweite* [4] **bear out sth.** endure sth. [5] **edge of doom** end of time From: William Shakespeare, 'Sonnet 116', cf. *Context*, p. 85 Here, both love and time are personified. Love in particular is described as a person with the appearance of 'rosy lips and cheeks'.	
simile ['sɪməli] *Vergleich*	Like a *metaphor, a simile is a type of comparison. But while metaphors say that something *is* something else, a simile says that something *is like* something else and uses the words *like* or *as* to draw the comparison.	*Example:* My mistress eyes are nothing like the sun. <div align="right">From: William Shakespeare, 'Sonnet 18'</div>

Glossary

symbol ['sɪmbl] *Symbol*	A symbol is a thing, word or phrase signifying something concrete that stands not only for itself but also for a certain abstract idea. As in the case of a *metaphor or a *simile the meaning of a symbol goes beyond the literal. *Example:* A red rose is often a symbol of love.

> ■ TROUBLE SPOT
> **symbol of sth.**
> Not: ~~symbol for sth.~~

Sound

alliteration [ə,lɪtə'reɪʃn] *Alliteration*	Alliteration is the repetition of a sound, normally a consonant, at the beginning of neighbouring words or of stressed syllables within such words, to produce a usually rhythmic, but sometimes also comic effect. *Example:* Around the rugged rock the ragged rascal ran.

assonance ['æsənəns] *Assonanz*	Assonance is the repetition of the same or similar vowel sounds within stressed syllables of neighbouring words.	*Example:* Beside the lake, beneath the trees, Fluttering and dancing in the breeze. From: William Wordsworth, 'I wandered lonely as a cloud'
onomatopoeia [,ɒnə,mætə'piːə] *Lautmalerei*	Omatopoeia is the use of a word which imitates the sounds it refers to, e.g. *buzz* or *hum.* In a group of words or a phrase it may evoke a particular feeling, mood, sound or movement.	*Example:* Only the stuttering rifles' rapid rattle. From: Wilfred Owen, 'Anthem for doomed youth' The repetition of 't's and 'r's sounds like the shooting of rifles, which the words describe.

Structure

accumulation [ə,kjuːmjə'leɪʃn] *Akkumulation,* *Ansammlung*	Accumulation is a listing of words and expressions with similar meaning. Thus, the words are emphasized or become more descriptive. *Example:* Then shall our names / Familiar in his mouth as household words / Harry the King, Bedford and Exeter / Warwick and Talbot, Salisbury and Gloucester, / Be in their flowing cups freshly remembered. From: William Shakespeare, *Henry V* This excerpt displays an accumulation of several addresses for 'King Harry'.
analogy [ə'nælədʒi] *Analogie*	Analogy is the comparison of two things which are similar in several aspects. By comparing an object, situation or person to something familiar, the explanation becomes easier to understand. *Example:* What's in a name? That which we call a rose. / By any other word would smell as sweet. / So Romeo would, were he not Romeo called. From: William Shakespeare, *Romeo and Juliet* Juliet states that just like a rose that will always keep its sweet smell whichever name it is called, Romeo will stay the same even if he changes his name.

anaphora [əˈnæfərə] Anapher	Anaphora is a form of *parallelism which repeats the same word or group of words at the beginning of successive clauses.	*Example:* Come in, I say. Come in and eat with us. From: Imtiaz Dharker, 'The right word', cf. *Context* p. 89, ll. 31–32
enjambement [ɪnˈdʒæmbmənt] *Enjambement*	Enjambement describes incomplete syntax at the end of the line where the meaning runs over to the next line without any punctuation at the end. An enjambement is also called *run-on line.*	*Example:* The child steps in And carefully, at my door, Takes off his shoes. From: Imtiaz Dharker, 'The right word', cf. *Context* p. 89, ll. 33–35
enumeration *Aufzählung*	Enumeration is the listing of words, phrases or ideas. In instructive or argumentative texts the list of enumerated elements can be given numbers or bullet points so the reader can see each new element clearly.	*Example:* [...] go, my son, multiply, divide, conquer. From: Philip Levine, 'Corporate Head'; cf. *Context* p. 189
parallelism [ˈpærəlelɪzəm] *Parallelismus*	Parallelism is the deliberate repetition of similar or identical words, phrases, sentence constructions, etc. in the same or neighbouring sentences. Parallelism draws the attention of the reader to certain ideas that the writer may consider important. It may be used to show that the elements are of similar importance, or it may be used in a climactic sequence, with the most important element listed at the end.	*Example:* [...] Which alters[1] when it alteration finds, Or bends with the remover to remove[2]. [1] **alter** change [2] **remover** person who goes away From: William Shakespeare, 'Sonnet 116', cf. *Context* p. 85, ll. 3–4
repetition *Wiederholung*	Repetition is the deliberate use of a word or phrase more than once in a sentence or a text to create a sense of pattern or form, or to emphasize certain elements for the reader or listener.	

Miscellaneous

allusion [əˈluːʒn] *Allusion, Anspielung*	Allusion is the direct or indirect reference to something or somebody the reader or listener is supposed to recognize and respond to. An allusion may be to a work of literature, a historical event, a religious text like the Bible, etc. *Example:* 'This place is like the garden of Eden'. This allusion refers to the 'garden of God', i.e. paradise, which appears in the Bible.
cliché [ˈkliːʃeɪ]	A cliché denotes the fact that an expression has been overused to the extent that the original meaning has been lost. It may also refer to predictable events or actions.

Glossary

exaggeration [ɪɡˌzædʒəˈreɪʃn] *Übertreibung*	Exaggeration is the use of a strong overstatement. It may be used to create either a serious or comic effect. A single phrase containing an exaggeration is called hyperbole [hʌɪˈpɔːbəli]. (cf. also *understatement)	*Example:* I fear the day technology will surpass our human interaction. The world will have a generation of idiots. *Albert Einstein*
irony [ˈaɪrəni] *Ironie*	Irony is the term used when a person makes fun of somebody or something without openly doing so. A person using irony may use certain words and actually mean the opposite of what those words normally mean. Also, a person may appear to support someone or something while at the same time making it clear (e.g. by his or her tone of voice) that he or she is actually criticizing or revealing the contradictions in the other person's behaviour. A text which uses irony to ridicule or make fun of an institution, person, set of beliefs, etc. is called a satire [ˈsætaɪə].	
juxtaposition [ˌdʒʌkstəpəˈzɪʃn] *Gegenüberstellung*	Juxtaposition is a very strong contrast [ˈkɒntrɑːst] of opposing ideas, arguments, views, mostly introduced by words like *but*, *however* or *nevertheless*.	
rhetorical question *rhetorische Frage*	A rhetorical question is a question to which the answer seems obvious and is therefore not necessary. Such questions push the reader or listener to a certain conclusion. As such they are popular in political *speeches, etc. when a person is trying to influence others.	*Example:* What do the changes mean? They can either strengthen and unite us, or they can weaken and divide us. From: William J. Clinton, 'The changing face of America'; cf. *Context* p. 144, ll. 27–28 Here the rhetorical question is used to draw the reader/listener into the argument by posing a direct question. The reader/listener might feel a little under pressure, even manipulated to answer the question in a specific way.
understatement *Untertreibung*	Understatement is a statement in which the true magnitude of an idea, event or fact is minimized, so that something is deliberately presented as being much less important, valuable, etc. than it really is. Understatement is often used for *ironic effect, e.g. saying 'It is a bit cold today', when the temperature is 10 degrees below freezing. (cf. also *exaggeration)	
wordplay or **pun** [pʌn] *Wortspiel*	Wordplay (also called pun) is the use of a word which may be understood in two different ways or which may be put into a different context to alter the meaning. *Example:* The magician got so mad that he pulled his hair out. Here, the word *hair* alludes to *hare* (= *Hase*), an animal commonly associated with magicians.	

Alphabetical list of words in the Glossary

Words in **bold** print have their own entries in the Glossary; words in blue print do not have their own entry and appear as part of another entry.

Verbs for Tasks ('Operatoren')

Context uses the same special vocabulary ('Operatoren') for tasks that is used in standard tests, including the 'Abitur'. Be sure you understand what's required of you when you come across one of the verbs below.

'Anforderungsbereich I' COMPREHENSION
refers to text comprehension and definition.

'Anforderungsbereich II' ANALYSIS
focuses on text analysis and comparison, and stylistic devices.

'Anforderungsbereich III' BEYOND THE TEXT
concentrates on discussion, comment, evaluation and text production.

> Find a further list of verbs for tasks, this one ordered by skills (writing, mediation, listening, speaking), here:
> **Webcode** context-58

The instructions say	Example	What you are expected to do
'Anforderungsbereich I' COMPREHENSION		
describe (*also:* **give/write a description of**) *beschreiben*	**Describe** the writer's invention and what it is used for.	*Give a detailed account of something.*
outline ['– –] *umreißen, skizzieren*	**Outline** the writer's views on …	*Give the main features, structure or general principles of a topic, omitting minor details.*
state *darlegen*	**State** the author's opinion on the main character's decision.	*Specify something clearly.*
present [prɪˈzent] *darstellen*	**Present** your ideas in a logical order.	*(Re)structure something and write it down.*
point out *benennen, erläutern*	**Point out** the keywords in the first paragraph of the text.	*Find and explain certain aspects.*
summarize (*also:* **give/ write a summary of; sum up**) *zusammenfassen*	**Summarize** the incident in the church in no more than four sentences.	*Give a concise account of the main points of something.*
'Anforderungsbereich II' ANALYSIS		
analyse *(BE)*, **analyze** *(AE)* [ˈænəlaɪz] / **examine** [ɪgˈzæmɪn] *analysieren, untersuchen*	**Analyse** the main elements of the poster. **Examine** the writer's attitude towards the protagonist.	*Describe and explain certain aspects and/or features of the text in detail.*
characterize (*usu. AE*), **give/write a characterization of** [ˈkærəktəraɪz, ˌkærəktəraɪˈzeɪʃn] *charakterisieren, detailliert beschreiben und erklären*	**Write a characterization of** the mother in the story.	*Describe and examine the way in which the characters are presented.*

explain *erklären*	**Explain** the main character's reaction to her mother in the first scene.	*Describe and define in detail.*
illustrate ['ɪləstreɪt] *erläutern,* *veranschaulichen*	**Illustrate** the author's use of metaphorical language.	*Use examples to explain something or make it clear why something is as it is.*
interpret [ɪn'tɜːprɪt] *interpretieren, deuten,* *auswerten*	**Interpret** the message the author wishes to convey.	*Analyse the form and content of something and explain its meaning in a wider context. Cite examples as evidence to support your interpretation.*
compare *vergleichen*	**Compare** how the characters are portrayed in the film and in the novel.	*Point out similarities and differences between two or more things.*

	'Anforderungsbereich III' BEYOND THE TEXT	
comment on ['kɒment] *kommentieren, Stellung* *nehmen zu*	**Comment on** the speaker's belief that …	*State clearly your opinions on the topic in question and support your views with evidence.*
discuss *diskutieren, erörtern*	**Discuss** how education influences attitudes towards immigration.	*Investigate or examine by argument; give reasons for and against.*
justify *begründen, rechtfertigen*	**Justify** your answer.	*Show adequate grounds for decisions or conclusions.*
evaluate [ɪ'væljueɪt] *einschätzen, bewerten*	**Evaluate** the author's view of the impact Obama's speech had on his audience.	*Form an opinion after carefully considering and presenting advantages and disadvantages.*
assess [ə'ses] *auswerten, beurteilen,* *bewerten*	**Assess** the effectiveness of the government's approach to fighting poverty.	*Consider the points for and against something in a balanced way.*
contrast [kən'trɑːst] *kontrastieren,* *gegenüberstellen*	**Contrast** the rights of African Americans in the 1960s and today.	*Emphasize the differences between two or more things.*

Charts

The British System of Government

Monarch

official head of state (mostly representative functions), signs bills passed by Parliament thereby making them law

officially appoints

The Government

Prime Minister
head of the government
leader of the strongest party in the House of Commons

Cabinet
about 20 of the most important Ministers
(heads of government departments)

officially appoints
(on the recommen-
dation of the PM)

Parliament

House of Lords
ca. 700 members (life peers, 26 Anglican bishops,
and 92 hereditary peers)
scrutinizes bills passed by the House of Commons

House of Commons
650 MPs from constituencies
makes laws
elected for each constituency in a first-past-the-post system,
elections are held at least every five years

is accountable to

elects

Electorate
all men and women over the age of 18

The US System of Government

System of Checks and Balances

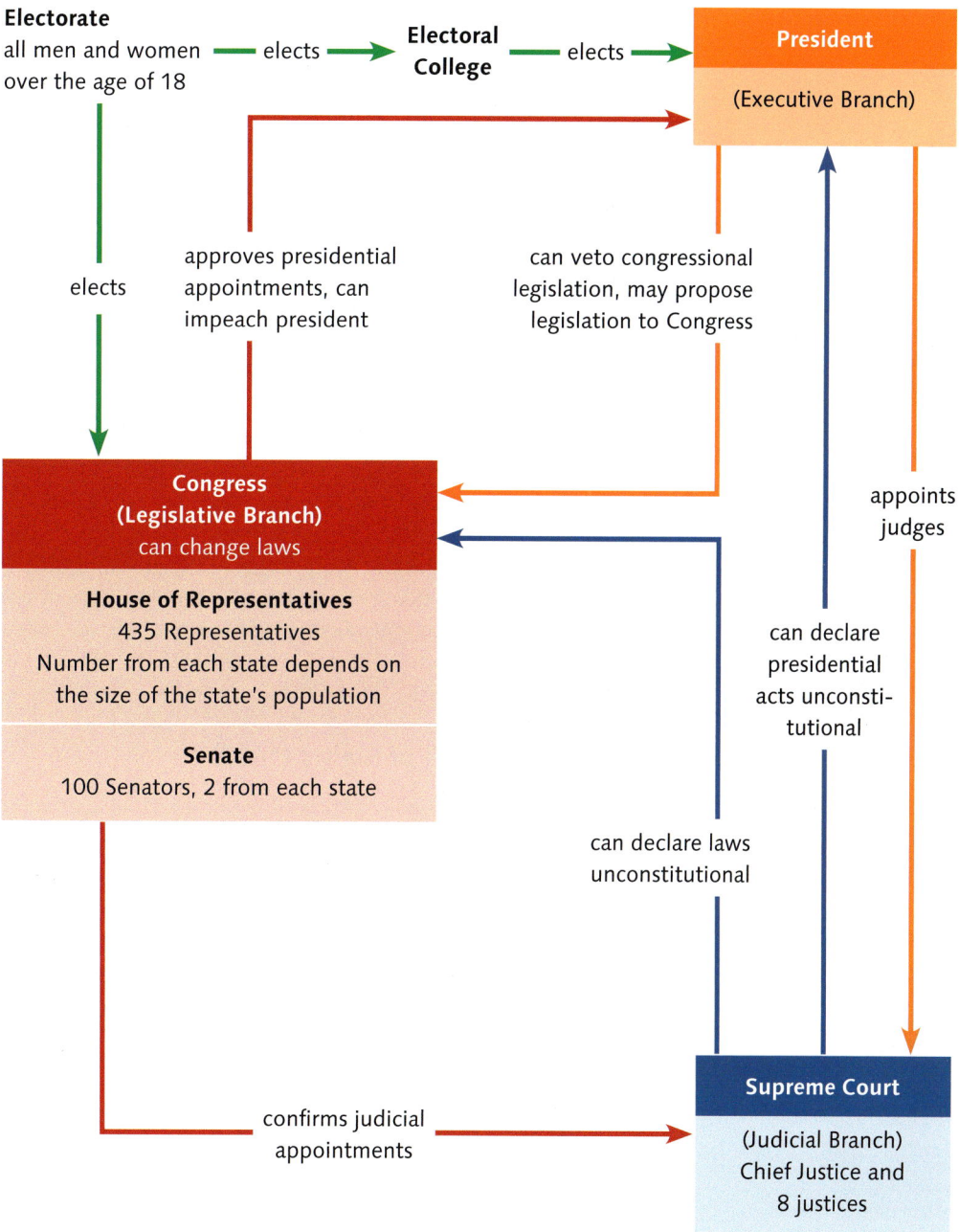

Historical Documents

Excerpts from the Magna Carta (1215)

Until King John (king from 1199–1216) was forced by his barons to sign a document called the Magna Carta ('great charter'), the will of the king had been law. The Magna Carta was the first step on the long road which led to the constitutional principle that the 'Law is King'. Six of its 63 articles are printed here.

(12) No scutage or aid shall be imposed in our kingdom, unless by the general council of our kingdom; except for ransoming our person, making our eldest son a knight and once for marrying our eldest daughter; and for these there shall be paid no more than a reasonable aid. [...]

(14) And for holding the general council of the kingdom concerning the assessment of aids, except in the three cases aforesaid, and for the assessing of scutage, we shall cause to be summoned the archbishops, bishops, abbots, earls, and greater barons of the realm, separately by our letters. [...]

(20) A freeman shall not be amerced for a small offence, except in accordance with the degree of the offence and for a grave offence he shall be amerced according to its gravity, without imperilling his status; and a merchant similarly without imperilling his stock-in-trade; and similarly a villain shall be amerced always without loss of wainage – if their liability is to us. And none of the aforesaid amercements shall be imposed except by the sworn evidence of worthy men of the neighbourhood.

(38) In future no official shall put anyone to trial merely on his own testimony, without reliable witness produced for this purpose.

(39) No freeman shall be taken or imprisoned, or deprived of his freehold, or outlawed, or banished, or in any way destroyed, nor will we take or order action against him, unless by the lawful judgment of his peers, or by the law of the land.

(40) We will sell to no man, we will not deny to any man, either justice or right.

Excerpts from the Bill of Rights (1689)

When James II (king from 1685–1688) tried to restore Catholicism to Britain, he met with resistance from all sides. Parliament forced James into exile in the 'Glorious Revolution' of 1688. Prince William of Orange and his wife, Princess Mary, were offered the throne on the condition that they accepted the 'Bill of Rights'. Thus Britain's constitutional monarchy was established. From then on, the British monarch ruled not by the grace of God, but by the grace of Parliament.

The said Lords Spiritual and Temporal, and Commons [...] do declare:

(1) That the pretended power of suspending of laws, or the execution of laws, by regal authority, without consent of Parliament, is illegal.

(2) That the pretended power of dispensing with laws or the execution by laws by regal authority as it has been assumed and exercised of late is illegal.

(4) That levying money for or to the use of the Crown by pretence of prerogative, without grant of Parliament, for longer time or in other manner than the same is or shall be granted, is illegal.

---

1 **scutage** ['skjuːtɪdʒ] (in feudal times) money paid by a knight instead of doing military service, or by a landowner instead of personal service
6 **aforesaid** [–'––] mentioned before
7 **summon sb.** (*fml*) order sb. to come to you
9 **freeman** ['––] (in feudal times) a citizen
amerce sb. [ə'mɜːs] make sb. pay a fine
in accordance with sb./sth. *in Übereinstimmung mit jdm./etwas*
11 **imperil sth.** [–'––] endanger sth.
12 **stock-in-trade** goods kept on sale by a merchant
villain ['vɪlən] (hier) Leibeigene/r
13 **wainage** (*old use*) profit or produce from the cultivation of land
if their liability is to us if the offence they committed was against us
14 **sworn evidence** *Aussage unter Eid*
16 **official** (*n*) person in a position of authority
18 **freehold** ['––] ownership of land

1 **said** (*adj; fml*) mentioned before
Lords Spiritual archbishops and bishops
Lords Temporal ['tempərəl] lords who are concerned with worldly affairs, rather than with spiritual things; together with the Lords Spiritual they constitute the House of Lords
Commons House of Commons consisting of representatives of counties and towns
5 **of late** in recent times
6 **by pretence of prerogative** ['prɪ'tens, prɪ'rɒgətɪv] by claiming that the king has the right to do sth.

(5) That it is the right of the subject to petition the King, and all commitments and
prosecutions for such petitioning are illegal.

(6) That the raising or keeping a standing army within the kingdom in time of
peace, unless it be with the consent of Parliament, is against law.

(8) That elections of members of Parliament ought to be free.

(9) That the freedom of speech, and debates and proceedings in Parliament, ought
not to be impeached or questioned in any court or place out of Parliament.

(10) That excessive bail ought not to be required nor excessive fines imposed; nor
cruel and unusual punishment inflicted.

(13) And that for redress of all grievances, and for the amending, strengthening,
and preserving of the laws, Parliament ought to be held frequently.

9 **commitment** *(old use)* =
committal act of sending sb. to
prison

15 **impeach sth.** (here) prevent sth.

16 **bail** *Kaution*
impose a fine demand money
as punishment

18 **redress of grievances** *(fml)*
correction of sth. considered
unfair

Excerpts from the Declaration of Independence (1776)

*Unhappiness with British rule had been on the rise in the American colonies
during the 1760s. In 1775, open fighting broke out between British troops and
American colonists – the beginning of the Revolutionary War. When Congress
adopted the Declaration of Independence on 4 July, 1776, this ended more than a
century and a half of colonial dependency, even though the war was to go on until
1783.*

When in the Course of human events, it becomes necessary for one people to
dissolve the political bands which have connected them with another, and to
assume among the powers of the earth, the separate and equal station to which the
Laws of Nature and of Nature's God entitle them, a decent respect to the opinions
of mankind requires that they should declare the causes which impel them to the
separation.

We hold these truths to be self-evident, that all men are created equal, that they
are endowed by their Creator with certain unalienable Rights, that among these
are Life, Liberty and the pursuit of Happiness. That to secure these rights, Governments are instituted among Men, deriving their just powers from the consent of
the governed. That whenever any Form of Government becomes destructive of
these ends, it is the Right of the People to alter or to abolish it, and to institute new
Government, laying its foundation on such principles and organizing its powers
in such form, as to them shall seem most likely to effect their Safety and
Happiness.

3 **assume sth.** *etwas übernehmen*
station *(old-fashioned or fml)*
status

5 **impel sb. to sth.** [–'–] force sb.
to do sth.

8 **endow sb. with sth.** [ɪn'daʊ]
(fml) give sb. sth.
unalienable *(old use)*
= **inalienable** [ɪn'eɪliənəbl] *(fml)*
that cannot be taken away

9 **pursuit of sth.** *(fml)* act of trying
to achieve sth.

10 **consent** [–'–] *(n)* agreement

The Bill of Rights (1791)

*At the time the Constitution of the USA was discussed and ratified, critics felt it
did not sufficiently protect individuals against abuse of their civil liberties and
rights by the federal government. Therefore, ten amendments to the Constitution
known as the Bill of Rights were proposed by Congress and passed in 1791.*

First Amendment Congress shall make no law respecting an establishment of
religion, or prohibiting the free exercise thereof; or abridging the freedom of
speech, or of the press; or the right of the people peaceably to assemble, and to
petition the government for a redress of grievances.

1 **respecting** concerning

2 **the free exercise thereof**
deren freie Ausübung
abridge sth. limit sth.

4 **redress of grievances** *(fml)*
correction of sth. considered
unfair

6 **infringe sth.** *(fml)* *etwas verletzen*

8 **but** except

11 **effects** *(pl; fml)* personal property
seizure ['siːʒə] *Beschlagnahme*

12 **warrant** *Durchsuchungs- oder Haftbefehl*

13 **affirmation** [ˌæfə'meɪʃn] *eidesstattliche Erklärung*

15 **hold sb. to answer for sth.** accuse sb. of sth. (in a court of law)

16 **infamous** ['ɪnfəməs] evil, shameful
presentment [– '– –] *formelle Anschuldigung*
indictment [ɪn'daɪtmənt] *Anklage*
grand jury *(AE)* panel of 12 or 23 citizens who investigate accusations and officially charge criminals to be tried before a jury if there is sufficient evidence

19 **in jeopardy of life and limb** ['dʒepədi] *in Gefahr für Leib und Leben*

21 **due process of law** proper legal procedures

26 **ascertain sth.** [ˌæsə'teɪn] *(fml)* determine sth.

28 **obtain sb.** (hier) *jdn. vorladen*
counsel lawyer giving legal advice

30 **common law** unwritten law based on custom, usage and former decisions of courts of law

31 **trial by jury** *Verfahren vor Geschworenen*

32 **try sth.** examine and decide sth. in a court of law

34 **bail** *Kaution*

37 **construe sth.** [– '–] interpret sth.
disparage a right [dɪs'pærɪdʒ] *ein Recht schmälern*

Second Amendment A well-regulated militia, being necessary to the security of a free state, the right of the people to keep and bear arms shall not be infringed. 5

Third Amendment No soldier shall, in time of peace be quartered in any house, without the consent of the owner, nor in time of war, but in a manner to be prescribed by law.

Fourth Amendment The right of the people to be secure in their persons, houses, 10 papers, and effects, against unreasonable searches and seizures, shall not be violated, and no warrants shall issue, but upon probable cause, supported by oath or affirmation, and particularly describing the place to be searched, and the persons or things to be seized.

Fifth Amendment No person shall be held to answer for a capital, or otherwise 15 infamous crime, unless on a presentment or indictment of a grand jury, except in cases arising in the land or naval forces, or in the militia, when in actual service in time of war or public danger; nor shall any person be subject for the same offense to be twice put in jeopardy of life or limb; nor shall be compelled in any criminal case to be a witness against himself, nor be deprived of life, liberty, or property, 20 without due process of law; nor shall private property be taken for public use, without just compensation.

Sixth Amendment In all criminal prosecutions, the accused shall enjoy the right to a speedy and public trial, by an impartial jury of the state and district wherein the crime shall have been committed, which district shall have been previously 25 ascertained by law, and to be informed of the nature and cause of the accusation; to be confronted with the witnesses against him; to have compulsory process for obtaining witnesses in his favor, and to have the assistance of counsel for his defence.

Seventh Amendment In suits at common law, where the value in controversy shall 30 exceed twenty dollars, the right of trial by jury shall be preserved, and no fact tried by a jury, shall be otherwise re-examined in any court of the United States, than according to the rules of the common law.

Eighth Amendment Excessive bail shall not be required, nor excessive fines imposed, nor cruel and unusual punishments inflicted. 35

Ninth Amendment The enumeration in the Constitution, of certain rights, shall not be construed to deny or disparage others retained by the people.

Tenth Amendment The powers not delegated to the United States by the Constitution, nor prohibited by it to the states, are reserved to the states respectively, or to the people. 40

Preamble to the Charter of the United Nations (1945)

Drafted immediately after the Second World War, the Charter of the United Nations set out to formulate the aims of this new organization.

2 **scourge** [skɜːdʒ] *(fig)* person or thing that causes suffering

4 **reaffirm sth.** *etwas erneut bekräftigen*

WE, THE PEOPLES OF THE UNITED NATIONS, DETERMINED,

to save succeeding generations from the scourge of war, which twice in our lifetime has brought untold sorrow to mankind, and

to reaffirm faith in fundamental human rights, in the dignity and worth of the human person, in the equal rights of men and women and of nations large and 5 small, and to establish conditions under which justice and respect for the obligations arising from treaties and other sources of international law can be maintained, and

to promote social progress and better standards of life in larger freedom,

10 AND FOR THESE ENDS

to practise tolerance and live together in peace with one another as good neighbours, and

to unite our strength to maintain international peace and security, and

to ensure, by the acceptance of principles and the institution of methods, that

15 armed force shall not be used, save in the common interest, and

to employ international machinery for the promotion of the economic and social advancement of all peoples,

HAVE RESOLVED TO COMBINE OUR EFFORTS TO ACCOMPLISH THIS AIM.

7 **obligation** *Verpflichtung*
10 **end** aim, purpose
14 **ensure sth.** *(BE) = (AE)* **insure sth.** guarantee sth.
18 **resolve** [rɪ'zɒlv] decide firmly

Preamble to the Universal Declaration of Human Rights (1948)

The Universal Declaration of Human Rights, which was adopted by the General Assembly of the United Nations on 10 December, 1948, outlines a basic view of human rights, but it is not a legally binding document.

Whereas recognition of the inherent dignity and of the equal and inalienable rights of all members of the human family is the foundation of freedom, justice and peace in the world,

Whereas disregard and contempt for human rights have resulted in barbarous
5 acts which have outraged the conscience of mankind, and the advent of a world in which human beings shall enjoy freedom of speech and belief and freedom from fear and want has been proclaimed as the highest aspiration of the common people,

Whereas it is essential, if man is not to be compelled to have recourse, as a last
10 resort, to rebellion against tyranny and oppression, that human rights should be protected by the rule of law,

Whereas it is essential to promote the development of friendly relations between nations,

Whereas the peoples of the United Nations have in the Charter reaffirmed their
15 faith in fundamental human rights, in the dignity and worth of the human person and in the equal rights of men and women and have determined to promote social progress and better standards of life in larger freedom,

Whereas Member States have pledged themselves to achieve, in co-operation with the United Nations, the promotion of universal respect for and observance of
20 human rights and fundamental freedoms,

Whereas a common understanding of these rights and freedoms is of the greatest importance for the full realization of this pledge,

Now, therefore, the GENERAL ASSEMBLY proclaims this UNIVERSAL DECLARATION OF HUMAN RIGHTS as a common standard of achievement for all
25 peoples and all nations, to the end that every individual and every organ of society, keeping this Declaration constantly in mind, shall strive by teaching and education to promote respect for these rights and freedoms and by progressive measures, national and international, to secure their universal and effective recognition

1 **whereas** because of the fact that **inalienable** [ɪn'eɪliənəbl] *(fml)* that cannot be taken away from you
4 **disregard** *(n) Missachtung* **contempt** feeling that sb./sth. is without value and deserves no respect
5 **outrage sb.** make sb. very shocked and angry **advent of sth./sb.** ['‒‒] coming of sth./sb. (an important event, person, technology, etc.)
9 **compel sb. to do sth.** [‒ '‒] *(fml)* force sb. to do sth. **have recourse to sth.** *Zuflucht zu etwas nehmen* **as a last resort** [rɪ'zɔːt] *als letzten Ausweg*
14 **reaffirm sth.** *etwas erneut bekräftigen*
18 **pledge yourself to sth.** formally promise to do sth.

30 jurisdiction *Zuständigkeit, Gerichtsbarkeit*

and observance, both among the peoples of Member States themselves and among the peoples of territories under their jurisdiction.

Preamble to the Treaty of Rome (1957)

The European Economic Community (EEC), the precursor to today's much larger European Union, was established on 27 March, 1957, when the six founding members – France, West Germany, Italy, Belgium, the Netherlands and Luxembourg – signed the Treaty of Rome, which is also called the Treaty Establishing the European Community.

5 determined [dɪˈtɜːmɪnd] *(adj)* having made a firm decision to do sth.
7 resolved [rɪˈzɒlvd] *(adj)* *(fml)* having made a firm decision to do sth.
11 concerted [– ˈ – –] *(adj)* *gemeinsam, gemeinschaftlich*
13 anxious to do sth. [ˈæŋkʃəs] wanting to do sth. very much
15 backwardness state of having made less progress than normal
17 abolition [ˌæbəˈlɪʃn] *Abschaffung*
21 pool sth. collect sth. (money, information, etc.) from different people or groups so that it can be used by all of them
resource supply of sth. that a country, an organization or a person has and can use, esp. to increase their wealth

His Majesty the King of the Belgians, The President of the Federal Republic of Germany, The President of the French Republic, The President of the Italian Republic, Her Royal Highness the Grand Duchess of Luxembourg, Her Majesty the Queen of the Netherlands,

DETERMINED to lay the foundations of an ever closer union among the peoples of Europe,

RESOLVED to ensure the economic and social progress of their countries by common action to eliminate the barriers which divide Europe,

AFFIRMING as the essential objective of their efforts the constant improvements of the living and working conditions of their peoples,

RECOGNIZING that the removal of existing obstacles calls for concerted action in order to guarantee steady expansion, balanced trade and fair competition,

ANXIOUS to strengthen the unity of their economies and to ensure their harmonious development by reducing the differences existing between the various regions and the backwardness of the less favoured regions,

DESIRING to contribute, by means of a common commercial policy, to the progressive abolition of restrictions on international trade,

INTENDING to confirm the solidarity which binds Europe and the overseas countries and desiring to ensure the development of their prosperity, in accordance with the principles of the Charter of the United Nations,

RESOLVED by thus pooling their resources to preserve and strengthen peace and liberty, and calling upon the other peoples of Europe who share their ideal to join in their efforts,

HAVE DECIDED to create a EUROPEAN COMMUNITY ...

Texts

pp. 16–17: Excerpts from READY PLAYER ONE by Ernest Cline, © 2011 by Dark All Day, Inc. Used by permission of Crown Books, an imprint of the Crown Publishing Group, a division of Random House LLC. All rights reserved.; **pp. 20–21:** Gerhard Witossek von www.muc.kobis.de, mit freundlicher Genehmigung; **pp. 22–23:** Adapted from www.debate org 2014; **pp. 24–25:** Adapted from www.whitehouse.gov 2014; **p. 26:** Ellie Zolfagharifard, used by permission; **pp. 27–28:** Excerpts from Vernon God Little by DBC Pierre, Faber and Faber Limited, 2003.; **p. 34:** Laura Roberts , used by permission; **pp. 36–37:** Nick Dear, used by permission; **p. 40:** Bob Holmes, used by permission; **p. 43:** Tim Franks, used by permission; **p. 45:** Zoltan Istvan, used by permission; **p. 48:** Agora-Energiewende, mit freundlicher Genehmigung; **pp. 56–57:** © 2002 M.T. Anderson. From FEED by M.T. Anderson. Reproduced by permission of Walker Books Ltd., London SE111 5HJ www.walker.co.uk; **pp. 60–61:** David Kleingers, mit freundlicher Genehmigung; **pp. 62–63:** Excerpts from THE CIRCLE by Dave Eggers, © 2013 by Dave Eggers. Used by permission of Alfred A. Knopf, an imprint of the Knopf Double-day Publishing Group, a division of Random House LLC. All rights reserved; **pp. 66–67:** © Margaret Atwood, 2004, Oryx and Crake, Bloomsbury Publishing Plc.; **pp. 69–70:** George Orwell, used by permission; **p. 85:** James Simmons, Poems 1956–1986 (Bloodaxe Books, 1986); **p. 89:** Imtiaz Dharker, The terrorist on my table (Bloodaxe Books, 2006); **p. 90:** © William Marr, 2014, used by permission; **pp. 96–97:** Alan Bennett, used by permission; **pp. 102–104:** Mike Bartlett, used by permission; **p. 106:** Halal Events Ltd, London, used by permission; **p. 107:** Amelia Gentleman, used by permission; **pp. 108–109:** phw, used by permission; **p. 110:** Stewart Wood, used by permission; **pp. 117–118:** Gurcharan Das, India Unbound, used by permission of Janklow & Nesbit, USA; **pp. 119–121:** Chetan Bhagat, used by permission; **p. 126:** Carolin Roder, Sandra Kurz, Maxim Derenko, Hochschule Heilbronn, Campus Künzelsau, Reinhold-Würth-Hochschule, Daimlerstr. 35, 74653 Künzelsau; **pp. 128–130:** "English Lessons" was originally published in English Lessons and Other Stories copyright © 1996 by Shauna Singh Baldwin. Reprinted by permission of Goose Lane Editions.; **p. 136:** Liz Balmaseda, Carnegie Foundation, http://greatimmigrants.carnegie.org/your-stories/, used by permission; **pp. 137–138:** June Sochen, used by permission; **pp. 141–142:** Bruce Norris, used by permission; **pp. 144–145:** William J. Clinton Commencement Address at Portland State University in Portland, Oregon; **pp. 150–151:** Todd Strasser, used by permission; **pp. 153–154:** Anne Applebaum, used by permission; **pp. 162–163:** Liz Alderman, used by permission; **p. 164:** Sascha Schmierer, used by permission; **p. 167:** Lucy Siegle, used by permission; **pp. 168–169:** Elko Born, used by permission; **p. 171:** Aoife Mannix, www.tall-lighthouse.co.uk, used by permission; **p. 172:** Michelle Warwicker, used by permission; **pp. 172–173** and **289:** R.L.G., used by permission; **p. 180:** Franklin D. Roosevelt, State of the Union Message to Congress, January 11, 1944. http://www.fdrlibrary.marist.edu/archives/address_text.html; **pp. 181–182:** President Barack Obama's State of the Union Address, January 28, 2014; **p. 183:** Felix Oberholzer-Gee, used by permission; **pp. 185–186:** Sean Coughlan, used by permission; **p. 188:** Uwe Jean Heuser, mit freundlicher Genehmigung; **pp. 190–191:** Carl Deuker, Graphia / Houghton Mufflin Harcourt, used by permission; **pp. 192–193:** Mark King used by permission; **pp. 193–194:** Emanuel Wetterqvist, used by permission; **p. 264:** Clare Whitmell, used by permission; **p. 268:** Ariane Sherine, used by permission; **p. 273:** Gavin Ewart, used by permission; **p. 293:** Hanif Kureishi, used by permission; **p. 302:** Milton and Rose Friedman, Houghton Mifflin Harcourt, used by permission; **p. 304:** Jonas Huticker, used by permission; **p. 312:** Ewan MacAskill, used by permission; **pp. 313–314:** Alan Bennett, used by permission; **p. 315:** Anna Schmid, used by permission

Illustrations / Graphics

Roland Beier, Berlin (p. 276; p. 277); **Petra Eberhard (designcollective)**, Berlin (p. 9 bottom; p. 24; p. 47; p. 83 storyboard; p. 85; p. 198; p. 258; p. 260); **Andreas Fischer**, Köln (p. 34; p. 52 B; p. 66; p. 68); **Yvonne Thron (designcollective)**, Berlin (p. 108; pp. 112/113 caleidoscope; p. 123 top; p. 166 bottom)

Photos

A1PIX – YOUR PHOTO TODAY, Taufkirchen (p. 12: SPL_SciencePhotoLibraryRF; p. 65 bottom left: Karl_Thomas); **action press**, Hamburg (p. 26: Exclusivepix; p. 44: Bas Czrwinski / ANP Photo; p. 58: Collection Christophel; p. 74 top: Everett Collection, bottom: Rex Features; p. 84 left and right:

TSW/Rex Features; p.96 bottom: SOLO SYNDICA-TION; p.111: Collection Christophel; p.121: ZUMA PRESS INC.; p.123: Everett Collection; p.125: ZUMA PRESS, INC.; p.149 bottom: EXTRAPRESS; p.174 top and bottom: GEORG NOWOTNY; p.193: QKD/Rex Features); **akg-images**, Berlin (p.53 E; p.65 bottom right: Wien, Kunsthistorisches Museum; p.114 bottom: Album; p.132 A: Joseph Martin; p.140 top (and bottom) © VG picture-Kunst, Bonn 2015; p.168; p.258: IAM); **Andertoons.com** (p.177 D: Mark Anderson; p.179: Mark Anderson); **BBC** (p.196 bottom); **beingfivecomics** (p.10 bottom: George Sfarnas); **bpk-images**, Berlin (p.122 bottom: Jürgen Schadeberg); **Bush Theatre/nabokov** (p.103: with kind permission from Nabokov and the Bush Theatre); **Cagle Cartoons**, Santa Barbara (p.25: Nate Beeler; p.139: Cameron Cardow); **CartoonStock**, Bath (p.19: John Martin; p.29: 2012 Jeff Stahler, dist. by Universal Uclick; p.32: S. Harris; p.37: Grizelda; p.38: Universal Uclick; p.50 bottom: Gizelda; p.91: Delgado, Roy; p.134: Peter Steiner; p.158: Karsten Schley; p.177 E: Abbot, Bill; p.242: Rex May Baloo; p.248: Royston Robertson; p.262: Baloo Rex May; p.321 A: Jackson Graham, B: Clive Goddard); **ClipDealer** (p.65 top left: AdstockRF; p.245: Sergej Khackimullin; p.264: Markus Gann); **Colourbox** (p.131 flag: Ruskpp; p.219 top: Pressmaster); **Corbis**, Düsseldorf (p.30 D: Science Photo Library; p.31 F: Jason Horowitz; p.36: Robbie Jack; p.45 top: Science Photo Library; p.46 bottom: Science Photo Library; p.51 left: Sergei Karoukhin/Reuters; p.53 D: Imaginechina; p.72 bottom: Corbis; p.95 top: Gail Orenstein/NurPhoto; p.96 top glasses (M): Vladimir Godnik/moodboard; p.98 bottom: POOL/Reuters; p.106 top: Sabiha Mahmoud; p.109: Paul Davey; p.113 E: Lindsay Hebberd; p.120: Dinodia; p.126 bottom right: Purcell-Holmes; p.131 dancers: Juls Ibanez/Demotix; p.132 B: GraphicaArtis, C: Bettmann; p.136 top: Brett Hufziger/Retna Ltd; p.147: Leon Harris/cultura; p.149 top: Ariel Skelley; p.155: Sigrid Olsson/PhotoAlto; p.169: Jose Breton/Cordon Press; p.172: Korolyova Kristina/ITAR-TASS Photo; p.180: Bettmann; p.182: Edmund D. Fountain/ZUMA Press; p.188: Roy McMahon; p.273: 2/Ocean; p.284: POOL/Reuters); **culture-images**, Köln (p.141: Lebrecht Music & Arts); **dpa Picture-Alliance**, Frankfurt/Main (p.43: Andreas Frank; p.122 top: AP Photo; p.126 centre: Robert Harding Imagery; p.133 E:

Everett Collection; p.161 A: Zentralbild, B: dpa, C: ASSOCIATED PR, D: ASSOCIATED PR, E: dpa/dpaweb, F: ASSOCIATED PR; p.184: dpa); **explainity®** (p.166); **F1 online digitale pictureagentur**, Frankfurt/Main (p.192 bottom: Flirt); **Fotofinder**, Berlin (p.51 right: Stillpictures/images.de; p.60 bottom: COLOR FORCE/Kobal Collection/images.de; p.79: The Art Archive/images.de; p.177 C: CHAPLIN/UNITED ARTISTS/Kobal Collection/Max Munn Autrey/images.de); **Fotolia** (p.27 (and 201): kiono; pp.30/31 background computer electronic circuit board: joephotostudio; p.0 B: Africa Studio, C: Sergey Nivens; p.40: freshidea; p.48 top, centre and bottom: Luigi Giordano; p.55: Andre B.; p.56: snapgalleria; p.57: style67; p.69: Uolir; p.73 abstract starburst light background: striZh; p.98 top: Beboy; p.99 bottom: rabbit75_fot; p.105 top: determined; p.106 bottom: photollurg; p.127: paul_brighton; p.128: Andrew Lever; p.129: 9photos; pp.156/157: niroworld; p.157 picture C: Lance Bellers, picture D: william87; p.159: koya979; p.164: Kzenon; p.167 Made in Bangladesh label (and 214): Jörg Lantelme; p.197 bottom: peshkova; p.200 Andrea Danti; p.202: science photo; p.203: Sophia Winters; p.220: Claudio Divizia; p.226: visceralimage; p.227: digitalstock; p.229: sgursozlu; p.236 fottoo; p.239: Natalia Bratslavsky; p.241 top: Bikeworldtravel, centre: Darren Green, bottom: dbrnjhrj; p.243 top: Andrei Nekrassov, bottom left: Brian Jackson; p.263: rasstock; p.279: Syda Productions); **Gannet-USA Today** (p.15 From USA Today 2015 © Gannett-USA Today. All rights reserved. Used by permission and protected by the Copyright Laws of the United States. The printing, copying, redistribution, or retransmission of this Content without express written permission is prohibited); **Ben Goode** (p.204); **Glow Images**, München (p.30 A: Image Source; p.100; p.107: imagebroker.com; p.185: StockbrokerXtra; p.223: Image Source); **Shawn Gruver**, Hermosa Beach (p.189 left); **Houghton Mifflin Harcourt Publishing** (p.190: 2010 by Carl Deuker. Reprinted by permission of Houghton Mifflin Harcourt Publishing Company); **INTERFOTO**, München (p.81: Sammlung Rauch; p.87: Writer Pictures Ltd/Rogan Coldes; p.89: Writer Pictures Ltd/Derek Adams; p.114 top: Mary Evans/Ronald Grant Archive; p.117 right: Mary Evans/Nigel Sorrell Collections; p.133 F: Danita

Delimont/David R. Frazier; p.291 top, centre and bottom: NG Collection); **Nick Kim**, Wellington, New Zealand (p.261); **laif – Agentur für Photos & Reportagen**, Köln (p.105 bottom: 2014 Nils Jorgensen/i-Images/Polaris; p.131 bottom right: Luke Duggleby 2010/Redux; p.148: Polaris; p.150: Willie Davis 2008/Redux; p.181: Polaris); **Lions Gate Entertainment Inc.** (p.59 top, bottom left and right: The Hunger Games © 2012 Lions Gate Entertainment Inc.; p.60 top left and right: The Hunger Games © 2012 Lions Gate Entertainment Inc.); **LOOK Die pictureagentur der Fotografen**, München (p.42 bottom: Glasshouse Images); **mauritius images**, Mittenwald (p.16: Alamy/Carol and Mike Werner; p.23 top: Alamy/Gary Lucken, bottom: Raimund Linke; p.54: Radius Images; p.62: Alamy/Massimo Petranzan; p.76 top: United Archives; p.78: Alamy/brenton west p.88: Alamy/GARY DOAK; p.94 bottom: Alamy/Justin Kase z12z; p.95 bottom: Alamy/Peter Alvey; p.101 bottom: Alamy/Classic Image; p.102: United Archives; p.105 centre: Alamy/Adrian P. Chinery/Nelson's Ship in a Bottle by Yinka Shonibare © VG picture-Kunst, Bonn 2015; p.115: imagebroker/Olaf Krüger; p.117 left: United Archives; p.133 D: Alamy/Archive Pics; p.136 bottom: Alamy/RosaIreneBetancourt 2; p.167 Made in India label (and 214): Alamy/Carolyn Jenkins, Made in U.S.A. label (and 214): Alamy/Independent Picture Service; p.175 right (and 215): Alamy/brianafrica; p.178: Alamy/Roger Bamber; p.183: Alamy/Eric Anthony Johnson; p.189 right: Alamy/Robert Landau; p.197 top: Alamy/Mick Sinclair; p.208: Alamy/MICHAEL DUNLEA; p.213: Alamy/D Legakis; p.243: Alamy/The Protected Art Archive); **Amy Mohammed** (p.14 top); **Nobelmedia** (p.160); **Patricia Piccinini and Tolarno and Roslyn Oxley9 Galleries** (p.39: Courtesy of the artist and Tolarno and Roslyn Oxley9 Galleries); **Photoshot** (p.42 top: BSIP; p.119: Xinhua; p.126 left: World Illustrated/Bill Coster; p.145: RICHARD B. LEVINE; p.244: Imagebroker/Ingeborg Knol); **Reuters** (p.45 bottom: Kevin Lamarque; p.50 top: Fred Prouser; p.112 A: X80002; p.153: US Marines/Handout; p.156 A: Johannes Eisele; p.157 E: Pawel Kopczynski); **Royal Shakespeare Company** (p.76 bottom: Stewart Hemley; p.80 (and 206): Stewart Hemley); **Sheila Burnett** (p.82 (and 206)); **Shutterstock** (p.10 top: Christopher Titze; p.11: Rawpixel; p.14 bottom: Photographee.eu;

p.20 left icons (M): Palsur, whiteboard: Nerthuz; light bulb icon (M): Alvaro Cabrera Jimenez; p.21 top: tmcphotos; p.22 classroom (M): Monkey Business Images, camera (M): Vasin Lee; p.31 E: Fisher Photostudio, G: Shevs, H: Vuk Varuna; p.33: Vuk Varuna; p.46 top: Ase; p.52 A: ktynzq; p.53 picture C: MaleWitch; p.63: Valerio Pardi; p.65 top right: olavs; p.67: Unholy Vault Designs; p.71: Xeron; p.83: Peshkova; p.86 T-shirt (M): Syda Productions, Shakespeare portrait (M): Stefanina Hill; pp.92/93 flag (M): Rsinha; p.94 top: jorgen mcleman; p.99 like/unlike: Alhovik, crown: Sashkin; p.101 top: Maran Garai; p.104: Frank L Junior; p.110: AGIF; p.113 C: Jeremy Richards, D: gnomeandi; p.116 India: Tupungato, Qutb Minar: Chris Pole, mountain railways: Attila JANDI, Sanchi: saiko3p, Taj Mahal: RuthChoi, Ellora Caves: Jeremy Richards, Chola Temples: msankar4; p.131 camera (M): photka, map in camera (M): Katsiaryna Pleshakova, food: Joe Gough, p.133 Statue of Liberty: Marcio Jose Bastos Silva; p.138: 1970s; p.156 B: Cyril Hou; p.162: michaeljung; p.167 cotton label (and 214): STILLFX; p.170: phoenixman; p.173: Reeed; p.176 A: Lurin, B: AVAVA; p.187: Robert Kneschke; p.192 top: takayuki; p.196 top: Goodluz; p.209: ruskpp; p.219 bottom: tassel78; p.222: Featureflash; p.225: emin kuliyev; p.234: Stokkete; p.235: Barbara Delgado (M); p.246: Syda Productions; p.271: bikeriderlondon; p.272: Ron Ellis; p.274: Ed Samuel; p.275: alexwhite; p.281: hxdbzxy; p.287: Andrey_Popov); **toondoo.com** (p.21 bottom: Hanoverscience); **toonpool.com** (p.28: © Claudia Reinhardt – all rights reserved); **TOPICMedia Service**, Putzbrunn (p.20 bottom right tablet (M) (and 72): Simon Belcher); **Visum Foto**, Hamburg (p.112 B: Philippe Lissac/Godong/Panos Pictures; p.118: Mark Henley; p.144 top: Panos Pictures, bottom: Andrew Lichtenstein/The Image; p.175 left (and 215): Panos Pictures)

Cover

Corbis, Düsseldorf (skyscrapers: Pawel Libera)